AWARD EDITION

HOUGHTON MIFFLIN
The Literature Experience
READING

Celebrate reading with us!

Cover illustration by Walter (Bud) Kemper III.

Acknowledgments appear on page 715.

Printed in the U.S.A.

ISBN: 0-395-61091-5

56789-D-96 95 94

BRIGHT GLORY

Senior Author
John J. Pikulski

*Senior Coordinating
Author*
J. David Cooper

*Senior Consulting
Author*
William K. Durr

Coordinating Authors
Kathryn H. Au
M. Jean Greenlaw
Marjorie Y. Lipson
Susan E. Page
Sheila W. Valencia
Karen K. Wixson

Authors
Rosalinda B. Barrera
Edwina Bradley
Ruth P. Bunyan
Jacqueline L. Chaparro
Jacqueline C. Comas
Alan N. Crawford
Robert L. Hillerich
Timothy G. Johnson
Jana M. Mason
Pamela A. Mason
William E. Nagy
Joseph S. Renzulli
Alfredo Schifini

Senior Advisor
Richard C. Anderson

Advisors
Christopher J. Baker
Charles Peters
MaryEllen Vogt

HOUGHTON MIFFLIN COMPANY   BOSTON
Atlanta   Dallas   Geneva, Illinois   Palo Alto   Princeton   Toronto

3

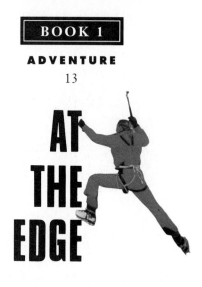
🎗 Award Winner

BOOK 2

BOOK 3

SOCIAL STUDIES

191

TOURING ANCIENT

THEME BOOKS
Oracle Bones, Stars, and Wheelbarrows:
Ancient Chinese Science and Technology
by Frank Ross, Jr.
Marco Polo: Voyager to the Orient
by Carol Greene

POETRY
263

ARTISTS IN CONCERT

REALISM
297

Choices

BOOK 6

FANTASY
385

HALL OF MIRRORS

NOVEL

The Pushcart War

 by Jean Merrill

ADVENTURE

BOOK 1

AT
THE
EDGE

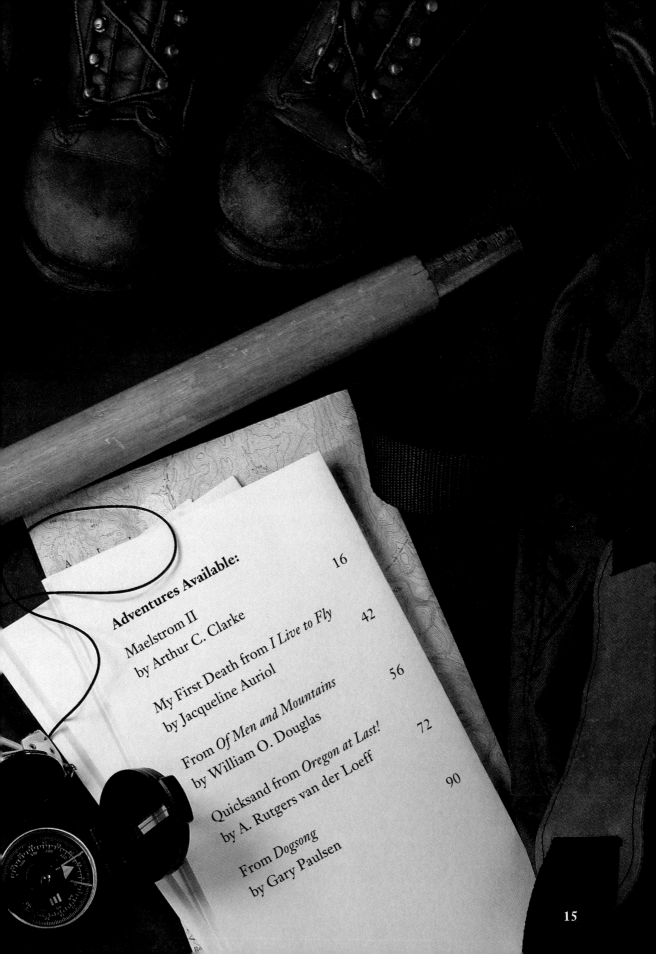

MAELSTROM II

by Arthur C. Clarke

He was not the first man, Cliff Leyland told himself bitterly, to know the exact second and the precise manner of his death. Times beyond number, condemned criminals had waited for their last dawn. Yet until the very end they could hope for a reprieve; human judges can show mercy.

But against the laws of nature, there is no appeal.

And only six hours ago, he had been whistling happily while he packed his ten kilos of personal baggage for the long fall home. He could still remember (even now, after all that had happened) how he had dreamed that Myra was already in his arms, that he was taking Brian and Sue on that promised cruise down the Nile. In a few minutes, as Earth rose above the horizon, he might see the Nile again; but memory alone could bring back the faces of his wife and children. And all because he had tried to save nine hundred and fifty sterling dollars by riding home on the freight catapult, instead of the rocket shuttle.

He had expected the first twelve seconds of the trip to be rough, as the electric launcher whipped the capsule along its ten-mile track and shot him off the Moon. Even with the protection of the water-bath in which he would float during countdown, he had not looked forward to the twenty g's of take-off. Yet when the acceleration had gripped the capsule, he had been hardly aware of the immense forces acting upon him. The only sound was a faint creaking from the metal walls; to anyone who had experienced the thunder of a rocket launch, the silence was uncanny. When the cabin speaker had announced "T plus five seconds; speed two thousand miles an hour," he could scarcely believe it.

Two thousand miles an hour in five seconds from a standing start — with seven seconds still to go as the generators smashed their thunderbolts of power into the launcher. He was riding the lightning across the face of the Moon. And at T plus seven seconds, the lightning failed.

Even in the womblike shelter of the tank, Cliff could sense that something had gone wrong. The water around him, until now frozen almost rigid by its weight, seemed suddenly to become alive. Though the capsule was still hurtling along the track, all acceleration had ceased, and it was merely coasting under its own momentum.

He had no time to feel fear, or to wonder what had happened, for the power failure lasted little more than a second. Then, with a jolt that shook the capsule from end to end and set off a series of ominous, tinkling crashes, the field came on again.

When the acceleration faded for the last time, all weight vanished with it. Cliff needed no instrument but his stomach to tell that the capsule had left the end of the track and was rising away from the surface of the Moon. He waited impatiently until the automatic pumps had drained the tank and the hot-air driers had done their work; then he drifted across the control panel, and pulled himself down into the bucket seat.

"Launch Control," he called urgently, as he drew the restraining straps around his waist, "what the devil happened?"

A brisk but worried voice answered at once.

"We're still checking — call you back in thirty seconds." Then it added belatedly, "Glad you're O.K."

While he was waiting, Cliff switched to forward vision. There was nothing ahead except stars — which was as it should be. At least he had taken off with most of his planned speed, and there was no danger that he would crash back to the Moon's surface immediately. But he would crash back sooner or later, for he could not possibly have reached escape velocity. He must be rising out into space along a great ellipse — and, in a few hours, he would be back at his starting point.

"Hello, Cliff," said Launch Control suddenly. "We've found what happened. The circuit breakers tripped when you went through section five of the track. So your take-off speed was seven hundred miles an hour low. That will bring you back in just over five hours — but don't worry; your course-correction jets can boost you into a stable orbit.

We'll tell you when to fire them. Then all you have to do is to sit tight until we can send someone to haul you down."

Slowly, Cliff allowed himself to relax. He had forgotten the capsule's vernier rockets. Low-powered though they were, they could kick him into an orbit that would clear the Moon. Though he might fall back to within a few miles of the lunar surface, skimming over mountains and plains at a breath-taking speed, he would be perfectly safe.

Then he remembered those tinkling crashes from the control compartment, and his hopes dimmed again, for there were not many things that could break in a space vehicle without most unpleasant consequences.

He was facing those consequences, now that the final checks of the ignition circuits had been completed. Neither on MANUAL nor on AUTO would the navigation rockets fire. The capsule's modest fuel reserves, which could have taken him to safety, were utterly useless. In five hours he would complete his orbit — and return to his launching point.

I wonder if they'll name the new crater after me, thought Cliff. "Crater Leyland: diameter . . ." What diameter? Better not exaggerate — I don't suppose it will be more than a couple of hundred yards across. Hardly worth putting on the map.

Launch Control was still silent, but that was not surprising. There was little that one could say to a man already as good as dead. And yet, though he knew that nothing could alter his trajectory,[1] even now he could not believe that he would soon be scattered over most of Farside. He was still soaring away from the Moon, snug and comfortable in his little cabin. The idea of death was utterly incongruous — as it is to all men until the final second.

And then, for a moment, Cliff forgot his own problem. The horizon ahead was no longer flat. Something

---

[1]**trajectory** (trə jĕk′tə rē): the path of a moving body or particle.

more brilliant even than the blazing lunar landscape was lifting against the stars. As the capsule curved round the edge of the Moon, it was creating the only kind of earthrise that was possible — a man-made one. In a minute it was all over, such was his speed in orbit. By that time the Earth had leaped clear of the horizon, and was climbing swiftly up the sky.

It was three-quarters full, and almost too bright to look upon. Here was a cosmic[2] mirror made not of dull rocks and dusty plains, but of snow and cloud and sea. Indeed, it was almost all sea, for the Pacific was turned toward him, and the blinding reflection of the sun covered the Hawaiian Islands. The haze of the atmosphere — that soft blanket that should have cushioned his descent in a few hours' time — obliterated all geographical details; perhaps that darker patch emerging from night was New Guinea, but he could not be sure.

There was a bitter irony in the knowledge that he was heading straight toward that lovely, gleaming apparition. Another seven hundred miles an hour and he would have made it. Seven hundred miles an hour — that was all. He might as well ask for seven million.

The sight of the rising Earth brought home to him, with irresistible force, the duty he feared but could postpone no longer.

"Launch Control," he said, holding his voice steady with a great effort, "please give me a circuit to Earth."

This was one of the strangest things he had ever done in his life: to sit here above the Moon and listen to the telephone ring in his own home, a quarter of a million miles away. It must be near midnight down there in Africa, and it would be some time before there would be any answer. Myra would stir sleepily; then, because she was a spaceman's

---

[2]**cosmic** (kŏz′mĭk): of the universe.

wife, always alert for disaster, she would be instantly awake. But they had both hated to have a phone in the bedroom, and it would be at least fifteen seconds before she could switch on the light, close the nursery door to avoid disturbing the baby, get down the stairs, and . . .

Her voice came clear and sweet across the emptiness of space. He would recognize it anywhere in the universe, and he detected at once the undertone of anxiety.

"Mrs. Leyland?" said the Earthside operator. "I have a call from your husband. Please remember the two-second time lag."

Cliff wondered how many people were listening to this call, on either the Moon, the Earth, or the relay satellites. It was hard to talk for the last time to your loved ones when you didn't know how many eavesdroppers there might be. But as soon as he began to speak, no one else existed but Myra and himself.

"Darling," he began, "this is Cliff. I'm afraid I won't be coming home, as I promised. There's been a . . . a technical slip. I'm quite all right at the moment, but I'm in big trouble."

He swallowed, trying to overcome the dryness in his mouth, then went on quickly before she could interrupt. As briefly as he could, he explained the situation. For his own sake as well as hers, he did not abandon all hope.

"Everyone's doing their best," he said. "Maybe they can get a ship up to me in time. But in case they can't . . . well, I wanted to speak to you and the children."

She took it well, as he had known that she would. He felt pride as well as love when her answer came back from the dark side of Earth.

"Don't worry, Cliff. I'm sure they'll get you out, and we'll have our holiday after all, exactly the way we planned."

"I think so, too," he lied. "But just in case, would you wake the children? Don't tell them that anything's wrong."

It was an endless half-minute before he heard their sleepy, yet excited, voices. Cliff would willingly have given these last few hours of his life to have seen their faces once again, but the capsule was not equipped with such luxuries as vision. Perhaps it was just as well, for he could not have hidden the truth had he looked into their eyes. They would know it soon enough, but not from him. He wanted to give them only happiness in these last moments together.

Yet it was hard to answer their questions, to tell them that he would soon be seeing them, to make promises that he could not keep. It needed all his self-control when Brian reminded him of the moondust he had forgotten once before — but had remembered this time.

"I've got it, Brian; it's in a jar right beside me. Soon you'll be able to show it to your friends." (No: soon it will be back on the world from which it came.) "And Susie — be a good girl and do everything that Mummy tells you. Your last school report wasn't too good, you know, especially those remarks about behavior. . . . Yes, Brian, I have those photographs, and the piece of rock from Aristarchus. . . ."

It was hard to die at thirty-five; but it was hard, too, for a boy to lose his father at ten. How would Brian remember him in the years ahead? Perhaps as no more than a fading voice from space, for he had spent so little time on Earth. In the last few minutes, as he swung outward and then back to the Moon, there was little enough that he could do except project his love and his hopes across the emptiness that he would never span again. The rest was up to Myra.

When the children had gone, happy but puzzled, there was work to do. Now was the time to keep one's head, to be businesslike and practical. Myra must face the future without him, but at least he could make the transition easier. Whatever happens to the individual, life goes on; and to modern man life involves mortgages and installments due, insurance policies and joint bank accounts. Almost impersonally, as if they concerned someone else — which would soon be true enough — Cliff began to talk about these things. There was a time for the heart and a time for the brain. The heart would have its final say three hours from now, when he began his last approach to the surface of the Moon.

No one interrupted them. There must have been silent monitors maintaining the link between two worlds, but the two of them might have been the only people alive. Sometimes while he was speaking Cliff's eyes would stray to the periscope,[3] and be dazzled by the glare of Earth — now more than halfway up the sky. It was impossible to believe that it was home for seven billion souls. Only three mattered to him now.

It should have been four, but with the best will in the world he could not put the baby on the same footing as the others. He had never seen his younger son; and now he never would.

At last he could think of no more to say. For some things, a lifetime was not enough — but an hour could be too much. He felt physically and emotionally exhausted, and the strain on Myra must have been equally great. He wanted to be alone with his thoughts and with the stars, to compose his mind and to make his peace with the universe.

"I'd like to sign off for an hour or so, darling," he said. There was no need for explanations; they understood each other too well. "I'll call you back in — in plenty of time. Good-by for now."

---

[3] **periscope** (pĕr´ĭ skōp´): an instrument in which mirrors or prisms allow observation of objects that are not in direct sight.

He waited the two and a half seconds for the answering good-by from Earth; then he cut the circuit and stared blankly at the tiny control desk. Quite unexpectedly, without desire or volition, tears sprang from his eyes, and suddenly he was weeping like a child.

He wept for his family, and for himself. He wept for the future that might have been, and the hopes that would soon be incandescent vapor, drifting between the stars. And he wept because there was nothing else to do.

After a while he felt much better. Indeed, he realized that he was extremely hungry. There was no point in dying on an empty stomach, and he began to rummage among the space rations in the closet-sized galley. While he was squeezing a tube of chicken-and-ham paste into his mouth, Launch Control called.

There was a new voice at the end of the line — a slow, steady, and immensely competent voice that sounded as if it would brook[4] no nonsense from inanimate machinery.

"This is Van Kessel, Chief of Maintenance, Space Vehicles Division. Listen carefully, Leyland. We think we've found a way out. It's a long shot — but it's the only chance you have."

Alternations of hope and despair are hard on the nervous system. Cliff felt a sudden dizziness; he might have fallen had there been any direction in which to fall.

"Go ahead," he said faintly, when he had recovered. Then he listened to Van Kessel with an eagerness that slowly changed to incredulity.

"I don't believe it!" he said at last. "It just doesn't make sense!"

---

[4]**brook**: to tolerate.

"You can't argue with the computers," answered Van Kessel. "They've checked the figures about twenty different ways. And it makes sense, all right. You won't be moving so fast at apogee,[5] and it doesn't need much of a kick then to change your orbit. I suppose you've never been in a deep-space rig before?"

"No, of course not."

"Pity — but never mind. If you follow instructions, you can't go wrong. You'll find the suit in the locker at the end of the cabin. Break the seals and haul it out."

Cliff floated the full six feet from the control desk to the rear of the cabin and pulled on the lever marked EMERGENCY ONLY — TYPE 17 DEEP-SPACE SUIT. The door opened, and the shining silver fabric hung flaccid before him.

"Strip down to your underclothes and wriggle into it," said Van Kessel. "Don't bother about the biopack — you clamp that on later."

"I'm in," said Cliff presently. "What do I do now?"

"You wait twenty minutes — and then we'll give you the signal to open the air lock and jump."

The implications of that word "jump" suddenly penetrated. Cliff looked around the now familiar, comforting little cabin, and then thought of the lonely emptiness between the stars — the unreverberant abyss through which a man could fall until the end of time.

He had never been in free space; there was no reason why he should. He was just a farmer's boy with a master's degree in agronomy,[6] seconded from the Sahara Reclamation Project and trying to grow crops on the Moon. Space was not for him; he belonged to the worlds of soil and rock, of moondust and vacuum-formed pumice.

---

[5]**apogee** (ăp′ə jē′): the point in an orbit at which a satellite is farthest from the earth, moon, or planet being orbited.

[6]**agronomy** (ə grŏn′ə mē): scientific farming.

"I can't do it," he whispered. "Isn't there any other way?"

"There's not," snapped Van Kessel. "We're doing our damnedest to save you, and this is no time to get neurotic. Dozens of men have been in far worse situations — badly injured, trapped in wreckage a million miles from help. But you're not even scratched, and already you're squealing! Pull yourself together — or we'll sign off and leave you to stew in your own juice."

Cliff turned slowly red, and it was several seconds before he answered.

"I'm all right," he said at last. "Let's go through those instructions again."

"That's better," said Van Kessel approvingly. "Twenty minutes from now, when you're at apogee, you'll go into the air lock. From that point, we'll lose communication; your suit radio has only a ten-mile range. But we'll be tracking you on radar and we'll be able to speak to you when you pass over us again. Now, about the controls on your suit . . ."

The twenty minutes went quickly enough. At the end of that time, Cliff knew exactly what he had to do. He had even come to believe that it might work.

"Time to bail out," said Van Kessel. "The capsule's correctly oriented — the air lock points the way you want to go. But direction isn't critical. *Speed* is what matters. Put everything you've got into that jump — and good luck!"

"Thanks," said Cliff inadequately. "Sorry that I . . . "

"Forget it," interrupted Van Kessel. "Now get moving!"

For the last time, Cliff looked around the tiny cabin, wondering if there was anything that he had forgotten. All his personal belongings would have to be abandoned, but they could be replaced easily enough. Then he remembered the little jar of moondust he had promised Brian; this time, he would not let the boy down. The minute mass of the sample — only a few ounces — would make no difference to his fate. He tied a piece of string around the neck of the jar and attached it to the harness of his suit.

The air lock was so small that there was literally no room to move; he stood sandwiched between inner and outer doors until the automatic pumping sequence was finished. Then the wall slowly opened away from him, and he was facing the stars.

With his clumsy gloved fingers, he hauled himself out of the air lock and stood upright on the steeply curving hull, bracing himself tightly against it with the safety line. The splendor of the scene held him almost paralyzed. He forgot all his fears of vertigo and insecurity as he gazed around him, no longer constrained by the narrow field of vision of the periscope.

The Moon was a gigantic crescent, the dividing line between night and day a jagged arch sweeping across a quarter of the sky. Down there the sun was setting, at the beginning of the long lunar night, but the summits of isolated peaks were still blazing with the last light of day, defying the darkness that had already encircled them.

That darkness was not complete. Though the sun had gone from the land below, the almost full Earth flooded it with glory. Cliff could see, faint but clear in the glimmering earthlight, the outlines of seas and highlands, the dim stars of mountain peaks, the dark circles of craters. He was flying above a ghostly, sleeping land — a land that was trying to drag him to his death. For now he was poised at the highest point of his orbit, exactly on the line between Moon and Earth. It was time to go.

He bent his legs, crouching against the hull. Then, with all his force, he launched himself toward the stars, letting the safety line run out behind him.

The capsule receded with surprising speed, and as it did so, he felt a most unexpected sensation. He had anticipated terror or vertigo,[7] but not this unmistakable, haunting sense of familiarity. All this had happened before; not to him, of course, but to someone else. He could not pinpoint the memory, and there was no time to hunt for it now.

He flashed a quick glance at Earth, Moon, and receding spacecraft, and made his decision without conscious thought. The line whipped away as he snapped the quick-release. Now he was alone, two thousand miles above the Moon, a quarter of a million miles from Earth. He could do nothing but wait; it would be two and a half hours before he would know if he could live — and if his own muscles had performed the task that the rockets had failed to do.

And as the stars slowly revolved around him, he suddenly knew the origin of that haunting memory. It was many years since he had read Poe's short stories, but who could ever forget them?

He, too, was trapped in a maelstrom, being whirled down to his doom; he, too, hoped to escape by abandoning his vessel. Though the forces involved were totally different, the parallel was striking. Poe's fisherman had lashed himself to a barrel because stubby, cylindrical objects were being sucked down into the great whirlpool more slowly than his ship. It was a brilliant application of the laws of hydrodynamics. Cliff could only hope that his use of celestial[8] mechanics would be equally inspired.

How fast had he jumped away from the capsule? At a good five miles an hour, surely. Trivial though that

---

[7]**vertigo** (vûr′tĭ gō′): dizziness.
[8]**celestial** (sə lĕs′chəl): of or related to the sky.

speed was by astronomical standards, it should be enough to inject him into a new orbit — one that, Van Kessel had promised him, would clear the Moon by several miles. That was not much of a margin, but it would be enough on this airless world, where there was no atmosphere to claw him down.

With a sudden spasm of guilt, Cliff realized that he had never made that second call to Myra. It was Van Kessel's fault; the engineer had kept him on the move, given him no time to brood over his own affairs. And Van Kessel was right: in a situation like this, a man could think only of himself. All his resources, mental and physical, must be concentrated on survival. This was no time or place for the distracting and weakening ties of love.

He was racing now toward the night side of the Moon, and the daylit crescent was shrinking as he watched. The intolerable disc of the Sun, at which he dared not look, was falling swiftly toward the curved horizon. The crescent moonscape dwindled to a burning line of light, a bow of fire set against the stars. Then the bow fragmented into a dozen shining beads, which one by one winked out as he shot into the shadow of the Moon.

With the going of the Sun, the earthlight seemed more brilliant than ever, frosting his suit with silver as he rotated slowly along his orbit. It took him about ten seconds to make each revolution; there was nothing he could do to check his spin, and indeed he welcomed the constantly changing view. Now that his eyes were no longer distracted by occasional
glimpses of the Sun, he could
see the stars in thou-
sands, where

there had been only hundreds before. The familiar constellations were drowned, and even the brightest of the planets were hard to find in that blaze of light.

The dark disc of the lunar night land lay across the star field like an eclipsing shadow, and it was slowly growing as he fell toward it. At every instant some star, bright or faint, would pass behind its edge and wink out of existence. It was almost as if a hole were growing in space, eating up the heavens.

There was no other indication of his movement, or of the passage of time — except for his regular ten-second spin. When he looked at his watch, he was astonished to see that he had left the capsule half an hour ago. He searched for it among the stars, without success. By now, it would be several miles behind. But presently it would draw ahead of him, as it moved on its lower orbit, and would be the first to reach the Moon.

Cliff was still puzzling over this paradox when the strain of the last few hours, combined with the euphoria of weightlessness, produced a result he would hardly have believed possible. Lulled by the gentle susurration[9] of the air inlets, floating lighter than any feather as he turned beneath the stars, he fell into a dreamless sleep.

When he awoke at some prompting of his subconscious, the Earth was nearing the edge of the Moon. The sight almost brought on another wave of self-pity, and for a moment he had to fight for control of his emotions. This was the very last he might ever see of Earth, as his orbit took him back over Farside, into the land where the earthlight never shone.

---

[9]**susurration (soo'sə rā'shən):** a soft whispering or murmuring sound.

The brilliant antarctic icecaps, the equatorial cloud belts, the scintillation of the Sun upon the Pacific — all were sinking swiftly behind the lunar mountains. Then they were gone; he had neither Sun nor Earth to light him now, and the invisible land below was so black that it hurt his eyes.

Unbelievably, a cluster of stars had appeared *inside* the darkened disc, where no stars could possibly be. Cliff stared at them in astonishment for a few seconds, then realized he was passing above one of the Farside settlements. Down there beneath the pressure domes of their city, men were waiting out the lunar night — sleeping, working, loving, resting, quarreling. Did they know that he was speeding like an invisible meteor through their sky, racing above their heads at four thousand miles an hour? Almost certainly; for by now the whole Moon, and the whole Earth, must know of his predicament. Perhaps they were searching for him with radar and telescope, but they would have little time to find him. Within seconds, the unknown city had dropped out of sight, and he was once more alone above Farside.

It was impossible to judge his altitude above the blank emptiness speeding below, for there was no sense of scale or perspective. Sometimes it seemed that he could reach out and touch the darkness across which he was racing; yet he knew that in reality it must still be many miles beneath him. But he also knew that he was still descending, and that at any moment one of the crater walls or mountain peaks that strained invisibly toward him might claw him from the sky.

In the darkness somewhere ahead was the final obstacle — the hazard he feared most of all. Across the heart of Farside, spanning the equator from north to south in a wall more than a thousand miles long, lay the Soviet Range. He had been a boy when it was discovered, back in 1959, and could still remember his excitement when he had seen the first smudged photographs from Lunik III. He could never have dreamed that one day he would be flying toward those same mountains, waiting for them to decide his fate.

The first eruption of dawn took him completely by surprise. Light exploded ahead of him, leaping from peak to peak until the whole arc of the horizon was limned with flame. He was hurtling out of the lunar night, directly into the face of the Sun. At least he would not die in darkness, but the greatest danger was yet to come. For now he was almost back where he had started, nearing the lowest point of his orbit. He glanced at the suit chronometer, and saw that five full hours had now passed. Within minutes, he would hit the Moon — or skim it and pass safely out into space.

As far as he could judge, he was less than twenty miles above the surface, and he was still descending, though very slowly now. Beneath him, the long shadows of the lunar dawn were daggers of darkness, stabbing toward the night land. The steeply slanting sunlight exaggerated every rise in the ground, making even the smallest hills appear to be mountains. And now, unmistakably, the land ahead was rising, wrinkling into the foothills of the Soviet Range. More than a hundred miles away, but approaching at a mile a second, a wave of rock was climbing from the face of the Moon. There was nothing he could do to avoid it; his path was fixed and unalterable. All that could be done had already been done, two and a half hours ago.

It was not enough. He was not going to rise above these mountains; they were rising above him.

Now he regretted his failure to make that second call to the woman who was still waiting, a quarter of a million miles away. Yet perhaps it was just as well, for there had been nothing more to say.

Other voices were calling in the space around him, as he came once more within range of Launch Control. They waxed and waned as he flashed through the radio shadow of the mountains; they were talking about him, but the fact scarcely registered on him. He listened with an impersonal interest, as if to messages from some remote point of space or time, of no concern to him. Once he heard Van Kessel's voice say, quite distinctly: "Tell *Callisto's* skipper we'll give him an intercept orbit as soon as we know that Leyland's past perigee.[10] Rendezvous time should be one hour five minutes from now." I hate to disappoint you, thought Cliff, but that's one appointment I'll never keep.

Now the wall of rock was only fifty miles away, and each time he spun helplessly in space it came ten miles closer. There was no room for optimism now, as he sped more swiftly than a rifle bullet toward that implacable barrier. This was the end, and suddenly it became of great importance to know whether he would meet it face first, with open eyes, or with his back turned, like a coward.

No memories of his past life flashed through Cliff's mind as he counted the seconds that remained. The swiftly unrolling moonscape rotated beneath him, every detail sharp and clear in the harsh light of dawn. Now he was turned away from the onrushing mountains, looking back on the path he had traveled, the path that should have led to Earth. No more than three of his ten-second days were left to him.

And then the moonscape exploded into silent flame. A light as fierce as that of the sun banished the long shadows, struck fire from the peaks and craters spread below. It lasted for only a fraction

---

[10]**perigee (pĕr ʹə jē ʹ):** the point in an orbit at which a satellite is closest to the earth, moon, or planet being orbited.

of a second, and had faded completely before he had turned toward its source.

Directly ahead of him, only twenty miles away, a vast cloud of dust was expanding toward the stars. It was as if a volcano had erupted in the Soviet Range — but that, of course, was impossible. Equally absurd was Cliff's second thought — that by some fantastic feat of organization and logistics the Farside Engineering Division had blasted away the obstacle in his path.

For it was gone. A huge, crescent-shaped bite had been taken out of the approaching skyline; rocks and debris were still rising from a crater that had not existed five seconds ago. Only the energy of an atomic bomb, exploded at precisely the right moment in his path, could have wrought such a miracle. And Cliff did not believe in miracles.

He had made another complete revolution, and was almost upon the mountains, when he remembered that, all this while, there had been a cosmic bulldozer moving invisibly ahead of him. The kinetic energy of the abandoned capsule — a thousand tons, traveling at over a mile a second — was quite sufficient to have blasted the gap through which he was now racing. The impact of the man-made meteor must have jolted the whole of Farside.

His luck held to the end. There was brief pitter-patter of dust particles against his suit, and he caught a blurred glimpse of glowing rocks and swiftly dispersing smoke clouds flashing beneath him. (How strange to see a cloud upon the Moon!) Then he was through the mountains, with nothing ahead but blessed empty sky.

Somewhere up there, an hour in the future along his second orbit, *Callisto* would be moving to meet him. But there was no hurry now; he had escaped from the maelstrom. For better or for worse, he had been granted the gift of life.

There was the launching track, a few miles to the right of his path; it looked like a hair-line scribed across the face of the Moon. In a few moments he would be within radio range. Now, with thankfulness and joy, he could make that second call to Earth, to the woman who was still waiting in the African night.

Responding to "Maelstrom II"

Thinking and Discussing

What personal characteristics does Cliff reveal as he goes through his ordeal? How much does his behavior affect what happens to him?

Cliff's telephone call to Earth does not affect the events in the plot one way or the other. Why do you think the author includes the call?

A breakdown in space-age technology is responsible for putting Cliff in a life-threatening situation. What part does this technology play in his rescue?

Choosing a Creative Response

Reporting on the Situation Cliff wonders whether listeners on the moon or the earth might be overhearing his conversation with Myra. Imagine you are a reporter monitoring radio waves for late-breaking news stories. Jot down notes for a news broadcast based on what you overhear. What will you tell listeners who want details about the situation? Write a short news story.

Tracing Flight Paths Draw a map or diagram that shows the path Cliff means to take from the moon to Earth and the path he takes instead. You might want to include the Soviet Range and other places on the moon. Remember to show that Cliff launches from Farside.

Creating Your Own Activity Plan and complete your own activity in response to "Maelstrom II."

Thinking and Writing

Imagine that Cliff is asked to write a first-person account of his ordeal for a popular weekly magazine. Give the article a title; then write the first paragraph as you think Cliff might write it.

Exploring Language

When Cliff watches dawn break over the surface of the moon, he sees a scene the author describes in this way: ". . . the long shadows of the lunar dawn were daggers of darkness, stabbing toward the night land." What mood does this description suggest? Rewrite the description to make the scene sound peaceful and safe.

Writing

Have you ever been "at the edge" of danger? As you read the stories here, you may recall a time when you went through an adventurous experience. What did you feel in the face of danger? How did you respond to the situation? What do you feel now about your personal adventure?

Write about your adventure in an autobiographical incident. Remember the important details of your adventure and make your readers feel the excitement and danger that you experienced. Be sure to include your present-day thoughts about your personal adventure. If these stories give you another writing idea, try that one instead.

1. Prewriting   Before you begin writing, choose the adventure that you would like to share with others. Relive it in your mind. Recall all the details about the events — the sights, sounds, and smells of the experience. Jot down your memories of what you felt as you were swept up in the adventure.

2. Write a First Draft   As you write your autobiographical incident, think about your audience and purpose for writing. Answer the following questions to help you organize your ideas.

- Who was involved in the adventure?
- Can I recall any dialogue from the experience?
- Which details are most important?
- What did I feel as I experienced the adventure? What do I feel now?
- What did I learn from my experience?

3. Revise   Read your autobiographical incident to a partner. Have you established a strong sense of adventure? Is the sequence of events clear? Are your feelings clearly stated? Make any necessary changes.

4. Proofread   Check your auto-biographical incident for correct spelling, capitalization, and punctuation. Be especially careful about checking for errors if you included dialogue in your autobiographical incident.

5. Publish   Make a neat copy of your autobiographical incident. You may want to include drawings or photographs in order to heighten the adventure for your readers.

MY FIRST DEATH

from *I Live to Fly* by Jacqueline Auriol

The flight had begun well enough. Nothing is prettier than the sky of the Ile-de-France on a sunny late afternoon in autumn. I had taken off from Brétigny after the end of a day's work, for this was a practice flight and had no connection with normal test flights, and that kind of flight takes place late in the afternoon so as not to disturb the traffic.

So I took off then into a blue and almost empty sky, with instructions to place one or two sonic booms[1] over Brétigny and to wind up the last sonic boom with a display of aerobatics.[2] On the ground, in the monitoring room, was Guillaume, who guided and controlled my flights.

I was diving along an axis that would cause the sonic boom too far from the aerodrome for Guillaume to hear it, he began to get into a cold sweat as soon as his stop-watch told him that I must have crossed the sound barrier,[3] and he had not heard my 'top'. A few more seconds and the needle would show two minutes or two and a half minutes: for Guillaume this was mathematical proof that I was dead. Mathematically, after two or two and a half minutes in a nose-dive, I would have hit the ground.

---

[1]**sonic booms:** shock waves caused by aircraft traveling at supersonic speeds and often sounding like explosions.

[2]**aerobatics** (âr′ə băt′ĭks): stunts, such as rolls and loops, performed with an airplane or glider.

[3]**sound barrier:** the sudden sharp increase in air drag exerted by the atmosphere on an aircraft approaching the speed of sound.

The plane was in a tail-spin. The spin was tightening dreadfully and I was in darkness, not yet unconscious, but completely in darkness. I knew it was all over, that this was the catastrophe, the end of which all test pilots think from time to time, and I was filled with a feeling of immense curiosity. Yes, curiosity.

I was saying to myself:

"This is it! This is the moment of your death and the most fascinating moment of your life. No doubt about it. You're going somewhere you've never been before, from where no one has ever returned. Soon, now, you'll know at last. What luck: to spend your last waiting moments in the best circumstances in the world. I am probably going to crash now, but in fact I cannot tell. Maybe right now. Maybe in a few seconds. It's even more fascinating than going to India."

Yes, I thought about India. It was utterly preposterous, for I didn't think of India as a paradise. Only I had never been to India at that time and for years I had been wanting to go. India was the unknown that fascinated me, and at this instant that I believed to be my last, the name of this country sprang into my mind as the symbol of the unknown. I didn't know whether this unknown was going to be happy or unhappy, but I knew there was going to be something there, something different. And I was filled with an immense curiosity.

In a more diffuse way, but quite separate as if on another level, another thought was also crossing the

darkness of my brain: presently someone will telephone my children to tell them I have crashed. They are going to grieve. The thought of their unhappiness saddened me, obviously, but not in any acute way. Deep down I was already terribly withdrawn from life. I also thought of the friends who were waiting for me on the ground, who could hear me and must be in an agony of distress. Their distress mattered to me, but, once again, not too much. I grieved for them all, my children, my friends, but somehow it was only second-degree grief.

Nor was I overmuch saddened by my own fate. I was too curious, too excited by what was going to happen to me. I was living the most exciting moment of my life, because I thought that at last I was going to know.

This is how, on that fine October day in 1956, at the controls of my Mystère IV, I learned so many things. I learned more about myself in two or three minutes than in the course of my whole life.

I realized that I believed in a beyond, whereas I had thought I was no longer a believer. At that moment when I was sure I was going, sure I was about to die, I truly believed that something was going to happen. I was sure there was something on the other side of that barrier, more rarely met and harder to cross than the sound barrier I had just crossed a few seconds before. And I was terribly curious to know what it was. But the really big, the marvelous lesson I learned in that moment in my life that was as decisive as the moment of my birth, was that I was not afraid. Like many people, like many pilots especially, I had always wondered whether I would be afraid at such a moment. And I had always been afraid of being afraid at such a moment. Since that day, I have known that, when things are inexorable, it is not possible to be afraid. In those few moments I realized that in the face of death some kind of gear change takes place in one's brain, one somehow alters speed, and  that truly one is not afraid, not afraid at all. At least this is true of myself and I am certain it is equally true for many people at such a moment.

I lost consciousness, and that in itself was a little like death. Then I came to — I shall never know after how long, probably a few seconds. Unconsciously I must have thought of Guillaume and the mechanics who, down on the ground, were dying with me. I first became aware of my cockpit, then of the ground, the position of the plane — I was in a tail-spin.

I was still sure I was going to die, but I began to fight for my life. My mask was disconnected and, just as after an operation, when you have been put to sleep counting nineteen — twenty, and you come out of the anesthetic continuing with twenty-one — twenty-two — twenty-three (or at least that's what happens with me), my hand of its own accord completed my half-finished movement towards the connection point. And I put it back in place. Thanks to my mask, with its built-in mike, I could talk with ground control. Now I had recovered consciousness, one thing mattered greatly to me: to let ground control know what was happening and explain it to them.

'They won't know why I've been killed. And I really  don't want it to be the same with me as it has been nearly every time one of my colleagues has been killed. When they find all the bits of the plane with the poor fellow more or less in it, they never know, or almost never, why it happened, and afterwards there are always those big question marks. So, since I do know why I'm being killed, I'm going to tell them. They absolutely must know why this is happening.'

So then I told them:

"I have a stabilizer breakdown. I'm crashing because my stabilizer has jammed in a nose-up position."

This in fact was the second communication I had sent to the ground since the plane had started its tricks. Just before I fainted, I had told them:

"I can't hold the plane any more."

And now, as consciousness returned more and more, I continued to speak to them:

"I'm in a tail-spin."

I am sure that at one moment I even waxed[4] a little theatrical: I was wondering whether or not one ought to say something when one was about to die. I decided it would be appropriate if I said *au revoir*[5] to them. And so, still spinning like mad, I said:

---

[4]**waxed:** grew or became.

[5]**au revoir** (ō′ rə **vwär′**): French for "good-bye."

48

"*Au revoir* to you all."

At least, I think I said it . . .

But those moments were so charged with emotion that the truth as I saw it is not necessarily the truth as Guillaume saw it, or even the truth at all. Guillaume told me later that he clearly heard my first communications: 'I can't hold the plane any more,' and that he had equally heard my voice announcing that I was in a tail-spin, and,  luckily, my very last shout of pure relief 'I've pulled out!' On the other hand, he didn't hear me say anything about the stabilizer, which is a great pity, nor my *au revoir* either.

For his part, Guillaume assured me that he was sending me a series of communications. That he was telling me to do this or do that, yet I heard none of his advice. I suppose my mind was so full of what I was doing, of what I was thinking, that I was incapable of hearing anything coming from ground control.

So we have two completely different versions of the truth, Guillaume and I, for he lived through these moments seeing nothing, isolated in the monitoring room, and I lived them wholly and with such intensity in the plane. Perhaps I didn't say all I thought I'd said. Perhaps I said it but forgot to press the little button on the stick that switches on the mike. I've no idea. The fact is that I heard Guillaume's voice clearly, and could understand every word he said, only after the danger of death was past.

While I was unconscious, the plane did anything it wanted. First it must have gone into a tighter and tighter spin, and then it must have started spiraling and looping

and turning upside down. But with all these turns and loops, it was losing speed. And as it slowed, the centrifugal[6] acceleration diminished accordingly. You get — comparatively speaking — the same thing in a car: when you take a sharp bend at high speed, and you feel the centrifugal pull very strongly, but if the bend is less sharp or your speed is lower, you feel it less.

From the moment I recovered consciousness and started to talk, my friends on the ground felt greatly relieved. My silence had led them to believe I had already crashed. They couldn't have known what had happened, since they couldn't see the plane and I had been silent, unconscious, for an undetermined length of time.

So I was conscious, I could vaguely hear the voices from ground control, and I was beginning to see. My vision was still very limited: at first I could make out only the instrument panel, which wasn't very helpful in view of the circumstances. But then I began to see fields and a little village, between Brétigny and La Ferté-Allais, which was not particularly reassuring either: as a matter of fact I was thinking, that is where I am going to crash.

---

[6]**centrifugal** (sĕn **trĭf′**yə gəl): moving or directed away from a center.

The tail-spin that was killing me was in a class of its own: I was twisting in every direction, I kept turning upside down, I was dropping and whirling around at all angles. And I couldn't pull out of it. In a healthy spin, the plane dives nose down and turns on its own axis. You can stop it quite easily in a plane with straight wings by returning the controls to a central position. But the Mystère IV was one of the first planes to have swept-back wings, which considerably alter a spin.

As I plunged towards the ground I remembered a lunch I had had a week before with a colleague of mine, Elie Buges, who was working at Bordeaux, where I had gone to make some flights in the Mystère IV. As it happened, he was testing this very plane, and he told me about some trouble he had had a little while previously:

"I had a little bother trying a tail-spin in a Mystère IV," he told me. "Remember, Jacqueline, if ever you get into a tail-spin in this plane, do what I did: shove everything hard down, not central, hard down, Jacqueline.

"When you get into a tail-spin in this plane," he went on, "what you have to do is so contrary to approved procedure that you really have to kick yourself in the backside to make yourself do it. Instead of trying to stop the spin by putting everything in the central position, you must on the contrary accelerate the spin to the maximum by putting the rudder pedals, the control column, absolutely everything into the spin. She's got to have maximum acceleration, because it's only then that the plane dives nose first and the spin becomes healthy. And it's only then that you can return the controls to the central position to stop it."

I went through the maneuver Buges had described  and as I did I was thinking very precisely: "I have to do this and that" and then I did it exactly. The tail-spin had become healthy again. And at the right moment, from pure reflex, I returned the controls to central position. I had straightened out. I was still in a nose-dive heading straight for the ground, of course, but I was no longer in a spin.

My eyes functioned properly now — and I could see the ground rushing up to me with dizzy speed. To myself I said: "You *are* a champion and no mistake, but nobody will ever know because you're going to make your little hole just the same. You're too close to the ground. You'll never pull out of it at this rate. There isn't enough room for you to get by."

At that moment I was about twelve and a half miles from Brétigny, near La Ferté-Allais, and there were some mechanics on the ground who saw me and, as I heard later, said:

"I say . . . that chap's going to kill himself."

Exactly what I was thinking.

But I was thinking it quite calmly. And it is perhaps owing to this feeling of detachment, that, while being certain I was going to kill myself, I still felt a kind of obligation towards the plane and perhaps towards myself too, and went through the necessary actions.

I pulled back on the stick for all I was worth, I throttled back completely, and brought out everything I knew that would affect my turning radius (the slower you're going, the closer you can hug the curve, just as in a car) and . . . I got by.

I made it, over the fields, a few yards from the ground, but I had those few yards and I got by.

I was happy, very happy. "Made it!" I told ground control; "I've pulled out!"

And at that moment — now it was no longer a matter of death but life, now it was a  matter of coming back and being infinitely happy to be alive — communications between Guillaume and myself became perfect again. He heard my voice perfectly clearly announcing that I had pulled out, managed to get by, and I could perfectly clearly hear him telling me:

"You needn't be in a hurry to land. Do a lap. Relax."

But I wasn't at all tense. And so I told him: "No. I'm coming in now."

And I landed with a plane that was all out of true. You couldn't tell it was just by looking at it, the wings were still intact and seemed to be in their usual place, but in fact the plane was in an appalling condition, almost beyond salvaging. The terrible pressures to which it had been subjected had turned it into a kind of solidified spin. To land, I had to put the controls in positions in which one simply does not put them. Like turning the steering wheel of a car to the left in order to go to the right.

But I landed first shot and I was filled with happiness. A wild happiness at being alive.

Responding to "My First Death"

Thinking and Discussing

How does Jacqueline feel about facing death? What important things does she discover about herself during the events in this selection?

Since this selection is written in the first person, readers know the final outcome of the flight. How does the author still manage to keep up the suspense?

How do you explain Jacqueline's intense curiosity about death on the one hand and her "wild happiness at being alive" on the other?

Choosing a Creative Response

Assembling a Collage What does the narrator of "My First Death" see as her airplane spins toward the ground? What kinds of objects, shapes, and colors would you use in a collage to picture the action and setting of "My First Death"? Make notes about what you would want to include in your collage. If possible, collect pictures from old magazines — and other materials — and create a group collage to display in your classroom.

Planning Movie Music Imagine that "My First Death" is being made into a movie. With a partner, brainstorm to come up with the kind of music you would use in the background to highlight the mood of the selection. What music would best accompany the beginning of Jacqueline's flight? What music would complement the speed and urgency of her tailspin? Write down your suggestions and share them with your group.

Creating Your Own Activity Plan and complete your own activity in response to "My First Death."

Thinking and Writing

Jacqueline Auriol survives a near-death situation because she follows emergency instructions. Write a brochure containing instructions for other emergency procedures. Use any information in the selections you have read and anything else you know about dealing with emergencies to write the brochure. Include safety tips for emergencies in one or more of the following areas:

- camping
- bicycling
- hiking
- skiing
- mountain climbing
- other situations

You may wish to illustrate your brochure and share it with your class.

Of Men and Mountains

by William O. Douglas

William Orville Douglas was born in Maine, Minnesota, in 1898. His father died when Douglas was six years old, and his mother moved the family to Yakima, Washington, where he spent the rest of his childhood. Soon after he arrived, he developed polio, and both of his legs were paralyzed. Following the advice of a country doctor, his mother massaged his legs every two hours for many weeks. Eventually his mother's treatment restored his ability to walk.

Douglas's illness left him small and weak. Other children bullied him. He compensated by becoming a brilliant student and by building up his strength. Inspired by Mount Adams, the great peak of the Cascades mountain range visible from his mother's back porch, he took up hiking and mountain climbing. He pushed himself hard. At night his muscles twitched so badly he could not sleep, but he felt satisfied that his legs were growing stronger.

It was in 1913 when Doug was 19 and I was not quite 15 that the two of us made this climb of Kloochman. Walter Kohagen, Doug, and I were camped in the Tieton Basin at a soda spring. The basin was then in large part a vast rich bottomland. We were traveling light, one blanket each. The night, I recall, was so bitter cold that we took turns refueling the campfire so that we could keep our backs warm enough to sleep. We rose at the first show of dawn, and cooked frying-pan bread and trout for breakfast. We had not planned to climb Kloochman, but somehow the challenge came to us as the sun touched her crest.

After breakfast we started circling the rock. There are fairly easy routes up Kloochman, but we shunned them. When we came to the southeast face (the one that never has been conquered, I believe) we chose it. Walter decided not to make the climb, but to wait at the base of the cliff for Doug and me. The July day was warm and cloudless. Doug led. The beginning was easy. For 100 feet or so we found ledges six to twelve inches wide we could follow to the left or right. Some ledges ran up the rock ten feet or more at a gentle grade. Others were merely steps to another ledge higher up. Thus by hugging the wall we could either ease ourselves upward or hoist ourselves from one ledge to another.

When we were about 100 feet up the wall, the ledges became narrower and footwork more precarious. Doug suggested we take off our shoes. This we did, tying them behind us on our belts. In stocking feet we wormed up the wall, clinging like flies to the dark rock. The pace was slow. We gingerly tested each toehold and fingerhold for loose rock before putting our weight on it. At times we had to inch along sidewise, our stomachs pressed tightly against the rock, in order to gain a point where we could reach the ledge above us. If we got on a ledge that turned out to be a cul-de-sac,[1] the much more dangerous task of going down the rock wall would confront us. Hence we picked our route with care and weighed the advantages of several choices which frequently were given us. At times we could not climb easily from one ledge to another. The one above might be a foot or so high. Then we would have to reach it with one knee, slowly bring the other knee up, and then, delicately balancing on both knees on the upper ledge, come slowly to our feet by pressing close to the wall and getting such purchase with our fingers as the lava rock permitted.

In that tortuous way we made perhaps 600 feet in two hours. It was late forenoon when we stopped to appraise our situation. We were in serious trouble. We had reached the feared cul-de-sac. The two- or three-inch ledge on which we stood ended. There seemed none above us within Doug's reach. I was longer-legged than Doug; so perhaps I could have reached some ledge with my fingers if I

---

[1]**cul-de-sac** (kŭl′dĭ săk′): literally, a dead-end street; here, a ledge that leads nowhere.

Illustrations by Bob Brunsdon

59

were ahead. But it was impossible to change positions on the wall. Doug was ahead and there he must stay. The problem was to find a way to get him up.

Feeling along the wall, Doug discovered a tiny groove into which he could press the tips of the fingers of his left hand. It might help him maintain balance as his weight began to shift from the lower ledge to the upper one. But there was within reach not even a lip of rock for his right hand. Just out of reach, however, was a substantial crevice, one that would hold several men. How could Doug reach it? I could not boost him, for my own balance was insecure. Clearly, Doug would have to jump to reach it — and he would have but one jump. Since he was standing on a ledge only a few inches wide, he could not expect to jump for his handhold, miss it, and land safely. A slip meant he would go hurtling down some 600 feet onto the rocks. After much discussion and indecision, Doug decided to take the chance and go up.

He asked me to do him a favor: If he failed and fell, I might still make it, since I was longer-legged; would I give certain messages to his family in that event? I nodded.

"Then listen carefully. Try to remember my exact words," he told me. "Tell Mother that I love her dearly. Tell her I think she is the most wonderful person in the world. Tell her not to worry — that I did not suffer, that God willed it so. Tell Sister that I have been a mean little devil but I had no malice toward her. Tell her I love her too — that some day I wanted to marry a girl as wholesome and cheery and good as she.

"Tell Dad I was brave and died unafraid. Tell him about our climb in full detail. Tell Dad I have always been very proud of him, that some day I had planned to be a doctor too. Tell him I lived a clean life, that I never did anything to make him ashamed. . . . Tell Mother, Sister, and Dad I prayed for them."

Every word burned into me. My heart was sick, my lips quivered. I pressed my face against the rock so Doug could not see. I wept.

All was silent. A pebble fell from the ledge on which I squeezed. I counted seconds before it hit 600 feet below with a faint, faraway tinkling sound. Would Doug drop through the same space? Would I follow?

When you fall 600 feet do you die before you hit the bottom? Closing my eyes, I asked God to help Doug up the wall.

In a second Doug said in a cheery voice, "Well, here goes."

A false bravado took hold of us. I said he could do it. He said he would. He wiped first one hand then the other on his trousers. He placed both palms against the wall, bent his knees slowly, paused a split second, and jumped straight up. It was not much of a jump — only six inches or so. But that jump by one pressed against a cliff 600 feet in the air had daredevil proportions. I held my breath; my heart pounded. The suspense was over.

Doug made the jump, and in a second was hanging by two hands from a strong, wide ledge. There was no toehold; he would have to hoist himself by his arms alone. He did just that. His body went slowly up as if pulled by some unseen winch.[2] Soon he had the weight of his body above the ledge and was resting on the palms of his hands. He then put his left knee on the ledge, rolled over on his side, and chuckled as he said, "Nothing to it."

A greater disappointment followed. Doug's exploration of the ledge showed he was in a final cul-de-sac. There was no way up. There was not even a higher ledge he could reach by jumping. We were now faced with the nightmare of going down the sheer rock wall. We could not go down frontwards because the

---

[2]**winch:** a machine for lifting or pulling.

ledges were too narrow and the wall too steep. We needed our toes, not our heels, on the rock; and we needed to have our stomachs pressed tightly against it. Then we could perhaps feel our way. But as every rock expert knows, descent of a cliff without ropes is often much more difficult than ascent.

That difficulty was impressed on us by the first move. Doug had to leave the ledge he had reached by jumping. He dared not slide blindly to the skimpy ledge he had just left. I must help him. I must move up the wall and stand closer to him. Though I could not possibly hold his weight, I must exert sufficient pressure to slow up his descent and to direct his toe onto the narrow ledge from which he had just jumped.

I was hanging to the rock like a fly, twelve feet or more to Doug's left. I inched my way toward him, first dropping to a lower ledge and then climbing to a higher one, using such toeholds as the rock afforded and edging my way crabwise.

When I reached him I said, "Now I'll help."

Doug lowered himself and hung by his fingers full length. His feet were about six inches above the ledge from which he had jumped. He was now my responsibility. If he dropped without aid or direction, he was gone. He could not catch and hold to the scanty ledge. I had little space for maneuvering. The surface on which I stood was not more than three inches wide. My left hand fortunately found an overhead crevice that gave a solid anchor in case my feet slipped.

I placed my right hand in the small of Doug's back and pressed upward with all my might. "Now you can come," I said.

He let go gently, and the full weight of his body came against my arm. My arm trembled under the tension. My left hand hung onto the crack in the rock like a grappling hook.[3] My stomach pressed against the wall as if to find mucilage in its pores. My toes dug in as I threw in every ounce of strength.

Down Doug came — a full inch. I couldn't help glancing down and seeing the rocks 600 feet below.

---

[3] **grappling hook:** an iron bar with several claws at one end for grasping or holding something.

Down Doug moved another inch, then a third. My left hand seemed paralyzed. The muscles of my toes were aching. My right arm shook. I could not hold much longer.

Down came Doug a fourth inch. I thought he was headed for destruction. His feet would miss the only toehold within reach. I could not possibly hold him. He would plunge to his death because my arm was not strong enough to hold him. The messages he had given me for his family raced through my mind. And I saw myself, sick and ashamed, standing before them, testifying to my own inadequacy, repeating his last words.

"Steady, Doug. The ledge is a foot to your right." He pawed the wall with the toes of his foot, searching.

"I can't find it. Don't let go."

The crisis was on us. Even if I had been safely anchored, my cramped position would have kept me from helping him much more. I felt helpless. In a few seconds I would reach the physical breaking point and Doug would go hurtling off the cliff. I did not see how I could keep him from slipping and yet maintain my own balance.

I will never know how I did it. But I tapped some reserve and directed his right foot onto the ledge from which he had earlier jumped. I did it by standing for a moment on my left foot alone and then using my right leg as a rod to guide his right foot to the ledge his swinging feet had missed.

His toes grabbed the ledge as if they were the talons of a bird. My right leg swung back to my perch.

"Are you OK?" I asked.

"Yes," said Doug. "Good work."

My right arm fell from him, numb and useless. I shook from exhaustion and for the first time noticed that my face was wet with perspiration. We stood against the rock in silence for several minutes, relaxing and regaining our composure.

Doug said: "Let's throw our shoes down. It will be easier going." So we untied them from our belts and dropped them to Walter Kohagen, who was waiting at the rock field below us.

Our descent was painfully slow but uneventful. We went down backwards, weaving a strange pattern across the face of the cliff as we moved from one side to the other. It was perhaps midafternoon when we reached the bottom, retrieved our shoes, and started around the other side of the rock. We left the southeast wall unconquered.

But, being young, we were determined to climb the rock. So once more we started to circle. When we came to the northwest wall, we selected it as our route.

Here, too, is a cliff rising 1000 feet like some unfinished pyramid. But close examination shows numerous toe-and fingerholds that make the start at least fairly easy. So we set out with our shoes on.

Again it was fairly easy going for a hundred feet or so, when Doug, who was ahead, came to a ledge to which he could not step. On later climbs we would send the longer-legged chap ahead. And on other occasions Doug himself has used a rope to traverse this spot. But this day success of the climb depended at this point on Doug's short legs alone. The ledge to which he must move was up to his hips. There were few fingerholds overhead, and none firm enough to carry his whole weight. Only a few tiny cracks were within reach to serve as purchase for him. But Doug would not give up.

He hitched up his trousers, and grasped a tiny groove of rock with the tips of the fingers of his left hand, pressing his right hand flat against the smooth rock wall as if it had magical sticking power. Slowly he lifted his left knee until it was slightly over the ledge above him. To do so he had to stand tiptoe on his right foot. Pulling with his left hand, he brought his right knee up. Doug was now on both knees on the upper ledge. If he could find good purchase overhead for his hands, he was safe. His hands explored the wall above him. He moved them slowly over most of it without finding a hold. Then he reached straight above his head and cried out, "This is our lucky day."

He had found strong rough edges of rock, and on this quickly pulled himself up. His hands were on a ledge a foot wide. He lay down on it on his stomach and grasped my outstretched hand. The pull of his strong arm against the drop of 100 feet or more was as comforting an experience as any I can recall. In a jiffy I was at his side. We pounded each other on the shoulders and laughed.

My own most serious trouble was yet to come. For a while Doug and I were separated. I worked laterally[4] along a ledge to the south, found easier going, and in a short time was 200 feet or more up the rock wall. I was above Doug, 25 feet or so, and 50 feet to his right. We had been extremely careful to test each toe- and fingerhold before putting our trust in it. Kloochman is full of treacherous rock. We often discovered thin ledges that crumbled under pressure and showered handfuls of rock and dust down below. Perhaps I was careless; but whatever the cause, the thin ledge on which I was standing gave way.

---

[4]**laterally** (lăt′ər əl ē): along the sides.

As I felt it slip, I grabbed for a hold above me. The crevasse I seized was solid. But there I was, hanging by my hands 200 feet in the air, my feet pawing the rock. To make matters worse, my camera had swung between me and the cliff when I slipped. It was a crude and clumsy instrument, a box type that I carried on a leather strap across my shoulders. Its hulk was actually pushing me from the cliff. I twisted in an endeavor to get rid of it, but it was firmly lodged between me and the wall.

I yelled to Doug for help. He at once started edging toward me. It seemed hours, though it was probably not over a few minutes. He shouted, "Hang on, I'll be there."

Hang on I did. My fingers ached beyond description. They were frozen to the rock. My exertion in pawing with my feet had added to the fatigue. The ache of my fingers extended to my wrists and then along my arms. I stopped thrashing around and hung like a sack, motionless. Every second seemed a minute, every minute an hour. I did not see how I could possibly hold.

I would slip, I thought, slip to sure death. I could not look down because of my position. But in my mind's eye I saw in sharp outline the jagged rocks that seemed to pull me toward them. The camera kept pushing my fingers from the ledge. I felt them move. They began to give way before the pull of a force too great for flesh to resist.

Fright grew in me. The idea of hanging helpless 200 feet above the abyss brought panic. I cried out to Doug but the words caught in my dry throat. I was like one in a nightmare who struggles to shout — who is then seized with a fear that promises to destroy him.

Then there flashed through my mind a family scene. Mother was sitting in the living room talking to me, telling me what a wonderful man Father was. She told me of his last illness and his death. She told me of his departure from Cleveland, Washington to Portland, Oregon for what proved to be a fatal operation. His last words to her were: "If I die, it will be glory. If I live, it will be grace."

The panic passed. The memory of those words restored reason. Glory to die? I could not understand why it would be glory to die. It would be glory to live. But as Father said, it might take grace to live, grace from One more powerful than either Doug or I.

66

And so again that day I prayed. I asked
God to save my life, to save me from destruction on this rock wall. I asked God to make my
fingers strong, to give me strength to hang on.
I asked God to give me courage, to make me
unafraid. I asked God to give me guts, to give
me power to do the impossible.

My fingers were as numb as flesh that is
full of novocaine. They seemed detached from
me, as if they belonged to someone else. My
wrists, my shoulders, cried out for respite from
the pain. It would be such welcome relief if
they could be released from the weight that
was on them.

Hang on? You can't hang on. You are a
weakling. The weaklings die in the woods.

Weakling? I'll show you. How long
must I hang on? All day? OK, all day then. I'll
hang on, I'll hang on. O God, dear God, help
me hang on!

I felt someone pushing my left foot upwards. It was Doug. As if through a dream his
voice was saying, "Your feet are 18 inches below
your toehold." Doug found those toeholds for
my feet.

I felt my shoes resting in solid cracks. I
pulled myself up and leaned on my elbows on
the ledge to which my hands had been glued. I
flexed my fingers and bent my wrists to bring
life back.

Doug came up abreast of me and said,
"We're even Stephen now."

"Even Stephen?"

"Today each of us has saved the other's
life."

Responding to *Of Men and Mountains*

Thinking and Discussing

Think about the risks the author and his companion take. Do you think the boys are courageous? Give reasons to support your answer.

How does the author use his physical and psychological or "inner" strength to help him? Why are both of these strengths important?

What do you think the author's attitude might have been later in life to the risks that he took in his youth? Explain your answer.

Choosing a Creative Response

Achieving a Goal The events in this selection point up the importance of cooperation between people to achieve goals. Because of their cooperation, the two climbers managed to scale part of the mountain without serious injury. Think of a situation in which cooperation among several people was important in achieving a goal. State the goal the group wanted to reach. Give details about the contribution each person made. Tell whether or not the goal was achieved.

Writing Messages If you were in a dangerous situation, what messages might you send to important people in your life? Write those messages.

Creating Your Own Activity Plan and complete your own activity in response to "Of Men and Mountains."

The Sager children in the next selection follow the Oregon Trail, which was traveled by pioneers during the nineteenth century. The Oregon Trail started at Independence, Missouri. After cutting northwest for 2000 miles, it ended in the wild but fertile Willamette Valley in the Oregon Territory. The trail followed three rivers: the Platte across the Great Plains, the Snake in the Rockies, and the Columbia in Oregon.

In 1804 Lewis and Clark became the first two whites to explore the northwestern part of the route. A Shoshone woman named Sacajawea served as their guide. In the 1820's and 1830's fur traders traveled the trail carrying beaver and otter skins to the East from the teeming Oregon forests. In 1841 sixty-nine people took the Oregon Trail,

THE OREGON TRAIL

and in 1850 approximately fifty-five thousand people made the trip. This flood of travelers began to subside only when the transcontinental railroad was completed in 1869. After that most settlers chose to go west by train, but as late as 1895 some people walked to Oregon.

Of the estimated half-million people who traveled the trail, about thirty-four thousand died — seventeen for every mile. Those who survived endured heat, cold, hunger, thirst, fatigue, and illness. They also faced hazards of the land, such as quicksand — loose, wet sand in which people or animals could sink and smother. Settlers arriving in the Willamette Valley could not even rest. Their new home was a wilderness, and they had to begin working immediately.

Map by Susanah Brown

Quicksand

from *Oregon at Last!* by A. Rutgers van der Loeff

In 1844 the Sager family sets out for Oregon from Independence, Missouri, following the Oregon Trail. Between Fort Bridger in Wyoming and Fort Hall in Idaho, Mr. Sager and his wife — who has just given birth to a child named Indepentia — die. Their thirteen-year-old son John faces seeing his brother and five sisters separated and raised by other families in the wagon train. John decides to keep the family together and to fulfill his father's dream of settling in Oregon. With only a few supplies, an ox named Walter, a cow named Anna, and a dog called Oscar, John leads the other Sager children through the wilderness toward Oregon.

Illustrations by Alexander Farquharson

They lost all count of the days. They walked and walked and walked. The nights grew longer, darker, colder.

In secret, John prayed that they would be able to stay down beside the river. As long as they could do that, they had grass and water at any rate. Game became scarcer. The mountain walls on both sides of the Snake [River] grew more menacing. John eyed those towering cliffs in dread that a moment should come when they would be able to get no farther.

They were not hungry; he was still always able to shoot something. In fact, they had not even touched their store of bacon and pemmican[1] yet. They did sometimes suffer from thirst, when, although close to the river, they had to toil along its high bank, without being able to get down to the water. But then they would sometimes find a little stagnant water in hollows in the rocks. They bailed it out into their waterskins, Louise boiled it in the kettle, and they drank the lukewarm, insipid stuff. Oscar had made a good recovery after his fight with the bear. They had rested for three days after that adventure, had slept a lot and eaten a lot. It had done them good, but they had been on the road again so long since then. So terribly long. . . .

Walter grew visibly weaker, but he still carried his load with patient good humor. Sometimes he would sink to his knees, but then he would scramble up again and struggle gamely on. Round his neck his skin hung in slack folds, and his shanks almost stuck through it, as sharp as arrows. On his knobbly backbone he had open wounds where the badly fitting packsaddles chafed him. Louise smeared the spots with rifle grease every night, and John slipped dry moss under the straps when loading up.

Anna, the cow, got leaner, but also more lithe and quicker, and she yielded milk regularly.

Indepentia grew on it, even though it did not make her fatter. Her little face and hands were red and swollen from gnat bites; she would beat the air desperately and clumsily with her short arms, but she could not keep the insects away. At times she wailed piteously; but sometimes she

---

[1]**pemmican (pĕm′ĭ kən):** a dried food made from pounded meat, berries, and fat.

slept for hours on end, for the greater part of the day. Her back and legs were red and sore, in spite of the rifle grease Louise smeared on them.

"I'm so afraid it'll be gone soon," she said once.

"That's nothing to worry about," said John.

That day he shot two mountain goats, and picked out the fattest parts. Louise melted them down and the result was a thick, yellowish ointment which stank but answered the purpose admirably.

The children grew thinner.

Their hair straggled over their shoulders, their clothes hung in tatters; Louise no longer repaired anything. But she tried to sew moccasins, as she had seen Indian women do. She used deerskin for the purpose, and sewed with sinews which she had previously chewed soft and split. But she made hardly any progress, the first pair had yet to be finished.

The children were still walking in their old boots. John had cut the toes off all of them; the children's feet were too swollen and painful for them to wear them normally. In fact, the only way of getting the boots on in the morning was to make them sopping wet, so that the leather became supple and soft. In the course of the day it got dry and hard, and at night, when the boots were pulled off, they sometimes took with them the skins of blisters which had burst in walking, dried, and stuck to the leather. That gave rise to many crying fits, and Francis never used so many long, strange words as when he was pulling off his boots. John was silent, as always.

The harder things became, the more severe he grew toward the children. They became frightened of him, and he noticed it. It hurt him, but he did not change his attitude. He *had* to be strict, otherwise they would get snowed up there in the Snake Valley before the winter came.

Night frosts were already occurring; at night they all huddled close together, each in his or her separate blanket, with the canvas of the tent over the lot. In the west, the mountain ridges were already covered with snow; the number of the white peaks constantly increased.

They *had* to get on.

John lashed them forward with threats and rough words. And they obeyed, for without John they were lost. But they grew frightened, all the same, and shrank from him. Even Francis did not always understand him. They did not see that he always demanded much more from himself than from them.

Of all of them, he looked the worst. His bleached hair hung round a livid, gaunt face, with eyes sunk deep in sockets surrounded by dark rings: his body was nothing but bone, muscle, and skin. But the children only saw that he looked stern and hard. Nevertheless, Matilda still sometimes felt for his hand, and she could look up at him with eyes which said, "Come, John, be nice! Laugh — just once!"

But he could not laugh.

Often he took Indepentia in his arms for consolation. He would walk on in front of the others, hugging the baby to his chest, his eyes looking into hers. The round, trusting eyes of Indepentia called out the best in John. He bowed his head, and sometimes tears dripped down on Indepentia's little face. He felt so lonely, and the task he had taken on his shoulders was much too heavy. Perhaps more than any of the others he felt a deep homesickness, a craving for the support and love of his father and mother.

The narrow, shut-in valley became marshier; it began to look like a swamp. For the feet of the Sager children, it was a blessed relief. Their shoes remained pliable and soft all day, and their feet cool. But the heavy pack animals found the going difficult.

One day, the valley began to broaden out. The sound of running water grew louder. It looked as if the mountains were moving apart.

At the end of a long day's march, the children stood before a narrow tributary which flowed into the Snake at a sharp angle. The strips of bank beside the river were broad and green; the water, which was shallow everywhere at the end of that dry summer, flowed swiftly into the wilder water of the Snake. There were forests of whispering yellow rushes, with dark-yellow feathery plumes, which glinted and became lighter in color when the wind ruffled them. It was much less forbidding and threatening than in the dark, narrow valley of the Snake.

"The ground's too damp for camping here," said John. "We'll go a little way back from the river, as far as those cedar trees under the mountain slope. Tomorrow we'll have to cross this. We've got to keep following the Snake."

They woke up feeling fresh and cheerful the following morning. John had been out very early and shot three rabbits; Louise roasted them, and sprinkled a tiny pinch of gunpowder on them — a wretched substitute for pepper and salt. But it was a delicious breakfast, all the same.

John went into the river first, in order to find the best place at which to ford it. In all probability, the water would not come higher than his knees, but he tied a rope round his waist and gave the end of it to Francis to hold. "You never know."

He walked across the boggy bank to the river, and cleared a path for himself through the dense reeds — carefully, for the edges of the leaves were as sharp as knives.

The bed of the river consisted of firm, grayish sand, which was hard and tacky. But no sooner did he stand still than it closed like a vise round his toes and heels. Quickly, he pulled his feet out, and shouted behind him, "Quicksand!"

He went on moving his feet up and down, and in that way made some slow progress. By now he was up to his knees in the water; it came no higher. "It's just about the same depth everywhere," he called back over his shoulder, "but the bed's probably all quicksand."

The children sat and watched him.

Constantly moving, never standing still for a moment, he reached the other side and tied the rope securely to a bush of red willow. Then he came back, and tied the loose end of the rope round a cottonwood tree on their side of the river. After doing that, he took his hunting knife and cut a wider path, with sweeping strokes, through the reeds which bordered the bank in a dense fringe. When he was finished his arms were bleeding from many fine, shallow cuts. He walked back a few steps and splashed the ice-cold water over them until they ceased to bleed.

He joined the others again. Louise looked at his arms. "Too sharp for the little ones," was all he said.

"Francis and I will carry the baggage across," he added shortly. "It'll be difficult enough to get the animals over unloaded."

Francis made the crossing through the icy water three times and John six times, heavily laden and never standing still for a second.

"Now, for the animals."

John made a soft clucking noise with his tongue, in order to coax them up to him. They came, full of trust. He patted their necks, stroked their noses.

Then he said to Francis, "Cut off a couple of stout sticks, will you?"

He continued to pat and stroke the cow and the ox. It was as if he wanted to ask their forgiveness in advance for what he would have to do to them.

When Francis came back with the sticks, his face set hard and tense again. "They mustn't stop for one moment," he said. "We've got to chase 'em along as fast as they can go."

"Let Matilda go to the other side first and call them," Louise suggested.

That was a good idea. John took Indepentia in his arms, Francis took the hands of Matilda and Lizzy.

"No," said John vehemently. "I'll carry Lizzy later. She'll have to wait, that's all. Don't forget, Matilda, you must never stand still. Just go on moving your feet up and down, up and down; don't stop, not even for a second. And you've got to walk along beside that rope. If you feel the ground sucking you down, grab the rope. D'you understand?"

The child nodded. John was never really frightened on her account; she always obeyed him to the letter. She also knew, almost instinctively, what was dangerous and what not. Now she walked, kicking out with her feet through the cold water, which came almost up to her middle. She did not utter a murmur. They reached the other side in safety.

John and Francis splashed back behind each other along the rope. The sun was already high in the sky; hours had passed. John was tired.

Once on the bank, he gave his orders. "Louise and Francis, you two must take Anna and Walter by the halters; I'll follow behind with the sticks. Cathie and Lizzy, stay here till I come and fetch you."

The animals began to hesitate as soon as they reached the reeds, but a smart whack against the backs of their legs worked wonders. Once in the water they did not flinch; only when they noticed how their hoofs caught fast in the heavy, gripping sand did they become uncertain again. John never stopped hitting their legs, with both sticks, left and right. Francis and Louise pulled on the halters as hard as they could, ceaselessly trampling in the water.

From the other side, Matilda called in her high, childish voice: "Anna! Walter! *Come* on, now! Anna! Walter!"

The cow mooed anxiously, but things went well. And they continued to go well. Once they had passed the halfway point, John hardly needed to strike them any more. The flanks of the animals heaved with exertion, and with blind terror of a danger they did not understand. Of their own volition they did their utmost to reach the other bank as soon as possible. All five were immeasurably relieved when they climbed up it.

John would have liked to fling himself down on the ground, as he had done after he had almost got drowned with Charley in crossing the North Platte. But that was impossible now — he had more responsibilities than he had had then. At once he set out on the return journey. His feet, which at first had hurt from the cold, had now become numbed blocks of ice. And he was so weary that it was as much as he could do to constantly lift them up and set them down. But he got there.

He took Lizzy on his back, and motioned to Cathie to walk behind him. This time he did not repeat his warning that she was under no circumstances to stand still for a moment. To him it had become so obvious that he did not think of impressing it again on Cathie.

They stepped into the water. Lizzy was heavy. John labored on, without looking round. Suddenly he heard a voice calling him from behind, "John! John! Shall I catch you a lovely silver fish?"

He looked round. There stood Cathie, bending down over the water with hands outstretched, laughing.

Keeping his feet constantly moving, he stayed where he was, and shouted angrily, "Cathie, come here at once!"

She tried to come, but she couldn't. Great fear could suddenly be read on her astonished face. She pulled and pulled. She could not get free. Her feet were fast, as if in iron traps. The sand had already closed round her ankles.

"John!" came in a small, pitiful wail from her lips. "John, I'm caught!"

The boy, who had been red with anger, went as white as chalk. "Francis!" he called hoarsely. "Take Lizzy over for me!"

Francis let himself down from the bank and ran into the water. The two boys rushed to meet each other. John set Lizzy down in the river and Francis seized her hand; they ran. At the water's edge, Louise was standing ready with something red that was supposed to be a shirt; at any rate it was dry.

In the meantime, John had reached Cathie. He threw his arms round her waist and pulled, tugged, pulled — as hard as he could. But he could not bring much force to bear because he had to keep his own feet constantly in motion. The sweat of fear stood out on his forehead.

"Ow, John, you're squashing me flat," Cathie panted.

"Be quiet!" John snarled. His brain was working feverishly. It was obvious that this was not helping at all. His strength was not enough. With lightning movements he began to haul in the slack rope. He fished the end out of the water, tied it three times round Cathie's thin little body, and made an enormous knot in it. Then he left his little sister alone. Without looking round he splashed off.

Immediately Cathie began to squirm and twist in all directions. It was such a horrible feeling, round her feet, and it was so tight. The calves of her legs hurt as if someone was pinching them very hard. She twisted forward, to left, to right, back, tugging at her legs. Suddenly she lost her balance and fell over backwards in the water. John heard the splash, turned round with a furious face, and came back and helped her up again.

"Confound you, child, stand still, d'you hear?"

He trampled off once more, as fast as he could. He felt exhausted. It was as if hundreds of needles were pricking the muscles of his thighs. Finally, he climbed up that bank again.

The others stood waiting anxiously; no one said a word. Everyone looked on in suspense at everything John was doing, so accustomed were they to the fact that John always came to the rescue, always knew how to meet every situation.

He picked up the rope, told Francis to untie it from the willow shrub round which it had been fastened, and walked with it to the only sizable tree which was not too far away, on the highest part of the bank. He climbed up into it with the rope, selected the most suitable place where two main branches forked, cast the rope over the fork, and then climbed down again.

He called Walter. The ox looked at him, but did not come.

Matilda and Francis both walked up to him, and Francis seized the halter. Matilda tapped his dirty hind legs, softly. The animal swished his tail, but began to run. John did not even go to meet him, he was so tired. . . .

"Louise, the girth from the packsaddle!" was all he said. Even his voice no longer had any strength. He tied the broad strap round the ox's body, but left some play. The free end of the rope was tied to the strap. And then, "Pull!" John commanded.

He gave the ox a gentle slap on his angular shanks. Francis took the halter again. He led the animal away from the river. The rope began

to tighten over the fork of the tree, with Cathie at the other end. The ox pulled, the rope was taut; the ox pulled even more, urged on by everyone.

Cathie screamed.

Nobody paid any attention. Of course Cathie screamed. As the rope tightened round her body, it felt as if she was being cut through the middle. But her feet were beginning to come free, albeit with tormenting slowness. In spite of the pain, Cathie suddenly became brave, and screamed as little as possible.

The ox went on pulling. He did not slacken off for a second, but the children on the bank could not see that it helped and Cathie could not tell them. She felt as if she was being torn in two. She no longer stood, she half lay in the water; she did not feel how cold it was, her hands were clenched convulsively round the taut rope.

The children on the bank looked on in desperation. It did not help at all, they thought. No matter how hard Walter pulled.

"Cathie!" Louise shouted from the edge of the water. "Try harder, or you'll die!"

"I'm not *going* to die!" Cathie screamed back in smothered tones.

They were so used to contradicting each other that Louise almost shouted, "Oh yes, you are!" But she checked herself just in time.

Cathie was now lying on one knee in the water, with her other leg stretched out behind her. She could feel that the foot of her outstretched leg was almost free. And the other was very nearly as loose, though now the sand had also got a hold round her knee. She was still pulling as hard as she possibly could on the rope; when she did that, the loops round her body did not hurt so much. Louise stood wringing her hands at the river's brink.

The ox pulled steadily on.

Suddenly he plunged forward. The rope was no longer taut and vibrating. Cathie was being dragged through the shallow water. "Whoa!" shouted John, and Francis pulled the animal back by his halter. Walter stood still.

Half-choked, Cathie scrambled to her feet, dripping wet. Sobbing, she splashed toward land, where hands were stretched out to pull her up. Oscar ran to and fro along the bank, barking loudly and wagging his tail.

"It was awful — it was *so* awful!" Cathie got out, in a trembling voice, between sobs.

There was a dry towel handy, there was sun, and there were warm hands full of bunches of dry grass. But that was not enough. "Make a fire!" John commanded.

Everyone went to look for wood except Louise, who remained with Cathie. Even little Lizzy was picking up twigs. In a very short time there was a big heap, and the fire was blazing up high. Cathie basked in the warmth; the color came back to her face. She laughed, those comical dimples reappeared in her cheeks, and she shook her long curls like a wet poodle.

"So you see, I *didn't* die!" she suddenly said to Louise. It sounded almost spiteful, but they all laughed. That was Cathie all over: spiteful and cheerful, bubbling with high spirits, touchy, full of rebellion, full of unexpected co-operativeness. That was Cathie, and that was how they liked her. They had never realized it so clearly as now.

Everyone looked gratefully and gladly at John when he said, "We're not going any farther today. We'll stay where we are."

But no game came within range of his gun, and they had to break into their stores for the first time. John did not like that at all, for he feared that the day would come when they might need it more than they needed it now. But when he saw the happy faces gathered round the bacon spluttering in the pan, he smiled wearily. It didn't matter — the important thing was, they had got Cathie back again.

Responding to "Quicksand"

Thinking and Discussing

List John's responsibilities to his brother and sisters during the journey. How is John affected by these responsibilities?

In this selection, the conflict arises from a dangerous environment. How does the author use the quicksand incident to reveal the children's characters?

In "Maelstrom II," Cliff Leyland reminds himself that "this was no time or place for the distracting and weakening ties of love." Do you think John would agree or disagree with this idea? Explain your answer.

Choosing a Creative Response

Planning Your Journey Imagine that it is the 1800's, and you are about to begin a two-thousand-mile overland journey west. You will cross deserts, rivers, and mountains in hot, mild, and cold weather. What are the most important things you can think of to take along? Keeping in mind that you may only have a wagon to pack your belongings in and that you will be walking most of the way, write a list of the items you will need for your journey.

Illustrating the Setting Draw a map or an illustration of the setting of "Quicksand." Before you begin, you might want to locate the Snake River in an atlas, or you might choose to reread descriptions of the setting in the selection. Then use your imagination to complete your map or illustration.

Creating Your Own Activity Plan and complete your own activity in response to "Quicksand."

What is quicksand? How dangerous is it? What can you do to help someone who is caught in it?

Places to watch out for quicksand are broad, flat streambeds and sandbars along the shore. Quicksand occurs where dense clay (or other material) forms a solid layer under a patch of loose, fine sand. When water flows into the sand, it cannot drain out because of the clay barrier. The trapped water keeps the individual grains of sand suspended so that they cannot support any weight. The sand — quicksand — then behaves like a liquid, and people or animals that step on it are in danger.

Anyone caught in quicksand should remain calm. People can float on quicksand just as they can on water, and if victims do not struggle, they will not sink. They should fall gently on their backs and extend their arms. They should then try to roll slowly toward firm ground.

The Arctic Ocean is covered by a giant, floating sheet of ice called **pack ice.** Pack ice is frozen sea water that frequently breaks up into chunks called **floes,** which range in size from several square feet to several square miles.

Floes are always moving. They   drift   apart   and then   crash backtogether, at times with such force that they raise ridges up to fifty feet high. These ridges sometimes quickly crash back down to surface level.

Pack ice drifts on the ocean currents in a slow,

clockwise circle around the Arctic.

Floes may drift for years

before they are carried

into the North Atlantic

where they

eventually

melt.

DOGSONG

by Gary Paulsen

Fourteen-year-old Russel wants to return to the time before men and machines from Outside changed life for people in the village. The blind wise man Oogruk reveals the ancient ways to Russel, who absorbs the old man's wisdom while in a trance. Russel takes Oogruk's sled and team of dogs and, remembering the trance, begins to rediscover the old Inuit life and lands.

Sea ice is not the same as fresh-water ice. The salt-water ice is stronger, more elastic, isn't as slippery. Also the sea ice moves all the time, even when it is thick. Sometimes whole cakes of the ice will go out to sea, miles across, sliding out to sea and taking anybody on the cake with it.

On the fourth day after taking the deer with the arrow Russel took the team out on the ice to find seals. Oogruk wanted oil for the lamp and he wanted some seal meat and fat to eat and he said these things in such a way that Russel felt it would be good to find a seal to take with the harpoon. It wasn't that he actually asked, or told Russel to go for seal, but he talked about how it was to hunt in the old days.

"Out on the edge of the ice, where it meets the sea but well back from the edge, sometimes there are seal holes. The seals come up through them and sit on the ice and if you are there when they come you can get the small harpoon point in them. That is the way it was done. Men would leave their dogs well back and pile a mound of snow in front of them and wait for the seal. Wait and wait." Oogruk had scratched with his nails on the wall of the house. "When the seal starts to come there is a scratching sound and the hunter must be ready to put the point in then."

"How long must one wait?" Russel asked.

"There is not a time. Waiting for seals is not something you measure. You get a seal, that is all. Some men go a whole winter and get none, some will get one right away. Hunting seals with the small point and the killing lance is part of the way to live."

So Russel went out on the ice. He took the team away in the daylight and was twenty miles out, working heavily through pressure ridges,[1] when the storm came off the sea.

He had seen many storms. In his years with the village, every winter brought violent storms off the sea, white walls of wind and driven snow. Twice he had been caught out on a snowmachine and had to run for the village ahead of the wall coming across the ice.

But with a dog team you did not run ahead of the wall. As he was crossing a pressure ridge, pushing the dogs up and over the broken,

---

[1]**pressure ridges:** raised areas on floating ice produced by strong winds or tides.

jagged edges, he heaved up on the sled and looked out across the ice, out to sea, and a great boiling wall of white was rising to the sky. In seconds it was impossible to tell where the sky ended and the sea ice began and Russel knew he would have to hide before it hit. He fought the sled down the pressure ridge and brought the dogs around into a small hole under an overlapping ice ledge. There was barely room to pull his legs in.

He tipped the sled over to make a rough door across the opening to block the wind and pulled the dogs in on top of him. Working as fast as he could he tried to pack snow into the slats of the sled bottom but before he could make any headway the wind roared into the pressure ridge.

Russel drew the hood tight on his parka and huddled into the dogs, closing the small opening in the front of his hood by burying his face in dog fur.

The dogs whined for a few moments, then squirmed into better positions, with their noses under their tails, and settled in to ride the storm out the same way dogs and wolves have ridden storms out forever — by sleeping and waiting.

Russel felt a couple of small wind-leaks around the edge of his parka and he stopped them by pulling the drawstrings tighter at the parka's bottom hem. When he had all air movement stopped he could feel the temperature coming up in his clothing and he listened to the wind as it tore at his shelter.

In what seemed like moments but might have been an hour, the wind had piled a drift over his hole and he used a free arm to pack the snow away and clear the space around his body. The dogs remained still and quiet, their heat tight around Russel.

After a time he dozed, and when he awakened it seemed that the wind had diminished to some degree. He used a mittened hand to clear away a hole and he saw that it was getting darker — the short day almost gone again — and that indeed the wind was dying.

He stood, broke through the drift and shrugged the snow off. It was still cloudy but everything seemed to be lifting. The dogs were curled in small balls covered with snow, each of them completely covered except for a small blowhole where a breath had kept the snow melted.

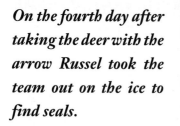

On the fourth day after taking the deer with the arrow Russel took the team out on the ice to find seals.

Each hole had a tiny bit of steam puffing up as the dogs exhaled and Russel was reluctant to make them stir. They looked so comfortable in their small houses.

Still he had to get home.

"Ha! Hay! Everybody up!" He grabbed the gangline[2] and shook it. The leader stood up and shook his fur clean of snow and that brought the rest of them up. Slowly they stretched and three of them evacuated, showing they understood work. A good dog will always leave waste before going to work, to not carry extra on the run.

In a minute he had them lined out, aimed for home — or where he thought the village was — and when he called them to run they went about thirty yards and stopped. It wasn't abrupt. They were running and they slowed to a trot and then a walk and finally they just stopped.

"What is it?" Russel snorted. "Are we still asleep in our houses? Hai! Get it up and go."

Again they started and went forty or so yards and stopped.

Russel swore. "Get up! Run now or I will find a whip."

And after a time, hesitating still, they finally got moving. Slowly. At a trot first, then a fast walk, then back up to a trot, they headed across the ice fields.

Russel nodded in satisfaction. He had not run dogs enough to know for certain what it meant when they didn't want to run, but he supposed that it was because they had anticipated staying down for a longer time.

But the man had to run the dogs. That's what Oogruk had said to him. "You must be part of the dogs, but you must run them. If you do not tell them what to do and where to go they will go where they want. And where a dog wants to go is not always the same as where the man wants to go."

The wind had stopped almost as suddenly as it came, in the way of arctic storms, but before it died it seemed to have changed a bit. When it first came it was out of the west, straight in from the sea, but before it

---

[2]**gangline:** the strap used to tie together a team of sled dogs.

stopped Russel noted that it had moved around to the north, was coming down from the blue-black north, the cold places.

Twice more the dogs tried to come to the right, but he made them go back and run his way. At last they lined out and went to work and Russel looked for the lights of the village. He had come out a way, but as the wind died he knew they should show, especially the light up on the hill near the fuel tanks.

He saw nothing. The clouds were still thick and low so he couldn't see the stars. He had nothing to help him tell his true direction.

He ran for several hours, letting the dogs seek their own speed, and once he was sure he should have run into the village he called them down and set the snowhook.

He was going the wrong way.

What has happened, he thought, is that during the storm the ice has caked and turned. A whole, huge plate of ice with Russel and the dogs had rotated and changed all his directions. That's why the dogs had hesitated, held back. They knew the way home and had wanted to head back to the house.

He could have let them run and they would have taken him home. But now — now what would they do?

More now, he thought. More is coming now. It was getting cold, colder than he'd ever seen it. He could feel the cold working into his clothing, see the white steam of the dogs' breath coming back over their backs. His feet were starting to hurt. He was lost and the cold was working in and he did not know where to go.

There were just the dogs — the dogs and the sled and him. And the ice, and the snow and the northern night. Nobody would come to look for him because they expected him to be out late — or didn't expect anything at all. He had told nobody other than Oogruk that he was going out for seals and since he was staying at Oogruk's house nobody else could know that he was gone. And Oogruk would not expect him back because Russel was hunting the old way.

He was alone.

And a part of him grew afraid. He had seen bad weather many times. But he'd always had the chance to get out of it. On a snowmachine, unless it broke down, you could ride to safety. But he would have to face the cold now.

He debated what to do for three or four minutes. If he went down without a fire the cold would get bad later — maybe too bad. He had nothing to burn and there was no wood or fuel on the ice.

And what had Oogruk said about that? He fought to remember the trance but nothing came. He knew about problems growing in the cold, or during a storm, from other people. But Oogruk had said nothing about being lost on the ice.

Lost on the ice.

People died when they were lost on the ice. He had heard stories of people dying, of whole families lost. The ice moved out and away from land and the people had starved to death or drowned when the ice broke up beneath them, stories that came down in the long nights, sad stories.

And now Russel. Now Russel lost on the ice with a dog team and sled.

In the sled bag he had a small piece of meat left over from when he and Oogruk had cooked the deer. He could eat. That would help him stay warm. And then what?

He could wait until the clouds cleared off and he could see stars and they would guide him home. But it might be many days. Sometimes the clouds stayed for weeks.

"So." He talked aloud to the dogs, saw a couple of tails wag in the darkness with his voice. "So there is some trouble. What should we do?"

The leader looked around at him, although it was too dark for Russel to see his face. Still, there was something there, a desire to understand or to help. Russel smiled, a quick sign back in the fur of his hood.

The dogs.

They were the answer. He could not trust himself, couldn't see anything to help him, but he could trust the dogs. Or he thought he could. He would let them run and decide where to go.

"Hai! Enough rest. It is time to take me home. Take me back to the village."

He squeaked with his lips and they got up and started off. At first they traveled in the direction Russel had forced them to go. But as they settled into their trot the leader moved them gently to the right, more and more to the right until he had them going where he had first started them off before Russel had corrected him.

Russel nodded, let them run. They had a purpose in their backs, a pulling sense that he could believe in. He was learning about dogs, just in the few runs he'd taken. He was learning.

And one thing he had to know was that in some ways they were smarter than men. Oogruk had said that to him.

"Men and dogs are not alike, although some men try to make them so. White men." Oogruk had laughed. "Because they try to make people out of dogs and in this way they make the dogs dumb. But to say that a dog is not smart because it is not as smart as a man is to say that snow is not smart. Dogs are not men. And as dogs, if they are allowed to be dogs, they are often smarter than men."

The problem, Russel knew, was learning when to recognize that dogs were smart. The dogs knew how to run in the dark and see with their heads, with their feet, with their hair and noses. They saw with everything.

At last Russel *knew* that they were heading back for the village in the cold and dark, knew it because he felt it inside.

But they were not home yet.

Running in the dark, even in the tight dark of the north when there is no moon, it is possible to see out ahead a great distance. The snow-ice is white-blue in the dark and if there is no wind to blow the snow around, everything shows up against the white.

Now, suddenly, there was a dark line ahead of the lead dog. A dark line followed by a black space on the snow, an opening of the ice. A lead[3] of open water, so wide Russel could not see across.

Open water. Steam rising into the cold. The ice was moving and he was moving with it.

---

[3]**lead** (lēd): an area of exposed water in a large, flat mass of ice.

The team stopped. The lead dog whined and moved back and forth across the edge of the ice. The dogs hated open water, hated to get wet, but they knew that the way home was across the lead.

For a few moments the leader continued to whine and pull back and forth. "Haw! We go left along the ice and see."

The leader slammed to the left gratefully, happy to be relieved of the responsibility.

But the open lead was long. They ran mile after mile along the broken edge of the ice, in and out of the steam wraiths that came from the sea water. New ice was forming rapidly in the deep cold but it was not safe and would not be safe for several days, if then. Besides, it kept breaking away with the shifting of the cake that Russel was running on.

Yet the fear was gone. The fear had come from the unknown, from not acting, and now that he had made a decision to act the fear had gone. He might not make it, he might die on the ice, but he would not die with fear. He would die working to not die.

That was something he could tell Oogruk when he got back. If he got back. The thing with dying was to try to not die and make death take you with surprise.

And with the end of the fear came a feeling of strength. The cold was less strong along the lead because the warmth from the sea water came up as steam. The steam froze on everything, on the gangline and the sled and the dogs. Soon everything glistened with ice, even the dogs looked like jewels running ahead of him in the dark with the ice frozen on their backs.

It was a beauty he could not measure. As so much of running the dogs proved to be — so much of it had a beauty he saw and took into himself but could not explain.

And while he was looking at the beauty he saw that the lead had narrowed. There was still open water, but there were large chunks floating in it and the idea came to him of bridging the open water with one of the chunks.

He stopped the team.

The leader whined. It is perhaps possible that Oogruk has done this, Russel thought, and the dog is scared because he's done it before.

Or it was possible that the dog was reading Russel's mind and knew what they were going to do. Or it might be that the dog had figured out what had to be done on his own.

Whatever the reason, the dog knew and he didn't like it. Russel set the hook and took the harpoon with the line on it out of the sled. He walked to the edge of the lead, holding back to make sure he wouldn't break off the edge and fall in. Death would come instantly with the water. With the weight of the parka and pants wet, he would go down like a stone.

There were several chunks floating in the lead, which had now narrowed to thirty or so feet. Most of them were smaller than he could use, but one was about twenty feet long and four feet wide. It lay sideways, halfway across the opening.

He laid the harpoon line on the ice, in a small loop, and held one end with his left hand. With his right he hefted the harpoon and with an easy toss threw it across the large chunk of ice.

Then he tried to ease it back so that the butt end of the harpoon would hang up on an edge. It was harder than it looked and took him ten or twelve tries before the harpoon shaft caught in a small hole. When it drew tight the point jammed and he took up the strain until he had the weight of the chunk moving. Slowly he pulled the ice through the dark water, slowly and gently heaving on the great weight.

He gradually brought the chunk across the lead until the end butted against the edge he stood on, then, using the harpoon as a prod he jammed and pushed until the ice lay the long way across the lead.

When it was in position he went back to the sled and pulled out the hook. "Up! Up and across the ice."

The leader knew what he wanted, but he held back, whining louder now. The ice didn't look that steady, didn't look safe. He didn't move to the side, but he wouldn't go, either.

Twice more Russel urged him from the sled but the dog wouldn't go and Russel threw the sled over on its side and walked to the front. The leader shook and crouched down but didn't move away. Russel took his mittens off and hung them by their cords behind his back. Then he grabbed a handful of hair on the dog's neck and another at the root of his tail and heaved the dog out onto the chunk.

The leader fought for balance, found it on the teetering ice, then drove with all his might for the other side of the lead, clawing and scrabbling.

So powerful was his tearing struggle that he pulled the next two dogs after him, and those three then pulled the rest of the team and the sled in a great leap onto the floating ice bridge.

Russel grabbed the handle as it went by and barely got his feet on the runners. A kick left, another to the right and the sled flew across the gap of water at the far end, splashed once as Russel threw his feet up to stay out of the water — and he was across.

Across onto the land ice. Off the floating pack ice. Safe.

Safe with the dogs. Safe and heading for the village. Safe and moving to where he could now see the light of the fuel tank on the hill. Safe out of the steam of the water and back on the solid ice.

Responding to *Dogsong*

Thinking and Discussing

How does Russel realize he has made a mistake and is heading in the wrong direction?

Russel feels great fear when he realizes he is lost on the ice. What causes his fear to disappear?

What do you think Russel has learned about taking a dog sled out on the ice after going through this experience? What has Russel learned about himself? Explain your answer.

Choosing a Creative Response

Talking About Animals Russel relies on his dogs for survival — for transportation, for warmth, for knowing how to get home. In what other situations do people rely on animals for survival? Think of two or three such situations and describe them.

Relating Past Adventures Imagine that Russel is now an old man. What might he tell his grandchildren about his experience? In your group, take turns being Russel, and tell your version of what happened.

Creating Your Own Activity Plan and complete your own activity in response to *Dogsong*.

Exploring Language

In *Dogsong*, the author hints that Russel is going in the wrong direction before this fact is revealed. What clues does the author give? Does this use of foreshadowing increase the suspense? Why?

Thinking About Adventure

Conducting a Panel Discussion Conduct a panel discussion in which authors talk about adventure stories. Choose five people in your class to play the roles of the authors of the selections in "At the Edge." Discussion may be based on what you have learned from the selections and any other information you have about adventure stories. The rest of the class should work in groups to develop questions for the panelists. Some questions might be about the following:

- authors' reasons for writing adventure stories
- characteristics of adventure stories
- importance of setting and conflict
- how authors create suspense
- how authors use adventure to show how characters learn about themselves

Creating an Adventure Almanac An almanac is a book that is published each year, providing information about history, science, space, the world, sports, climate, and other areas of interest.

With your group, find out as much as you can about the setting of one of the selections you have just read. Use your information to put together an adventure almanac. You might consider including information about some of the following:

- plant and animal life
- population
- climate
- size
- history
- exploration of the region

Decorate the pages of your almanac, and design a cover for it.

Designing a Poster   The selections in this section provide a variety of interesting settings. With your group, create a lively poster of one of the settings. You may use paints, crayons, magazine pictures, or any other objects to illustrate the scene. You may wish to include some of the characters in your poster.

Developing a Suspense Thesaurus   In the box below are some interesting words used in connection with danger and suspense in the selections. Create a thesaurus with these words. As you may already know, a thesaurus is a book of synonyms.

First put the words in alphabetical order. If necessary, find their meanings in the Glossary or in a dictionary. With a partner, think of as many synonyms as you can for each word. You may add other danger and suspense words to your thesaurus.

alert	strain	panic	anxiously
disaster	terror	menacing	tremble
ominous	tortuous	dread	tension

About the Authors

Jacqueline Auriol was born in France in 1917. She took up flying initially as a hobby. In 1949 she was involved in a plane crash that crushed her face. Since flying had injured her, she decided that one day she would make flying repay her. She sustained her determination to become a professional pilot through more than fifteen operations to repair her face. After the final operation, Auriol talked her way into the French government school for test pilots and became the world's only officially qualified woman test pilot. She has won the world women's flying speed record five times and has been awarded the Harmon Trophy, America's top flying award, three times.

Arthur C. Clarke was born in England in 1917. He became interested in science early and built a working telescope when he was thirteen.

Following his graduation from King's College in London, Clarke began writing and selling articles and science fiction stories to magazines in England and the United States. In 1951, he began writing full-time.

Among Clarke's best-known works are *Against the Fall of Night, The Other Side of the Sky, A Fall of Moondust,* and *Rendezvous with Rama.* He has won the Hugo Award of the World Science Fiction Convention twice and has received the Nebula Award of the Science Fiction Writers of America three times. He lives in Sri Lanka.

William O. Douglas was born in 1898 in Minnesota but moved with his family to Washington State when he was still a young child. In 1939 he was appointed Justice of the United States Supreme Court, a position he held until 1975.

Throughout his life Douglas loved the mountains. He climbed the Himalayas and wrote several books about his experiences as a world traveler and a mountain climber. He died in 1980.

A. Rutgers van der Loeff was born in 1910 in the Netherlands. She began her writing career as a translator and later discovered that she found writing her own books uplifting. Her books for adults and young people have been translated into many languages, including English, Finnish, Indonesian, Hebrew, Japanese, Portuguese, and Czech. Rutgers van der Loeff also enjoys gardening, traveling, and painting. She lives in the Netherlands.

Gary Paulsen was born in Minnesota in 1939. He has worked as a teacher, field engineer, editor, soldier, actor, director, farmer, rancher, truck driver, trapper, migrant farm worker, singer, sailor — and writer. "I write because it's all I can do," he says. "Every time I've tried to do something else. . . [I] have to come back to writing."

Paulsen has published over forty books for young people. His novel *Dogsong* came out of his experiences as a competitor in the annual 1100-mile Iditarod Trail Sled Dog Race. *Dogsong* was named a Newbery Honor Book in 1986.

Upcoming Adventures

Trial by Wilderness by David Mathieson (Houghton, 1985)

Stranded in the wilderness of British Columbia after a plane crash, Elena must find a way to survive before the northern winter overtakes her.

High Elk's Treasure by Virginia Driving Hawk Sneve (Holiday House, 1972)

A terrifying storm, a stolen horse, a mysterious guest, and young Joe's discovery of an ancient treasure pitch the High Elk family into unexpected excitement.

Banner in the Sky by James Ramsey Ullman (Harper/Lippincott, 1954, 1988)

Rudi Matt struggles to become the first person to reach the peak of the Citadel, the greatest mountain in Switzerland, even though his father died in the attempt.

Amelia Earhart by Blythe Randolph (Watts, 1987)

America's most famous woman aviator accomplished many outstanding feats. Her determination and adventurous spirit led her to make the round-the-world flight that ended when she mysteriously disappeared.

Matthew Henson by Michael Gilman (Chelsea House, 1988)

Details of Henson's many expeditions highlight this exciting biography. Henson, an African American, traveled to the North Pole with explorer Robert Peary in 1908.

TRADITIONAL TALES

WELCOME
to The Annual
TALE-TELLING CONTEST

Three Areas of Competition:
Folk Heroes, Numskulls, and Tricksters
Place: Your Classroom
Time: Regular School Hours
Judges: Readers of These Tales

Contestants will tell tales from various oral traditions.
Be entertained! Learn a lesson! Understand occurrences
in nature! Experience the time-honored art of storytelling!

PROGRAM

Folk Heroes, Numskulls, and Tricksters

EVENT NO.1

Competition of Folk Heroes

At one time, these heroes may have been real people living in real places, but the realistic details have long ago given way to exaggerated feats. Now the tales are larger than life, as are the heroes.

The Ballad of JOHN HENRY

John Henry is a famous American folk hero whose feats are usually told in song. "The Ballad of John Henry" is one of the most widely sung folk ballads in the United States.

When John Henry was a little baby
Sittin' on his mama's knee,
He picked up a hammer and a piece of steel
Said, "It's gonna be the death of me."

The captain said to John Henry,
"Gonna bring me a steam drill around.
Gonna take that drill to the Big Bend tunnel
And mow that old mountain down."

John Henry went to the tunnel.
They put him in the lead to drive.
The rock so tall, John Henry so small,
He put down his hammer and he cried.

John Henry said to his captain,
"Well, a man ain't nothin' but a man.
Before I let this steam-drill beat me down
I'll die with this hammer in my hand."

The man that invented the steam drill
Thought he was mighty fine.
John Henry drove his drill fourteen feet
And the steam drill only made nine.

John Henry said to his shaker,[1]
"Well, now, shaker why don't you sing?
I'm throwin' nine pounds from my hips on down
Just listen to the cold steel ring."

The captain said to John Henry,
"I believe the mountain's sinkin' in."
John Henry laughed at the captain and said,
"It's just my old hammer suckin' wind."

John Henry said to his shaker,
"Well, now, shaker why don't you pray?
'Cause if I miss just one piece of steel
Tomorrow'll be a buryin' day."

John Henry hammered on the mountain
He hammered till half past three,
"This Big Bend Tunnel on the C&O road
Is gonna be the death of me."

John Henry hammered in the mountain
Till the hammer caught on fire.
And the very last words I heard him say
Were "Cool drink of water 'fore I die."

Well, they took John Henry to the mountain
On the mountain top so high
He drove so hard he broke his poor heart
He laid down his hammer and he died.

(Anonymous)

Illustrated by James Grashow

---

[1] **shaker**: a steel driver's partner, who holds the drill in place and turns it occasionally so that it can cut through rock more effectively with each blow of the driver's hammer.

Responding to

The Ballad of JOHN HENRY

Thinking and Discussing

What is the conflict in "The Ballad of John Henry"? How is John Henry both a winner and a loser in this conflict?

Which one of the following statements do you think best expresses the theme of the ballad? Give reasons for your choice.

- People are superior to machines.
- Machines are superior to people.
- A hero prefers death to defeat.

Choosing a Creative Response

Writing a Ballad A **ballad** is a lively poem, often with refrains and repeated lines, in which a story is told. What book, television, or movie character of today might be celebrated in a ballad? Choose one such person, and write a few stanzas that tell about his or her important accomplishments.

Telling a Tale Expand "The Ballad of John Henry" into an oral tale. Base your tale on the ballad, but make up additional details to describe the setting and characters more fully. Be sure to include dialogue in the tale, too. You may wish to tell the tale to your classmates.

Creating Your Own Activity Plan and complete your own activity in response to "The Ballad of John Henry."

Exploring Language

How is John Henry's fate hinted at in the first stanza? What other examples of **foreshadowing,** or the technique of giving hints about what will happen in a story, can you find in the ballad?

Writing a Story

Imagine a society without movies, television, or even books, where telling tales is an important part of everyday life. You too might become a storyteller in such a society. What tale would you tell to provide entertainment or teach a lesson?

Now that you've begun to read some traditional tales, think about writing one of your own. You might already have one inside you! You may decide to begin now or wait until you've read more tales in "Folk Heroes, Numskulls, and Tricksters." If you have another idea for a story, write about that one.

1. Prewriting

Is there a story that a parent, grandparent, other relative, or neighbor has told you? Choose a favorite tale to retell. Remember that you, as storyteller, can add or change details in order to give your tale a personal touch. If you prefer, you may even create an original tale that is all your own.

Write down the names of your characters, what they look like, how they act, and the problems they face. Make a few notes about how the tale develops and ends. Keep in mind that every good tale has a beginning, a middle, and a satisfying ending.

2. Write a First Draft

Organize your notes and ideas about the tale. Remember that traditional tales usually introduce the main character, the main character's personality traits, and the main problem right away. Write the first draft of your tale. Include some dialogue to bring your characters to life.

3. Revise

Read your first draft to a partner. If new ideas occur to you as you read, jot them down. Listen to your partner's suggestions, and use those you like. Make any needed changes.

4. Proofread

Now proofread your tale. Check for correct spelling, capitalization, and punctuation. If you wish, use a colored pencil to make corrections.

5. Publish

Write or type a neat copy of your tale. Think of an interesting way to share it. If you share your tale aloud, remember that changing your tone of voice and facial expressions or using hand gestures and other movements can make the tale especially entertaining. You might also illustrate your tale and present it to someone as a gift.

Tony Beaver

retold by Anne Malcolmson

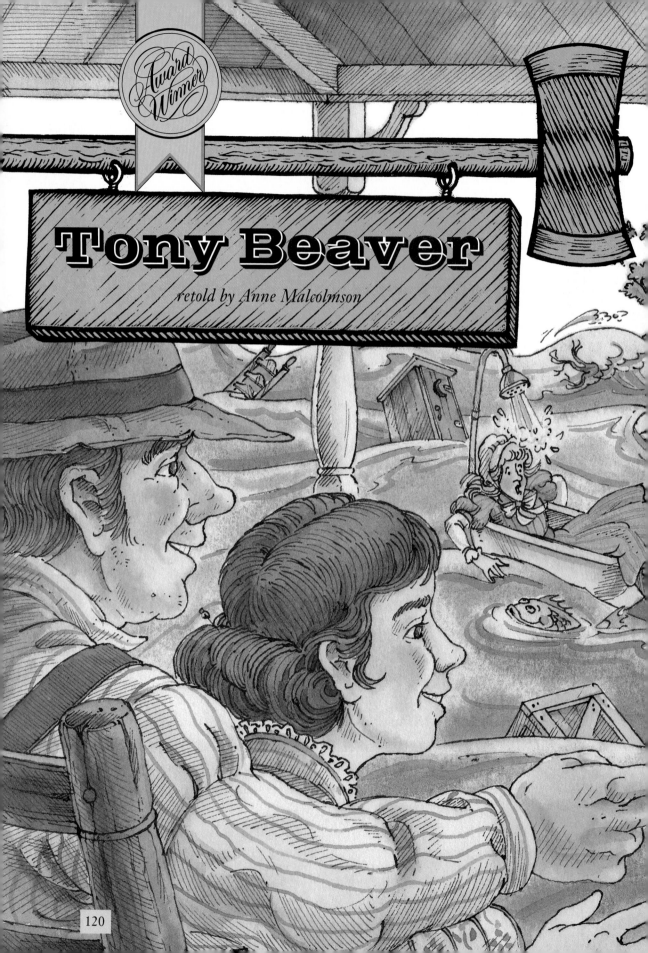

ony Beaver, the great lumberjack of the South, lived "up Eel River." You won't find Eel River on any maps. The geographers haven't decided where to put it. The people of Louisiana and Arkansas are sure that it's in the cypress swamps. Georgians are just as sure that it's in the turpentine hills. North Carolinians insist that it's in the Smoky Mountains. But West Virginians, who know most about Tony, say that Eel River is high up in their own Alleghenies.

The most interesting person at the Eel River Camp is, of course, Tony Beaver. He's too great a person to describe. You'll have to see him for yourselves. And until you do, you'll have to be satisfied with stories of some of the wonderful things he's done.

Some years after he'd given up farming and gone into the lumber business, Tony still kept a small garden of a few thousand acres on which he raised peanuts. His "goobers," as he called them, were sold at circuses and baseball games all over the United States. He had also a stand of molasses maple trees, which produced the sweetest, most delicious syrup you ever poured over a flapjack. They say Paul Bunyan used to send for a small ocean of it every year.

Tony Beaver never could learn to do things in a small way. One season he produced so many goobers and so much molasses that even he was swamped. The circus people complained that peanut shells were heaped so high in the tents the audiences couldn't see the rings. The Eel River warehouses were bursting with unsold goods.

To add to Tony's troubles it began to rain. It rained for days and nights without stopping, until the hill country above Tony's private town of Eel River Landing was flooded. At first the townsfolk didn't mind. They found it entertaining to be able to sit on their own front porches and watch henhouses and church steeples sweeping past them downstream.

Still it poured. They began to be alarmed. Their own levees were about to break. It looked as though Eel River Landing itself might be washed out into the Gulf of Mexico.

A committee was elected and sent to ask Tony if he could do something to stop the flood. He shook hands with all the members and sat down in front of the bunkhouse fire to smoke his pipe and think. Soon a Big Idea came to him.

The members were sent home to collect all their friends and relations at the peanut warehouses. The loggers were sent to the molasses stores. Big Henry and Sawdust Sam, his foreman, hitched the big oxen to the vinegar cruet[1] and the salt box, and drove them to the riverside. The big logger himself borrowed a wooden spoon from the cookhouse and followed after.

As soon as everyone had met, Tony gave his directions. The townsfolk shelled the peanuts as fast as they could and tossed the nuts into the river. The lumberjacks emptied the molasses barrels into the water from the other side. Sam dumped in the salt. Big Henry poured in the vinegar. Great Tony Beaver straddled the flood, one foot on one side, one on the other, and stirred that river for all he was worth.

---

[1] **cruet** (krō′it): a small glass bottle for holding vinegar or oil.

The goobers and 'lasses stuck to the reeds. They clogged the river bed. The current began to slacken. Eel River was oozing, not racing, toward the town.

Then the sun came out, the hot noonday sun. A sweet-smelling mist arose as its rays heated the mixture. Still Tony swished his spoon from bank to bank. Bubbles appeared gradually along the shores, little pearl bubbles at first, then big balloon bubbles. Finally the whole river boiled up. The steam rose higher than the mountains. The odor was delicious!

Tony's spoon churned faster and faster. As the river bubbled and hissed and spouted, its brown speckled waters thickened. From time to time the big lumberjack lifted his ladle and let it drip. Each time the drops fell more slowly, until at last one spun out into a fine hard thread.

With that, Tony Beaver tossed the spoon aside and jumped to the bank. With a jerk he yanked a cloud across the sun. Immediately the river cooled. The thick, sticky mass stopped seething and began to harden. The current had stopped completely. There above Eel River Landing stretched a dam and a broad lake, as brown and quiet and hard as a rock. Except for the white pebbly specks made by the goobers, it was as smooth as a skating rink.

The townsfolk cheered. A holiday was declared and the committee gave Tony a vote of thanks for saving the village. The kids ran home for their ice skates. Soon everyone was gliding in and out among the peanut bumps. People for miles around came to help celebrate.

It was the best party West Virginia ever had, except that there were no refreshments. These were easily supplied, however.

"Break yourself off a piece of the dam," Tony suggested to a hungry-looking youngster. "It tastes mighty good."

The boy thought Tony was joking. But when the big logger reached down and broke off a hunk, he agreed to try it. M-m-m-m! It certainly did taste good. One or two other brave fellows tried it. Soon there was a scramble for the sweet nutty stuff.

Tony had not only saved the town. He had invented peanut brittle.

Illustrated by Ed Parker

RESPONDING TO
Tony Beaver

Thinking and Discussing

What qualities make Tony Beaver a folk hero of larger-than-life dimensions? Explain your answer.

Choosing a Creative Response

Writing a News Story Imagine you are a newspaper reporter covering Tony Beaver's efforts to stop the flood. Write the headline and the first paragraph of your news story. Be sure that your paragraph reports on the "Five W's" of the event: *Who, What, When, Where,* and *Why*. You may want to read your news story to the class.

Thinking of Solutions With your group, think of problems people face today, such as solid waste disposal, shoreline erosion, and air pollution. Then think of humorous ways in which Tony Beaver might go about solving these problems. As a group, present the problem and Tony Beaver's outrageous solution to the rest of the class.

Creating Your Own Activity Plan and complete your own activity in response to "Tony Beaver."

Many legendary heroes in American folklore were real people. Pioneer Daniel Boone, born in 1734 in Pennsylvania, began hunting at age twelve. Throughout his life, he was a skilled hunter and knew the ways of the woods. He also helped many Americans settle in Kentucky.

DAVY CROCKETT

Davy Crockett was born in 1786. A frontiersman and politician, he fought and died at the battle of the Alamo in Texas. Exaggerated tales about him claimed that he could "run faster, jump higher, squat lower, dive deeper, stay under longer, and come out drier than any other man."

DANIEL BOONE

126

HEROES

Annie Oakley, or "Little Sure Shot," was a sharpshooter who could shoot a playing card thrown in the air ninety feet away. She lived from 1860 to 1926.

ANNIE OAKLEY

Other legendary heroes sprang from the vivid imaginations of Americans. Paul Bunyan, for example, was a giant logger who helped settle the frontier with his huge blue ox, Babe. According to legend, Paul Bunyan invented logging in the Pacific Northwest, and dug Puget Sound so that he could float logs to the mill. He also scooped out the Great Lakes to provide drinking water for Babe!

PAUL BUNYAN

Pecos Bill

AND HIS BOUNCING BRIDE

retold by Anne Malcolmson

There were two loves in the life of Pecos Bill. The first was his horse Widow-Maker, a beautiful creamy white mustang. The second was a girl, a pretty creature named Slue-Foot Sue.

Widow-Maker was the wildest pony in the West. He was the son of the White Mustang. Like his father he had a proud spirit which refused to be broken. For many years cowboys and *vaqueros*[1] had tried to capture him. At last Pecos Bill succeeded. He had a terrible time of it. For a whole week he lay beside a water hole before he could lasso the white pony. For another week he had to ride across the prairies, in and out of canyons and briar patches, before he could bring the pony to a walk. It was a wild ride indeed. But after Bill's ride on the cyclone it was nothing.

---

[1]**vaqueros** (vä-kâr´ōz): Spanish for *cowhands*.

At last the white stallion gave up the struggle. Pecos patted his neck gently and spoke to him in horse language. "I hope you will not be offended," he began as politely as possible, "but beauty such as yours is rare, even in this glorious state of Texas. I have no wish to break your proud spirit. I feel that together you and I would make a perfect team. Will you not be my partner at the I.X.L. Ranch?"

The horse neighed sadly. "It must be," he sighed. "I must give up my freedom. But since I must, I am glad that you are the man who has conquered me. Only Pecos Bill is worthy to fix a saddle upon the son of the great White Stallion, the Ghost King of the Prairie."

"I am deeply honored," said Pecos Bill, touched in his heart by the compliment.

"It is rather myself who am honored," replied the mustang, taking a brighter view of the situation.

The two of them went on for several hours saying nice things to each other. Before they were through, the pony was begging Pecos to be his master. Pecos was weeping and saying he was not fit to ride so magnificent a beast. In the end, however, Pecos Bill made two solemn promises. He would never place a bit in the pony's mouth. No other human would ever sit in his saddle.

The story of Bill's other love, Slue-Foot Sue, is a long one. It began with the tale of the Perpetual Motion Ranch. Bill had bought a mountain from Paul Bunyan. It looked to him like a perfect mountain for a ranch. It was shaped like a cone, with smooth sides covered with grassy meadows. At the top it was always winter. At the bottom it was always summer. In between it was always spring and fall. The sun always shone on one side; the other was always in shade. The cattle could have any climate they wished.

Bill had to breed a special kind of steer for his ranch. These had two short legs on one side and two long legs on the other. By traveling in one direction around the mountain, they were able to stand up straight on the steep sides.

The novelty wore off, however, and at last Bill sold the Perpetual Motion Ranch to an English duke. The day that the I.X.L. boys moved out, the lord moved in. He brought with him trainload after trainload of fancy English things. He had featherbeds and fine china and oil paintings and real silver and linen tablecloths and silk rugs. The cowboys laughed themselves almost sick when they saw these dude things being brought to a cattle ranch.

Pecos Bill didn't laugh. He didn't even notice the fancy things. All he could see was the English duke's beautiful daughter. She was as pretty as the sun and moon combined. Her hair was silky and red. Her eyes were blue. She wore a sweeping taffeta dress and a little poke bonnet with feathers on it. She was the loveliest creature Pecos Bill had ever seen.

She was as lively as she was pretty. Bill soon discovered that Slue-Foot Sue was a girl of talent. Before anyone could say "Jack Robinson," she changed into a cowboy suit and danced a jig to the tune of "Get Along, Little Dogies."

Bill soon lost all his interest in cowpunching. He spent his afternoons at the Perpetual Motion Ranch, teaching Sue to ride a broncho. Sue could ride as well as anyone, but she pretended to let him teach her. After several months of Bill's lessons, she put on a show. She jumped onto the back of a huge catfish in the Rio Grande River and rode all the way to the Gulf of Mexico, bareback. Bill was proud of her. He thought she had learned her tricks all from him.

Sue's mother was terribly upset by her daughter's behavior. She didn't care much for Bill. She was very proper. It was her fondest hope that Sue would stop being a tomboy and marry an earl or a member of Parliament.

130

As soon as she realized that her daughter was falling in love with a cowboy, she was nearly heart-broken. There was nothing she could do about it, however. Slue-Foot Sue was a headstrong girl who always had her own way.

At last the duchess relented. She invited Bill to tea and began to lecture him on English manners. She taught him how to balance a tea-cup, how to bow from the waist, and how to eat scones and marmalade[2] instead of beans and bacon. He learned quickly, and soon the duchess was pleased with him. She called him Colonel.

When the boys from the I.X.L. Ranch saw what was going on they were disgusted. Here was their boss, their brave, big, cyclone-riding Pecos Bill, mooning around in love like a sick puppy. They laughed at his dude manners. They made fun of his dainty appetite. When he dressed up in his finery to call on his girl, they stood in the bunkhouse door. They simpered and raised their eyebrows and said to one another, "La-dee-da, dearie, ain't we fine today!"

But for all their kidding they were broken-hearted. None of them had anything against Sue. They admired the way she rode a horse and played a guitar and danced a jig. But the thought of losing Bill to a woman was too much. Even worse was the thought that Bill might get married and bring a woman home to live with them. That was awful.

In spite of their teasing and the duchess's lessons, Bill asked Slue-Foot Sue to marry him. She accepted before he could back out. Her father, the lord, had always liked Bill and was terribly pleased at the match.

On his wedding day Pecos Bill shone like the sun in his new clothes. His boys were dressed in their finest chaps and boots for the occasion. Half of them were going to be groomsmen. The

---

[2]**scones and marmalade:** biscuit-like pastries and jam traditionally served in England.

other half were going to be bridesmen. At first Bill asked them to be bridesmaids, but they refused. They said that was going too far.

They rode to the Perpetual Motion Ranch in a fine procession, Bill at the head on Widow-Maker. The white horse pranced and danced with excitement.

At the ranch house waited the rest of the wedding party. The lord had sent back to England for a bishop to perform the ceremony. There stood His Eminence in his lace robes. On his one hand stood the duke in a cutaway coat. On his other hand stood the duchess in a stiff purple gown right from Paris.

Down the stairs came the bride. She was a vision of beauty. She wore a white satin dress cut in the latest fashion. It had a long lace train, but its chief glory was a bustle. A bustle was a wire contraption that fitted under the back of the dress. It made the skirt stand out and was considered very handsome in those days.

As Slue-Foot Sue danced down the steps even the cowhands forgot their sorrow. They jumped down from their horses and swept their sombreros from their heads. Pecos Bill lost his head. He leapt down from Widow-Maker and ran to meet her. "You are lovely," he murmured. "I promise to grant you every wish you make."

That was a mistake. A devilish gleam twinkled in Sue's eye. For months she had been begging Bill to let her ride Widow-Maker. Bill, of course, had always refused.

Now Sue saw her chance. Before she allowed the wedding to proceed, she demanded that Bill give her one ride on his white mustang.

"No, no!" cried Pecos Bill. Before he could stop her Sue dashed down the drive and placed her dainty foot into the stirrup. The duchess screamed. The bishop turned pale.

Widow-Maker gave an angry snort. The promise to him had been broken. He lifted his four feet off the ground and arched his back. Up, up, up shot Slue-Foot Sue. She disappeared into the clouds.

"Catch her, catch her!" roared Bill at the boys. They spread themselves out into a wide circle. Then from the sky came a scream like a siren. Down, down, down fell Sue. She hit the earth with terrible force.

She landed on her bustle. The wire acted as a spring. It bounced. Up again she flew.

Up and down, up and down between the earth and sky Sue bounced like a rubber ball. Every time she fell her bustle hit first. Back she bounced. This went on for a week. When at last she came back to earth to stay, she was completely changed. She no longer loved Pecos Bill.

The wedding was called off and the boys returned to the I.X.L. with their unhappy boss. For months he refused to eat. He lost interest in cow-punching. He was the unhappiest man Texas had ever seen.

At last he called his hands to-gether and made a long speech. He told them that the days of real cow-punching were over. The prairie was being fenced off by farmers. These "nesters," as he called them, were ruining the land for the ranchers. He was going to sell his herd.

The I.X.L. had its last roundup. Bill gathered all the prime steers together and put them on the train for Kansas City. Then he divided the cows and calves among his boys. He himself mounted Widow-Maker and rode away.

The boys hated to see him go, but they knew how he felt. "Nesters" or no "nesters," the real reason for his going was his broken heart.

None of them ever saw him again. Some of them thought he had gone back to the coyotes. Others had an idea that Slue-Foot Sue had changed her mind and that she and Bill were setting up housekeeping in some private canyon. But they never knew.

Some years later an old cowhand claimed that Bill had died. The great cowpuncher had met a dude rancher at a rodeo. The dude was dressed up in an outfit he had bought from a movie cowboy. The dude's chaps were made of doeskin. His boots were painted with landscapes and had heels three inches high. The brim of his hat was broad enough to cover a small circus. Bill took a good look at him and died laughing.

Illustrated by Ed Parker

Responding to

Pecos Bill and His Bouncing Bride

Thinking and Discussing

How well does Pecos Bill fit into the world of Slue-Foot Sue's family? How well does Slue-Foot Sue fit into Pecos Bill's world?

In what ways is Pecos Bill like the folk heroes Tony Beaver and John Henry? Do you think Slue-Foot Sue is a folk hero, too? Give reasons for your answers.

Many folk heroes perform impossible deeds, but readers rarely know how they feel as people. In this tale, however, Pecos Bill is treated differently. What do the events before and after the intended wedding reveal about Pecos Bill's character?

Choosing a Creative Response

Describing a Visit Suppose Pecos Bill and Slue-Foot Sue actually marry and settle down on a ranch. Imagine that your class visits them on a field trip. Can you picture how Pecos Bill and Slue-Foot Sue would react if a flood, an earthquake, or a blizzard were to occur during your visit? Pick some natural disaster, and tell what happens.

Creating Your Own Activity Plan and complete your own activity in response to "Pecos Bill and His Bouncing Bride."

Thinking and Writing

Write an engagement announcement that might appear in a local newspaper when Slue-Foot Sue and Pecos Bill decide to marry. Include an illustration of the couple and larger-than-life, exaggerated details such as those found in the tale.

EVENT

NO.2

Competition of Numskulls

Found in traditional tales all over the world, numskulls are simpletons who leave trails of chaos and confusion. Oddly enough, however, these trails lead directly to happy endings.

Four Brothers
Who Were
Both Wise and Foolish

retold by Virginia Haviland

nce, long ago, and this is the truth, there lived in Spain a farmer who had four sons: Ricardo, Roberto, Alfredo, and Bernardo.

The three older sons were wild and reckless. To plow the fields — that was a hateful task. To plant corn and wheat was a dull way to spend one's life. To milk goats was both foul-smelling and stupid.

"This is no sort of life for adventurous lads like us," said the three.

But Bernardo, the youngest, was cut from a different piece of cloth. He liked the push of the plow under his hands. He sang as he sowed the grain. And when he milked the goats, he had pleasant thoughts.

By working hard all together, yesterday, today, and tomorrow, their father had at last saved one silver peso. It was not much, but it was better than nothing.

He called his sons in from the fields and said to them: "This is my entire fortune. You have worked well. Divide this among you and go wherever your fancy leads you."

The four lads split the peso into quarter-pieces. Each put one in his pocket.

"Now we can seek our fortunes," said Ricardo.

"After that we will seek adventures," said Roberto.

"One of us must marry a King's daughter," said Alfredo.

But Bernardo shook his head. "I don't care much about doing any of those things. I had far rather stay at home."

His brothers scoffed. They called him a fool. They called him a silly fellow, a buffoon. They said he did not know when he was well off.

So, when they took their departure, Bernardo went with them. Hay foot, straw foot,[1] each followed his brother's heels until they came to a place where four roads crossed. Here they halted.

"Let us separate now," said Ricardo. "Let each of us follow his own road and find what fortune awaits him. At the end of a year, we will meet here. Is it agreed?"

"Agreed," said Roberto and Alfredo.

But Bernardo shook his head: "I don't care about going any farther. I'd rather go home."

But the others pulled him about, and called him a simpleton.

"I will take the road going north," said Ricardo.

"I will take the road going east," said Roberto.

"And I — the road south," said Alfredo.

That left for Bernardo the road going west. He took it with small comfort and tramped off without looking back.

On the road north, Ricardo was set upon by a band of robbers. They tied him to a donkey, after they took his quarter-piece of peso and beat him for having so little wealth. Then they bore him off to their hideaway in the mountains.

In six months their leader died. Ricardo by now had shown

[1]**Hay foot, straw foot:** left foot, right foot.

138

himself so reckless and clever that they made him chief of the band.

On the road going east, Roberto traded his silver for an old gun. By performing a trick here and another there, he managed to keep himself in food and his gun in bullets. He practiced shooting all day and every day, until his marksmanship became so perfect that he could clip the smallest leaf from its tree a half-mile away.

On the road south, Alfredo overtook a small man wearing enormous spectacles.

"Your glasses fit you badly," said Alfredo, "and what are you looking at?"

"Not much," said the man. "Just taking a look at China. They are having a great flood there."

"Marvelous," said Alfredo.

"Tiresome," said the small man. "When you look at China, you forget Spain. When you look inside a house in Persia, you forget there is a cozy little house waiting for you in Andalusia. I have grown rich seeing too much. Now I think I will go home and look no farther than the walls around my patio. You can have the spectacles for whatever you happen to have in your pocket."

"Agreed," said Alfredo.

And he gave the small man his quarter-piece of peso.

Bernardo, the youngest brother, wandered a day and a night along his road and found nothing. He was about to turn back, when he came across a coppersmith's shop.

All that second day he watched the coppersmith mending kettles, fitting copper bands about great casks, making pots and ladles and all sorts of useful things.

"If I can't be a farmer," he thought, "I will become a coppersmith." So he gave the fellow his quarter-piece to teach him his trade.

At the end of the year the four brothers met at the crossroads.

"I have become a robber chief. Anything in the world that I like I can take for my own," said Ricardo.

"I have become the greatest marksman in Spain," said Roberto, showing off his fowling-piece. "Show me the smallest object at the farthest distance, and I can hit it."

Alfredo put on his spectacles. "I can see the Emperor of China sitting down to tea in his garden and a fly that is crawling on his nose."

Bernardo hung his head. He could not look his fine brothers in the eye.

"Come, speak up, stupid one," said the others. "What have you to show for your year?"

"Nothing worth talking about. I am just a poor coppersmith. I can mend a pot or a kettle — that is all. Now let us go home."

The others laughed till their sides ached, calling him a goose — a simpleton — a buffoon — the worst one in all of Spain. "If we let you go home now you would remain a simpleton all your life. You shall come with us on our adventure."

Alfredo looked all around the world to see in what direction adventure might lie. "Oh — oh!" he said at last, and pointed to the east. "Yonder lies the sea. On the sea lies an island. On the island sleeps a captive Princess, guarded night and day by a giant sea serpent."

"We will rescue her!" shouted Ricardo.

"Agreed!" shouted Roberto and Alfredo.

Bernardo shook his head. "I don't care much about sea serpents, or rescuing a Princess. I'd rather go home."

But the others pulled him along. And before he knew it, they were looking across the sea. They fitted up a small vessel and set sail for the island. How many days they sailed does not matter. They reached there in the dark of dawn.

140

Alfredo put on his spectacles and looked. "The serpent sleeps," said he. "But he is coiled around the Princess to the height of the tower."

"Does the Princess sleep?" asked Bernardo.

"Of course she sleeps. What has that to do with it?" Alfredo was scornful.

"A sleeping Princess is not apt to scream. A screaming Princess could waken a sea serpent. Let us have our coffee first."

For once the others agreed. They had their coffee. Then Ricardo was put softly ashore.

"Watch me," he whispered. "Now I will steal the Princess, for that is my profession."

Everything went well until the last moment. Then Ricardo caught his foot on the serpent's tail. That woke him and he gave a great roar. That woke the Princess and she screamed. That set Ricardo running, hot for the beach. He swam and the serpent swam. Ricardo boarded the ship and set down the Princess. The serpent came close, very close.

"Now," said Roberto, "I will shoot the serpent, for that is my profession."

Shoot him he did, clean through the middle. But the serpent gave three dying lashes with the end of his tail. *Flip-flap-flop!* It cut the ship nearly in two. The three brothers and the Princess were terrified, for drowning looked very near.

"There is nothing to be scared of," said Bernardo. "Mending is my profession." He proceeded to get his tools and some long strips of copper and he welded the two parts of the ship together until she was as good as new. "Safe and snug," said he.

They lifted anchor and sailed to the country where the Princess's father was King. I cannot tell you if it was Greece or Persia or Asia. All I know is that the ship got there.

The King was enormously pleased to have his daughter rescued. He had been too busy with affairs of state to do it himself. And he was more than willing to reward the one who had done it. He would do it very handsomely — not only with the Princess herself, but with a large sack of gold as well.

"I rescued her," said Alfredo. And when the others looked surprised, he added, "Had I not put on my spectacles and discovered her, she would still be on the island."

"I rescued her," said Ricardo. "Didn't I steal her from the middle of the serpent's coils?"

"And stepped on his tail and woke him," reminded Roberto. "Had I not shot the serpent, where would we all be? Dead!"

The King listened solemnly. Then he pointed a finger at Bernardo: "*You* — what did you do?"

"Nothing much," said Bernardo. "When the serpent cut the ship in two, I mended it."

"Then *you* rescued the Princess." The King said it with such kingly authority that no one dared dispute him. "You shall marry the Princess."

Bernardo shook his head. "I don't care much about being the husband of a Princess," he said. "I would rather go home."

"Come, come!" said the King.

"Come, come!" said the brothers.

"Come," said the Princess. "I'll go with you. I've always wanted to milk a goat."

So they all separated. Ricardo took the road north and went back to his robber band. Roberto took his gun and went east. Alfredo put on his spectacles and stepped high into the south. But Bernardo and the Princess went west, singing all the way home.

Illustrated by Carol Schwartz

142

Responding to

Four Brothers
WHO WERE BOTH WISE AND FOOLISH

Thinking and Discussing

How does Bernardo's experience contrast with the experiences of his brothers during their first year away from home?

Throughout the tale, Bernardo says he wants to go home. What does this statement reveal about him?

This tale begins, "Once, long ago, and this is the truth, there lived in Spain . . ." How does this opening statement add to the humor in the tale?

Choosing a Creative Response

Writing a Tale At the end of the story, the brothers separate. Pick one of the brothers — Ricardo, Roberto, or Alfredo — and imagine future adventures he might have. Describe the adventures in a written tale of your own.

Describing the Perfect Gift You have been invited to Bernardo and the Princess's wedding, but you are unable to attend. Based on what you know about these characters, what gift would you like to send them? Write Bernardo and the Princess a brief note to say what the gift is and why you chose it for them. You might want to decorate your note.

Creating Your Own Activity Plan and complete your own activity in response to "Four Brothers Who Were Both Wise and Foolish."

When Shlemiel Went to Warsaw

by Isaac Bashevis Singer

Though Shlemiel was a lazybones and a sleepyhead and hated to move, he always daydreamed of taking a trip. He had heard many stories about faraway countries, huge deserts, deep oceans, and high mountains, and often discussed with Mrs. Shlemiel his great wish to go on a long journey. Mrs. Shlemiel would reply: "Long journeys are not for a Shlemiel. You better stay home and mind the children while I go to market to sell my vegetables." Yet Shlemiel could not bring himself to give up his dream of seeing the world and its wonders.

A recent visitor to Chelm had told Shlemiel marvelous things about the city of Warsaw. How beautiful the streets were, how high the buildings and luxurious the stores. Shlemiel decided once and for all that he must see this great city for himself. He knew that one had to prepare for a journey. But what was there for him to take? He had nothing but the old clothes he wore. One morning, after Mrs. Shlemiel left for the market, he told the older boys to stay home from cheder[1] and mind the younger

---

[1] **cheder** (kād′ər): a school where 7- to 13-year-old boys are taught to read Hebrew.

children. Then he took a few slices of bread, an onion, and a clove of garlic, put them in a kerchief, tied it into a bundle, and started for Warsaw on foot.

There was a street in Chelm called Warsaw Street and Shlemiel believed that it led directly to Warsaw. While still in the village, he was stopped by several neighbors who asked him where he was going. Shlemiel told them that he was on his way to Warsaw.

"What will you do in Warsaw?" they asked him.

Shlemiel replied: "What do I do in Chelm? Nothing."

He soon reached the outskirts of town. He walked slowly because the soles of his boots were worn through. Soon the houses and stores gave way to pastures and fields. He passed a peasant driving an ox-drawn plow. After several hours of walking, Shlemiel grew tired. He was so weary that he wasn't even hungry. He lay down on the grass near the roadside for a nap, but before he fell asleep he thought: "When I wake up, I may not remember which is the way to Warsaw and which leads back to Chelm." After pondering a moment, he removed his boots and set them down beside him with the toes pointing toward Warsaw and the heels toward Chelm. He soon fell asleep and dreamed that he was a baker baking onion rolls with poppy seeds. Customers came to buy them and Shlemiel said: "These onion rolls are not for sale."

"Then why do you bake them?"

"They are for my wife, my children, and for me."

Later he dreamed that he was the king of Chelm. Once a year, instead of taxes, each citizen brought him a pot of strawberry jam. Shlemiel sat on a golden throne and nearby sat Mrs. Shlemiel, the queen, and his children, the princes and princesses. They were all eating onion rolls and spooning up big portions of strawberry jam. A carriage arrived and took the royal family to Warsaw, America, and to the River Sambation, which spurts out stones the week long and rests on the Sabbath.

Near the road, a short distance from where Shlemiel slept, was a smithy. The blacksmith happened to come out just in time to see Shlemiel carefully placing his boots at his side with the toes facing in the direction of Warsaw. The blacksmith was a prankster and as soon as Shlemiel was sound asleep he tiptoed over and turned the boots around. When Shlemiel awoke, he felt rested but hungry. He got out a slice of bread, rubbed it with garlic, and took a bit of onion. Then he pulled his boots on and continued on his way.

He walked along and everything looked strangely familiar. He recognized houses that he had seen before. It seemed to him that he knew the people he met. Could it be that he had already reached another town, Shlemiel wondered. And why was it so similar to Chelm? He stopped a passer-by and asked the name of the town. "Chelm," the man replied.

Shlemiel was astonished. How was this possible? He had walked away from Chelm. How could he have arrived back there? He began to rub his forehead and soon found the answer to the riddle. There were two Chelms and he had reached the second one.

Still it seemed very odd that the streets, the houses, the people were so similar to those in the Chelm he had left behind. Shlemiel puzzled over this fact until he suddenly remembered something he had learned in cheder: "The earth is the same everywhere." And so why shouldn't the second Chelm be exactly like the first one? This discovery gave Shlemiel great satisfaction. He wondered if there was a street here like his street and a house on it like the one he lived in. And indeed he soon arrived at an identical street and house. Evening had fallen. He opened the door and to his amazement saw a second Mrs. Shlemiel with children just like his. Everything was exactly the same as in his own household. Even the cat seemed the same. Mrs. Shlemiel at once began to scold him.

"Shlemiel, where did you go? You left the house alone. And what have you there in that bundle?"

The children all ran to him and cried: "Papa, where have you been?"

Shlemiel paused a moment and then he said: "Mrs. Shlemiel, I'm not your husband. Children, I'm not your papa."

"Have you lost your mind?" Mrs. Shlemiel screamed.

"I am Shlemiel of Chelm One and this is Chelm Two."

Mrs. Shlemiel clapped her hands so hard that the chickens sleeping under the stove awoke in fright and flew out all over the room.

"Children, your father has gone crazy," she wailed. She immediately sent one of the boys for Gimpel, the healer. All the neighbors came crowding in. Shlemiel stood in the middle of the room and proclaimed: "It's true, you all look like the people in my town, but you are not the same. I come from Chelm One and you live in Chelm Two."

"Shlemiel, what's the matter with you?" someone cried. "You're in your own house, with your own wife and children, your own neighbors and friends."

"No, you don't understand. I come from Chelm One. I was on my way to Warsaw, and between Chelm One and Warsaw there is a Chelm Two. And that is where I am."

"What are you talking about. We all know you and you know all of us. Don't you recognize your chickens?"

"No, I'm not in my town," Shlemiel insisted. "But," he continued, "Chelm Two does have the same people and the same houses as Chelm One, and that is why you are mistaken. Tomorrow I will continue on to Warsaw."

"In that case, where is my husband?" Mrs. Shlemiel inquired in a rage, and she proceeded to berate Shlemiel with all the curses she could think of.

"How should I know where your husband is?" Shlemiel replied.

Some of the neighbors could not help laughing; others pitied the family. Gimpel, the healer, announced that he knew of no remedy for such an illness. After some time, everybody went home.

Mrs. Shlemiel had cooked noodles and beans that evening, a dish that Shlemiel liked especially. She said to him: "You may be mad, but even a madman has to eat."

"Why should you feed a stranger?" Shlemiel asked.

"As a matter of fact, an ox like you should eat straw, not noodles and beans. Sit down and be quiet. Maybe some food and rest will bring you back to your senses."

"Mrs. Shlemiel, you're a good woman. My wife wouldn't feed a stranger. It would seem that there is some small difference between the two Chelms."

The noodles and beans smelled so good that Shlemiel needed no further coaxing. He sat down and as he ate he spoke to the children.

"My dear children, I live in a house that looks exactly like this one. I have a wife and she is as like your mother as two peas are like each other. My children resemble you as drops of water resemble one another."

The younger children laughed; the older ones began to cry. Mrs. Shlemiel said: "As if being a Shlemiel wasn't enough, he had to go crazy in addition. What am I going to do now? I won't be able to leave the children with him when I go to market. Who knows what a madman may do?" She clasped her head in her hands and cried out: "God in heaven, what have I done to deserve this?"

Nevertheless, she made up a fresh bed for Shlemiel; and even though he had napped during the day, near the smithy, the moment his head touched the pillow he fell fast asleep and was soon snoring loudly. He again dreamed that he was the king of Chelm and that his wife, the queen, had fried for him a huge panful of blintzes. Some were filled with cheese, others with blueberries or cherries, and all were sprinkled with sugar and cinnamon and were drowning in sour cream. Shlemiel ate twenty blintzes all at once and hid the remainder in his crown for later.

In the morning, when Shlemiel awoke, the house was filled with townspeople. Mrs. Shlemiel stood in their midst, her eyes red with weeping. Shlemiel was about to scold his wife for letting so many strangers into the house, but then he remembered that he himself was a stranger here. At home he would have gotten up, washed, and dressed. Now in front of all these people he was at a loss as to what to do. As always when he was embarrassed, he began to scratch his head and pull at his beard. Finally, overcoming his bashfulness, he decided to get up. He threw off the covers and put his bare feet on the floor. "Don't let him run away," Mrs. Shlemiel screamed. "He'll disappear and I'll be a deserted wife, without a Shlemiel."

At this point Baruch, the baker, interrupted. "Let's take him to the Elders. They'll know what to do."

"That's right! Let's take him to the Elders," everybody agreed.

Although Shlemiel insisted that since he lived in Chelm One, the local Elders had no power over him, several of the strong young men helped him into his pants, his boots, his coat and cap and escorted him to the house of Gronam the Ox. The Elders, who had already heard of the matter, had gathered early in the morning to consider what was to be done.

As the crowd came in, one of the Elders, Dopey Lekisch, was saying, "Maybe there really are two Chelms."

"If there are two, then why can't there be three, four, or even a hundred Chelms?" Sender Donkey interrupted.

"And even if there are a hundred Chelms, must there be a Shlemiel in each one of them?" argued Shmendrick Numskull.

Gronam the Ox, the head Elder, listened to all the arguments but was not yet prepared to express an opinion. However, his wrinkled, bulging forehead indicated that he was deep in thought. It was Gronam the Ox who questioned Shlemiel. Shlemiel related everything that had happened to him, and when he finished, Gronam asked: "Do you recognize me?"

"Surely. You are wise Gronam the Ox."

"And in your Chelm is there also a Gronam the Ox?"

"Yes, there is a Gronam the Ox and he looks exactly like you."

"Isn't it possible that you turned around and came back to Chelm?" Gronam inquired.

"Why should I turn around? I'm not a windmill," Shlemiel replied.

"In that case, you are not this Mrs. Shlemiel's husband."

"No, I'm not."

"Then Mrs. Shlemiel's husband, the real Shlemiel, must have left the day you came."

"It would seem so."

"Then he'll probably come back."

"Probably."

"In that case, you must wait until he returns. Then we'll know who is who."

"Dear Elders, my Shlemiel has come back," screamed Mrs. Shlemiel. "I don't need two Shlemiels. One is more than enough."

"Whoever he is, he may not live in your house until everything is made clear," Gronam insisted.

"Where shall I live?" Shlemiel asked.

"In the poorhouse."

"What will I do in the poorhouse?"

"What do you do at home?"

"Good God, who will take care of my children when I go to market?" moaned Mrs. Shlemiel. "Besides, I want a husband. Even a Shlemiel is better than no husband at all."

"Are we to blame that your husband left you and went to Warsaw?" Gronam asked. "Wait until he comes home."

Mrs. Shlemiel wept bitterly and the children cried too. Shlemiel said: "How strange. My own wife always scolded me. My children talked back to me. And here a strange woman and strange children want me to live with them. It looks to me as if Chelm Two is actually better than Chelm One."

"Just a moment. I think I have an idea," interrupted Gronam.

"What is your idea?" Zeinvel Ninny inquired.

"Since we decided to send Shlemiel to the poorhouse, the town will have to hire someone to take care of Mrs. Shlemiel's children so she can go to market. Why not hire Shlemiel for that? It's true, he is not Mrs. Shlemiel's husband or the children's father. But he is so much like the real Shlemiel that the children will feel at home with him."

"What a wonderful idea!" cried Feyvel Thickwit.

"Only King Solomon[2] could have thought of such a wise solution," agreed Treitel the Fool.

"Such a clever way out of this dilemma could only have been thought of in our Chelm," chimed in Shmendrick Numskull.

"How much do you want to be paid to take care of Mrs. Shlemiel's children?" asked Gronam.

For a moment Shlemiel stood there completely bewildered. Then he said, "Three groschen a day."

"Idiot, moron, ass!" screamed Mrs. Shlemiel. "What are three groschen nowadays? You shouldn't do it for less than six a day." She ran over to Shlemiel and pinched him on the arm. Shlemiel winced and cried out, "She pinches just like my wife."

The Elders held a consultation among themselves. The town budget was very limited. Finally Gronam announced: "Three groschen may be too little, but six groschen a day is

---

[2]**King Solomon:** a tenth century B.C. king of Israel who was noted for his wisdom.

154

definitely too much, especially for a stranger. We will compromise and pay you five groschen a day. Shlemiel, do you accept?"

"Yes, but how long am I to keep this job?"

"Until the real Shlemiel comes home."

Gronam's decision was soon known throughout Chelm and the town admired his great wisdom and that of all the Elders of Chelm.

At first, Shlemiel tried to keep for himself the five groschen that the town paid him. "If I'm not your husband, I don't have to support you," he told Mrs. Shlemiel.

"In that case, since I'm not your wife, I don't have to cook for you, darn your socks, or patch your clothes."

And so, of course, Shlemiel turned over his pay to her. It was the first time that Mrs. Shlemiel had ever gotten any money for the household from Shlemiel. Now when she was in a good mood, she would say to him: "What a pity you didn't decide to go to Warsaw ten years ago."

"Don't you ever miss your husband?" Shlemiel would ask.

"And what about you? Don't you miss your wife?" Mrs. Shlemiel would ask.

And both would admit that they were quite happy with matters as they stood.

Years passed and no Shlemiel returned to Chelm. The Elders had many explanations for this. Zeinvel Ninny believed that Shlemiel had crossed the black mountains and had been eaten alive by the cannibals who live there. Dopey Lekisch thought that Shlemiel most probably had come to the Castle of Asmodeus, where he had been forced to marry a demon princess. Shmendrick Numskull came to the conclusion that Shlemiel had reached the edge of the world and had fallen off. There were many other theories. For example, that the real Shlemiel had lost his memory and had simply forgotten that he was Shlemiel. Such things do happen.

Gronam did not like to impose his theories on other people; however, he was convinced that Shlemiel had gone to the other Chelm, where he had had exactly the same experience as the Shlemiel in this Chelm. He had been hired by the local community and was taking care of the other Mrs. Shlemiel's children for a wage of five groschen a day.

As for Shlemiel himself, he no longer knew what to think. The children were growing up and soon would be able to take care of themselves. Sometimes Shlemiel would sit and ponder. Where is the other Shlemiel? When will he come home? What is my real wife doing? Is she waiting for me, or has she got herself another Shlemiel? These were questions that he could not answer.

Every now and then Shlemiel would still get the desire to go traveling, but he could not bring himself to start out. What was the point of going on a trip if it led nowhere? Often, as he sat alone puzzling over the strange ways of the world, he would become more and more confused and begin humming to himself:

"Those who leave Chelm
End up in Chelm.
Those who remain in Chelm
Are certainly in Chelm.
All roads lead to Chelm.
All the world is one big Chelm."

Illustrated by Ed Parker

Thinking and Discussing

Is Shlemiel the only fool in this tale? Explain your answer.

Chelm is the traditional home of fools in Jewish folklore. The author ends the tale by saying, "All the world is one big Chelm." What do you think he suggests by this observation?

Choosing a Creative Response

Writing Dialogue   Imagine Bernardo and Shlemiel together on a talk show, discussing their actions and attitudes toward life. Decide what each character might say. Suppose the two numskulls get into an argument about which one is happiest. What facts would each use to support his claim?

Creating Your Own Activity   Plan and complete your own activity in response to "When Shlemiel Went to Warsaw."

Exploring Language

New words and phrases come into the English language constantly. *Whopper* first appeared in 1858, and *tall tale* appeared in the 1920's. Other interesting words and phrases describing exaggeration arrived as follows: *fish story*, 1819; *flapdoodle*, 1850's; *hot air*, 1873; *hogwash*, 1904. Make a list of other words that describe exaggeration, and share it with your group. You may want to use a thesaurus or a dictionary of slang terms.

EVENT

No.3

Competition of Tricksters

Tricksters are wily pranksters who improvise for fun and profit. It's always amusing to watch them plan their tricky plots. Even more satisfying is seeing tricksters trapped in their own too-clever schemes.

Brother Coyote and Brother Cricket

retold by J. Frank Dobie

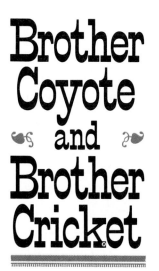

One summer evening about sundown a coyote trotting across the plain put his foot down on a tuft of grass wherein a cricket was singing *"Sereno en aquellos campos"* — "Serene in those fields."

The cricket jumped out and cried, "But, Brother Coyote, why are you destroying my palace?"

"I really did not know you lived here until you revealed yourself," the coyote said.

"You are crude and you insult me," the cricket said. He was ready to spring away.

"Insult you!" the coyote jeered. "Why, you dwarf, I am merely seeking my living, and now that I have you, I am going to eat you up. I had rather have a red watermelon or a fat kid, but I eat a cricket or a grasshopper when it's handy. Maybe you will fill the hollow in one of my molars."

"But, Brother Coyote," the cricket said, now in his soothing way, "it is not fair."

The coyote sat down on the carpet of grass. "Brother Cricket," he said, "you know that when nature offers itself, it is fair for nature to accept."

159

"But, Brother Coyote, you haven't given me a chance."

"Chance?" exclaimed the coyote. "Why, what sort of chance do you expect?"

"I want to fight a duel."

"You fight a duel with me?" And the coyote laughed.

"Yes, fight a duel with you," the cricket said.

"If I win, then my song will go on. If you win, then I'll fill the hollow in one of your respectable teeth."

The coyote looked away off across the plain, and saw a crow flying down in play at the waving tail of a striped skunk. "Well," he said, "perhaps the people need a comedy. All right, we'll have your duel, Brother Cricket."

"Oh, thank you very much, Brother Coyote."

"Now I sit here trembling at the sight of your armor and weapons," the coyote said. "But go on and name your terms."

"It is agreed," said the cricket. "You go and get your army together, and I will go and get my army together. Tomorrow when the sun is straight overhead, you have your army on the prairie just above the water called the Tank of the Seven Coons, and I will have my army in the thicket in the draw just below the dam to this tank. On the hour we shall engage in mortal combat."

"That is clear, General Cricket," said the coyote. "Until tomorrow at high noon, *adiós.*"

"*Adiós*, General Coyote."

That night General Coyote went east and west, north and south, summoning in high voice his forces to gather on the prairie above the Tank of the Seven Coons. He summoned the lobo,[1] the badger, the tiger of the deep canyon, the panther of the rimrock, the wildcat of the chaparral, the coon, the possum, the sharp fox, and all the other people with claws and teeth.

And in a singsong, General Cricket summoned his forces — the horseflies, the mosquitoes, the honey bees, the bumblebees, the yellow jackets, the black hornets, and even a colony of red ants — all the people that have stingers and can stick. He told them to gather in the thicket in the draw below the Tank of the Seven Coons.

Long before high noon, the people of fang and claw were assembling on the prairie above the water tank. General Coyote was trotting about, looking this way and that way, smelling and listening. The sun stood straight up, and still he could not see one sign of General Cricket's army.

Finally he called the fox and ordered him to scout out the position of the enemy. With his long nose pointed ahead, his ears alert and his eyes peeled, the fox went trotting down the draw. General Coyote was watching him. When he came to the edge of the thicket, the fox flattened to the ground and began twisting into the brush. Just as he was poking his keen snout into a clump of whitebrush to see and smell more closely, General Cricket ordered a battalion of black hornets to assault him.

They did, all at once. They stuck their stingers into his ears, into the corners of his eyes, into his nostrils, into his flanks, into every spot of his body where hair is short and skin is tender. He snapped and pitched, but only for a minute. He turned seventeen somersaults on the ground, and the black hornets came thicker. Then he streaked for the tank of water. He dived to escape his assaulters, and went to the bottom.

---

[1] **lobo:** Spanish for *wolf.*

161

But in a minute he had to come back up for air. Then, sticking his long, long mouth out of the water, he cried at the top of his voice, "General Coyote, retreat! The enemy are upon us!"

General Cricket had already ordered the yellow jackets to attack the army of giants on the prairie, and the war cries of the bumblebees were in the air.

"Retreat!" the fox shrieked again.

General Coyote tucked his tail between his legs and retreated and every soldier in the army tucked his tail and retreated also — all except the bobcat. He retreated without tucking his tail. That is how General Cricket won the duel with General Coyote.

Thus a person should avoid being vainglorious
and considering himself shrewder than he is.
He may be outwitted
by his own vanity.

Illustrated by Carol Schwartz

Brother Coyote and Brother Cricket

Thinking and Discussing

In this tale, the trickster is tricked — he is trapped in his own plot. What weaknesses in his character lead to his downfall?

Do you believe General Coyote and his army ever had a chance of winning the duel? Give reasons for your answer.

Choosing a Creative Response

Charting Character Traits People often assign particular character traits to certain animals because of the way the animals look or behave. For example, a coyote is often seen as a tricky, wily, sneaky character. Ants are seen as busy, and owls are considered wise. Choose two animals from General Cricket's army and two from General Coyote's, and make a chart of their traits. If you like, think of other animals with interesting traits, and add them to your chart.

Planning Strategy Suppose you are a spy for General Coyote in the camp of General Cricket. What information will you take back to your leader? What suggestions will you make for meeting the challenge of the "stingers and stickers"? With a partner make strategy notes, and share them with your group.

Creating Your Own Activity Plan and complete your own activity in response to "Brother Coyote and Brother Cricket."

COYOTE and LITTLE BLUE FOX

retold by Gail Robinson and Douglas Hill

When all the parts of the earth were still glossy with new-ness, Coyote felt a great enmity for one of the People, Little Blue Fox. It seemed to Coyote that Little Blue Fox was always somehow in his way, upsetting his plans, interfering with his life.

When Coyote went fishing, Little Blue Fox was usually to be found upstream, catching the best fish and leaving none for Coyote. If Coyote were trying to dig a rabbit out of its burrow, Little Blue Fox would lie in wait at the second hole leading out of the burrow, to snap up the rabbit as it escaped. If Coyote wanted a swim in a pool, Little Blue Fox would surely have been there first, stirring up silt and mud into the clear water. If Coyote went to have a meal at a human village, every time Little Blue Fox would be there before him, filling his belly and laughing.

Coyote spent a great deal of time thinking about how often he had been thwarted and disappointed by Little Blue Fox. As he thought about these things he grew angrier and angrier, so that the anger built up like the pressure of water behind a beaver dam. In that state, one day, Coyote saw Little Blue Fox out in open country ahead of him, ambling along, and the dam burst — so that Coyote's anger spilled out in a great shout.

"Little Blue Fox," Coyote shouted, "you have caused me enough pain and trouble — you will cause me no more! I am going to tear you to pieces!"

"Oh, please, don't do that, Coyote," Little Blue Fox said quickly. "At least not until I have had my fill of prairie chickens."

"What prairie chickens?" Coyote asked, suddenly both hungry and suspicious at the same time.

"Do you see that great tree?" said the Fox, pointing to a mighty pine whose lower branches left marks like those of brooms on the ground. "A large family of prairie chickens will soon come to meet me there. I have tricked them into believing that I am very ill, and dying, and the mother prairie chicken has promised to bring some medicinal herbs and seeds to cure me. I convinced her that her whole family should come too, so that they could bring me a large supply of seeds. They will be along any minute."

"Then they will be too late," Coyote growled, "for they will find you dead — and not from an illness!" And Coyote gathered himself to spring.

"No, please!" cried Little Blue Fox. "How can you be so cruel? All my life I have wanted to eat my fill of prairie chicken — just once. And now, when at last my wish is about to come true, you want to kill me. Please, Coyote, let me have my wish, and then kill me — and I will die happily."

Coyote thought for a moment. "All right," he said finally, "you may have your wish. And then I will have *my* wish — to see you dead."

"Thank you," said Fox. "You are the most generous of the People. And there will probably be enough prairie chicken for you as well."

"There had better be," said Coyote, licking his lips.

"Of course," said Little Blue Fox, "if they see you here they might turn away. Perhaps you should hide — but somewhere nearby where you can keep an eye on me," he added hastily.

Coyote nodded. "A sound idea. Now, I wonder where I could hide?"

"Perhaps you could hide up in the tree itself, and watch me from there," Little Blue Fox suggested.

"Perhaps I could hide in the tree," said Coyote as if Little Blue Fox had not spoken, "and watch you from there."

"Brilliant!" said Little Blue Fox. "Why did I not think of that?"

165

Coyote looked hard at him to see if there was mockery in his expression, but Little Blue Fox's face was still and unsmiling. Never once taking his eyes off the Fox, Coyote turned and began to climb the great tree.

Now, climbing trees was not something that Coyote did well — and large pine trees are unpleasant for any climber. Soon Coyote had to take his eyes off the Fox as he fought to squeeze between tightly tangled branches, or to stretch across spaces where there were no branches. The porcupine-sharp needles of the tree scratched him and seemed unerringly to aim for his eyes. Short twigs on the branches stabbed him; gluey pine gum matted his hair and stuck to his skin; dead branches broke away beneath his feet; scaly bark scrapings fell grittily into his eyes and mouth. It was a slow, arduous and painful climb, but finally — sore, sticky and bleeding — Coyote tucked himself into a high crotch of the tree and peered hopefully down, expecting to see a flock of prairie chickens hurrying to their appointment with Little Blue Fox.

Instead, he saw the Fox himself hurrying off across the plain, kicking up little puffs of dust as he ran.

For a moment Coyote sat perfectly still and quiet in the tree-top. Then he howled — a high, drawn-out howl of pain and rage and humiliation.

Afterwards, he began the slow and tortuous climb down from the tree.

On the ground again, Coyote hurried as fast as his

sore feet would allow along the trail left by Little Blue Fox. In spite of his soreness, he was still the fastest runner of the plains — so it was not long before he began to catch sight of the dust trail of Little Blue Fox in the distance every time he topped a rise of land. But Little Blue Fox was looking back, and he too could see the dust-line of Coyote. When Little Blue Fox saw his hunter, he quickly changed direction, seeking the rocky beds of dried streams, or clutches of thorn-bush surrounded by toe-blistering sand. But Coyote stayed on his trail, though it had become a more painful one to follow.

Shortly Coyote came round a rock outcropping and found himself at a spot where the plain rose suddenly, forming a high, flat-topped hump of land with sheer cliffs along one side of it, slabbed with scales of rock. There, to his astonishment, was Little Blue Fox, standing with his back against the cliff, his legs braced, pushing against the cliff-face with all his strength.

Before Coyote could say anything, Little Blue Fox shouted, "Thank goodness you have come! Help me quickly — I don't think I can hold it by myself!"

"Hold what?" said the puzzled Coyote. "What do you think you're doing?"

"The cliff!" shouted the Fox. "The cliff began to fall and I am holding it back — but I need your help!"

"I'm not listening to any more of your tricks," Coyote snarled. "I've listened to you enough. This time I really am going to tear you to bits."

"Then we will both die," Little Blue Fox told him, "for if I let this cliff wall go, it will surely fall on both of us."

"Lies!" Coyote said. "That cliff wall has been standing since the beginning of the world and will probably be still standing at the end."

"No, it is falling!" Little Blue Fox protested, still pushing against the cliff as hard as he could. "As I came past, some bits of rock trickled down, and I saw that I had to prop up the cliff before all of it collapsed."

As he spoke, far above them a rabbit became disturbed at the sound of their voices and scrambled into its hole near the edge of the cliff, dislodging a few loose pebbles. They spattered down along the cliff-face and fell directly past Coyote's nose.

"There you are!" cried Little Blue Fox delightedly. "I am telling you the truth! Now you must help me, for I cannot hold the cliff alone much longer!"

Coyote had given a start of fright as the pebbles fell. Now, convinced, he leaped to the Fox's side and leaned his shoulder as hard as he could against the cliff.

"Push harder!" Little Blue Fox cried. "Push!" And Coyote strained and heaved against the wall.

"What are we going to do?" Coyote gasped. "We can't stand here forever holding up this cliff."

"If only one of us were strong enough to hold it by himself for a while," said Little Blue Fox, panting with the effort of pushing.

"Why, I'm sure I could hold it," Coyote said.

"I'm sure you could too," said Little Blue Fox. "If you take all the weight, I will go and find a log to prop up the cliff."

"All right," said Coyote. He began to push so hard against the cliff that his eyes bulged out and turned red all round their edges. "Off you go, then," he grunted. "But hurry!"

Little Blue Fox pulled away from the wall slowly, as if to make sure that Coyote could really take the strain, stepping back gingerly, then moving away softly as if a heavy footstep might bring the whole cliff crashing down on top of them both.

"Hurry!" Coyote repeated.

"I'll try," said Little Blue Fox, "but it may take me a little while to find a log strong enough. Be patient!"

And he rushed off as if his life depended on it — which, of course, it did.

Coyote remained still, his teeth bared and his muscles knotted with strain, forcing his shoulder as hard as he could against the unyielding rock. Soon the shoulder began to feel sore. As time went on, it began to ache fiercely. By then, also, Coyote's head was throbbing from the heat of the sun's direct beams, doubly strong because reflected off the rock wall of the cliff, and his throat was dry and clenched with thirst.

"Where is that Fox?" he muttered to himself. "Perhaps he is not strong enough to bring a large log quickly. Poor weak thing — it's as well that I came along to hold up this cliff."

And, proudly, he leaned even harder into the cliff-face and tried to ignore the agony in his shoulder and the fact that his tongue had glued itself to the roof of his mouth with thirst.

But finally, as the day waned and as dusk came to cling to the cliff, he could no longer pretend that he was not suffering.

"I'll have to let the cliff fall, and risk being caught under it," he said to himself, "for I will certainly die of thirst if I stay here longer."

So he gathered up his legs, carefully and slowly, without releasing the pressure against the cliff. Then he made an enormous leap backwards, turning in the air as he went, and ran away from the cliff as fast as only Coyote can run.

Behind him the stillness of the evening remained unbroken. Coyote was not at first aware of the silence. But when he heard no rumble of falling rock, he slowed his pace and looked back over his shoulder.

The cliff had not fallen. It did not look to be in the remotest danger of ever falling, throughout all time.

Coyote could not contain his rage. He howled, he shrieked, he leaped into the air, he rolled on the ground, he ran around in small circles snapping at shadows.

"Now he has gone too far!" Coyote screamed. "Too far! I will tear out his tongue! I will pull off his head! I will . . ." Unable to think of any more terrible things to do to Little Blue Fox, he raced off through the evening in the direction the Fox had taken.

Soon Coyote's nose told him he was approaching a small lake, which reminded him all over again how painfully thirsty he had been, before his anger turned his mind away from it.

"Little Blue Fox is thirsty too," Coyote muttered to himself. "Now I will catch him."

Through a small stand of trees Coyote rushed down to bury his face in the lake's cool surface. But there he slid to a hasty stop, unable to believe his eyes.

As if nothing had happened, Little Blue Fox was standing quietly by the side of the lake, outlined by the light of the moon that had just climbed above the nearby trees.

"Drink before you do anything else," Little Blue Fox said gently. "It will make you feel much better."

"I will not!" shouted the raging Coyote. "I will never again do anything you say! I am going to tear you to pieces this minute, without delay!"

"Don't be foolish," Little Blue Fox said, stepping nearer to Coyote. "You ought to have a drink before killing me, so you can enjoy it more. Here — if you hold on to my arm you will know I cannot get away, so you may drink in peace. The water is cool from fresh underground streams."

By then, all the talk of drinking had made Coyote's thirst even more desperate. Without a word, he roughly grasped Fox's wrist and turned to plunge his face into the water, gulping until he had to stop for breath.

"I'm glad you came along," Little Blue Fox said genially. "I was hoping some strong swimmer would come to help me retrieve that large maize[1] cake out there in the water."

Coyote raised his dripping face and looked at the lake. As the ripples from his drinking smoothed, he saw what seemed to be a large yellow disc lying in the darkened water.

"I went to a great deal of trouble to get that cake from the humans," Fox went on. "Now if someone doesn't hurry and dive for it, it will sink beyond reach. Just look at the size of it."

Coyote looked, and his stomach turned over with hunger.

"How did the cake come to be in the lake?" Coyote asked with suspicion.

"I was on my way back to you," Little Blue Fox said airily, "when I stopped here for a drink and stupidly let the cake drop into the water."

Coyote paused, unable to think clearly for the noise his stomach was making. "I don't think even I can dive that deeply."

"There is a way," Fox said thoughtfully. "You could tie a large stone round your neck, which would make you heavy enough to sink down to the cake."

---

[1]**maize** (māz): corn.

"Perhaps I could tie a large stone round my neck," Coyote said, again as if Little Blue Fox had not spoken, "and let it sink me down to the cake."

"Wonderful!" said Little Blue Fox. "How clever you are."

"I can already taste the delicious flavour of maize cake," said Coyote gleefully.

He bounded off and found the biggest rock he could carry, while Fox swiftly twisted together some grass fibres to make a short and sturdy rope. Then he tied the rope to the rock. Coyote helpfully lifted his chin while Fox tied the other end round his neck. Then they went to the edge of the lake, where a ledge of mossy rock jutted out above the deepest part.

"Now," said Little Blue Fox, "I will throw the rock as far as I can from this edge and at the same time you jump."

Coyote peered over the edge at the still surface of the lake. "Are you quite sure . . . ?" he began.

But Fox cut in quickly. "Remember the delicious taste of maize cake," he said. "All you need to do is jump, and soon your belly will be full."

As if it had heard, Coyote's stomach gave a loud rumble. "All right," said Coyote, "here I go."

Little Blue Fox picked up the rock and, with a mighty heave, threw it over the edge of the outcropping, and Coyote leaped out and plunged down into the water.

Chuckling to himself, Fox watched for a moment as the rock dragged Coyote down into the black depths, with Coyote looking this way and that for the maize cake. But it was not to be found, for of course the yellow disc had been the reflection of the full moon, which Coyote had been too hungry and too impatient to notice. Then, still laughing, Little Blue Fox ran off into the darkness.

What seemed a very long time later, Coyote came to the surface of the lake and scrabbled weakly out of the water. There on the lake's edge he lay still — exhausted, half-starved, half-drowned. By the time he was able to stand up, Little Blue Fox was far, far away.

"I think I will leave that Fox alone from now on," Coyote thought to himself as he stumbled back to his home, "for he will surely kill me dead if we meet again."

Illustrated by Vince Caputo

COYOTE AND LITTLE BLUE FOX

Thinking and Discussing

On three occasions, Little Blue Fox successfully tricks Coyote. How does this repetition affect the suspense and humor of the tale?

List the tricks Little Blue Fox plays on Coyote. Why does Coyote fall for all of Little Blue Fox's tricks even though he is suspicious of each one?

What similar lesson, or moral, do "Brother Coyote and Brother Cricket" and "Coyote and Little Blue Fox" suggest?

Choosing a Creative Response

Drawing Coyote Comics Suppose Coyote foolishly decides to go after Little Blue Fox once more. Create a comic strip to show how the cool, clever fox outsmarts — for the fourth time — the angry but gullible coyote. As an alternative, you could show Coyote finally outwitting Little Blue Fox. How does he do it? How does Little Blue Fox respond? Be sure to include speech balloons for the characters.

Creating Your Own Activity Plan and complete your own activity in response to "Coyote and Little Blue Fox."

The Story of the King's Lettuce

from *Watership Down* by Richard Adams

Watership Down is the story of a small band of rabbits who, when their home is threatened with destruction, set out on a quest to establish a new and better society. Along the way, they face many dangers and hardships. However, even in the worst of times, they huddle together for comfort and tell tales about the most legendary rabbit of them all — El-ahrairah.

They say that there was a time when El-ahrairah[1] and his followers lost all their luck. Their enemies drove them out and they were forced to live down in the marshes of Kelfazin. Now, where the marshes of Kelfazin may be I do not know, but at the time when El-ahrairah and his followers were living there, of all the dreary places in the world they were the dreariest. There was no food but coarse grass and even the grass was mixed with bitter rushes and docks. The ground was too wet for digging: the water stood in any hole that was made. But all the other animals had grown so suspicious of El-ahrairah and his tricks that they would not let him out of that wretched country and every day Prince Rainbow used to come walking through the marshes to make sure that El-ahrairah was still there. Prince Rainbow had the power of the sky and the power of the hills and Frith[2] had told him to order the world as he thought best.

One day, when Prince Rainbow was coming through the marshes, El-ahrairah went up to him and said, "Prince Rainbow, my people are cold and cannot get underground because of the wet. Their food is so dull and poor that they will be ill when the bad weather comes. Why do you keep us here against our will? We do no harm."

"El-ahrairah," replied Prince Rainbow, "all the animals know that you are a thief and a trickster. Now your tricks have caught up with you and you have to live here until you can persuade us that you will be an honest rabbit."

"Then we shall never get out," said El-ahrairah, "for I would be ashamed to tell my people to stop living on their wits. Will you let us out if I can swim across a lake full of pike?"

"No," said Prince Rainbow, "for I have heard of that trick of yours, El-ahrairah, and I know how it is done."

"Will you let us go if I can steal the lettuces from King Darzin's garden?" asked El-ahrairah.

---

[1]**El-ahrairah:** pronounced Elil-hrair-rah with stresses the same as in the phrase "Never say die."
[2]**Frith:** the rabbits' major deity.

Now, King Darzin ruled over the biggest and richest of the animal cities in the world at that time. His soldiers were very fierce and his lettuce garden was surrounded by a deep ditch and guarded by a thousand sentries day and night. It was near his palace, on the edge of the city where all his followers lived. So when El-ahrairah talked of stealing King Darzin's lettuces, Prince Rainbow laughed and said,

"You can try, El-ahrairah, and if you succeed I will multiply your people everywhere and no one will be able to keep them out of a vegetable garden from now till the end of the world. But what will really happen is that you will be killed by the soldiers and the world will be rid of a smooth, plausible rascal."

"Very well," said El-ahrairah. "We shall see."

Now, Yona the hedgehog was nearby, looking for slugs and snails in the marshes, and he heard what passed between Prince Rainbow and El-ahrairah. He slipped away to the great palace of King Darzin and begged to be rewarded for warning him against his enemies.

"King Darzin," he sniffled, "that wicked thief El-ahrairah has said he will steal your lettuces and he is coming to trick you and get into the garden."

King Darzin hurried down to the lettuce garden and sent for the captain of the guard.

"You see these lettuces?" he said. "Not one of them has been stolen since the seed was sown. Very soon now they will be ready and then I mean to hold a great feast for all my people. But I have heard that that scoundrel El-ahrairah means to come and steal them if he can. You are to double the guards: and all the gardeners and weeders are to be examined every day. Not one leaf is to go out of the garden until either I or my chief taster gives the order."

The captain of the guard did as he was told. That night El-ahrairah came out of the marshes of Kelfazin and went secretly up to the great ditch. With him was his trusty Captain of Owsla,[3] Rabscuttle. They squatted in the bushes and watched the doubled guards patrolling

[3] **Owsla:** the palace guard.

up and down. When the morning came they saw all the gardeners and weeders coming up to the wall and every one was looked at by three guards. One was new and had come instead of his uncle who was ill, but the guards would not let him in because they did not know him by sight and they nearly threw him into the ditch before they would even let him go home. El-ahrairah and Rabscuttle came away in perplexity and that day, when Prince Rainbow came walking through the fields, he said, "Well, well, Prince with the Thousand Enemies, where are the lettuces?"

"I am having them delivered," answered El-ahrairah. "There will be rather too many to carry." Then he and Rabscuttle went secretly down one of their few holes where there was no water, put a sentry outside and thought and talked for a day and a night.

On the top of the hill near King Darzin's palace there was a garden and here his many children and his chief followers' children used to be taken to play by their mothers and nursemaids. There was no wall round the garden. It was guarded only when the children were there: at night it was empty, because there was nothing to steal and no one to be hunted. The next night Rabscuttle, who had been told by El-ahrairah what he had to do, went to the garden and dug a scrape. He hid in the scrape all night; and the next morning, when the children were brought to play, he slipped out and joined them. There were so many children that each one of the mothers and nursemaids thought that he must belong to somebody else, but as he was about the same size as the children and not much different to look at, he was able to make friends with some of them. Rabscuttle was full of tricks and games and quite soon he was running and playing just as if he had been one of the children himself. When the time came for the children to go home, Rabscuttle went, too. They came up to the gate of the city and the guards saw Rabscuttle with King Darzin's son. They stopped him and asked which was his mother, but the King's son said, "You let him alone. He's my friend," and Rabscuttle went in with all the others.

Now, as soon as Rabscuttle got inside the King's palace, he scurried off and went into one of the dark burrows; and here he hid all day. But in the evening he came out and made his way to the royal storerooms, where the food was being got ready for the King and his chief followers and wives. There were grasses and fruits and roots and even nuts and berries, for King Darzin's people went everywhere in those days, through the woods and fields. There were no soldiers in the storerooms and Rabscuttle hid there in the dark. And he did all he could to make the food bad, except what he ate himself.

That evening King Darzin sent for the chief taster and asked him whether the lettuces were ready. The chief taster said that several of them were excellent and that he had already had some brought into the stores.

"Good," said the King. "We will have two or three tonight."

But the next morning the King and several of his people were taken ill with bad stomachs. Whatever they ate, they kept on getting ill, because Rabscuttle was hiding in the storerooms and spoiling the food as fast as it was brought in. The King ate several more lettuces, but he got no better. In fact, he got worse.

After five days Rabscuttle slipped out again with the children and came back to El-ahrairah. When he heard that the King was ill and that Rabscuttle had done all he

wanted, El-ahrairah set to work to disguise himself. He clipped his white tail and made Rabscuttle nibble his fur short and stain it with mud and blackberries. Then he covered himself all over with trailing strands of goose grass and big burdocks and he even found ways to alter his smell. At last even his own wives could not recognize him, and El-ahrairah told Rabscuttle to follow some way behind and off he went to King Darzin's palace. But Rabscuttle waited outside, on the top of the hill.

When he got to the palace, El-ahrairah demanded to see the captain of the guard. "You are to take me to the King," he said. "Prince Rainbow has sent me. He has heard that the King is ill and he has sent for me, from the distant land beyond Kelfazin, to find the cause of his sickness. Be quick! I am not accustomed to be kept waiting."

"How do I know this is true?" asked the captain of the guard.

"It is all one to me," replied El-ahrairah. "What is the sickness of a little king to the chief physician of the land beyond the golden river of Frith? I will return and tell Prince Rainbow that the King's guard were foolish and gave me such treatment as one might expect from a crowd of flea-bitten louts."

He turned and began to go away, but the captain of the guard became frightened and called him back. El-ahrairah allowed himself to be persuaded and the soldiers took him to the King.

After five days of bad food and bad stomach, the King was not inclined to be suspicious of someone who said that Prince Rainbow had sent him to make him better. He begged El-ahrairah to examine him and promised to do all he said.

El-ahrairah made a great business of examining the King. He looked at his eyes and his ears and his teeth and his droppings and the ends of his claws and he inquired what he had been eating. Then he demanded to see the royal storerooms and the lettuce garden. When he came back he looked very grave and said, "Great King, I know well what sorry news it will be to you, but the cause of your sickness is those very lettuces by which you set such store."

"The lettuces?" cried King Darzin. "Impossible! They are all grown from good, healthy seed and guarded day and night."

"Alas!" said El-ahrairah. "I know it well! But they have been infected by the dreaded Lousepedoodle, that flies in ever decreasing circles through the Gunpat of the Cludge — a deadly virus — dear me, yes! — isolated by the purple Avvago and maturing in the gray-green forests of the Okey Pokey. This, you understand, is to put the matter for you in simple terms, insofar as I can. Medically speaking, there are certain complexities with which I will not weary you."

"I cannot believe it," said the King.

"The simplest course," said El-ahrairah, "will be to prove it to you. But we need not make one of your subjects ill. Tell the soldiers to go out and take a prisoner."

The soldiers went out and the first creature they found was Rabscuttle, grazing on the hilltop. They dragged him through the gates and into the King's presence.

"Ah, a rabbit," said El-ahrairah. "Nasty creature! So much the better. Disgusting rabbit, eat that lettuce!"

Rabscuttle did so and soon afterward he began to moan and thrash about. He kicked in convulsions and rolled his eyes. He gnawed at the floor and frothed at the mouth.

"He is very ill," said El-ahrairah. "He must have got an exceptionally bad one. Or else, which is more probable, the infection is particularly deadly to rabbits. But, in any event, let us be thankful it was not Your Majesty. Well, he has served our purpose. Throw him out! I would strongly advise Your Majesty," went on El-ahrairah, "not to leave the lettuces where they are, for they will shoot and flower and seed. The infection will spread. I know it is disappointing, but you must get rid of them."

At that moment, as luck would have it, in came the captain of the guard, with Yona the hedgehog.

"Your Majesty," he cried, "this creature returns from the marshes of Kelfazin. The people of El-ahrairah are mustering for war. They say they are coming to attack Your Majesty's garden and steal the royal lettuces. May I have Your Majesty's order to take out the soldiers and destroy them?"

"Aha!" said the King. "I have thought of a trick worth two of that. 'Particularly deadly to rabbits.' Well! Well! Let them have all the lettuces they want. In fact, you are to take a thousand down to the marshes of Kelfazin and leave them there. Ho! Ho! What a joke! I feel all the better for it!"

"Ah, what deadly cunning!" said El-ahrairah. "No wonder Your Majesty is ruler of a great people. I believe you are already recovering. As with many illnesses, the cure is simple, once perceived. No, no, I will accept no reward. In any case, there is nothing here that would be thought of value in the shining land beyond the golden river of Frith. I have done as Prince Rainbow required. It is sufficient. Perhaps you will be so good as to tell your guards to accompany me to the foot of the hill?" He bowed, and left the palace.

Later that evening, as El-ahrairah was urging his rabbits to growl more fiercely and run up and down in the marshes of Kelfazin, Prince Rainbow came over the river.

"El-ahrairah," he called, "am I bewitched?"

"It is quite possible," said El-ahrairah. "The dreaded Lousepedoodle —"

"There are a thousand lettuces in a pile at the top of the marsh. Who put them there?"

"I told you they were being delivered," said El-ahrairah. "You could hardly expect my people, weak and hungry as they are, to carry them all the way from King Darzin's garden. However, they will soon recover now, under the treatment that I shall prescribe. I am a physician, I may say, and if you have not heard as much, Prince Rainbow, you may take it that you soon will, from another quarter. Rabscuttle, go out and collect the lettuces."

Then Prince Rainbow saw that El-ahrairah had been as good as his word, and that he himself must keep his promise, too. He let the rabbits out of the marshes of Kelfazin and they multiplied everywhere. And from that day to this, no power on earth can keep a rabbit out of a vegetable garden, for El-ahrairah prompts them with a thousand tricks, the best in the world.

Illustrated by Vince Caputo

Responding to

The Story of the King's Lettuce

Thinking and Discussing

How does El-ahrairah's understanding of the king's character help him to succeed? What does this understanding reveal about El-ahrairah's character?

Why might El-ahrairah be considered both a trickster and a hero?

Choosing a Creative Response

Talking Nonsense As part of his effort to trick King Darzin, El-ahrairah resorts to nonsensical language, claiming the king's disease is caused by "the dreaded Lousepedoodle, that flies in ever decreasing circles through the Gunpat of the Cludge . . . isolated by the purple Avvago and maturing in the gray-green forests of the Okey Pokey."

Write a brief persuasive argument using a similar mixture of real and nonsensical words. For example, you could try to persuade a parent to let you go somewhere or do something, or you could try to talk a friend into doing a chore or task for you.

Training Tricksters Write a training manual entitled "How to Be a Trickster." Use what you have learned about the characteristics and actions of tricksters. Remember to include a definition of "trickster," a detailed description of a trickster's characteristics, and pointers on how to become a successful trickster. Compare manuals as a group.

Creating Your Own Activity Plan and create your own activity in response to "The Story of the King's Lettuce."

THINKING ABOUT TRADITIONAL TALES

Judging the Contest

Now that you've read a variety of traditional tales, vote for your favorite in each event — folk heroes, numskulls, and tricksters. Which one was most entertaining? Most humorous? Most instructive? Make a ballot like the one on your program, and mark your choices. Then add up the votes of everyone in the class to find out which tales are the winners!

Predicting Oral Traditions

The ballad and tales you read in "Folk Heroes, Numskulls, and Tricksters" are part of various oral traditions. Some expressions you hear every day will eventually become part of our oral tradition. What stories and sayings will survive to become part of the oral tradition in your life? You may want to consider stories, song lyrics, jump-rope rhymes, jokes, riddles, commercials, and humorous words and phrases used in your community or part of the country.

Talk to people in your community for ideas. Working with a group, collect as many examples as you can. Then create a book, illustrating it as you wish.

Acting Out Emotions

Storytellers use precise, effective words to show that a character is experiencing emotions such as happiness, shyness, and excitement. An angry character might *scream* or *growl*. A shy character might *whisper* or *murmur*. In "Coyote and Little Blue Fox," Coyote *growls* and *snarls* to show his anger.

Write the names of ten emotions on slips of paper. Have a group member draw an emotion and act it out while the other group members guess which emotion is being portrayed.

Collecting Cartoons of Tales

Working with a group, create one-frame cartoons or comic strips of your favorite characters and scenes in "Folk Heroes, Numskulls, and Tricksters." Include humorous captions or speech balloons if you wish. Then combine your cartoons with those of other groups to make a book entitled *Cartoons of Tales*.

ABOUT THE AUTHORS

Anne Malcolmson was born in 1910 and has taught school for many years. She became frustrated in her search for a book of American folktales for her students and decided to write one herself, using the tales of Pecos Bill, Paul Bunyan, and other American folk heroes she had heard of as a child.

Malcolmson's first collection of folktales, *Yankee Doodle's Cousins*, appeared in 1941. She has since published more books of folktales as well as books on other subjects.

Virginia Haviland was born in 1911 in New York State but grew up in New England. After graduating from Cornell University in 1933, she became a librarian. In 1963 she began working as the head of the Children's Book Section at the Library of Congress in Washington, D.C. She was best known as the editor and compiler of the *Favorite Fairy Tales* series that includes volumes of stories from around the world. Haviland died in 1988.

Isaac Bashevis Singer was born in Poland in 1904 and grew up in Warsaw. Singer was trained to be a rabbi, but he decided — against his family's wishes — to become a writer. He emigrated to the United States in 1935.

Zlateh the Goat, Singer's first book for young people, was published in 1966. His other works for youngsters have included *When Shlemiel Went to Warsaw*, *A Day of Pleasure*, *Alone in the Wild Forest*, and *The Power of Light*.

Singer was awarded the Nobel Prize for Literature in 1978 for his contribution to literature for both adults and children. He died in 1991.

J. Frank Dobie was born in 1888 and spent his childhood on a ranch in the brush country of southwestern Texas. He taught English and English literature at several universities in Texas and Oklahoma, but his real love was folklore. In 1921 Dobie helped to organize the Texas Folklore Society and began "setting down the lore of Texas and the Southwest." *I'll Tell You a Tale* is one of his collections of folktales. He died in 1964.

Gail Robinson is a Canadian poet whose works have been published in Great Britain and North America. She has lived among the Native Americans of Canada and the United States and has heard many of their tales directly from them. A number of these tales appear in *Coyote, the Trickster*.

Douglas Hill, born in 1935 in Manitoba, Canada, is a poet and author of science fiction and history books. At one point he lived among the Native Americans of North America and heard many of their tales firsthand. His interest in folklore has led to frequent contributions to *Man, Myth & Magic*, a weekly encyclopedia of folklore and magic. He is a co-author of *Coyote, the Trickster*.

Richard Adams was born in 1920 in England. He worked in England's Department of Environment until 1974, when he became a full-time writer. His book *Watership Down* won both Britain's Guardian Award and Britain's Carnegie Medal as an outstanding book for young people. *Watership Down* was also very popular in the United States, where it was sold as a book for adults. Adams's other books include adult novels and two books about nature. Adams lives on the Isle of Man, west of the Scottish coast.

Future Entries and Contestants

Grandfather Tales
collected and retold by
Richard Chase (Houghton, 1976)
Mr. Chase has captured for
all time the rich humor of these
folktales from North Carolina and
Virginia. The zestful mountain
speech that characterizes the tales
makes enjoyable reading for
all ages.

Shlemiel and Other Fools of Chelm
by Isaac Bashevis Singer (Houghton, 1993)
In this new collection, six favorites
from *When Shlemiel Went to Warsaw* appear
with *The Fools of Chelm and Their History*.
The Yiddish folklore of eastern Europe
delights and amuses readers who love tales.

Joe Magarac and His U.S.A. Citizen Papers
by Irwin Shapiro (University of Pittsburgh Press, 1979)

This is an exciting tale about an American folk hero, Hungarian-born Joe Magarac of the Pennsylvania steel mills.

The Merry Adventures of Robin Hood of Great Renown in Nottinghamshire
by Howard Pyle (Scribner, 1976)

In old ballads and tales of medieval England, the folk hero Robin Hood and his outlaw band steal from the rich and give to the poor. This classic is wonderfully illustrated by Howard Pyle.

A Natural Man: The True Story of John Henry by Steve Sanfield (Godine, 1986)

A noted storyteller writes his version of "The Ballad of John Henry," from John Henry's birth to his race with a steam drill.

BOOK 3

TOURING
ANCIENT
CHINA

191

A Link with the Past

Before you stands the Great Wall of China. It stretches out as far as the eye can see, to faraway places, to faraway times. Imagine an age when fortified borders determined the fate of ancient kingdoms. It was in just such an age when the Chinese Empire was born. The Great Wall is a reminder of that time. And it is a reminder of the frontier that helped shape the history of ancient Chinese civilization.

Historic Sites

From *Across the Centuries,* a social studies textbook

The Flowering of Chinese Civilization

What were the most significant achievements of the Tang and Sung dynasties?

Key Terms

- aristocrat
- meritocracy
- mandate
- Confucianism

➤ *Here is a part of the Chinese text of the poem by Li Bo. The landscape next to it is painted in ink on silk, and has been attributed to the Tang artist Li Ssu–hsun. Guo Xi, one of the greatest artists of the Sung dynasty, said that enjoying a landscape could be a substitute for wandering through the mountains.*

Quiet Night Thoughts
*Beside my bed the bright moonbeams bound
Almost as if there were frost on the ground.
Raising up, I gaze at the mountain moon;
Lying back, I think of my old home town.*

Li Bo

If you were asked to write a poem about a nature scene where you live, what would your poem be like? How would it resemble the poem above? How would it be different?

194

The poem was written by Li Bo, the most beloved poet in China's history. He lived during the Tang dynasty, which began when the Duke of Tang took power in 618. This dynasty was followed by the Sung dynasty, which lasted until 1279. Together, these two dynasties were among the most artistically brilliant eras in Chinese civilization.

Poetry and painting are two areas in which Tang and Sung artists excelled. A favorite theme of both poets and painters was the harmony they saw in the natural world. In the poem, Li Bo remembers the place where he grew up.

He notes that the moon that he sees in the poem is the same mountain moon that shines on his hometown. Nature is a soothing influence in the poem. It also unites two different times and places.

Chinese painters did not simply draw what they saw, but they tried to represent the spirit, or essence, of the subject. This feeling of harmony with their subject helped them to create a sense of life in their work. A Chinese artist named Wang Wei explained the art of Chinese painting this way:

> *S uch paintings cannot be achieved by the physical movements of the fingers and the hand, but only by the spirit entering into them. This is the nature of the painting.*
>
> from *Introduction to Painting* by Wang Wei

During the Tang dynasty, pottery figures such as this fashionable lady were made in molds and painted. A pale, round face was thought to be most beautiful.

The Civil Service System

Painting and poetry were not the only areas of great Chinese achievement from 617 to 1279. The Tang and Sung dynasties also developed a fair and effective administration system.

More Schools for More People

Previous rulers had used examinations to find good candidates for public office. But only an **aristocrat**, or member of a wealthy and influential family, could afford to study for the exams. Preparing for the tests took years and required traveling to special schools in the capital. As a result, aristocrats held more than 90 percent of all government jobs.

▶ *Chinese civil service examinations were stamped with seals such as this.*

▼ *This character used by an emperor of the Sung dynasty means "by order of the emperor." Calligraphy was a subject on the civil service examination.*

The Tang and Sung governments recruited civil servants from other classes. Though most peasants still could not afford to spend years studying, during the Sung dynasty nearly half of all government workers came from social ranks other than the aristocracy.

A System Based on Merit

Officials appointed under earlier dynasties often held their positions for life, even if they were not very good at their jobs. Under the Tang and Sung dynasties, civil servants who did their jobs well were promoted. Those who did poorly were demoted, or even fired. Such a system, in which people are chosen and promoted on the basis of their performance, or merit, is called a **meritocracy**. The Chinese were the first people to establish a meritocracy. Other countries, such as the United States and France, set up similar administration systems a thousand years later.

Power to the Emperor

The Chinese believed that each emperor received a **mandate**, or order to govern, from heaven, so they called him the "Son of Heaven." The Chinese believed the emperor held absolute power. In practice, he shared his power with wealthy, landowning families.

Under the meritocracy, aristocrats found it harder to gain influence or power. They received fewer positions, and risked punishment if they did not perform their jobs well. The new, successful officials, on the other hand, were gaining power. Grateful for their positions, they tended to be more loyal to the emperor. The emperor could trust them to enforce his laws, even in regions far from the capital. ■

■ *Why did the aristocracy find it more difficult to gain influence under the civil service system?*

The Birth of a New Economy

To manage government business efficiently, official inspectors, tax collectors, and messengers needed to travel throughout the empire. To aid this work the government under the Tang and Sung dynasties built an extensive system of roads and waterways. These, in turn, spurred trade and encouraged the spread of ideas within China.

Better Roads and Waterways

By the late 700's, relay hostels, or inns, with horses and food for traveling bureaucrats were in use along all main

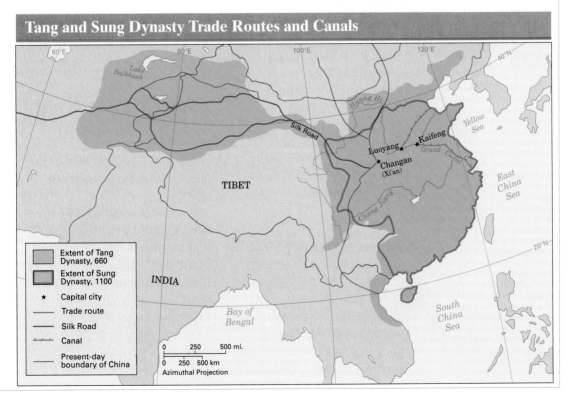

Tang and Sung Dynasty Trade Routes and Canals

Extent of Tang Dynasty, 660
Extent of Sung Dynasty, 1100
★ Capital city
Trade route
Silk Road
Canal
Present-day boundary of China

0   250   500 mi.
0   250   500 km
Azimuthal Projection

Lake Balkhash
Silk Road
Hyang He
Yellow Sea
Luoyang ★   ★ Kaifeng
Grand Canal
★ Changan (Xi'an)
TIBET
Chang Jiang
East China Sea
INDIA
Bay of Bengal
South China Sea

roads. Mounted messengers and foot runners carried government mail. According to one observer of the day, "It took only a few days for all the news from distant places to reach the authorities." Runners also carried official goods this way. Some 9,600 runners regularly supplied fresh seafood to the Tang capital of Changan from coastal cities as much as 800 miles away.

The government also improved the waterways for the growing number of sailboats, hand-driven paddle-wheel boats, and rowing ships. They built river relay hostels, extended the canal system, and found ways to help ships navigate through difficult or dangerous places in the rivers.

By 850 the rivers and canals formed a network covering much of China. On the map on page 197, trace the route Tang officials used to travel from Luoyang to the East China Sea. How long is this route? What canals and rivers did you use?

New Crops and Farming Methods

Though built at first for government use, the large network of roads and waterways would soon aid trading activity throughout China. Chinese farming became more productive thanks to new crops intro-

duced by outsiders. Traders from India, southeast Asia, and Arab regions taught the Chinese about new crops. They also introduced a new, fast-ripening rice that enabled farmers to plant two crops of rice per year instead of just one.

New agricultural techniques also made farming more productive. Government officials taught farmers to build irrigation ditches, dams, and pumps driven by human, water, or wind power. With these techniques, farmers

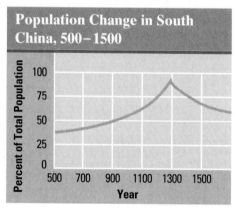

Population Change in South China, 500–1500

could turn dry land into paddies, or wet fields, to grow more rice.

A population shift also contributed to the boom in agriculture. Nomad invasions in the north forced many Chinese to flee to the more fertile south. Many of the southerners became hired hands or tenants on large farms.

Farmers soon produced

➤ *According to the graph at right, what percentage of the total population of China lived in the south around 620? What percentage lived in the south around 1280?*

more food than they needed. They sold the extra food, or surplus, to people in other regions. They, too, used the new trade routes, in order to sell their crops.

A Thriving Merchant Class

A growing number of merchants entered the shipping business. Relying on the network of canals and rivers, they transported products efficiently and inexpensively in Chinese ships, called junks. They also carried goods along the coast. In 1088 an observer wrote this description of a northern coastal city.

M*erchants from [southern and central provinces] come to this town in seagoing junks to sell such dutiable goods as spices. . . . [Northern] merchants come bringing copper cash, silk thread, silk floss, silk gauze and thin silk, and do an extremely thriving trade with them.*

from *The Continuation of the Comprehensive Mirror for Aiding Government*

The merchants carried their cash on strings that held up to a thousand copper or iron coins. In earlier times, both cash and goods, such as silk or grain, were used in trading. As trade increased, merchants found it easier to trade in cash.

But cash was heavy. Imagine carrying fifty dollars in coins in your pocket! In 1024 the Sung government used a plate like the one on this page to print the first national paper currency. The new paper money made business easier for both big merchants and small shopkeepers.

As cash became the most common item exchanged for other goods, a money economy developed. Trading became easier because of the wide use of money. Money was now the standard by which people judged the value of a bushel of rice or a length of silk. The business of trade required more shopkeepers, bankers, inspectors, tax collectors, storehouse workers, and others, so the merchant class grew. This new merchant class tended to live in cities, where trading activity was heaviest. Many rural workers flocked to the cities to fill jobs related to trade. Thus cities grew in size, and small market towns emerged in rural areas. General prosperity led to a continued increase in population, especially in the south. ■

■ *What factors led to a money economy in China?*

A Continuing Heritage

Although the Chinese prospered through their thriving new trade network, they continued to value their ancient traditions. One such tradition was **Confucianism**, a set of beliefs that focused on proper conduct, respect for elders, scholarship, and government service. The civil service exams still required candidates to study the Confucian classics, works based on the ideas of the philosopher Confucius, who was born around 551 B.C. These became widely available after the invention of printing in the late 700's. Historians call this renewed emphasis on Confucian ideas Neo-Confucianism.

Respect for the past, however, did not keep the Chinese from moving forward. Between A.D. 100 and 1200, the Chinese developed many new inventions. Look at the time line below. Notice that most Chinese discoveries predate similar discoveries in Europe. Matches, for example, were in use in China as early as A.D. 577. At what time did this invention come into use in the West?

Printing

Some of the most significant of the many Chinese inventions were developed during the Tang and Sung periods. Of these, printing was probably the most significant. By making books, calendars, and government pamphlets available to all people, printing hastened the spread of knowledge throughout China.

Woodblock printing was the earliest form of printing. The Chinese began to use the method in the late 700's, about 600 years before Europeans learned about this method. To make a woodblock print, skilled craftspeople carved raised characters on the surface of a wooden "page." They brushed ink onto this page and laid a piece of paper over it to make a print. The entire

Inventions in China and Europe

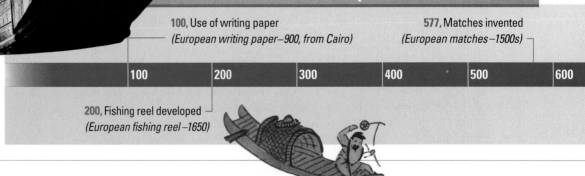

100, Use of writing paper
(European writing paper—900, from Cairo)

577, Matches invented
(European matches—1500s)

| 100 | 200 | 300 | 400 | 500 | 600 |

200, Fishing reel developed
(European fishing reel—1650)

process was done by hand.

How long do you think it would take you to carve the words in this sentence onto a block of wood? The Chinese spent twenty-one years carving and printing all 130 volumes of the Confucian classics.

A less time-consuming method of printing, using movable type, was invented around 1045 by a Chinese commoner named Pi Sheng. He cut ideographs, the Chinese characters, out of sticky clay and baked them until they were hard. Then he made each page by placing the necessary characters into an iron frame. This method of printing was very quick and efficient for printing large quantities of copies.

By A.D. 1100, scholars used books on law, medicine, mathematics, and science to learn from both the past and the present. New techniques for treating a disease or planting a crop, for example, spread much more quickly in printed form than by word of mouth or by demonstration. An observer in the southern coastal county of Fujien wrote:

> **E**very peasant, artisan and merchant teaches his sons how to read books. Even herdsmen, and wives who bring their husbands food at their work in the fields, can recite the poems of the men of ancient times.
>
> Fang Tatsing

Gunpowder

Another Chinese invention was gunpowder, which may have been discovered as early as the 600's. By the 1200's the Chinese manufactured gunpowder in large quantities. A document written in 1221 states: "On the same day were

c. 8th century, Paper money developed
(European bank note issued —1661)

1041–1048, Movable type developed
(European movable type–1450)

| 700 | 800 | 900 | 1000 | 1100 | 1200 |

976, Chain drive developed for clocks
(European chain drive for silk-reeling machine —1770)

produced 7000 gunpowder crossbow arrows, 10,000 gunpowder ordinary arrows, 3000 barbed gunpowder packages and 20,000 ordinary gunpowder packages."

Inventions for Travel

Many Chinese inventions made traveling easier. Travel abroad from China was often by sea. The Chinese relied on their charts of the stars and a compass called a "fish" to help them find their way.

Chinese astronomers began to map the stars as early as 300 B.C. Star charts dating from around A.D. 940 show many common constellations.

The Chinese compass, developed for use on ships in the 1100's, used a magnetic rock called a lodestone. The compass maker cut a thin sheet of metal into the shape of a fish and rubbed it with the lodestone to make it magnetic. The metal fish, when floated in a

container of water, pointed north and south. A description of how sailors used the magnetic fish at sea appeared in a report written in 1119:

T he sailors are sure of their bearings. At night they judge by the stars. In daytime they tell by the sun. When it is cloudy, they rely on the south-pointing needle.

R E V I E W

1. **FOCUS** What were the major achievements of the Tang and Sung dynasties?
2. **CULTURE** What common theme runs through many poems and paintings of the Tang and Sung dynasties?
3. **ECONOMICS** How did the growth of Chinese agriculture contribute to the money economy that developed?
4. **CRITICAL THINKING** Would you say that most schools are meritocracies? Explain.
5. **ACTIVITY** Assume that you are the inventor of one of the inventions mentioned in the text. Describe your invention to your classmates, who have never heard of it before. Be sure to point out how your device could improve their lives.

China and the Larger World

Geography helped protect ancient China from the outside world. In ancient times, the Himalaya Mountains to the southwest and the Takla Makan Desert to the west limited Chinese contact with India, Persia, and other civilizations. China was vulnerable in the north, however. There, a huge open **steppe**, or grassy plain, left China open to attack by outside invaders.

In 1211, mounted Mongol warriors led by Genghis Khan swept into China from the north. They were unstoppable.

THINKING FOCUS

What factors caused China to open trade in some years and remain isolated from the rest of the world in others?

Key Terms

* steppe
* khan

◄ *In this portrait of Kublai Khan, he is dressed in the traditional clothing of a Chinese emperor.*

[T]he Mongols] wear defensive armor made of the thick hides of buffaloes and other beasts, dried by the fire, and thus rendered extremely hard and strong. They are brave in battle, almost to desperation, setting little value upon their lives, and exposing themselves without hesitation to all manner of danger. Their disposition is cruel.

They are capable of supporting every kind of [hardship], and when there is a necessity for it, can live for a month on the milk of their mares, and upon such wild animals as they may chance to catch. Their horses are fed upon grass alone, and do not require barley or other grain.

The men are accustomed to remain on horseback during two days and two nights, without dismounting; sleeping in that situation while their horses graze. . . . When the service is distant, they carry but little with them, and that, chiefly what is requisite for their encampment, and utensils for cooking.

. . . Each man has, on an average, eighteen horses and mares, and when that which they ride is fatigued, they change it for another. . . . [In battle their] horses are so well broken-in to quick changes of movement, that upon the signal given, they instantly turn in every direction; and by these rapid maneuvers many victories have been obtained.

From *Marco Polo* . . .
Edited by Richard J. Wells

The Mongols Take Over

While south China prospered under the Sung dynasty, Genghis Khan and his mounted warriors took control of northern China. The skillful horsemen traveled for weeks at a time, mounting surprise attacks along the Chinese frontier. With very few horses and inferior riding skills, the cumbersome Chinese armies were rarely able to pursue or defeat the Mongols. By 1234 all of north China was under the Mongol rule.

The New Khan Ruler

Kublai Khan, a grandson of Genghis, was chosen as the great **khan**, or ruler, in 1260. In 1267 Kublai moved his imperial capital from Mongolia to Beijing (ba jĭng´) in north China in order to be closer to his subjects.

Kublai adopted certain

Chinese traditions of government to make it easier for him to rule and be accepted by the Chinese. For example, he rebuilt the capital in the traditional Chinese style and declared himself Emperor and Son of Heaven. He even founded his own dynasty, called the Yuan (yoo än´), which lasted until 1368.

Kublai Khan and the Mongols did not support Chinese culture, however. They used some Chinese systems of government, but only to strengthen Mongol rule. The most important government positions were held by Mongols or other non-Chinese. The Chinese themselves were given the least important jobs. Government documents were written in Mongolian and then translated into Chinese.

Kublai staged many attacks on the Sung dynasty in south China. When his forces finally overpowered the last group of Sung defenders in 1279, Kublai became the first foreigner to rule all of China.

An Interruption in Progress

Although the Mongols maintained the basic Chinese government structure, their occupation of China disrupted economic and social development. Millions of Chinese were killed or injured during the Mongol invasions. In some areas, such as the eastern province of Anhwei, the whole population died or fled.

The Mongols squandered the wealth of the Tang and Sung dynasties by burning cities and using vast areas of fertile farmland as pastures for their horses. They neglected canals and irrigation systems, and fertile fields soon turned parched and barren. Farmers lost their land and civil servants lost their jobs.

In the south, the Mongols hoped to win support from the wealthy landowners by letting them keep their lands. Instead, the Mongols seized land from the peasants, forcing them to seek work as hired hands on large estates. Thus the rich remained rich, while the poor became even poorer.

A Direct Link to the West

The Mongols disrupted Chinese life and culture, but they also fostered China's links to the rest of the world. Camel caravans traveled throughout the vast Mongol empire, from Beijing through central Asia to the Black Sea, carrying silks and ceramics for the western

This is a ceramic model of the type of small, sturdy horse ridden by Mongol warriors. It was found in a tomb from the Tang dynasty.

market. The Mongols also expanded the Chinese system of postal relays, establishing stations with supplies and horses for travelers who crossed the Asian steppe.

Meanwhile, travelers who crossed the Indian Ocean to China found thriving port cities, such as Guangzhou (**gwăng´jō´**), and Quanzhou (**Kwăn´jō**). Merchants and diplomats from the Arab world gathered in south China's seaports. Through Arab merchants, who acted as go-betweens, many goods from the West and from southeast Asia traded hands in Chinese ports.

Increased contacts with the world not only expanded trade in China but also aided the spread of ideas in the West. For example, knowledge of printing and gunpowder probably spread from China to West Asia and Europe during the Mongol period. ■

■ *In what ways did the Mongol conquest of China affect the livelihood of most Chinese people?*

The Ming Dynasty

Some merchants prospered under Mongol rule. But most Chinese were eager to expel the foreigners who squandered China's riches while neglecting its people. The Chinese rebelled against the Mongols and founded a new dynasty in 1368. The rebel leader and founder of the Ming dynasty was Emperor Taitsu (tī **tsōō´**). He ruled until his death in 1398, the year in which the Chinese drove the last Mongols out of China. The Ming dynasty continued to rule all of China until 1644.

Familiar Traditions
Emperor Taitsu turned to familiar traditions for help in restoring the empire. He reestablished the civil service examination system and encouraged promising scholars.

Like earlier emperors, Emperor Taitsu undertook public works projects. He repaired irrigation systems, built reservoirs, and extensively repaired and rebuilt the Great Wall. He helped homeless people move to regions devastated by the Mongols. The immigrants received land, seeds, tools, and livestock. Unlike earlier Chinese emperors, Emperor Taitsu also seized large estates, abol-

➤ *Ming ceramics, with their distinctive blue and white glazes, were popular items of trade and are now quite valuable. The cobalt used to produce the blue color on this vase was first imported during the Mongol period.*

ished slavery, and raised the taxes of the rich. Such measures narrowed the gap between rich and poor.

More Power to the Emperor

The Ming emperors made themselves extremely powerful. For example, Emperor Taitsu abolished the position of the prime minister, who had served as the link between the emperor and the six departments of government. Now the emperor controlled the departments directly.

While earlier emperors had welcomed open discussion of issues, Ming emperors made decisions in secret councils. Emperor Taitsu even created a secret police force to spy on officials. Historians estimate that he accused at least 100,000 people of corruption or treason and then executed them. Such a ruler, who holds absolute power and uses it abusively, is called a despot.

The Ming emperors ordered a splendid new capital built on the site of the old Mongol capital of Beijing. During the early 1400's, about one million workers labored to complete the new city. Great walls, 40 feet high, surrounded a central area known as the Imperial City. Here, grand halls, courtyards, lakes, and gardens provided a costly and lavish setting for the business of government.

Yet another wall and a moat surrounded the inner-most square, called the Forbidden City. The Forbidden City contained separate palaces for the members of the imperial family, most of whom received generous allowances. Here, too, was the Hall of Supreme Harmony, where the emperors often held court.

The Son of Heaven sat on his throne on the highest terrace, far above his audience. Only the most privileged ministers could see and hear the emperor. The emperor set himself physically above and apart from his subjects to encourage the notion that he was truly superior.

A Superior Naval Power

The emperors wanted to show the world the power and prestige of the Ming dynasty. Chinese contacts with southeastern Asia, Japan, and India grew during the Ming reign. Between 1405 and 1433, court official Cheng Ho gathered a fleet of ships and made seven voyages to the Middle East and to the east coast of Africa. These voyages earned respect for China as a naval force.

But the Ming emperors were wary of foreign influence and soon decided that the world had little of value to offer China. They forbade further explorations and ended the costly voyages after 1433. They even made it a crime for any Chinese to leave the country by sea.

Contact with the West

The Ming emperors discouraged Chinese merchants from trading with foreign countries. They wanted to reap China's trade profits for the court and prevent Chinese contact with people they regarded as inferior.

Despite the trade restrictions imposed by Ming emperors, however, the rest of the world discovered China. The first Portuguese ship reached China in 1514, and by 1557 the Portuguese managed to establish a settlement on China's coast at Macao, near Guangzhou. Jesuit missionaries opened Catholic missions and began to convert some Chinese to Christianity.

These missionaries, who were well educated in mathematics, astronomy, and the arts, carried knowledge and inventions between East and West. For example, Europeans learned how to build Chinese arched bridges, and the Chinese learned about European astronomy and mathematics.

European traders seeking Chinese tea, silk, and porcelain brought with them new crops such as sweet potatoes and corn from the Americas. They also introduced beef and dairy cattle to the Chinese, who began to raise them in the fertile pastures of the south. The increased trade also increased the amount of gold and silver in circulation in China.

Yet throughout the Ming dynasty, despotic rulers attempted to restrict trade. They also wasted money on lavish court life and withdrew ever further from day-to-day affairs within China. Eventually, the people grew tired of heavy taxation and careless government. In the early 1600's, these problems led southern peasants to rebel against the despots. ■

■ *In what ways did the Ming dynasty affect trade and other contacts with the West?*

R E V I E W

1. **FOCUS** What factors caused China to open trade in some years and remain isolated from the rest of the world in others?
2. **CONNECT** What impact did Mongol rule have upon economic development of the Tang and Sung dynasties?
3. **ECONOMICS** How did the Ming attitude toward foreigners affect trade?
4. **POLITICAL SYSTEMS** Discuss the abuses the Chinese suffered under the Mongols.

5. **CRITICAL THINKING** Do you think the Mongol rulers would have had as much contact with the rest of the world if they had supported the Chinese culture and government more?
6. **ACTIVITY** You are a farmer whose land has been seized by Mongol invaders. Write a paragraph in which you describe the Mongols, their attack on your land, and how you will support yourself now that you have no farm.

Across the Centuries

Thinking and Discussing

If you had lived in ancient China, where might you have felt most vulnerable to an attack from outsiders? Why? How would you have defended this area of the country?

In what ways did the Tang and Sung dynasties affect the occupations of the Chinese people? How did the Mongol invasion affect them later?

Why do you think the author included firsthand reports from people who actually lived in ancient China? What effect do these personal accounts have on the reader?

Applying Historical Concepts

Trading with Ancient China Imagine you are a European trader who has just returned from an ancient Chinese port with a shipload of goods. Write a paragraph describing what food and merchandise you have returned with and explain why you think Westerners will buy these items. Did any of your products originally come from Arabian markets? From India? Did you bring home any invention that you will have to explain to people? Drawing a diagram might help demonstrate how it works.

Writing an Eyewitness Memoir

Three of the selections you are about to read are eyewitness accounts of life in ancient China. The authors — Abu Zeid al Hasan, Marco Polo, and Ibn Battuta — were explorers. They knew that most people back home would never be able to travel all the way to China. So they tried to describe what they had seen there as vividly as they could.

Perhaps you too have visited a place that you would like your friends to know about. Try describing it for them in your own eyewitness memoir. You might want to write about a place that impressed you in another town, region, or country. You could choose to describe a place near home, such as another school or neighborhood, a factory, or another family's house.

If you think of a different topic, feel free to try it instead.

Prewriting

Take some time to think before you begin writing. Close your eyes and try to picture the place clearly. Imagine walking through it and around it. What do you see? What sounds and smells do you notice? What strikes you as most remarkable? Do you associate this place with any particular people, or with an event? What is your opinion of the place? How did your visit affect you?

Jot down some of your impressions. Perhaps you have some photographs or journal entries that you can review to stimulate your memory. If the place is nearby, perhaps you can revisit it and take some notes.

Write a First Draft
Think about your audience. Try to get them as interested in the place as you are, right from the very start: You might want to begin with some particularly striking fact, person, or incident.

Use sensory details. You want your readers to see, hear, and smell the place as vividly as if they too had been there.

Revise
If time permits, set your first draft aside for a few days. Then read it as if you had never seen it before. Can you picture the place from the description? Are all the details important? Should you leave some out, and add others that are more expressive?

Proofread
Check that spelling, punctuation, and capitalization are correct. Your readers will not trust your observations if the writing itself is not accurate.

Publish
Copy your eyewitness memoir neatly. You might want to illustrate it with photographs, drawings, or maps. You and your classmates can assemble your memoirs into a travel magazine.

The First Emperor

from *The Tomb Robbers*
by *Daniel Cohen*

The Tomb of the First Emperor

Ch'in Shih Huang Ti, the first emperor of China, was a stern and powerful ruler. Originally a king of a minor Chinese state, he conquered neighboring rival states and brought them together under one centralized government. This form of government, the Chinese Empire, lasted over 2,000 years.

In 1974, Chinese archaeologists unearthed the remarkable tomb of Ch'in Shih Huang Ti. Today archaeologists estimate that the construction of the tomb spanned decades and required the efforts of 700,000 builders.

On these pages, clay warriors unearthed near the tomb of Ch'in Shih Huang Ti. On the following pages, an infantryman, or foot soldier; a chariot driver; and a cavalry soldier with his horse.

Perhaps the greatest archaeological find of modern times, one that may ultimately outshine even the discovery of the tomb of the Egyptian boy-king Tutankhamun, is the tomb of the Emperor Ch'in Shih Huang Ti.[1] Now admittedly the name Ch'in Shih Huang Ti is not exactly a household word in the West. But then neither was Tutankhamun until 1922. The major difference is that while Tutankhamun himself was historically insignificant, Ch'in Shih Huang Ti was enormously important in Chinese history. In many respects he was really the founder of China.

The future emperor started out as the king of the small state Ch'in. At the time, the land was divided up among a number of small states, all constantly warring with one another. Ch'in was one of the smallest and weakest. Yet the king of Ch'in managed to overcome all his rivals, and in the year 221 B.C. he proclaimed himself emperor of the land that we now know as China. From that date until the revolution of 1912, China was always ruled by an emperor. The name China itself comes from the name Ch'in.

Shih Huang Ti ruled his empire with ferocious efficiency. He had the Great Wall of China built to keep out the northern barbarians. The Great Wall, which stretches some fifteen hundred miles, is a building project that rivals and perhaps surpasses the Great Pyramid. The Great Wall took twelve years to build and cost the lives of countless thousands of laborers. Today the Great Wall remains China's number one tourist attraction.

---

[1]This name is also written Qin Shi Huang-di, or just Qin Shihuang, or Shi Huangdi. It is pronounced Chǐn Shûr Hwäng Dē.

As he grew older, Shih Huang Ti became obsessed with the prospect of his own death. He had survived several assassination attempts and was terrified of another. He traveled constantly between his 270 different palaces, so that no one could ever be sure where he was going to be. He never slept in the same room for two nights in a row. Anyone who revealed the emperor's whereabouts was put to death along with his entire family. Shih Huang Ti searched constantly for the secret of immortality. He became prey to a host of phony magicians and other fakers who promised much but could deliver nothing.

The emperor heard that there were immortals living on some far-off island, so he sent a huge fleet to find them. The commander of the fleet knew that if he failed in his mission, the emperor would put him to death. So the fleet simply never returned. It is said that the fleet found the island of Japan and stayed there to become the ancestors of the modern Japanese.

In his desire to stay alive, Shih Huang Ti did not neglect the probability that he would die some day. He began construction of an immense tomb in the Black Horse hills near one of his favorite summer palaces. The tomb's construction took three times as long as the construction of the Great Wall.

The emperor, of course, did die. Death came while he was visiting the eastern provinces. But his life had become so secretive that only a few high officials were aware of his death. They contrived to keep it a secret until they could consolidate their own power. The imperial procession headed back for the capital. Unfortunately, it was midsummer and the emperor's body began to rot and stink. So one of the plotters arranged to have a cart of fish follow the immense imperial chariot to hide the odor of the decomposing corpse. Finally, news of the emperor's death was made public. The body, or what was left of it, was buried in the tomb that he had been building for so long.

Stories about that tomb sound absolutely incredible. It was said to contain miniature reproductions of all the emperor's 270 palaces. A map of the entire empire with all the major rivers reproduced in mercury, which by some mechanical means was made to flow into a miniature ocean, was also part of the interior of the tomb. So was a reproduction of the stars and planets. According to legend, the burial chamber itself was filled with molten copper so that the emperor's remains were sealed inside a gigantic ingot.[2]

It was also said that loaded crossbows were set up all around the inside of the tomb, and that anyone who did manage to penetrate the inner chambers would be shot full of arrows. But just to make sure that no one got that far, the pallbearers who had placed Shih Huang Ti's remains in the tomb were sealed inside with it. They were supposed to be the only ones who knew exactly how to get in and out of the intricate tomb. All of this was done to preserve the emperor's remains from the hands of tomb robbers. Did it work? We don't really know yet.

There are two contradictory stories about the tomb of Ch'in Shih Huang Ti. The first says that it was covered up with earth to make it resemble an ordinary hill and that its location has remained unknown for centuries.

But a more accurate legend holds that there never was any attempt to disguise the existence of the tomb. Ch'in Shih Huang Ti had been building it for years, and everybody knew where it was. After his death

---

[2]**ingot** (ĭng′gət): A mass of metal shaped in the form of a bar or block.

the tomb was surrounded by walls enclosing an area of about five hundred acres. This was to be the emperor's "spirit city." Inside the spirit city were temples and all sorts of other sacred buildings and objects dedicated to the dead emperor.

Over the centuries the walls, the temples, indeed everything above ground was carried away by vandals. The top of the tomb was covered with earth and eventually came to resemble a large hill. Locally the hill is called Mount Li. But still the farmers who lived in the area had heard stories that Mount Li contained the tomb of Ch'in Shih Huang Ti or of some other important person.

In the spring of 1974 a peasant plowing a field near Mount Li uncovered a life-sized clay statue of a warrior. Further digging indicated that there was an entire army of statues beneath the ground. Though excavations are not yet complete, Chinese authorities believe that there are some six thousand life-sized clay statues of warriors, plus scores of life-sized statues of horses.

Most of the statues are broken, but some are in an absolutely remarkable state of preservation. Each statue is finely made, and each shows a distinct individual, different from all the others.

This incredible collection is Shih Huang Ti's "spirit army." At one time Chinese kings practiced human sacrifice so that the victims could serve the dead king in the next world. Shih Huang Ti was willing to make do with models. Men and horses were arranged in a military fashion in a three-acre underground chamber. The chamber may have been entered at some point. The roof certainly collapsed. But still the delicate figures have survived surprisingly well. Most of the damage was done when the roof caved in. That is why the Chinese archaeologists are so hopeful that when the tomb itself is excavated, it too will be found to have survived surprisingly well.

The Chinese are not rushing the excavations. They have only a limited number of trained people to do the job. After all, the tomb has been there for over two thousand years. A few more years won't make much difference.

Though once denounced as a tyrant, Ch'in Shih Huang Ti is now regarded as a national hero. His name is a household word in China. The Chinese government knows that it may have an unparalleled ancient treasure on its hands, and it wants to do the job well. Over the next few years we should be hearing much more about this truly remarkable find.

ADVICE TO THE FIRST EMPEROR

The ancient Chinese philosopher Confucius taught that there could be good government only when good people governed. He said that "Virtuous behavior by rulers has a greater effect in governing than laws and codes of punishment." By the third century B.C., however, popular Chinese thought held that it was more important for a ruler to have complete control and never permit criticism of the state. Two leading supporters of this theory were Hanfeizi and Li Si. Li Si was able to personally promote these ideas and put them into practice when he became an advisor to the first emperor, Ch'in Shih Huang Ti.

HANFEIZI

When the wise man rules the state, he does not count on people to do good on their own, but uses such methods as will keep them from doing any evil. If he counts on people behaving themselves without strict rules, there will not be more than ten such people in the whole country. But if he uses such methods as will keep them from doing evil, then the entire state can be brought up to an acceptable level of behavior.

If one should have to depend on finding arrows which are naturally straight, there would be no arrows in a hundred generations. If one could make wheels only from pieces of wood which are naturally circles, there would be no wheels in a thousand generations. Although in a hundred generations there is neither wood that is naturally straight for arrows nor wood that comes naturally in circles for wheels, people in every generation still have wheels for their carts and shoot arrows at birds. Why is that? It is because the tools for straightening and bending wood are used. Though without the use of such tools there might happen to be a naturally straight arrow or a naturally round wheel, the skilled carpenter will not value that object, because many more arrows and wheels must still be shaped out of imperfect pieces of wood. Similarly, though there might happen to be an individual who is naturally good, the intelligent ruler will not prize him but will follow a course that will make certain the majority do not do evil.

LI SI

The fact that intelligent rulers were able for a long time to hold high position and great power is due only to their ability always to apply severe punishments. It was for this reason that none in the empire dared to be rebellious. If a ruler does not take care to prevent rebellion, but instead acts like the loving mother who spoils her children, indeed he has not understood the principles of the wise men who came before him. When a ruler fails to practice the advice for governing the state left by the sages, what else does he do except make himself the slave of the empire? Is this not a pity?

The First Emperor

Thinking and Discussing

What does the existence of the Great Wall tell historians about the problems of ancient China? Do you think that it was better for a whole country unified under one ruler to try to solve this problem rather than several smaller kingdoms? Why or why not?

How would you summarize the advice that Hanfeizi and Li Si gave to the first emperor? Do you think Shih Huang Ti generally followed their advice? Give evidence from the selection to support your answer.

What three types of sources have provided historians with information about Shih Huang Ti? Which types of sources are more reliable? Why? Why are all sources of information important when investigating remote periods of history?

Applying Historical Concepts

Researching the Great Wall The Great Wall of China was an incredible achievement and remains one of the great wonders of the world. Do research on the Great Wall and plan a way to share the information you gather with others. You might make a replica of the Great Wall and label it with facts. Or you might publish an illustrated booklet entitled "Amazing Facts About the Great Wall of China."

Ancient Chinese *Art*

Science in Ancient China

by George Beshore

When traders returned to their native lands from ancient China, they brought with them many things that most people had never seen before. Porcelain, silk, and Chinese inventions quickly became popular because they were so beautiful and rare. Today most of these items are so common that they are taken for granted. But if you had lived centuries ago, how do you think you would have reacted examining a kite for the very first time? What would you have thought of it? Would you have guessed that it could fly?

Above: a silk moth; below: Emperor T'ai-tsung of the Tang dynasty in a silk robe

Silk

The Chinese applied practical technology to the manufacture of fine products. One of the best known of these is the lustrous cloth called silk. Long before most people in the West knew where China was located or what the people there looked like, the wealthy merchants of Greece, Rome, and Persia were crossing deserts and mountains to trade for this highly prized material.

No one knows when the Chinese first learned to raise silkworms, collect and unwind their cocoons, and weave a fine cloth from the tiny threads that silkworms produce. Tradition says that the legendary Emperor Huang-Ti taught them how to do this. Other legends say that it was Huang-Ti's wife, the Empress Hsilina Shih, who discovered the technique. Some versions of these myths cite the year 2640 B.C. as the time when this happened.

The exact truth about how the Chinese learned to raise silkworms and convert their cocoons into cloth may never be known, but we do know that silk production has flourished in the Yellow River valley area for over four thousand years.

Then, as now, the first step was to raise silkworms, which live on mulberry trees and feed on the leaves. The silkworm moth lays between two hundred and five hundred eggs,

each about as big as a pinhead. The eggs hatch into larvae — wiggly creatures that look much like caterpillars.

A silkworm larva grows from about a quarter of an inch (6 mm) to three inches (76.2 mm) long in about six weeks. During that time it feeds on huge quantities of mulberry leaves. A growing silkworm caterpillar often eats *its own weight* in leaves each day.

After about six weeks of feeding and growing, the silkworm settles down on a leaf and begins to spin a cocoon around itself. The tiny silken thread that the insect wraps around and around its body makes a continuous strand from 1,200 to 3,000 feet (365 to 900 m) long. These cocoons are collected and heated to kill the larvae inside.

Then comes the tedious process of unwinding the tiny filament of silk without breaking it. The cocoons are soaked in hot water to loosen the sticky material that holds them together. Then the thread is unwound. A Chinese worker takes several cocoons at one time and twists their thin strands together to form the silken thread that will later be woven into cloth. The length of the thread depends on the number of cocoons; this will vary according to the use that is planned for the finished material.

In ancient China much of the silk was woven into cloth by people working in their

A Chinese woman spinning silk

223

own homes. Women usually unwound the co-coons by hand, but men often helped weave the threads into cloth. Looms used for the weaving process go back beyond recorded history, although they were constantly being improved. Other labor-saving methods were gradually adopted to replace the slower hand methods of ancient times. A treatise written in A.D. 1090 describes a silk-winding device operated by a foot treadle. Spinning wheels, which are used to twist together short threads at the end of each cocoon, originated in India. They replaced hand-spinning techniques in China early in the thirteenth century. Water wheels came into use during the tenth and eleventh centuries to drive the silk-winding, spinning, and weaving machines.

Chinese women weaving silk

Porcelain and Bronze

Another Chinese specialty is a fine pottery called porcelain. The Germans and Austrians later learned to produce fine porcelain pieces, but experts say that they have never been able to do as well as the Chinese did at the height of their porcelain production in the tenth century A.D. To this day fine dishes are called

Porcelain lions, often used to guard the entrance to a house or a temple

china, regardless of whether they are made in the East or the West.

Pottery production in the East goes back beyond any historic record. Archaeological evidence shows that the people who lived along the Yellow River were making pots from clay at least four thousand years ago.

They used two kinds of clay. One was gray; Chinese artisans learned to coat it with glazes containing metallic elements that turned bright red or green or other pleasing colors when the piece was

fired. A second kind of clay was white; from it they developed a delicate pottery so thin that light can shine through it. This could also be glazed to produce colorful vases and urns. From this clay the Chinese produced the porcelain pieces that have been highly prized throughout history. Designs were painted on by workers using delicate brushes. So detailed and specialized was this work that an artist was trained for his or her entire lifetime in a particular type of design instead of trying to do a mixture of trees and animals or landscapes and plants.

Beautifully crafted porcelain from the Ming and Ching dynasties

Over three thousand years ago the Chinese created another specialty: casting fine bronze vases and figures. Bronze is the mixture of 80 to 85 percent copper and 15 to 20 percent tin that ancient peoples of many cultures learned to work long before they found out how to cast iron. Since it is softer, bronze is also more delicate than iron.

In order to make a fine bronze piece, an artisan first carved an exact model of the vessel in wax. All designs were carefully carved out or impressed on its surface. When the form was exactly right, the artisan began to brush on a mixture of clay and water so thin that it went into the tiniest openings. This was allowed to dry, and additional layers were brushed on.

Finally the clay was built up to a sufficient thickness. A few holes were left in the outside, and the clay was baked. The heat hardened the clay and melted the wax, which was drained out. Molten bronze, heated so that it flowed like a liquid, was then poured in the clay mold through the holes. When it cooled, the artisan had an exact copy in bronze of the original wax form.

The clay mold was broken away to reveal the bronze statue or urn beneath, so only one piece could be made from each mold. Holes left to drain out the wax and pour in the bronze were carefully filed and smoothed over. Then the finished piece was ready for the marketplace.

Top left: a bronze acrobat of the Eastern Chou dynasty; middle left: a Shang dynasty ceremonial vessel; bottom left: a bronze lion from the imperial palace in Beijing; below: bronze tigers from the middle Chou period

From Steel
to Seismographs

In the second century B.C. the Chinese began heating iron in charcoal. This gave their metal the proper carbon content to make steel, which is harder than cast iron. Steel bits could be used to drill wells as deep as 2,000 feet (600 m). Many of these wells were used to supply water for entire villages; others brought up brine that was processed into salt.

To drill the deep wells, a group of people would jump on and off each end of a crossbeam to give it the up-and-down motion needed for drilling. Meanwhile, others rotated the drill cable so that the bit would cut into the earth. This is essentially the same process used almost two thousand years later in the southwestern United States to drill some of that country's first oil wells. In the United States it was called "kicking down" a well.

A Chinese astronomer, Chang Hêng, invented the seismograph, a device that detects earthquakes, in the second century A.D. His seismograph had eight metal dragons arranged around a pendulum in the center. Each dragon faced a different direction and held a copper ball in its mouth. When an earthquake shook the structure, a ball dropped, making a loud *clang* when it hit the metal surface below. This attracted the attention of an attendant, who could tell the direction of the quake by drawing a line out from the dragon that had dropped the ball.

People thought Chang Hêng was a clever person until one day when a ball dropped but no one felt an earthquake. They made fun of him, saying that his invention was a fake. This went on for a couple of days until a messenger arrived from a province several hundred miles to the northwest. This messenger reported that an earthquake had indeed occurred at the time when Chang Hêng's seismograph had reported it. His instrument could detect an earthquake so far away that no one could feel the tremor!

Kite flying depicted on a paper handscroll from the Sung dynasty or later

Kites and Balloons

Chinese records sometimes give the name of the general or emperor who first used a new device rather than the name of the person who invented it. For example, the Chinese knew about kites for several centuries B.C. and drew pictures of them in the fourth century B.C. Their records say that a general named Han Hsin was the inventor.

Actually, Han Hsin lived over a hundred years after those pictures of kites were drawn. Instead of inventing the kite, he made the first known military use of it in the third century B.C. An army he was fighting had fortified itself inside a city that Han Hsin's troops could not conquer. He put some of his men to work digging a tunnel under the walls. At the same time he had others fly a kite over the city. By keeping track of the length of string they let out, he could compute the distance that his men would have to dig in order to come up inside the walls of the city instead of on the outside.

This is the first known use of an aerial device in warfare. Later Chinese generals used kites to signal each other during battles. Sometimes they would send aloft a kite containing whistles and other noise-makers to try to divert or frighten enemy forces. This was especially effective at night, when foes had no way to see what was causing the strange sounds up in the sky.

The Chinese experimented with balloons over two thousand years ago. First they emptied eggshells and made them float by heating the air inside. Later they developed hot-air balloons, which were often shaped like dragons or birds and floated overhead during special celebrations. This was common practice in the East more than fifteen hundred years before the Montgolfier brothers sent up the first hot-air balloon in France in 1783.

Always a practical people, the Chinese concentrated their scientific efforts on developing the technologies they needed to live better lives and protect the country against enemies. This effort led them to develop many practical inventions long before such discoveries were known elsewhere in the world.

A porcelain cup from the Ming dynasty

THE PERFECTION OF ART IN CHINA

by Abu Zeid al Hasan

Today, more is known about what Abu Zeid al Hasan saw in China than of the author himself. He is believed to have been a Moslem who traveled to Asia to trade with Chinese merchants. It was nearly a thousand years after he recorded his observations that they were finally published in his native Arabic language. Abu Zeid al Hasan's account of early Chinese culture was later translated into English in 1718.

The Chinese surpass all nations in all arts, and particularly in painting; and they perform such perfect work as others can but faintly imitate. When an artificer [craftsman] has finished a fine piece, he carries it to the Prince's palace to demand the reward he thinks he deserves for the beauty of his performance; and the custom is for the Prince to order him to leave his work at the palace gate, where it stands a whole year. If, during that time, no person finds a fault therein, the artificer is rewarded, and admitted into the body of artists; but if the least fault be found, it is rejected, and the workman sent away empty.

It happened once that one of these painters drew an ear of corn, with a bird perched on it, upon a piece of silk; and his performance was so admirable, that all who beheld it were astonished. This piece stood exposed to public view, till one day a crooked fellow passing by the palace, found fault with the picture, and was immediately conducted to the Prince or Governor of the city, who at the same time sent for the painter. Then he asked this crooked fellow what fault he had to find with this piece; to which he answered, "Everybody knows that a bird never settles upon an ear of corn but it bends under him, whereas this painter has represented his ear bolt upright, though he has perched a bird upon it; this is the fault I have to find." The objection was held just, and the Prince bestowed no reward upon the artist. They pretend by this, and other such means, to excite their workmen to such perfection, by engaging them to be extremely nice and circumspect in what they undertake, and to apply their whole genius to what is to go out of their hands.

Ancient Chinese Art

Thinking and Discussing

What does each author think about the skill involved in Chinese art compared to artistic achievements elsewhere in the world at that time? What examples does each author use to support his opinion?

When was each piece written? How does this cause the focus of the two selections to differ?

Applying Historical Concepts

Presenting a Play Write a script that dramatizes the story told by Abu Zeid al Hasan in his observations about ancient Chinese art. Create roles for the prince, the artist, and the person who finds fault with the painting. You might also describe props and costumes you will use to suggest the setting. Write dialogue in which the painter and the faultfinder give the prince their opinions of the painting and tell whether or not the artist deserves to be paid. Then have the prince explain why he decides against the painter after weighing both arguments. Rehearse your play and present the scene to the class.

Listing Chinese Creations Make a list of all the Chinese art forms and inventions discussed in the text, writing them in the order in which they appear. Include in each entry the materials, tools, or instruments involved in the creation of the art form or invention. Which art form or invention impresses you most?

233

Sons of the Steppe

by Hans Baumann

illustrated by Mou-Sien Tseng

In Sons of the Steppe, *Hans Baumann's fictional account of the Mongol invasion of China, you will meet real people, some of whom you have already read about. You will meet the fierce Mongols who invaded China from the north across the steppe. You will meet their harsh leader, Genghis Khan, and his young grandsons, Kublai Khan and Arik-Buka. Other historic figures in this novel are Yeliu, a Chinese sage who remains loyal to his people though he is forced to serve Genghis Khan, and Chepe, an officer in Genghis Khan's army. It is around the lives of these ordinary men that Baumann weaves his story and captures the drama of real life in the pages of his historical novel.*

It was a cloudless night and the moon was full. It stood sharply out-lined against the sky. The Steppe was bathed in silver light, and even the horsemen's yurts[1] glistened.

Chepe and the princes[2] rode up to the sentries, handed over their horses and mingled with the crowd. The *Orluk* was recognized at once, so in spite of the crush of people it was easy for him and the princes to push their way to the middle of the camp. The warriors had been drink-ing; they were grumbling noisily, and again and again Chepe and the princes heard them saying: "It will be singed! The beautiful beard will be singed off!"

Chepe tried to obtain more detailed information, but he could get nothing out of the men.

The yurt in the center of the camp towered over all the others. Beside it stood a gigantic mast from which was hanging a white standard, as big as a sail, with nine points. White horse-tails were fastened to the ends of these points. This was the *Tug*, the Khan's standard. The horse-tails were the insignia of the nine *Orluks*.

A wide space was left clear around the yurt with the *Tug*. The men who formed Genghis Khan's bodyguard, all of them well-grown men and all a foot taller than the other horsemen, stood around, forming a loose cordon. There was room enough between them — but no one pressed forward. The men of the bodyguard were not drunk — that could be seen at once by their sure, firm step.

A guard wanted to make way for the *Orluk* at once, but Chepe re-mained standing. What was to be seen on the open space astonished even him; and the princes were simply spellbound. The Khan's throne was in front of the entrance to the yurt. At each side of it there were seats, five on the right and four on the left. They were the *Orluks'* seats.

---

[1]**yurt** (yûrt): a circular, domed, portable tent.
[2]Chepe is a Mongol warrior leader called an *Orluk*. The princes are two grandsons of Genghis Khan: Arik-Buka and Kublai.

Two of them were vacant; one had been reserved for Chepe and another for the *Orluk* Sorgan-Shira. The Khan was sitting on his throne. Seven *Orluks* were sitting on the seats, and all were being looked after by servants who came running with tankards. All the *Orluks* were in the best of humour.

Chepe was thirsty after the ride, but he hesitated to take his seat. He did not think it wise to disturb the Khan just then. Obviously something special was going on.

The only fire to be seen in the camp was burning in a bowl placed right at the Khan's feet, and a servant was looking after it and keeping it blazing well. A few paces away stood a post to which a man dressed in silk was bound. The cloak which he wore shone in the moonlight more brightly than the leather jerkins of the *Orluks*. A band was wound round the man's forehead and fastened to the post, so that the head inclined backwards and the face was turned towards the moon. The man's beard, a long, black shining beard, stood forward in front of him. The beard, too, was tied up. A man was holding it by a silken cord, so that it could not fall on his breast. Another attendant was holding a large hour-glass.

"What is it all about?" asked Arik-Buka.

"I fancy it has something to do with the moon," said Chepe.

"What is there unusual about the moon?"

"Sometimes when the sky is bright it disappears," said Chepe. "The night swallows it; you know that yourself; and that is a spectacle which the Khan loves. But he always wants to know in advance when this is going to happen."

"And the man at the post?" asked Kublai. "Why is he bound? And his beard — why, even the Khan hasn't such a long beard!"

"That is much to be regretted," said Chepe. "If he had, he probably wouldn't have so much time for long beards — and for people like that man there, who wear long beards."

"But he doesn't seem to treat him with special favour," said Arik-Buka.

"That has yet to be seen, if I am not mistaken . . . that is, if the man with the beard is not mistaken."

At that moment the man who was holding the hour-glass made a sign to the Khan, who then raised his hand. Immediately there was a roll of drums, and then silence reigned over the wide square. The Khan spoke: "The time is up, astrologer. The sand has run out," he said.

"The sand was in too great a hurry, O Khan," said the man at the post, in a firm voice.

"You are too sure of yourself."

"The heavens do not err, O Khan."

"But it seems to me that you do. I'm very sorry about your beautiful beard. I agreed that you could keep it if you proved that you understand the heavens. But you can see for yourself that what you foretold has not happened. The eclipse has not come to pass."

"It will come as I have said, O Khan," said the man tied to the post.

"The sand has run out, and my patience too!" Genghis Khan made a sign to the man who was guarding the fire, and the latter lifted up the bowl and stood with it right beside the bound man. Now the man's face could be seen more distinctly; it was the fairest face in the whole camp. Kublai saw that it was different from the faces of the horsemen. There was not the slightest trace of either ferocity or fear in it.

"May I speak again, O Khan?" asked the man at the post.

"Speak! But if you speak foolish things I shall have your mouth singed too."

"That is all within your power, O Khan," said the bound man. "But you will offend heaven if you trust it less than the sand in an hour-glass."

They should singe his mouth! thought Arik-Buka. And Chepe thought: None of them has taken such a liberty as that till now. Kublai glanced over at the Khan. The Khan seemed to be pondering the matter.

"May I speak again, O Khan?" asked the strange man once more.

"Well, speak on! But it is the last time."

"Wait for the space of a thousand heart-beats, O Khan! If the moon has lost none of her fullness by then, cut off my head!"

"He knows how to bargain," whispered Arik-Buka.

"Like all the people of the South," hissed Chepe. "But this one here beats them all!"

"Loose him!" ordered the Khan. He turned his face towards the moon, which was standing clear against the sky. And while the man who had been holding the fire cut the ropes and the other one freed the beard from its imprisonment, a round shadow began to move over the face of the moon. Before the space of a thousand heart-beats was up, anyone who looked at the moon could perceive it.

The Khan signed to the man in the silken coat to come up to him.

"You have put the astrologers whom I have had up till now to shame. And the *shamans* too. They said that no eclipse was to be expected so soon. I need a man who is on good terms with the heavens. I am told your name is Yeliu."

"Yeliu Chutsai of the Liao family," the stranger confirmed.

"That is a family which has had much to suffer from the Chin Emperor," said the Khan with emphasis, "and so I have also avenged you."

"I was in the service of the Emperor of Chin by my own free will, as my father was before me," said Yeliu. "I was a counsellor and minister of the Emperor. It would not be fitting for me to speak ill of him just because he has perished."

A murmur passed through the line of horsemen at these words. But the Khan showed no sign of displeasure.

"It seems you are accustomed to say what you think. I like that. Come to the supper-table with me! I should like to learn more from you."

The Khan looked up at the moon. "The eclipse is moving forward quite distinctly. A good omen! You, my Mongols, shall move forward like that, and take one kingdom after another. Light the fires! And if you like, go on drinking. Your Khan has found someone who is on good terms with the heavens!"

At a sign from the Khan a seat was brought along for Yeliu.

"A fine reception!" said Arik-Buka. Chepe gripped the prince's arm. "It's best for us not to go to the Khan until tomorrow," he said. "Or do you wish to sit beside this Yeliu?"

Chepe put up the princes in his yurt. He invited them to stay with him permanently, and the princes immediately agreed to do so. And although the noise continued in the lanes throughout the camp for a long time, the three quickly fell asleep. The twelve-day ride had taken it out of them.

As he dropped off to sleep Kublai saw Yeliu's face before him just as it had looked when the fire was blazing up right beside it.

I could ask him about the names of the stars, he thought.

The camp was being broken up, but the Khan detained Chepe and the princes, who had presented themselves to him early in the morning, in his yurt. He pushed the best morsels of food over to them and questioned them ceaselessly. He was full of jokes, and his grey eyes shone when he laughed. He reproached the three for not having come to him during the night.

"There was so much going on," said Chepe hesitantly; "the new astrologer —"

"A man such as I have not met before amongst those of the South," said the Khan so definitely that Chepe preferred not to touch on the subject again.

The Khan was just about to rise from the table when an officer of the life guard arrived and announced that a prisoner had been captured by the sentries who were roaming the countryside, just as he was about to creep into a hole in the ground.

Anyone who tried to flee condemned himself to death; everyone who had endured the "sieving" process[3] and been declared a useful person knew this. Up to now no one had dared to make off and seek a way back to freedom. The Steppe offered too few hiding-places — and the Gobi, that deadly barrier, stood between them and the South.

"I wish to see him," ordered the Khan.

The man was dragged in by two life guards. His hands were tied together. His face was scratched. There were traces of blood in his beard.

"He refused to walk," the Guards officer announced. "We had to drag him."

"Free him!" said the Khan. The horsemen freed him. The man fell forward and remained lying down with his face pressed to the ground.

"Is he too weak to stand up?" inquired the Khan.

"He doesn't want to stand up," said the officer. Then he pushed the man with his foot. "Look here, won't you speak to the Khan?" he said.

The man on the ground did not utter a word.

"Lift him up!" ordered the Khan. "I want to see how he looks at me."

The man was lifted up. He looked at the ground in front of him.

"I wish you to look at me!" said the Khan. "Look at me, or you will lose your eyes!"

The man stood there, his face unmoved. He did not raise his eyes a hair's breadth.

---

[3]**"sieving" process:** A *sieve* (sĭv) is a utensil for separating liquids and fine particles from more solid substances. Here the *sieving process* refers to the way in which the Mongols separated the Chinese into categories of "useless" and "useful."

"What's the man's name?"

"Tang Liweng," said the officer. "He's an expert on the old script. He belongs to the Liao clan."

"Call Yeliu!" said the Khan at once.

Then the man said: "I would prefer to look at you than at that one!" and he stared into the Khan's face.

"What does that mean?"

"That I despise him a hundred times more than I do you! You were born a devil, but he made himself a devil by entering your service!"

"Free him!" ordered the Khan.

Why doesn't he strike him down? thought Arik-Buka.

Tang Liweng was an old man, but he stood erect. Then he said: "When you made him appear ridiculous bound to the post I was glad, and I hoped his beard would be burnt."

An officer entered. "Yeliu is outside the yurt," he said.

"Send him in."

Yeliu entered. Tang Liweng looked at him with hatred.

"He didn't want to look at you," said the Khan to Yeliu. "Do you know this man?"

"He is a great scholar," said Yeliu.

"He is the greatest blockhead ever born," said the Khan furiously. "He has abused you because you entered my service."

"He was my pupil," said Tang Liweng, "but now I am ashamed that he was. We were related; now we are no longer so."

Yeliu remained silent.

"Why did you want to flee?" the Khan asked Tang Liweng.

"I wanted to go to the country to which I belong."

"And what did you want to do there?"

"To gnaw," said Tang Liweng excitedly.

"What's that you wanted to do?"

Then Tang Liweng whispered: "You turned us into ants to drag burdens for you. I wanted to go from one ant to another and remind them all that only one thing remained for us to do: to gnaw . . . to gnaw at your throne until it would collapse."

"You have no doubt forgotten that I have broken your jawbones," said the Khan mockingly.

"One can gnaw even with broken jaws — provided one isn't too half-hearted," said Tang Liweng.

"What nonsense!" said the Khan. "You do not understand how things are since I have been in power. Even if you had escaped and incited others against me, you would only have become their murderer. I would have had to crush the breakers of the new order which I have set up. You forget that I am everywhere — wherever my horsemen have marked the ground with the hooves of their horses. You have even forgotten the Gobi, great scholar! Or do you think the desert would have spared you?"

"You are the desert!" said Tang Liweng so violently that the scars on his face began to bleed.

Why does the Khan not strike him down? thought Arik-Buka again.

"And you are the darkness which makes the desert even more terrible," said Tang Liweng, turning to Yeliu. "Have you forgotten what he has done to your people — the people who speak your language and are of your mind? He trod them down until they mingled with the earth. He trampled down the towns because he suspected that freedom dwelt in them. And he is only beginning. He aims at making these countries, these gardens of the earth, into Steppe. He intends to quench millions of lives. And you, creature of fear, are walking in his shadow because you fear for your life!"

Yeliu remained silent. The Khan looked at him.

"Have you nothing to say to that?"

"No, O Khan!" said Yeliu, with an impassive face. The Khan observed him more sharply.

"Do you regret having entered my service?"

"No, O Khan," answered Yeliu.

Thereupon Tang Liweng took two steps towards Yeliu and dealt him a blow in the face with his clenched fist. Yeliu staggered, but again stood firm when the men of the life guard pulled Tang Liweng back.

"Are you not going to hit back?" asked the Khan angrily.

"No, O Khan," said Yeliu.

"Then beat him, you!" cried the Khan. "And let all those whom we are feeding be present, although they have forfeited their lives, so that they see how we treat ants who emit poison instead of doing what they should do."

Tang Liweng stood there just as if what the Khan was saying did not concern him at all. The Khan suddenly interrupted himself. Pointing to Yeliu, he said to Tang Liweng: "You are a Liao, so is he. For his sake I shall give you an hour. If you make up your mind . . ."

"I do not want to die," said Tang Liweng, "and this alone would be death: to enter your service."

"They will make short work of you."

"You cannot kill me," said Tang Liweng. "You cannot kill what alone is important to me. You can destroy my body, but you cannot subjugate my mind. You cannot stamp out the spark of freedom which I am."

"You talk insanely," said the Khan. He turned to the officer. "I have never seen a greater fool," he said. "Take him out! No one is to look on. He is to disappear and be forgotten for ever!"

The guard led Tang Liweng away.

"A madman, isn't he?" said the Khan, turning to Yeliu.

"No," said Yeliu.

There was an eerie silence. Chepe and the princes looked at Yeliu spellbound.

"You do not consider that rebel to be mad, then?"

"He went *his* way," said Yeliu quietly. "He saw that way clearly
before him."

"You do not despise him, do you?" asked the Khan.

"Tang Liweng was a great man," said Yeliu.

The Khan fixed Yeliu with cold eyes. "And why, then, do you not
do the same as he does?"

"His way is not mine," said Yeliu. "I am no rebel. My star has led
me into your service. I knew for a long time past that that would happen.
My father, who foretold to the Chin Emperor the exact day of his downfall, told me that I would end my life in the service of the lord of half the
world."

"I shall one day be lord of the whole world," said the Khan angrily.

Yeliu shut his eyes. "The heavens are not mistaken," he said.

"Speak!" said the Khan. "I want to know what the heavens know."

Yeliu still kept his eyes shut. He looked as if he was being tortured by some vision. He began to speak in an altered voice: "All will tremble before you, O Khan, and you will establish an enormous empire such as no one before you ever thought of, and your sons shall extend your power still farther. But it is only your grandson who shall inherit it fully." Yeliu opened his eyes. He looked around as if searching for someone. Then he pointed to Kublai and said: "It will be that one."

Kublai saw the hand pointing to him, and his face began to burn.

"How do you know that?" asked the Khan, startled by the force of Yeliu's words. "And why Kublai?"

"Feng Huang, the phoenix, ruler of all the three hundred and sixty-five feathered creatures, stepped through your yurt, O Khan. Without taking notice of the others, the bird walked up to Kublai, and with his beak he touched the spot on the breast beneath which the heart beats. Feng Huang has three voices. In the morning he calls: *Ho shi* — May things go well in the world! At midday: *Ki-tshang* — Turn at the right time! In the evening: *Shan dsai* — Now all is well! Up to the present the bird phoenix has been seen three times. Under the Yellow Emperors of olden times he lived at the southern gate of the Imperial Palace. When the Chao music originated under the Chin emperor, he came flying, and danced to the Emperor's songs. Now he has appeared for the third time. The Emperors of olden times had the power which is without blemish; Emperor Chin had the music, which directs men and animals and even the growth of plants, without force; and in Kublai, your grandson, wisdom shall dwell."

Chepe and Arik-Buka looked at each other, dumbfounded. This man is more dangerous than Tang Liweng, they both thought, and Chepe cast an icy glance at Yeliu. Restraining himself with an effort, he said in a casual tone: "Forgive me, O Khan, if I speak now! I have not seen in the yurt the bird of which the astrologer speaks. But perhaps that is because I am only one of your warriors — not a wise man."

"I didn't notice any bird either," said Arik-Buka contemptuously.

The Khan took no notice of these remarks. He seemed to have eyes only for Yeliu. Looking at him keenly, he said: "One who is of my blood should attain to the knowledge which is yours. I wish you to become Kublai's teacher." The Khan's voice became threatening. "He shall learn to see what is hidden from me. He shall be able to read what Tatatungo writes out for me. And you shall remain near me always so that I may be able to see which way you lead him."

Only then did the Khan turn to Chepe. "And now we shall ride on!" he said.

Sons of the Steppe

Thinking and Discussing

What information in the selection is probably factual and true? What elements of the novel are probably fictional? Why should an author be careful when inventing ideas for use in historical fiction?

What kind of ruler do you think Genghis Khan will prove to be? What kind of ruler do you think young Kublai Khan will be later? How do your predictions compare with what you read earlier in *Across the Centuries*?

Why might an author write about this theme through fiction rather than nonfiction? How does historical fiction help you understand history?

Applying Historical Concepts

Writing a Letter Home Imagine you are traveling with Chepe, Arik-Buka, and Kublai Khan. Write a letter home, giving a summary of the events at Genghis Khan's camp. Which events will you cover at greatest length? How do the events affect you? Think about the tone of your letter — are you in awe of Genghis Khan? What image of Genghis Khan would a modern reader form by reading your letter? Do you think the picture would be accurate?

Kublai Khan: Eyewitness Accounts

The Great Khan

by Marco Polo

Born to an Italian merchant in 1254, Marco Polo learned at an early age to handle foreign money and estimate the value of merchandise. At seventeen years of age, he left Venice, Italy, with his father and uncle to go to China. Planning to go by sea, they ended up traveling across land by camel and didn't reach the court of Kublai Khan until three years later. The Polos spent the next sixteen or seventeen years serving the Khan and touring the kingdom. When he and his family returned to Italy in 1295, Marco Polo wrote about their many adventures in a book called Description of the World. *It became the most widely read book of its time in Europe.*

Kublai-khan is a comely [attractive], handsome man of middle stature, with a fresh complexion, bright black eyes, a well-formed nose, and every way well proportioned. He has four lawful wives, every one of whom has the title of empress, and the eldest born son of these wives is to succeed him in the empire. Each of these empresses has her own magnificent palace and peculiar court, and is attended by three hundred women. . . .

During the three winter months of December, January, and February, Kublai-khan generally resides in Cambalu [Beijing] which is at the north-east border of Kathay [or Cathay, an ancient name for China]: on the southern part of the new city stands the great palace of the khan, which is the largest and most magnificent of any in the world.

When the khan holds a solemn court on any particular day of festival, his table is raised higher than all the rest, and is set on the north side of the hall, having his face to the south, his first or principal queen being placed on his left hand, and his sons and nephews, and other princes of the blood-royal being arranged on his right; but their table is placed so much lower, that their heads are hardly so high as the khan's feet. By this means the khan, as he sits at table, can see all that feast along with him in the hall. There are not tables for all who are admitted to the feast but the greatest part of the soldiers and captains sit down on carpets, where they

Tomb figures from the Tang dynasty

are served with victuals [food] and drink. At all the doors there are two gigantic fellows with cudgels, who observe carefully if anyone touches the threshold in going in; and whoever does so, forfeits his garment, or receives a certain number of blows of the cudgel. Those who serve the khan or sit at his table, have their mouths covered with silken veils lest their breath should touch the meat or drink which he is to use. When he drinks, the damsel who carries the cup kneels down and then all the barons and others present kneel likewise, and all the musicians sound their instruments, till the khan has done drinking. If I were to describe all the pomp and magnificence of these festivals, and all the dainties and delicate dishes which are served up, I should become prolix [long-winded] and tiresome.

The money of the great khan is not of gold or silver, or other metal, but a species of paper, which is thus made: They take the middle bark of the mulberry tree, which they make firm in a particular manner, and this is cut out into round pieces of various sizes, on which the seal or mark of the khan is impressed. Of this paper money, an immense quantity is fabricated in the city of Cambalu, sufficient to supply the currency of the whole empire; and no person, under pain of death, may coin or spend any other money, or refuse to accept of this, in all the kingdoms and countries which are subject to his dominions [control]. All who come into his dominions are prohibited from using any other money, so that all merchants coming from countries however remote, must bring with them gold, silver, pearls, or precious stones, for which they receive the khan's

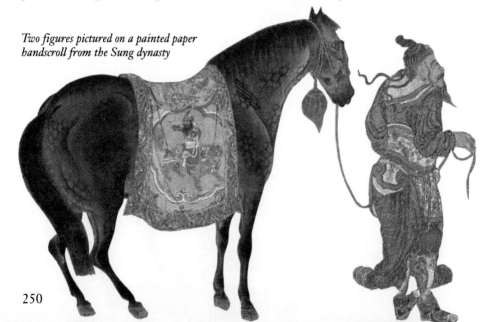

Two figures pictured on a painted paper handscroll from the Sung dynasty

paper money in exchange: And as that money is not received in other countries, they must exchange it again in the empire of the great khan, for merchandise to carry with them on their return. The khan pays all salaries, stipends, and wages to his officers, servants, and army, in this money, and whatever is required for the service of his court and household is paid for in the same. By all these means, there is no sovereign in the world who equals the great khan in extent of treasure; as he expends none in the mint, or in any other way whatever.

The khan sends every year to the different provinces of his empire, to inquire whether any injuries have been sustained to the crops by tempests, locusts, worms, or any other calamity; and when any province or district has suffered damage, the tribute is remitted for that year, and he even sends corn for food and seed from the public granaries: For in years of great abundance, he purchases large quantities of grain, which is carefully preserved for three or four years, by officers appointed for the purpose; by which means, when a scarcity occurs in any province, the defect may be supplied from the granaries of the khan in another province.

All barons or others, who approach within half a mile of the residence of the great khan, must be still and quiet, no noise or loud speaking being permitted in his presence or neighbourhood. Every one who enters the hall of presence, must pull off his boots, lest he soil the carpets, and puts on furred buskins of white leather, giving his other boots to the charge of servants till he quits the hall; and every one carries a small covered vessel to spit in, as no one dare spit in the halls of the palace.

An archer and horse pictured on a handscroll

The Land of China

by Ibn Battúta

Born in the North African city of Tangier in 1304, Moslem adventurer Ibn Battúta saw more of the world in his lifetime than most tourists see today in the age of jet airplanes. Known as the "traveler of Islam," Ibn Battúta journeyed more than 75,000 miles despite rugged conditions and primitive forms of transportation. He visited every Moslem country of his day, as well as the non-Moslem countries of Ceylon and China, and the Christian city of Constantinople. When he was thirty-eight years old, Ibn Battúta led a mission from India through Northern China to Beijing and back, noting customs and traditions of the Chinese people along the way.

The land of China is of vast extent, and abounding in produce, fruits, grains, gold and silver. In this respect there is no country in the world that can rival it. . . . In the land of China there is abundant sugarcane, equal, nay superior, in quality to that of Egypt, as well as grapes and plums. . . . All the fruits which we have in our country are to be found there, either much the same or better quality. Wheat is very abundant in China, indeed better wheat I have never seen, and the same may be said for their lentils and chick-peas.

The Chinese pottery [porcelain] is manufactured only in the towns of Zaytún and Sín-kalán. It is made of the soil of some mountains in that district which takes fire like charcoal. . . . They mix this with some stones which they have, burn the whole for three days, then pour water over it. This gives a kind of clay which they cause to ferment. The best quality of [porcelain is made from] clay that has fermented for a complete month, but no more, the poorer quality [from clay] that has fermented for ten days. The price of this porcelain there is the same as, or even less than, that of ordinary pottery in our own country. It is exported to India and other countries, even reaching as far as our own lands in the West, and it is the finest of all makes of pottery. . . .

The Chinese infidels[1] eat the flesh of swine and dogs, and sell it in their markets. They are wealthy folk and well-to-do, but they make no display either in their food or their clothes. You will see one of their principal merchants, a man so rich that his wealth cannot be counted, wearing a coarse cotton tunic. But there is one thing that the Chinese take pride in, that is gold and silver plate. Every one of them carries a stick, on which they lean in walking. . . . Silk is very plentiful among them, because the silk-worm attaches itself to fruits and feeds on them without requiring much care. For that reason it is so common to be worn by even the very poorest there. Were it not for the merchants it would have no value at all, for a single piece of cotton cloth is sold in their country for the price of many pieces of silk. It is customary amongst them for a merchant to cast what gold and silver he has into ingots, each weighing a

---

[1]The writer, as a Moslem, considers the Chinese to be *infidels* — "unfaithful ones."

hundred-weight or more or less, and to put those ingots above the door of his house. . . .

The Chinese are of all peoples the most skilful in the arts and possessed of the greatest mastery of them. . . . In regard to portraiture there is none, whether Greek or any other, who can match them in precision. I myself saw an extraordinary example of this gift of theirs. I never returned to any of their cities after I had visited it a first time without finding my portrait and the portraits of my companions drawn on the walls and on sheets of paper exhibited in the bazaars. When I visited the sultan's city I passed with my companions through the painters' bazaar on my way to the sultan's palace. We were dressed after the Iraqui fashion. On returning from the palace in the evening, I passed through the same bazaar, and saw my portrait and those of my companions drawn on a sheet of paper which they had affixed to the wall. Each of us set to examining the other's portraits [and found that] the likeness was perfect in every respect. I was told that the sultan had ordered them to do this, and that they had come to the palace while we were there and had been observing us and drawing our portraits without our noticing it. This is a custom of theirs, I mean making portraits of all who pass through their country. In fact they have brought this to such perfection that if a stranger commit any offence that obliges him to flee from China, they send his portrait far and wide. A search is then made for him and wheresoever the [person bearing] a resemblance to that portrait is found he is arrested.

Kublai Khan:
Eyewitness Accounts

Thinking and Discussing

From the time Marco Polo was young, he was a favorite of Kublai Khan. As a man, he grew wealthy in the Khan's service. Do you think these experiences might have influenced Marco Polo when he wrote his historical account of Chinese society? Can you find examples of bias in the selection?

How does Ibn Battúta's account of Chinese customs differ from that of Marco Polo? How are their impressions of Chinese society during the reign of Kublai Khan similar?

Applying Historical Concepts

Tracing the Old Silk Road The Old Silk Road was a caravan route that ran from Cadiz, Spain, to Shanghai, China. For more than two thousand years, it was the longest road in the world. Marco Polo followed this route for part of the time when going to Beijing, China, to visit the emperor Kublai Khan.

In an encyclopedia or nonfiction book on ancient China, look up a map showing the Old Silk Road. Then, on a map of contemporary Europe and Asia, trace its path across these continents to the Chinese capital. You may wish to color-code different features of the route and identify what the colors mean in a key.

Judging Historical Writing

As you have seen in this unit, there are various ways in which a reader can learn about the past — through historical fiction, eyewitness reports, and textbooks. Work with two other classmates to present a panel discussion debating the advantages and disadvantages of each approach. Have the group members play the role of a historical novelist, a scholarly researcher, or a textbook publisher during the debate. Present the points of view of these experts. Be sure to give specific examples from the unit to show how a particular type of writing helped the reader understand Chinese history. At the end, ask the audience which opinions and arguments were most persuasive, and which type of writing they think was most effective.

Celebrating Chinese Arts and Crafts

Hold a classroom fair celebrating the arts and crafts of China. Divide into groups and decide which art or craft to explore. Possibilities include poetry, painting, silk embroidery, pottery, puppet making, kite making, paper cutting, ivory and jade carving, straw collage, and rug weaving.

Research and write a paragraph about the history of the craft in China and its significance to Chinese culture. Display actual samples or photographs of the final product, along with diagrams showing how it is made.

If you like, try completing a project of your own in kite making, paper cutting, haiku, or straw collage. Then give demonstrations on the day of your fair.

Planning a Mini-Series

Imagine you are a television director preparing a historical mini-series about ancient China. Based on what you have learned in this unit, plan the events you will cover in the program.

First, select scenes that are dramatic enough for television and decide how many episodes will be broadcast. Then outline the plot in words or by drawing pictures of the scenes on pieces of cardboard or poster board.

Which historical details will be fact, and which will be fiction? Who will your main characters be? Do you know which movie stars you will cast in those roles? What props and costumes will you need? What will be the title of your feature? Make notes about all these aspects of your plan.

About the

HANS BAUMANN

Hans Baumann was born in Bavaria in the Federal Republic of Germany, where he still lives. He has worked as a poet, editor, and playwright, but in America he is best known for his works of historical fiction for young people. These include *The Caves of the Great Hunters*, *I Marched with Hannibal*, *Lion Gate and Labyrinth*, and *Sons of the Steppe*, which received the *New York Herald Tribune* Spring Book Festival award for the best juvenile book in 1958.

GEORGE BESHORE

A full-time free-lance writer, George Beshore has been writing about scientific and environmental subjects for more than twenty-five years. Most of his work up to this point has been published in newspapers and magazines, but he is currently at work on a book about science and technology in other cultures and other times. Beshore lives in Alexandria, Virginia.

Authors

DANIEL COHEN

Daniel Cohen was born in Chicago in 1936. He received a degree in journalism from the University of Illinois and worked for *Time* magazine and *Science Digest*. Cohen has written more than one hundred and twenty nonfiction books for young people, on topics ranging from ESP, ghosts, and sea monsters to video games and crime.

    Cohen thinks of himself as a writer and craftsman, but not as an artist. He says since he has little imagination, he feels most confident writing nonfiction books. "At best I'm professional, never brilliant. . . . I simply try to do the best job that I possibly can and still make a living."

Above: a gilt-bronze dragon; left: a clay sculpture of an archer discovered near the tomb of Ch'in Shih Huang Ti

ON YOUR OWN IN CHINA

Marco Polo: Voyager to the Orient
by Carol Greene (Childrens, 1987)
Marco Polo's travels to
China and his adventures at the
court of Kublai Khan are described
simply and, at times, humorously
in this fascinating glimpse of the
Orient as seen by one of the
world's first "tourists."

Oracle Bones, Stars, and Wheelbarrows
by Frank Ross, Jr. (Houghton, 1982)

This eye-opening book looks at the scientific and technological discoveries made by the Chinese centuries before such advances were achieved in the West.

Builders of the Ancient World (National Geographic, 1986)

Handsome photographs and detailed text describe ancient creators and their impressive structures, including some of China's oldest bridges, monuments, and temples.

Young Fu of the Upper Yangtze
by Elizabeth Foreman Lewis (Holt, 1932)

In this Newbery Award–winning book, Young Fu is apprenticed to a coppersmith in the city of Chungking. There he learns to succeed at his trade and bring honor to his widowed mother.

The Great Wall of China
by Leonard Everett Fisher (Macmillan, 1986)

The Pulitzer Prize–winning artist uses striking illustrations to present a brief history of China's 3750-mile-long Great Wall, built over two thousand years ago to keep out Mongol invaders.

Genghis Khan by Judy Humphrey (Chelsea House, 1987)

This biography about one of the most famous world figures is enlivened by quotations from the writings of Genghis Khan himself and from his contemporaries. Photographs illustrate similarities between the dress, customs, and lifestyle of today's Mongolians and those of nine hundred years ago.

POETRY

BOOK 4

The Circus by Georges Seurat, circa 1890, oil on canvas

ARTISTS IN
CONCERT

Images

Lines

Sounds

The Blue Bird by Jean Metzinger, circa 1915, oil on canvas

Award Winner

IMAGES

Butterfly Habitat by Joseph Cornell, 1940, wood, paper, and glass

Wild Life Cameo, Early Morn

Lawrence Ferlinghetti

By the great river Deschutes
        on the meadowbank greensward
    sun just hitting
        the high bluffs
    stone cliffs sculpted
        high away
    across the river

At the foot of a steep brown slope
        a mile away
    six white-tail deer
    four young bucks with branched antlers
    and two small does
        mute in eternity
        drinking the river
  then in real time raising heads
  and climbing up and up
        a steep faint switchback
  into full sun

I bring them close in the binoculars
        as in a round cameo
  There is a hollow bole in a tree
        one looks into
One by one they
    drink silence
        (the two does last)
  one by one
    climb up so calm
        over the rim of the canyon
  and without looking back
        disappear forever
Like certain people
  in my life

Windshield Wiper

Eve Merriam

fog smog	fog smog
tissue paper	tissue paper
clear the blear	clear the smear
fog more	fog more
splat splat	downpour
rubber scraper	rubber scraper
overshoes	macintosh
bumbershoot	muddle on
slosh through	slosh through
drying up	drying up
sky lighter	sky lighter
nearly clear	nearly clear

clearing clearing veer
clear here clear

SEPARATION

Your absence has gone through me
Like thread through a needle.
Everything I do is stitched with its color.

W. S. Merwin

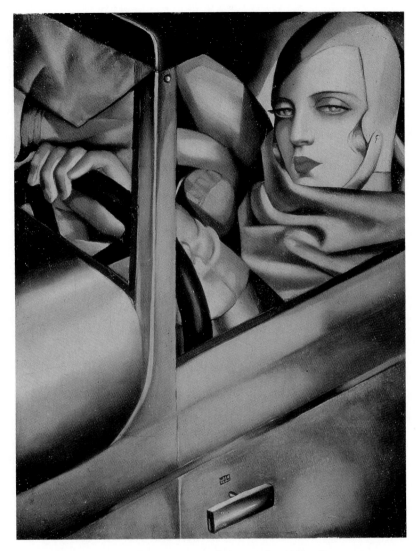

Self Portrait in a Car by Tamara de Lempicka, 1932, oil on canvas

Seneca by Paul Klee, 1922

ZINNIAS

Zinnias, stout and stiff,
Stand no nonsense: their colors
Stare, their leaves
Grow straight out, their petals
Jut like clipped cardboard,
Round, in neat flat rings.

Even cut and bunched,
Arranged to please us
In the house, in water, they
Will hardly wilt — I know
Someone like zinnias; I wish
I were like zinnias.

Valerie Worth

This morning

This morning
The sun broke
my window
and came in laughing

Javier Gálvez

On Getting a Natural

For Gwendolyn Brooks

She didn't know she was beautiful
though her smiles were dawn,
her voice was bells,
and her skin deep velvet Night.
She didn't know she was beautiful,
although her deeds,
kind, generous, unobtrusive,
gave hope to some,
and help to others,
and inspiration to us all. And
beauty is as beauty does,
they say.
Then one day there blossomed
a crown upon her head,
bushy, bouffant, real Afro-down,
Queen Nefertiti again.
And now her regal woolly crown
declares,
I know
I'm black
AND
beautiful.

Dudley Randall

WAR

Dawn came slowly,
almost not at all.
The sun crept over the hill
cautiously
fearful of being hit
by mortar fire.

Dan Roth

The Twentieth Century by Max Ernst, 1955, oil on canvas

The Dream Keeper

Bring me all of your dreams,
You dreamers,
Bring me all of your
Heart melodies
That I may wrap them
In a blue cloud-cloth
Away from the too-rough fingers
Of the world.

Langston Hughes

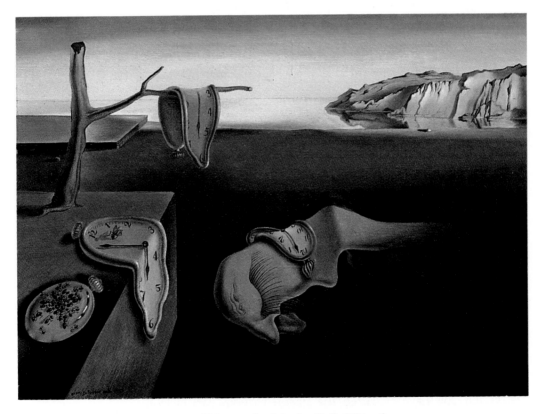

The Persistence of Memory by Salvador Dali, 1931, oil on canvas

Responding to

IMAGES

Thinking and Discussing

The poets in "Images" use strong visual images to convey the meaning of the poems. What images in these poems are your favorites? Give reasons for your answer.

Poets often use comparisons to express feelings. What comparisons did the poets use to express feelings about a separation, zinnias, waking up on a sunny day, Gwendolyn Brooks, war, and dreams? Which comparison is most powerful? Explain your answer.

Choosing a Creative Response

Capturing Images The poets in "Images" use descriptive words to capture images, but people can capture images in other ways. Think of an image and try to capture it in one of the following ways:

- drawing
- describing in a paragraph
- taking a picture
- making a collage
- writing song lyrics

When you have captured the image to your satisfaction, share it with your group.

Creating Your Own Activity Plan and complete your own activity in response to the poems in "Images."

276

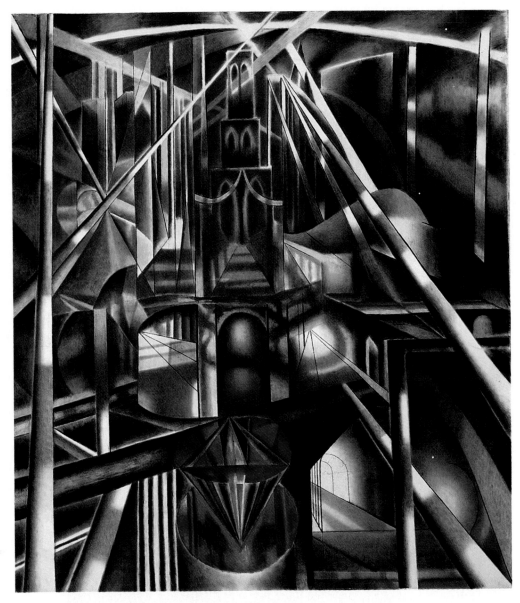

Old Brooklyn Bridge by Joseph Stella, oil on canvas

LINES

Portrait of a Black Man by André Derain, circa 1928, oil on canvas

Past

I have all these parts   stuffed in
                              me
    like mama's chicken
                    and
            biscuits,
                    and
    daddy's apple pie, and a tasty
                        story
    from the family
            tree.
    But I know that tomorrow
                    morning
        I'll wake up
            empty, and hungry for that
                                next
                                bite
    of my new
            day

Arnold Adoff

the /

sky /

was

the
    sky
        was
can dy lu
minous
        edible
spry
    pinks shy
lemons
greens coo   l choc
olate
s.
        un der,
    a lo
  co
mo
    tive s pout
        ing
            vi
            o
            lets

e. e. cummings

North Sea Picture by Paul Klee, 1923, watercolor

CHAIRS

Chairs
Seem
To
Sit
Down
On
Themselves, almost as if
They were people,
Some fat, some thin
Settled comfortably
On their own seats,
Some even stretch out their arms
To
Rest.

Valerie Worth

Dream Song

as my eyes
search
the prairie
I feel the summer
in the spring

(*Chippewa*)

Of the Achievements of Great Civilizations
from the *Teapot Opera* series by Arthur Tress, 1980, cibachrome

Responding to

LINES

Thinking and Discussing

The poems in "Lines" include some lines that consist of one word or one syllable. How do these short lines strengthen the images or themes? Give an example from each poem to support your answer.

Choosing a Creative Response

Writing a Visual Poem The arrangement of lines in "the/ sky/was" suggests the wisps of clouds and smoke that the poet describes. The lines in "Chairs" are arranged in the shape of a chair. The poets have used lines not only to help convey their thoughts, feelings, and ideas but also to create a visual image of their subjects. Think of a familiar object, and write a short, vivid description of the object. You may or may not name the object. Arrange your words in the shape of the object. Share your description with your group.

Creating Your Own Activity Plan and complete your own activity in response to the poems in "Lines."

Three Musicians by Pablo Picasso, summer 1921, oil on canvas

SOUNDS

Stopping by Woods on a Snowy Evening

Whose woods these are I think I know.
His house is in the village though;
He will not see me stopping here
To watch his woods fill up with snow.

My little horse must think it queer
To stop without a farmhouse near
Between the woods and frozen lake
The darkest evening of the year.

He gives his harness bells a shake
To ask if there is some mistake.
The only other sound's the sweep
Of easy wind and downy flake.

The woods are lovely, dark and deep.
But I have promises to keep,
And miles to go before I sleep,
And miles to go before I sleep.

Robert Frost

Time Transfixed by René Magritte, 1938, oil on canvas

Night Train

Across the dim frozen fields of night
Where is it going, where is it going?
No throb of wheels, no rush of light.
Only a whistle blowing, blowing.
Only a whistle blowing.

Something echoing through my brain,
Something timed between sleep and waking,
Murmurs, murmurs this may be the train
I must be sometime, somewhere taking,
I must be sometime taking.

Robert Francis

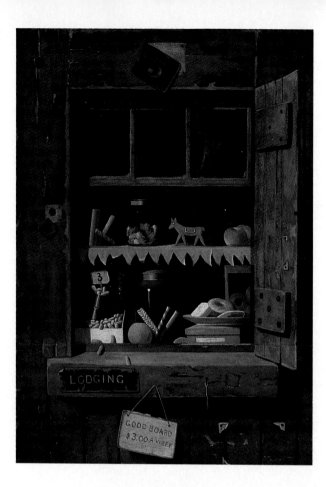

The Poor Man's Store
by John Frederick Peto,
1885, oil on canvas and wood

The Great Figure

Among the rain
and lights
I saw the figure 5
in gold
on a red
firetruck
moving
tense
unheeded
to gong clangs
siren howls
and wheels rumbling
through the dark city.

William Carlos Williams

TURTLE SOUP

Beautiful Soup, so rich and green,
Waiting in a hot tureen!
Who for such dainties would not stoop?
Soup of the evening, beautiful Soup!
Soup of the evening, beautiful Soup!
      Beau — ootiful Soo — oop!
      Beau — ootiful Soo — oop!
Soo — oop of the e — e — evening,
      Beautiful, beautiful Soup!

Beautiful Soup! Who cares for fish,
Game, or any other dish?
Who would not give all else for two p
ennyworth only of beautiful Soup?
Pennyworth only of beautiful Soup?
      Beau — ootiful Soo — oop!
      Beau — ootiful Soo — oop!
Soo — oop of the e — e — evening,
      Beautiful, beauti — FUL SOUP!

Lewis Carroll

Responding to

SOUNDS

Thinking and Discussing

"Stopping by Woods on a Snowy Evening" is a well-known American poem with distinct sound effects. What sound effects do you think have helped to contribute to the poem's popularity? Why?

What feeling do the rhythm and images of "Night Train" create? What sound might the rhythm imitate?

How does repetition in "Turtle Soup" increase the humor in the poem?

Choosing a Creative Response

Sounding Out a Poem Choose one of the poems in "Sounds" and with your group perform it for your class, using appropriate sound effects. Some members can clap softly or tap their feet. Other members who might play musical instruments can provide musical accompaniment.

Creating Your Own Activity Plan and complete your own activity in response to the poems in "Sounds."

Thinking About Poetry

Collecting Images Which poems in "Artists in Concert" do you remember most vividly because of the images? In your group collect pictures inspired by the poems. Then create a display of the images to present to the class. Your presentation might take the form of a photo display, a slide show, or even a video show.

Recording a Poetry Reading With your group, plan a radio poetry reading. Decide which poems are most appropriate for solo reading and which ones for choral reading. Then practice reading the poems aloud. Develop and include sound effects to make the readings dramatic, interesting, and inspiring. Give your radio show a name, write an introduction for it, record it, and play the recording for your class.

Authors

Arnold Adoff was a teacher in Harlem. When he could find no suitable anthologies of black literature for his students, he began to put together his own. His publications include *My Black Me: A Beginning Book of Black Poetry*.

Lewis Carroll is the pen name of Charles Dodgson, the British mathematician and photographer. He wrote *Alice in Wonderland* and its sequel, *Through the Looking Glass*.

e. e. cummings carried out radical experiments with language in his poetry. His poems are said to "reveal miracles in the commonplace."

Funerary Mask from the Gabon and Congo, circa late 19th to early 20th century, painted wood

Lawrence Ferlinghetti belonged to a group of writers of the 1950's who became known as the Beat Movement. His collection of poems, *A Coney Island of the Mind*, was a popular poetry book of the 1950's.

Robert Francis chose to live a simple life so he could devote himself to writing poetry. His best-known work is *Robert Francis: Collected Poems 1936–76*.

Robert Frost, perhaps the most popular American poet of his time, spent nearly all his life in rural New England. He won four Pulitzer Prizes. The first was awarded in 1924 for his collection *New Hampshire*.

Langston Hughes, the best-known poet of the Harlem Renaissance of the 1920's, used blues and jazz rhythms in his poetry. He also wrote plays, newspaper columns, and novels.

Eve Merriam's book of poetry, *The Inner City Mother Goose,* was successfully produced as a Broadway musical in 1971.

W. S. Merwin has won praise for his translations of classical and contemporary poetry. He received a Pulitzer Prize in 1971 for *A Carrier of Ladders.*

In 1965, **Dudley Randall** became publisher of Broadside Press, which was founded to publish books by young black poets. He is the author of several collections including *More to Remember.*

William Carlos Williams was a doctor as well as an important American poet. His most famous poem, *Paterson,* is a book-length portrait of Paterson, New Jersey.

Valerie Worth's many interests — astronomy, gardening, and meditation — have provided subjects for her poetry. Her collections include *The Crone's Book of Words* and *Small Poems.*

Efforts to locate biographical information about **Javier Gálvez** and **Dan Roth** have been unsuccessful. Information made available to the publisher will appear in the next edition.

POETIC ENCORES

Room for Me and a Mountain Lion: Poetry of Open Space selected by Nancy Larrick (M. Evans, 1974) contains over one hundred poems that celebrate nature.

Rhythm Road: Poems to Move To selected by Lillian Morrison (Lothrop, 1988) vividly expresses action.

Spaceways: An Anthology of Space Poetry compiled by John Foster (Oxford, 1987) uses many new poems and imaginatively covers a wide range of astronomical subjects.

Back to Class, poems by Mel Glenn (Clarion, 1988) describes in free verse the thoughts and feelings of students and teachers.

History of Electricity (detail) by Raoul Dufy, 1937, oil on canvas

REALISM

Choices

Choices

Boris

By
Jaap ter Haar

Illustrated by Jim Baldwin

During World War II, the Soviet city of Leningrad was besieged by the German army. For nine hundred horror-filled days, the citizens of Leningrad faced bombings, hunger, illness, and death. Twelve-year-old Boris has nightmares about the death of his father, who drowned while attempting to transport supplies across frozen Lake Ladoga. Boris's fourteen-year-old friend Nadia has lost her father and older brother to illness.

Despite their great sadness, Boris and Nadia want to survive. They must find food for themselves and for the remaining members of their families. Nadia has a plan. Before he died, her older brother Serjozja had told her where potatoes were buried. They lie in the dangerous territory between the German and Russian lines. Nadia and Boris decide to risk their lives to find those precious potatoes.

"Don't make a sound from now on," whispered Nadia.

They were crouched in a shell-hole close to the bank of a stream that lay frozen in the gully between two high embankments. A hundred yards farther on were the Russian lines. There the soldiers kept guard over the heavy artillery, the ammunition and the machine-guns. Nadia watched their movements carefully; she looked around on all sides; then she touched Boris on the shoulder.

"Now!"

They clambered out of the hole, tried to make themselves as small as possible, and ran the last part to the river. They slid and skidded breathlessly down its steep bank. Now at last they were out of sight of the soldiers. And now also Boris could see how they could get back beyond the lines unobserved. They had only to walk along the river-bed. The one dangerous bit would be the bridge. Would Serjozja have paused there and wondered about it too?

Nadia was standing still, listening intently to all sounds. She was out of breath, and little puffs of white came from her lips. They could hear quite clearly the voices and laughs of the Russian soldiers.

"Come on."

Without making a sound they crept through the stiff-frozen reeds towards the bridge. In the distance they heard a few scattered shots and the sound of a car starting.

Crack! The ice snapped under Boris's right foot. Nadia turned on him indignantly.

"Sssssssh!"

Boris made a face at her. How could he help it if the ice was thin?

Almost on all fours they made their way through the reeds to the bridge. Now they would have to forsake the bank and entrust themselves to the ice. To his horror, Boris saw that the water in the middle under the bridge was not frozen. Dark, cold and threatening, it rippled in the icy wind. Would the few feet of ice that had formed against the concrete sides of the bridge be strong enough to hold them? Boris felt terror creeping over him; under the bridge was just like his nightmare: ice and black holes.

Even Nadia hesitated. Then she stepped cautiously on to the ice. It held. Slowly she shuffled — foot after foot, in Serjozja's huge comical boots — on to the narrow strip of ice under the bridge. Once there she turned and waved for him to follow.

Boris glanced about himself in panic. Scenes from his nightmare flashed before his eyes: the snow-covered plain that was Lake Ladoga; the splintering ice; his father's hand gripping the steering-wheel . . .

For a moment or two he stood trembling, struggling against fear. Then suddenly he could almost hear his father talking to him, as he had before his last fatal ride.

"It's not a sin to be afraid, Boris, for we can be brave at the same time."

"Pssst!" Nadia was making frantic signs for him to hurry. Any second the soldiers might appear.

Boris took a deep breath. With a mighty effort, he tried to think about his mother, about the potatoes, about Serjozja. Keeping his eyes turned away from the dark water, he stepped on to the strip of ice which seemed to grow narrower and narrower.

Nadia was half-way across. To make herself as light as possible she was supporting herself with her hands against the wall.

"It's a good job," thought Boris ruefully, "that we're both so skinny." Inch by inch, he edged down until he too was under the bridge. The ice gave a creak and a crack shot through it. Black water began to seep through.

Boris moved forward as quickly as he dared; the sooner he was out of this dangerous spot the better. Then he realized Nadia was standing quite still. She raised her hand in warning. Boris heard for himself the marching footsteps of a detachment of troops. Their boots rang out on the bridge. Then a command: "At the double!" The footsteps drummed on the bridge, just above their heads.

Boris stood like a stone. He shut his eyes in order not to see the ice and the water.

Nadia peered out and up anxiously; then she turned and almost giggled at Boris — as if they were sharing a joke at the expense of the soldiers. Boris tried to smile back at her, but it was a feeble effort. He'd better think of something nice quickly — how many potatoes he was going to carry home; his mother, who would almost cry with joy — but he wished with all his heart he were safe at home now.

It seemed an eternity before the soldiers' footsteps died away . . .

"Come!" Nadia beckoned.

Clinging to the underside of the bridge, Nadia and Boris struggled painfully on. At last they were across the groaning, faintly heaving ice and on the other side of the bridge. Boris's heart lifted as he felt firm Russian soil beneath his feet once more — even if that soil was hard-frozen and hidden under a thick blanket of snow . . .

Boris gazed after Nadia — how incredibly brave she was! She had gone up the bank on the far side of the bridge, craning her neck and peering over to see if their way was clear. Boris felt ashamed that he had been such a coward. Cowards could never make fine soldiers. He resolved never again to be so unmanly.

Suddenly the sirens went off in Leningrad. From this distance they sounded much more ominous than when you were closer to them. Then Boris heard the monotonous drone of a group of bombers. Another attack from the air?

Nadia climbed back down hastily, her coat encrusted with snow.

"We're in luck," she said excitedly. "While there are planes over-head, no one will bother us."

Boris nodded, although he was not too happy about this kind of luck. How many bombs would rain down on the city this time? The drone in the sky grew louder. In the distance the guns began again. Boris hoped they would hit their target — though it was a dreadful thought that the men in the air would crash-dive in flames to their deaths.

"Boom! Boom!" Almost deafening came the return shots from the German lines.

"Come on," said Nadia, holding out her hand. As quickly as they could they ran along the bank. The distance between them and the bridge grew. They left behind them the witch's cauldron[1] of explosions and flames which was their city.

"We're in luck," Nadia had said. Perhaps they really were in luck, since they had got so far from the city without being noticed. But Boris still heard the bombs dropping on Leningrad, where his mother lay helpless in bed.

Boris ran after Nadia. He tried not to think any longer. The only thing that mattered now were the pits of potatoes in the lonely waste of No-man's-land. Boris could see them now, covered with straw and sand. He saw himself digging and then . . . thousands of potatoes heaped together like marbles . . .

---

[1]**cauldron** (kôl′drən): a large kettle for boiling.

They sat in the snow. They had walked for more than an hour from the bridge. Leningrad and the Russian lines round the city lay far behind them among the gentle rolling countryside. On the way they had come upon a farm which had been burned to the ground. They had poked around it, but they hadn't found anything to eat. In the desolate yard had been an empty dog-kennel. What had happened to the dog, Boris wondered? Was it still alive? Or had the Germans shot it, as they sometimes shot people? Somehow, the dog-kennel made Boris sadder than the blackened ruins of the farm. After all, didn't he see blackened ruins every day? Without saying very much they had set off again. It was hard going on the frosty, uneven ground, against the cold wind. Boris's lips felt frost-bitten, and a place on the inside of his thigh was rubbed raw with the rough material of his trousers. They began to walk more and more slowly. Nadia, too, seemed suddenly to have become very tired.

"Let's have a rest," she had said. And they had flopped down in the snow. They sucked pieces of snow to see if that would help their thirst, and perhaps also their gnawing hunger.

"Is it much farther?" Boris must have asked the same question at least ten times.

"It can't be much farther now," said Nadia. She pointed to a row of trees in the distance. "It must be over there."

The trees looked a long way off, but now that the end was at least in sight, Boris began to feel a bit more cheerful. The way back wouldn't be so bad. They'd have the wind at their backs, and they'd also have the potatoes. With that precious loot the journey would be nothing. From under his fur cap Boris watched Nadia, who had kept going so steadily the whole way. Now she was gasping from exertion. Her breath came out of her mouth like puffs of smoke and was blown away by the wind.

"Nadia, have you ever been afraid?"

Nadia nodded.

"When?"

Nadia thought for a bit. "When I'm at home," she said at last. "When I'm sitting in the room and feel that Father's got his eye on me . . ." Her voice trailed away. She had forgotten that her father and Serjozja were dead now. No wonder, with all the suspense of that afternoon.

It was deathly quiet in the white world around them. No sirens, no scraping of shovels, no guns. Shamefaced, because she had forgotten, Nadia gazed at the snow. She looked ready to burst into tears. Afterwards, when the war was over, he'd marry Nadia, Boris thought. Then he'd look after her, and she would never have to look so sad again. But what could he say to her now that would stop the trembling of her lips?

"I'm often afraid too!" he said softly.

"When I'm afraid I write my diary," said Nadia.

"Does that help?"

"Sometimes."

Boris stared into the distance. It might be an idea to keep a diary. You could write down things that you couldn't say aloud.

"We'd better go on," said Nadia. They had got stiff, sitting in the cold. They shivered as they stood up.

Now it was Boris's turn to hold out his hand and help Nadia along. After the first few steps his trousers began to rub against the same sore place on his leg.

Hand in hand they plodded on through that still, white world. The trees stood out like slender, grey twigs against the horizon.

"It's not much farther," said Boris cheerfully.

One foot after another. They *must* get there soon. But it was slow going, so slow. Three-quarters of an hour later they seemed to have covered hardly any ground. The trees in the distance that Nadia had kept pointing to were still in the distance. Boris began to worry again.

"Will we get back before it's dark?"

Nadia didn't answer. Perhaps she thought it was a stupid question. Or was she too exhausted to speak? For the last half-hour she hadn't said a single word, but just stared silently ahead. Was she thinking about her father and Serjozja?

One foot after another. At each step, Boris's worry grew. How on earth were they going to manage to walk back, if they had heavy bags of potatoes to carry? He decided not to look up from the ground until he had counted a hundred. Perhaps after that, when he looked up, they would be nearly at the trees. But no, when he had counted as slowly as possible and looked up, the thin little twigs still stood out against the sky. One foot after another. Nadia tripped. She would have fallen if Boris hadn't managed to hold her. He put his arm around her, but she almost tripped again. Was it because Serjozja's boots were far too big for her? She stopped and put her hand to her head.

"Shall we have a rest?" Boris asked her.

Nadia didn't answer. Because the row of trees was still far away, Boris thought they had better carry on. But it was getting difficult to drag Nadia along now. Perhaps it would be better to sit down for a few minutes to gather their strength for the last bit. He was just going to say this, when Nadia's hand slipped out of his. With a start Boris looked at her. What was the matter? Nadia was staggering as if she had lost her balance. She tottered for a few steps, then she collapsed in the snow.

In a flash Boris was on his knees beside her.

"Nadia! Nadia!" He shouted her name and shook her, but she didn't respond. Her eyes were half-closed.

"Nadia! Nadia, do you hear me?" She couldn't just lie there. This couldn't be real. It mustn't be real.

The wind whirled over the ground and blew snow into her hair. Boris tried to make her sit up. He began to be afraid. Nadia surely wasn't going to die, like that old man who had just sunk down among the ruins? That couldn't happen. That mustn't happen. "Nadia. Nadia." He said her name softly, pleading her to answer. Nadia, who was so brave and who knew where the potatoes were, Nadia couldn't die. Not now . . .

To his relief, he saw her lips move a little. She mumbled something, but Boris couldn't make out the words . . .

The horizon with the row of trees disappeared, as if a page of the white world had been turned over.

Far, far away, she heard Boris's voice. In a little while she'd speak to him, but now she just wanted to go to sleep. She couldn't do any more . . .

She felt Boris putting his arms round her. But she couldn't thank him. The whole world seemed to be growing tiny; black specks danced before her eyes . . . There was Mother, standing at the stove making pancakes; the creamy batter sizzled in the iron pan.

There was Father, his brown eyes twinkling . . . They were walking along the banks of the River Neva and Serjozja had given her a balloon . . . There was the Stipolevs' big dog, the one that had stolen her doll and chewed it up . . .

Farther and farther she wandered into the little world of her own memories. She was no longer aware of Boris and their quest for potatoes; of starving Leningrad . . .

The black spots dancing through her mind grew bigger and bigger . . .

"Nadia!" Boris had unbuttoned his coat and pulled out the old sack. He tried to push it under Nadia, but he couldn't move her. What should he do? Despairingly he looked around him. He couldn't leave her lying here in the snow. He managed to get her partly on to the sack, and fastened up her coat, which the wind had blown open. What else could he do?

Boris pondered. Nadia's life depended on him, he knew that. Could he drag her back to the city? Had he the strength for that?

"Nadia, oh please, Nadia!" If only he could ask her what he should do. But Nadia lay motionless. Perhaps it would be best to try and find help. He could cover Nadia with his coat. Boris started to get up, then stopped, half-crouched, half-standing. His heart stood still. For a moment he couldn't believe his eyes. He blinked. It was still there — a boot, right next to him in the snow. And above the boot, the rough green of a soldier's uniform. And above that, the edge of a white cape. His heart thumping, Boris let his gaze travel slowly upwards. There was no doubt about it. Over an arm lay a rifle with a hand on the trigger. And above . . .

Numb with fear, Boris stared into the face of a German soldier . . .

His whole body trembled; for a moment he was too shocked to think clearly. He just looked dazedly at the German. What could he do to save Nadia and himself? He could throw himself at the enemy's throat, and rid himself of all his terror and grief and hate by strangling this tall stranger. But he knew he wouldn't have a chance.

The soldier lowered his rifle. Boris crouched closer to the ground. Was he going to be beaten up? Would Nadia and he be flung into a concentration camp? What would happen to his mother? Tears of helpless rage sprang into his eyes. But his father had said he mustn't cry. And a German must never think that a young Russian was afraid. With a shaking hand he drew out the revolver in his pocket and pointed it at the soldier. Then he looked timidly up to see if the German was frightened by it. But the soldier showed no fear. He shook his head slowly from side to side; not angrily, not frowning, as you would have expected, but only slightly surprised, as if he knew quite well that the gun wasn't loaded. Disappointed, but also relieved, Boris let his hand drop.

"Du kleiner, was machst du hier?"[2]

These were foreign words that Boris didn't understand, but they sounded friendly, almost gentle. Did the soldier want to know what they were doing there?

"We wanted to get potatoes," said Boris and, because the German probably didn't understand Russian, he pointed to the row of trees in the distance and then to his mouth. The soldier would understand then that they hadn't come to fight them, but only to get food.

"Gott im Himmel!"[3] muttered the soldier. He threw down his rifle, laid his hand on Boris's head, and knelt down by Nadia. Still confused, Boris looked at the rifle lying so close to his hands. Should he pick it up? If he was quick enough, he could shoot the soldier. That was what he had always wanted to do — to kill Germans. Weren't Germans everyone's hated enemies?

But from the way that the soldier was looking at Nadia, from the way he put his arm round her and tried to make her sit up, Boris realized that he, at least, was no enemy. It was very bewildering.

"Ulli, Karl, Heinz, komm mal her!"[4] called the soldier over his shoulder. With a start Boris looked round. Only then did he notice more Germans; their heads were sticking out from a ditch. They had pulled their white capes over themselves, so as not to be seen against the snowy background. Were they a small patrol, out reconnoitering? Or were there thousands of white-caped soldiers in the snow, preparing to launch a huge attack on Leningrad?

The three soldiers crawled out of the ditch and came up. They were carrying rifles and machine-guns.

---

[2]**"Du kleiner, was machst du hier?"**: "You little one, what are you doing here?"
[3]**"Gott im Himmel!"**: "God in heaven!"
[4]**"Ulli, Karl, Heinz, komm mal her!"**: "Ulli, Karl, Heinz, come here!"

"Cognac!" said the soldier who was kneeling beside Nadia.

One of the soldiers handed him a flask. Carefully the soldier held it to Nadia's lips. A few drops dribbled down her chin but some went in her mouth.

Nadia stirred. "Thank you, Boris!" she murmured, almost too quietly to be heard. Then her eyes opened. She had no idea where she was. Her great brown eyes were dazed. Slowly she turned her head and looked at the Germans. Boris saw her shrink back, and her eyes grew even bigger with fear.

"Boris!" Nadia tried to get up, but she was too weak.

"They're German soldiers," Boris whispered helplessly.

"Hab keine Angst!"[5] said the kneeling man, softly.

"Oh, Boris," said Nadia. She shut her eyes and would have fallen back on the ground if the soldier had not held her tightly.

One of the other men took off his cape and pulled the haversack from his back. When he opened it Boris saw that it held a piece of sausage, and bread, and chocolate. His mouth watered. He watched the soldier break off a piece of chocolate and put it in Nadia's mouth.

Nadia gave a glimmer of a smile. The soldier nodded encouragingly at her. He gave her another piece and then another.

"Hier!"[6] Another of the Germans was holding a piece of sausage right in front of Boris's nose. He looked at it longingly and then indecisively at the soldier. Could you accept anything from people who were enemies? How many tales of heroism had he heard about Russians who had refused to accept any such German bribes? He felt his hunger gnaw.

"Ist gut!"[7] said the German.

Sorrowfully, Boris shook his head in refusal. He gulped. He realized just how tired he really was. The soldier seemed to sway before his eyes. Black spots danced among the snow.

"I must put my head down," thought Boris, and he slid slowly on to the snow-covered ground.

---

[5]**"Hab keine Angst!"**: "Don't worry!"
[6]**"Hier!"**: "Here!"
[7]**"Ist gut!"**: "It's good!"

Boris sat in the snow. He thought about his mother. What would she think if he never came home again? She would never know that he and Nadia had gone to No-man's-land to look for potatoes. No-man's-land — it was a foolish name, land of no man. And yet the Germans had come. He could hear their voices. The words that they spoke sounded hard and sharp. When he really began to listen to them, he could make out that there was some disagreement. He looked up in surprise. Yes, they were quarrelling, just like the children in Leningrad when they were playing at being at war, except that, he supposed, none of the Germans had wanted to play in the first place. Boris could not guess what this quarrel was about, but he could understand a few words: "die Kinder . . ."[8] and "sterben . . ."[9]

Nadia tried to sit up. With great frightened eyes she looked towards the Germans, who were still arguing fiercely among themselves.

"What are they saying, Nadia?" whispered Boris.

"They're talking about us," answered Nadia.

Anxiously, Boris looked from one soldier to another. They were beginning to lose their tempers and their voices were getting louder and angrier. It seemed to be three against one.

"Es ist Wahnsinn! Ich geh nicht!"[10] A soldier with a fair beard stamped his foot. The one who had given Nadia the brandy brought the quarrel to an end. He was certainly an officer, decided Boris, because now the others were listening attentively to him. When he had finished speaking, the soldier with the beard shrugged his shoulders.

---

[8]**"die Kinder . . .":** "the children . . ."

[9]**"sterben . . .":** "to die . . ."

[10]**"Es ist Wahnsinn! Ich geh nicht!":** "This is madness! I won't go!"

He tapped his finger against his forehead — he obviously thought the officer was out of his mind. Then he picked up his rifle and walked moodily away in the direction of the row of trees. Boris stared after him tensely. What was going to happen? Dear God, the soldier who had wanted to give him the sausage had pulled his bayonet out. He fixed it into his rifle. Were they going to be tortured? Or were the Germans going to shoot them? Boris held his breath. A shiver of fear ran through his whole body.

But the soldier didn't stab them. He pulled a white handkerchief out of his pocket and tied it to the bayonet.

Then the miracle happened. The officer in charge came over to Nadia and picked her up in his arms. He pulled his cape round her. Next, Boris felt himself lifted up.

"Hab keine Angst!" said the soldier again. His voice sounded gentle and friendly. His kind blue eyes, which looked as if they were used to laughter, were sad now. They began to walk. The man with the handkerchief on the bayonet went ahead. He held his rifle in the air, so that the handkerchief fluttered in the wind.

"Boris . . . Boris . . ." called Nadia. It was a shout of joy. "Boris, they're going to take us back to Leningrad!"

It was almost unbelievable, but they were going in the direction of the city. Again Boris looked at the face of the man who was carrying him. How was it possible that an enemy could have such a kind, friendly face?

"Ja, wir bringen euch nach Leningrad."[11] The soldier smiled and nodded at Boris, as if to assure him that everything was going to be all right.

Now Boris could smile too. It was quite clear to him that these three Germans were friends, not enemies. He felt even more sorry now that he had refused that lovely piece of sausage. The boots crunched through the snow. Each stride brought them nearer to Leningrad. It

---

[11]**"Ja, wir bringen euch nach Leningrad.":** "Yes, we are taking you to Leningrad."

was a comforting thought. Within a few hours he would be safe at home, if safe was a word that could still be used to describe any part of the besieged city . . .

After a good hour's marching, they came to a halt at the top of a long slope. Boris and Nadia were put down in the snow. Did the men want to have a rest? Their chests were heaving, and they stood to get their breath back, snorting like horses. They began to talk excitedly again, waving their hands in the air and pointing into the distance, where the black silhouette of Leningrad stood out clearly against the grey sky.

"What are they saying now?" whispered Boris.

"I think that they don't dare go any farther," replied Nadia.

"Why not?"

"If our soldiers see that they're German, they'll shoot at once."

Boris shuddered. Not for a moment had that thought occurred to him. He understood now why the soldier with the beard had stayed behind. It was not surprising that he feared the Russians.

"Do you think you could manage the last bit by yourself?" Boris asked anxiously. The Germans couldn't be expected to go any farther and there was still quite a way to go.

Nadia shrugged her shoulders. "I don't know," she murmured.

Alarm and uncertainty came flooding back with a great rush. His eyes wide with fear, Boris stared at the German soldiers. What would they decide? One of them was shaking his head — that was a bad sign.

"Hör mal zu!"[12] ordered the officer. His face was grave but his voice was not angry. The others listened respectfully to those phrases so strange to the children's ears.

"Die Kinder . . . gefährlich . . . Leningrad . . . die Russen . . . schiessen . . . !"[13]

Again Boris had the strongest feeling that these Germans were friends. In Leningrad everyone was convinced that all Germans were unfeeling murderers, that they killed helpless women and children without mercy, that they burned whole villages to the ground. Boris could not believe these three Germans capable of such horrors.

Once again the officer came over to them. Again a sad kind of smile appeared on his stern face. He slipped a piece of chocolate in each of their mouths.

How good it tasted! Boris shut his eyes tight so as not to lose a trace of the delightful creamy sweetness in his mouth.

"Thank you," said Nadia politely, after a moment.

"Oh yes, thank you very much," mumbled Boris. It was all right to accept presents from friends, he thought. It was just a pity that he couldn't take home a little bit of chocolate for his mother — especially as he'd be going back without any potatoes.

The Germans took off their white capes. They rolled them up neatly and pushed them between the straps of their haversacks. Boris couldn't think why they did that. They stood now in their green-grey uniforms, which looked all the darker and more noticeable against the snowy white background.

"Why did they do that?" Boris asked in a whisper.

---

[12]"**Hör mal zu!**": "Listen to me!"

[13]"**Die Kinder . . . gefährlich . . . Leningrad . . . die Russen . . . schiessen . . . !**": "The children . . . dangerous . . . Leningrad . . . the Russians . . . shoot . . . !"

Nadia shrugged her shoulders.

"Are they going to fight?" Perhaps it would be easier to fight without the long white capes.

"No," said Nadia. "The handkerchief on the rifle means that they don't intend to fight."

"Are they going to take us any farther?"

"I think so," said Nadia.

She was right. The officer came over to Boris and picked him up. He nodded to the children; for the first time his sad eyes looked slightly happy. One of the soldiers lifted Nadia in his arms.

"Jetzt gehen wir los!"[14]

"Gott im Himmel," muttered the soldier who was carrying the rifle with the handkerchief on it. He bit his lip, reluctant to go one step farther.

Once again the heavy boots crunched through the snow. They were walking now straight towards the Russian lines. That must take a lot of courage. Did these three German soldiers really know that so many people in Leningrad were dying of hunger? Did they realize how many men had drowned in Lake Ladoga? Did they know how many gunners dropped dead from sheer exhaustion behind their very guns? Bitter hate and a burning desire for revenge would greet them.

Boris peered anxiously into the distance. Would his fellow countrymen shoot as soon as they saw the three green German uniforms approaching over the snow? He was almost certain they would. In a fight for life or death there was no mercy. Could he warn his new friends about the danger? Or would that be treason against his own country? Boris tugged the officer's arm and pointed towards the Russian lines. "Bang, bang!" he said, hoping the man would know what he meant.

"Danke! Ich weiss!"[15] The officer nodded that he understood and once more smiled ruefully at Boris. He walked steadily on, like the brave soldier he was . . .

---

[14]**"Jetzt gehen wir los!"**: "Now we are leaving!"
[15]**"Danke! Ich weiss!"**: "Thank you! I know!"

One shot rang out and then another. The German soldiers came to an abrupt halt. Tensely they stared into the distance. Boris held his breath. Was he going to see some action?

"Sie kommen!"[16] grunted the officer in charge. He set Boris on the ground and gestured towards a forward post in the front line. At least fifteen Russian soldiers were to be seen approaching. They moved in close formation over the white ground, rifles at the ready.

"They've come to fetch us," cried Nadia joyfully. Her brown eyes shone.

"Why did they shoot?" asked Boris. He was a bit uneasy.

"They were warning shots," said Nadia. "They didn't want the Germans to come too close to their lines." She grasped Boris's hand and smiled at him. "You needn't be afraid any longer."

But Boris was afraid. The German soldier next to him, the one with the waving handkerchief tied to his rifle, raised the weapon higher in the air. He bit his lips nervously and the officer fingered his belt uncertainly. Were the Russians and the Germans going to fight? Fifteen against three isn't fair, thought Boris. Even the children in Leningrad had made each side equal in their war-games. But this was no game. Perhaps there was going to be fighting in real earnest.

With thumping heart Boris looked at the Russian soldiers as they marched over the snow towards them. He was very happy to see them. But why did they look so stern and forbidding. Why did their grey-coated figures and their rifles look so menacing against the white

---

[16]**"Sie kommen!":** "They are coming!"

background? It was impossible to read their thoughts or guess what their next actions would be.

A lieutenant walked on ahead. He was carrying a machine-gun, his right hand on the trigger. The earpieces of his fur cap flapped in the wind.

When they came to within about thirty yards, the Russian platoon spread out and formed a half-circle. And in this way they came up on three sides, with slow and threatening steps.

Boris swallowed. He gripped Nadia's hand, for they would soon know what was going to happen. For a moment he thought that Nadia was going to run to meet them, she looked so excited and happy. Didn't their stern, frowning faces discourage her at all? Why did none of the Russians seem pleased that they had got back safely?

When they had got right up to the Germans, the lieutenant held up his hand. The half-circle of his men stood motionless. There was absolute silence.

The officer in charge of the German patrol saluted and nodded a greeting to the Russians. But not one Russian returned his salute. Unmoving, they stared at their enemy. They would sooner kill them than smile at them, thought Boris.

A hopeless feeling of sorrow overwhelmed him. Why did everything have to be so complicated . . . ?

"Interpreter!" called the lieutenant.

An older man with glasses stepped forward.

"Ask them what they've come for." His voice sounded grim. The interpreter took another step forward and began to speak. He had some trouble with the harsh German words.

Boris peeped from under his cap at the Russians who stood around him. He saw distrust, hate, bitterness. Could no one begin to understand that these three Germans had shown themselves to be friends? The officer in charge gave his answer to the interpreter's question. Would he deign[17] to tell them how kindly he had treated Nadia?

---

[17]**deign** (dān): to be kind or gracious enough to do something.

"They were on patrol in the forward lines," said the interpreter to the Russian lieutenant, "when they came across the children. The little girl had collapsed."

The lieutenant looked sharply at Boris and Nadia. His eyes were hard and his voice abrupt.

"What's your name?"

"I'm Nadia Morozova," Nadia murmured. She looked down at the ground. Everything seemed to be going so differently from what she had expected.

"And you?"

"My name's Boris . . . Boris Makarenko," stammered Boris.

Why did the lieutenant look so stern? Was he angry because they had sneaked into No-man's-land? Or did he regard them as traitors — Russian children carried back in German arms? Boris hoped that Nadia would explain everything: about the air-raid, the rations, about his mother, about Serjozja who had died in the night. Surely the lieutenant would listen and understand.

"What were you doing so far outside the city?" The lieutenant looked sternly at Nadia again.

"We were looking for food," Nadia said softly.

"Come here!" The lieutenant beckoned.

Nadia and Boris went over to him. They stood beside the Russians, facing the Germans. Two sides, one against the other. Between them lay six feet of No-man's-land, where no one had any identity. Boris couldn't bring himself to look at the German officer, he felt so ashamed of the Russian soldiers' determination to hide any human feelings.

"Ask him why they've brought back the children," said the lieutenant to the interpreter.

Boris scraped the snow with his foot until the ground began to show. A few withered blades of grass still lingered in the frozen soil. Over his head the interpreter and the German officer exchanged question and answer.

"He says that the children had collapsed in the snow and were completely exhausted," the interpreter translated into Russian. "He says that even in an inhumane war people can show human feelings. Children have no part in the war. He couldn't find it in his heart to leave them lying in the snow. It was impossible to take them to the German lines. So he brought them here."

Boris held his breath and looked anxiously at the lieutenant. Would he understand now that these were good Germans?

Suddenly the sergeant stepped forward. His voice was as cold as steel.

"Lieutenant," he said, "let's take away their guns. Maybe they have done a good deed; but maybe they're spies. Let's take them back and see if we can get any information out of them. After all that's happened, I've lost my faith in good Germans."

Boris was filled with horror. He saw that the lieutenant was hesitating. Nadia pulled at his arm and looked fearfully at the sergeant.

"No, no, you can't do that," she whispered. But no man standing in No-man's-land heard her speak.

"Don't believe a word they say," put in another soldier from behind Nadia. His eyes gleamed with hatred. How much bitterness was bursting out of his heart?

"Shoot them right away, lieutenant. Shoot them right away." Even as he spoke the man took a step forward and pointed his rifle at the German officer. Mad with hate, he meant to shoot . . .

Boris sprang forward. He ran to the German and stood with his arms outstretched as if he could thus protect him.

"Don't shoot," he yelled, his voice breaking. "Don't shoot. They saved our lives."

It was deathly silent. No one said a word. No one moved.

"Come here," commanded the lieutenant. But Boris didn't come. He stood firmly in front of the German. A desperate, helpless wave of passion swept over him; tears of rage against the hatred, terror and madness of war filled his eyes.

"Nadia was lying in the snow." Boris screamed the words at the Russian. "She couldn't even speak to me. I couldn't carry her. I tried to, but I couldn't." He jerked his head at the German behind him. "He carried her. He's my friend." Frantically Boris tried to make them understand. "My friend, do you hear — my friend!" He was crying with rage.

Nadia came over to him.

"Boris, Boris dear," she said gently, but Boris shook with sobs.

Then Boris felt a firm hand on his shoulder, a friendly hand. He looked up into the German's face. Through his tears he saw the officer smiling at him. At once the terror began to fade from his tearful eyes.

Then Boris looked at the lieutenant. The harshness on his face had given way to astonishment. The soldier who had wanted to shoot had lowered his rifle and was scraping it idly in the snow; some of the other soldiers were gazing into the distance. The sergeant stared at Nadia. Again no one said a word . . .

Then the lieutenant turned to the interpreter. "Tell them they are free to go back, Ivan Petrovitch." He hesitated, as if searching for words. "Say to them that we are grateful; it would be shameful if we, in the brutality of war, should forget all humanity."

The interpreter translated his words.

The German soldiers made to turn on their heels, but the officer remained as he was.

"Ein Augenblick, bitte!"[18] He pulled his haversack from his shoulder and stopped to open it.

---

[18]**"Ein Augenblick, bitte!":** "Just a second, please!"

"Hier," he said to Boris and Nadia, and handed them each a piece of bread and sausage, and a tin with foreign words on the label.

Once again Boris felt that trustworthy hand on his shoulder. Then the officer stood up straight. Slowly he looked round the watching circle, with that same sad smile that Boris had already seen on his face, clapped his heels together and saluted. He stood as stiff and straight as a candle, the typical German soldier.

The young lieutenant of the Red Army stood smartly to attention. "Platoon," he ordered, "attention!" All the Russians sprang to attention. Slowly the lieutenant brought his hand up to his cap. It was as if he were saluting the Germans for their courage, their help, their humanity.

Boris looked at the officer. He would have liked to thank him again, but the German had turned on his heel. With firm steps he and the others walked away down the slope into the distance: men in No-man's-land.

Nadia waved hesitantly, but the Germans did not look back.

The snow-covered land no longer lay like an unwritten page under the grey sky. The prints of German boots had written a message on it for all to read . . .

Responding to Boris

Thinking and Discussing

Boris and Nadia set out to dig up some potatoes rumored to be buried in dangerous territory. What does this undertaking reveal about them and their situation?

The author portrays Boris as a complex character with many memories and emotions. What mixed feelings does he have regarding the German soldiers? Are his emotions justified? Explain your answer.

In this selection, Boris, Nadia, and the German soldiers show courage. Who do you think is the bravest? Give reasons for your answer.

Choosing a Creative Response

Contrasting War and Peace
The author describes a city besieged by war as a "witch's cauldron of explosions and flames. . . ." Think of figurative expressions you might use to describe a city during a time of peace, rather than war. Illustrate the contrasting descriptions if you wish. On each illustration, write the description that the picture represents.

Conducting an Interview
Imagine that you are a reporter conducting an interview with Boris, Nadia, or one of the German soldiers after their ordeal. Select a partner to play the role of the character you interview. You may want to make notes for questions before you begin.

Creating Your Own Activity
Plan and complete your own activity in response to *Boris*.

Thinking and Writing

The selection ends by saying "the prints of German boots had written a message on [the land] for all to read . . ." Write what you think that message is. You might want to express the message in the form of a song or poem.

Writing

A Firsthand Biography — Sketch

As you read the selections in "Choices," you will encounter characters who make choices that lead to personal growth. You probably know people who have made important decisions that resulted in emotional growth — perhaps a friend who parted with something treasured, a relative who had to make a difficult career choice, or a classmate who defended an unpopular opinion.

Write a firsthand biography about someone you know well who had this type of experience. In your biography, make your subject come alive for your readers by including important details. If you think of other ideas as you read these stories, you may want to try one of those instead.

1. Prewriting

Before you begin writing, identify the person who will be the subject of your firsthand biography. Make sure you know all the details of the situation your subject faced when he or she made an important decision that led to emotional growth. Plan the way in which you will present your subject and the significant events. Answer the following questions.

- How will I state the purpose of my biography?
- How will I introduce the subject to my readers?
- Which details of my relationship with my subject do I want to include?

2. Write a First Draft

Remember that you want your readers to get to know the subject of your firsthand biography and understand why the decision he or she made was meaningful. Think about the following things while you write.

- Do I have a strong beginning that immediately engages the reader's interest in my subject?
- Should I include dialogue?
- Have I organized the description of my subject, the details of the important events, and my thoughts and feelings in the best possible way?

3. Revise

Read your firsthand biography to a partner. Does your partner feel that the subject of your biography comes alive? Does your partner understand the significance of choices in your subject's life? Make any necessary changes.

4. Proofread

Check your firsthand biography for correct spelling, punctuation, and grammar. Be especially careful while proofreading dialogue.

5. Publish

Make a neat copy of your firsthand biography. You may wish to include a photograph of the subject of your biography on the title page. Share the biography with your classmates.

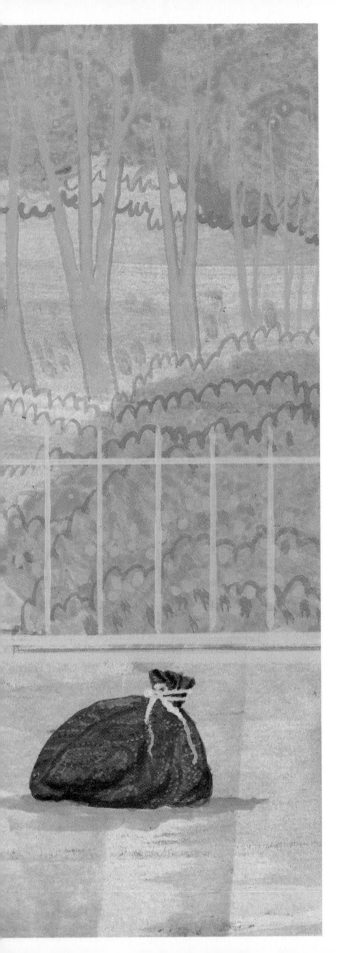

Escape to Freedom

A Play About Young Frederick Douglass

By Ossie Davis

Illustrated by Jim Baldwin

Frederick Douglass was born into slavery in Maryland around 1817. In Scene One of Escape to Freedom, *young Frederick learns that he will be sent to work for one of his master's relatives in Baltimore. As Scene Two begins, Frederick arrives in Baltimore.*

SCENE TWO

(While singing "Bright Glory," the cast arranges the set to suggest a neat back yard, with a white picket fence, a table, and a chair. On the table is a Bible and a plate of buttered bread.)

COMPANY: *You don't hear me praying here*
You can't find me nowhere (can't find me)
Come on up to bright glory
I'll be waiting up there
I'll be waiting up there, my Lord
I'll be waiting up there (be waiting)
Come on up to bright glory
I'll be waiting up there.
*(*COMPANY *continues to hum melody offstage as dialogue continues.)*
*(*FRED *and* JETHRO *enter.* FRED *is carrying a small bundle. They cross into yard.)*

JETHRO: Well, Frederick, here we are.

FRED: *(Looking around, taking it all in)* Baltimore.

JETHRO: *(Pointing)* And that's the house, right over there. Now, remember, mind your manners; show Mr. and Mrs. Auld what a good little slave you are — no sass, no back talk, remember your place. Keep your head bowed and your eyes on the ground — and whatever they tell you to do — do it! Right away — understand?

FRED: Yes, Jethro, but — do what?
(Humming offstage ends.)

JETHRO: Don't worry, they'll tell you. Now I got to be going —

FRED: But ain't you gonna take me in?

JETHRO: Look, Fred, you don't need nobody to take you in. Just obey the white folks — do whatever they tell you, and you'll be all right.

330

(JETHRO *exits, after a beat.* FRED *turns and takes a few tentative steps toward the house.*)

FRED: Here in Baltimore I saw what I had never seen before: it was a white face, beaming with the most kindly emotions — the face of my new mistress, Sophia Auld.

(WHITE WOMAN *enters during above. She sits at the table, picks up the Bible, and begins to read.*)

WHITE BOY: (*Enters from house and runs to* WHITE WOMAN.) Mother! Button up my shirt!

WHITE WOMAN: I declare, little Thomas, surely the least you can do is button your own shirt.

WHITE BOY: I want you to button it!

(WHITE WOMAN *reluctantly puts her Bible aside and buttons his shirt. Then she looks down.*)

WHITE WOMAN: And your shoes, Thomas, you haven't even tied your shoes —

WHITE BOY: I want you to tie them!

(*Exasperated, she starts to reach down, but catches sight of* FRED, *who has crossed to the back yard and is standing nearby.*)

WHITE WOMAN: Fred?

FRED: Yes, Miz Sophia.

WHITE WOMAN: (*Relieved*) Thank God, you've come at last. Thomas, this is Fred, your slave — your uncle sent him to stay with us and to be your body servant —

WHITE BOY: (*Excited by the prospect*) Is he really my slave?

WHITE WOMAN: Yes.

WHITE BOY: All mine, and nobody else's?

WHITE WOMAN: Yes — until your uncle takes him back.

WHITE BOY: Good! Come, Fred —

(WHITE BOY *signals* FRED *and starts off.*)

WHITE WOMAN: Wait a minute, Thomas, where are you going?

WHITE BOY:	To the dockyards, to show off my new slave. Come on, Fred —
WHITE WOMAN:	No, Thomas.
WHITE BOY:	We'll be right back.
WHITE WOMAN:	I said no. Your father will be home in a minute, and you haven't read your Bible for today.
WHITE BOY:	*(Angry)* I don't want to read the Bible for today. I want to show off my slave —
WHITE WOMAN:	*(Firmly)* There'll be plenty of time for that later. Now we read from the Bible. *(WHITE WOMAN picks up the Bible, finds the place, and hands it to WHITE BOY.)*
WHITE BOY:	*(Takes the book and pretends to try, then gives up.)* I don't want to —
WHITE WOMAN:	Come on, Thomas, show Freddie how well you can read.
WHITE BOY:	*(Shouting)* I don't want to! *(He flings the book down and runs into the house.)*
WHITE WOMAN:	Thomas! Thomas, honey, Mother didn't mean to hurt your feelings — *(She hurries off after him. FRED stands a minute; then, his curiosity getting the better of him, he picks up the Bible, opens it, trying to understand what is meant by reading. WHITE WOMAN re-enters, carrying a pair of sandals. FRED is so occupied he does not see her. She approaches and looks over his shoulder.)*
WHITE WOMAN:	Fred —
FRED:	*(Startled, putting the book down like a hot potato)* Yes, ma'am — *(He stands before her, guilty, his head bowed, his eyes cast down in a manner he has been taught is proper for a slave.)*
WHITE WOMAN:	*(Chiding, but kindly)* No, no, Fred, you mustn't bow your head to me like that. We are all of us still God's children — nor slave nor master makes a

difference to Him. It says so in the Bible — this book right here that you had in your hand.

(FRED, remembering his guilt, casts his eyes down again.)

FRED: I'm sorry, ma'am, I didn't mean to touch it, but —

WHITE WOMAN: Fred —

FRED: *(Still not looking up)* Yes, ma'am —

WHITE WOMAN: Here are some sandals for you to wear.

(FRED cannot manage to speak.)

Take them.

(He takes them.)

Put them on, they're yours.

(FRED tries to put the sandals on but is too nervous.)

Would you like for me to help you?

(She kneels and puts the sandals on FRED, who is stunned at such kind and gentle behavior from a white person.)

There you are —

(FRED stands before her, dumb, his eyes cast down, unable to say a word.)

(Kindly, with complete understanding) Don't you know how to say thank you?

FRED: *(Not daring to look up at her, he finally manages it.)*

Thank you, ma'am.

WHITE WOMAN: *(Suddenly occurring to her)* My lands, child, you must be starved. Have some bread and butter.

(She turns to the table and offers it to him. FRED takes it but can't seem to manage to get it into his mouth.)

WHITE WOMAN: Is something the matter?

FRED: *(Quickly)* No, ma'am — it's just that —

WHITE WOMAN: Yes?

(FRED looks intently at the Bible. It is not difficult for her to read his thoughts.)

Would you like for me to teach you to read?

FRED: Oh, yes, ma'am!

(She picks up the Bible and hands it to him.

FRED *quickly puts his bread aside and picks up the Bible, getting great pleasure out of just being able to hold a book in his hands.)*

WHITE WOMAN: This is the Bible, and it is spelled B-I-B-L-E. *(*FRED *looks at her in total confusion.)* What I mean is: "Bible" is a word — *(She stops and studies him. It is obvious that he has absolutely no understanding of anything she is telling him. She sits and pulls him to her, takes the book into her own hands, and begins pointing out each letter.)* — and every word is made up of letters, which we call the alphabet.

FRED: Alphabet.

WHITE WOMAN: Good. Now, the letter of the alphabet we use to begin the word "Bible" is called "B" —

FRED: "B" —

WHITE WOMAN: Very good, Fred, excellent. And this letter of the alphabet is called "I."

FRED: "I" — *(*WHITE MAN, *as Hugh Auld, enters and stops, scarcely believing his eyes.)*

WHITE WOMAN: Now the third letter in the word "Bible" is the same as the first letter of the word —

FRED: *(Snapping it up)* "B"!

WHITE WOMAN: *(Overjoyed at his obvious intelligence)* Excellent, Fred, excellent!

WHITE MAN: *(Shouting)* Sophia, stop! *(He dashes over and snatches the Bible from his wife's hand.)* What are you doing?

WHITE WOMAN: I'm teaching Freddie to read —

WHITE MAN: Freddie?

WHITE WOMAN: You asked your uncle to send you a slave to be a companion to little Thomas. Freddie, this is

Mr. Hugh Auld, your new master while you are in Baltimore.

(FRED *tries to find a proper response, but just at this moment* WHITE BOY *runs back on and grabs* FRED *by the arm and starts to pull.*)

WHITE BOY: Come on, Fred, I've got something to show you.

(FRED *looks to* WHITE WOMAN — *and* WHITE MAN — *for instructions.*)

Fred — I'm not ever gonna let you be my slave if you don't come on; I want to show you my new boat. Tell him, Mama —

WHITE WOMAN: *(Smiling)* It's all right, Fred.

(*A beat, then* FRED *and* WHITE BOY, *smiling at each other, run off.* WHITE MAN *watches them off, and then, to make sure he will not be overheard, he takes* WHITE WOMAN *by the arm and draws her aside.*)

WHITE MAN: What on earth are you trying to do to that boy, ruin him?

WHITE WOMAN: Ruin him? I was only teaching him to read.

WHITE MAN: But you can't do that, Sophia!

WHITE WOMAN: Why not? He's a very bright boy.

WHITE MAN: He's a slave — and to teach a slave to read is not only unlawful, it's unsafe, and I forbid it.

(FRED *starts back onstage in search of the bundle he was carrying, which he has left behind, but, hearing himself being talked about, he starts back out, then stops in a spot where he will not be seen, and listens.*)

WHITE WOMAN: *(Deeply disturbed)* Forbid it? But Freddie is human, and the Bible says —

WHITE MAN: Never mind what the Bible says — and for Heaven's sakes, stop talking like an abolitionist![1]

WHITE WOMAN: Abolitionist?

---

[1]**abolitionist** (ăb′ə **lĭsh′ə** nĭst): one who opposed slavery in the United States.

WHITE MAN: Yes, those Yankee do-gooders, always trying to tell us Southerners that black folks are no different from the rest of us — can you imagine such nonsense? Freddie is not human, not in the ways that you and I are.

WHITE WOMAN: How can you say that of a creature that has a soul and a mind?

WHITE MAN: But, darling, Freddie hasn't got a soul — he's black; he's a slave.

WHITE WOMAN: But all the same —

WHITE MAN: Listen to me, Sophia — reading's not only no good for a black boy like Fred; it would do him harm, make him discontent, miserable, unhappy with his lot.[2] Now, you wouldn't want that, would you? (WHITE WOMAN *ponders a moment.*)

WHITE WOMAN: No, but —

WHITE MAN: (*As they exit*) The worst thing in the world you can do for a slave — if you want to keep him happy — is to teach that slave to read, understand? (*From offstage we hear a low humming, which continues under the following.*) (*When* WHITE MAN *and* WHITE WOMAN *have gone,* FRED *comes out of hiding.*)

FRED: (*To audience*) My master's words sank deep into my heart. I now understood something that had been the greatest puzzle of all to me: the white man's power to enslave the black man. Keep the black man away from the books, keep us ignorant, and we would always be his slaves! From that moment on I understood the pathway from slavery to freedom. Come hell or high water — even if it cost me my life — I was determined to read!

---

[2]**lot:** situation in life; fate.

(Humming ends.)

(FRED looks around to make sure he is not being watched, then crosses to pick up the Bible, and tries to read. He walks up and down mumbling to himself, trying to make sense out of the words on the page, but without success. So deep in his preoccupation is he that he does not see that WHITE WOMAN has returned and stands for a moment watching. Not until he bumps into her does he lift his eyes.)

FRED: *(Apologetic, frightened)* Oh — Miz Sophia!

WHITE WOMAN: Fred, I made a mistake — about trying to teach you to read — it's — it's not right — it's against the law.

FRED: Why is it against the law?

WHITE WOMAN: *(Snapping, trying to steel herself for what she has to do)* Don't ask me why, it just is, that's all. And if I catch you with a book, I'll have to take it away, understand?

FRED: No, ma'am.

WHITE WOMAN: You *do* understand. You are not dumb — you have a good brain in that head of yours.

FRED: But if I do have a brain, then how —

WHITE WOMAN: And, anyway, you're my property. I own you like I own a horse or a mule. You don't *need* to read, you understand?

FRED: *(Tentative, searching, earnest, really trying)* You said that all people was equal before God — that being slave or being free didn't matter before God —

WHITE WOMAN: I am not talking about God! And anyway, what God said — about people being equal — doesn't apply to you.

FRED: Why don't it, Miz Sophia?

WHITE WOMAN: *(Growing more testy)* Because you ain't people, that's why —

FRED: But, ma'am, if I ain't people — what am I?

WHITE WOMAN: You are — some kind of animal that — that looks like people but you're not!

FRED: But I can talk — and you just said I got a good brain —

WHITE WOMAN: Don't you contradict me!

FRED: And I could read, too, if —

WHITE WOMAN: *(Shouting)* You will not read! Not in my house you won't! And if I should ever catch you —

FRED: But, please, Miz Sophia —

WHITE WOMAN: Shut your sassy, impudent mouth and get out of here! Get out of here!

(WHITE WOMAN is disturbed by what she has just done. Clutching the Bible, she hurries off.)

(Humming begins offstage.)

FRED: *(To audience)* Master Hugh wasted no time. With Miz Sophia's sudden change, I began to see that slavery was harmful to the slaveowner as well as the slave. As the months passed, if I was in a separate room for any length of time, she would search me out, sure that I had found a book — but by now it was too late. The first step had already been taken: Mistress Sophia, by teaching me what little she had, had set my feet on the highway to freedom, and I wasn't going to let her — or anybody else — turn me around.

(Humming ends.)

(WHITE BOY enters, this time as a schoolboy. He is barefoot, his clothes are patched and ragged; he is obviously much worse off than FRED. FRED watches as WHITE BOY passes, drawn like a magnet by the schoolbooks he carries under his arms. FRED suddenly has an idea, and as WHITE BOY passes, he snatches up the remainder of the bread and butter on the table and runs after him.)

FRED: Hey! Hey, boy!

(WHITE BOY *does not notice him.*)

Hey, boy, wait —

(Still no reaction)

Hey, white boy!

WHITE BOY: You calling me?

FRED: Yeah, I'm calling you — what's your name?

WHITE BOY: My name's Robert. What's yours?

FRED: My name's Fred. I'm a slave.

WHITE BOY: I know that — well, I gotta go.

(*He starts off, but* FRED *overtakes him.*)

FRED: Hey, does your father own slaves?

WHITE BOY: No —

FRED: Why not?

WHITE BOY: (*Embarrassed*) We're too poor. We don't even
have enough to eat.

(FRED *looks at* WHITE BOY. WHITE BOY *starts
off again.* FRED *conspicuously brings the bread
into view.*)

FRED: Hey, you hungry?

(WHITE BOY *stops, thinks a moment, then turns just in
time to see* FRED *shove a big chunk of bread into his
mouth.* WHITE BOY *says nothing.* FRED, *seeing the fish
is hooked, chews lustily.*)

FRED: Man, this is the best bread I ever tasted.

(FRED *breaks off a piece and holds it out.*)

Want a piece?

(WHITE BOY *hesitates a moment, then crosses over to*
FRED. *He reaches for the bread, but* FRED *pulls it back.*)

First, you got to answer me a question — you
go to school?

WHITE BOY: (*Eyes fastened hypnotically on the bread*) Yes.

FRED: That means you know how to read, right?

WHITE BOY: Yes —

FRED: Good.

(FRED *hands* WHITE BOY *the remainder of the bread.*

WHITE BOY *puts his books down, the better to deal with the bread, which he snatches and wolfs down hungrily. FRED, with equal hunger, snatches up the book and tries to read. When WHITE BOY is finished, he wipes his mouth and reaches for the book.)*

WHITE BOY: Can I have my book now?

FRED: Sure, as soon as you teach me how to read.

WHITE BOY: It's against the law to teach you to read. You are a slave.

FRED: Are you a slave?

WHITE BOY: Of course I'm not a slave — I'm white —

FRED: You are white, and you will be free all your life — but I am black —

WHITE BOY: *(Thinking about it)* — which means that you will be a slave all your life.

FRED: *(Vehemently)* I don't think that's right, do you?

WHITE BOY: *(Pondering for a moment)* No!

FRED: Then teach me to read —

WHITE BOY: What?

FRED: Master Auld say, teach a slave to read and he won't be a slave no more.

WHITE BOY: He did?

FRED: Yes — so as soon as I learn to read I'll be free, just like you. Teach me, Robert — teach me to read from your book — will you?
(WHITE BOY begins to respond to FRED's enthusiasm.)

WHITE BOY: *(Excited)* Of course I will.
(They take the book between them as they sit down on the floor — then they begin.)

WHITE BOY: First, the alphabet — "A" —

FRED: "A" —

WHITE BOY: "B" —

FRED: "B" —

WHITE BOY: "C" —

FRED: "C" —

WHITE BOY: "D" —

FRED: "D" —

(So caught up are they in the lesson that they do not see that WHITE WOMAN *has entered and is spying on them.)*

WHITE BOY: "E" —

FRED: "E" —

WHITE BOY: "F" —

FRED: "F" —

*(*WHITE WOMAN *sneaks up behind the two boys on the floor.)*

WHITE BOY: "G" —

FRED: "G" —

WHITE BOY: "H" —

*(*WHITE WOMAN *snatches the book from* WHITE BOY's *fingers.* FRED *and* WHITE BOY *jump up.)*

WHITE WOMAN: Caught you!

(She tears the book up and flings the pieces to the ground.)

WHITE BOY: Please, ma'am, we was only —

WHITE WOMAN: I know what you were doing — ruining a perfectly good slave! Now get out of here!

(She hands broom to FRED.*)*

And you get to your work!

(She chases WHITE BOY *offstage.)*

FRED: *(Crosses to pick up the torn pages of the book.)* From this time on she watched me like a hawk — because everything I could find with print on it I tried to read, even if I couldn't understand it all the time.

*(*FRED *opens the book and begins to read.)*

Frederick Douglass followed his convictions and did learn to read. When he was about twenty-one, he escaped from his master and traveled north, where he worked for the abolition of slavery.

341

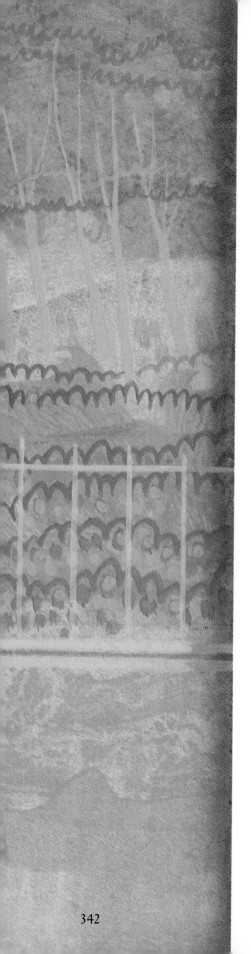

Responding to Escape to Freedom

Thinking and Discussing

What character traits does Fred show in his efforts to learn to read? Give examples of behavior that illustrate each trait you name.

Setting and characterization in a play are often revealed by a simple word or a few actions. How does the playwright let readers know where the action is set? How would you describe Thomas Auld? What actions and words reveal his character?

What does Fred mean by his observation that "slavery was harmful to the slaveowner as well as the slave"? Support your answer with an example from the selection.

Choosing a Creative Response

Investigating Frederick Douglass Young Frederick Douglass is a complex character. Even as he meekly follows the commands of his "owners," he struggles to learn to read, having had the insight that reading and writing are the key to freedom.

Research the later life of Frederick Douglass in an encyclopedia or other reference. What connections can you see between the strong character traits he displayed as a boy and his beliefs and accomplishments as an adult? Was he correct about the importance of literacy in his life?

Dramatizing a Scene With a partner or two, choose a portion of this scene to dramatize for your group. Pay careful attention to stage directions in parentheses. Remember to say your lines as the character would say them.

Discussing Reading The episode in the play took place over 150 years ago. What problems might a person who cannot read or write face in today's world? With your group, discuss ways in which illiteracy limits freedom.

Creating Your Own Activity Plan and complete your own activity in response to *Escape to Freedom*.

Thinking and Writing

Imagine what our society would be like if every citizen were *not* given the opportunity to learn to read. How would news gathering and reporting be affected? How would people buy and sell goods? What jobs might people have? How would everyday life be changed by not having children attend school? Write a brief essay that deals with these and any other questions that occur to you. Discuss your ideas about literacy with your group.

Dicey's Song

By Cynthia Voigt

Illustrated by Jim Baldwin

After Dicey Tillerman's mother disappears and is traced to a mental hospital where she lies unconscious, Dicey leads her brothers and sister on a long, difficult journey to find a home with the grandmother they've never met before. When they move in with Gram, Dicey hopes their troubles will be over. Yet, even with the building of new ties, old problems and sorrows do not go away by themselves. None of the Tillermans, and least of all Dicey, can forget about Momma.

Dicey looked out the window and made her legs stay still. Outside, wind blew the branches of the two big oaks, ripping off the last of the brown leaves and carrying them away. The sky was a bright blue, and the sun shone with a diamond hardness. The brightness of the sun and the coldness of the wind combined to mark out sharply the edges of her view. She could see each individual brick on the old building, as if the cold made each brick contract into itself. The angles of the main entranceway, the clear edge of the cement sidewalk, the flat lawn, bare and brown now, all looked as if they would be cold to touch.

Dicey crossed her ankles again, containing her impatience. She was wearing jeans and one of the rough old boys' sweaters, a bright red one that hung loose about her torso. She had chosen it because it seemed like the kind of color her Momma's brother Bullet would have liked, if she was right about the kind of person he had been.

Mr. Chappelle was putting off returning their papers until he had told them about the mistakes most of them had made. They were supposed to be writing these things down, the list of misspelled words, the grammar errors, the kind of topic sentence every paragraph was supposed to have. He was explaining and explaining. Everybody was quiet, just waiting for him to get finished. The thing that got Dicey was that he pretended he was doing this stuff first because it was more important than the grades. That was what he said, that the papers were a learning situation, and the grades didn't matter.

But Dicey suspected that he was doing this dull stuff first because he knew that once he handed the papers back nobody would pay any attention to him. It wasn't his fault, it was just the way classes went. You worked hard (or not so hard) for something, and when you got the results that job was over. The teacher might not think it was over, but the students sure did. The grade told you how well you had done (or what you got away with). The grade was what you looked for — not the red circles around mistakes. Sometimes, a teacher wrote a comment, *good work* (or *bad work*), and you looked at that, too. But mostly, everything they had to say they said in the grade. If there was something more important than the grade, Dicey wanted to know why didn't teachers ever say anything about that, like write you a note about it on your paper. If it wasn't worth his time to write down, how could he say it was worth hers?

She sat forward and sat back and sat forward. She looked at the clock — only fifteen minutes left; he'd have to hand the papers back soon.

"Now," Mr. Chappelle said, "you may be interested in seeing your essays." He smiled at his own joke, so a few kids made little fake laughing noises.

"Before I hand them out, there are two I'd like to read aloud to you." Dicey made herself lean back in her chair. She jammed her hands down into her pockets and stretched her legs out in front of her. "To share with you," Mr. Chappelle said, and reached down into his briefcase. He took out the pile of papers. He ran his hand through his red hair and looked around at everyone, his eyes sliding along the rows. He tried another joke. "Both of these essays were written by girls, but I don't want you boys to get discouraged. Everyone knows boys grow up more slowly."

Who *cares*, Dicey demanded silently.

He took up a paper and began to read.

There's this girl I know, you never know what she's thinking, even though everybody thinks they know this girl. You look at her face, but that doesn't tell you anything. Sometimes you know you don't know what's going on inside. Sometimes, you're not sure you don't know. I wonder about this girl. Here's what I've noticed.

Dicey thought this girl could be just about anyone, even Dicey. She could tell by the way the rest of the class was listening, they had the same feeling. The way it was written, it was just like somebody talking.

She's about the laughingest person you're liable to meet, if you live forever. Nothing but sets her off laughing. You could tell her you were flunking every course and about to be booted out of home and into the unemployment lines, and she'd laugh. She'd laugh until you might start laughing too. You could tell her you just got elected president of your class and captain of the football team and Prince Charming, all at once, and you know what she'd do — she'd laugh. Everywhere she goes it's nothing but laugh, laugh, until you feel like you're caught out in a rainstorm that won't never end. But I keep finding her crying when she thinks nobody's there to see. I catch her. And when I ask her, "Honey, why you crying so bad?" she never says one word to tell me. I stand there, passing out the Kleenex, and she's whooping and wailing and there's nothing can stop her once she's started.

By this time, Dicey thought she recognized who the person was describing: Mina. Because of the laughing. The crying wasn't anything Dicey had seen, but she guessed this was a pretty close friend of Mina's.

Another thing. She's always talking about you. Not behind your back, but right when you're having your conversation. "How are you, and what do you think, and *what do you like?"* She's mighty easy to talk with, this girl, because she's always interested in the other person. She listens and she remembers and she'll ask you, two years later, "Remember that fight you had with your father about your allowance? Do you still feel the same way?" I guess she's about the most unselfish person I know. But inside, she's always thinking about herself, patting herself on the back for being a caring, remembering person. She's got about the longest arms you'll ever see for patting herself on the back. So while you're telling her this sad, beautiful love story, and you're saying everything you feel — but everything — she's listening so hard you feel like she's curled up inside your own head and you think there never was such a person for listening to you. All the time, part of her's wondering if she's ever been in love or if she ever will be, and how it'll be for her, and she's thinking how great you think she is. This girl is just about something, and I sometimes wonder if even she knows what's going on.*

But, Dicey thought, the only person who could know all that about Mina was Mina. Dicey sat forward in her chair. Was it Mina's paper? She slipped her eye over to where Mina was sitting. The smooth brown cheeks looked as if they'd never heard this before. Mina was looking down at her open notebook. But she wasn't smiling, the way the rest of the class was while they listened. The way Dicey started to smile, figuring out what Mina had done. Dicey was impressed by this paper, the way Mina wrote about herself. Boy was that an idea — that was an idea and a half.

To see her, she's got all the answers. Everybody else has trouble making up their minds. Should I do this? Do I want to wear that? Is it the right answer? Not this girl, she just knows the heart out of everything and everybody. She doesn't hesitate, she just puts her big feet out in front of her and gets going. And worry? That's a word this girl never heard of. It's not in her dictionary. She knows north from south, and she knows which way she wants to go. No regrets, not for her. If she makes a mistake — well she's made a mistake and so what? Confident, you'd call her, and for all you know you're one hundred percent right, there wasn't anybody since the Garden of Eden as confident. But I've seen her do her hair one way then brush it out and do it another. I've seen her sit in one chair and then in another and then move to a bench and finally sit on the ground, until she hopped up to sit in the chair she tried first. I've seen her rip up ten starts on home-work papers and only hand one in because she ran out of time to rip it up in.

By this time, the class had figured out that it was Mina the essay was about. They whispered it and looked at Mina. They wondered — interrupting Mr. Chappelle but he didn't seem to mind, he seemed to want them to guess — who'd written it. They asked one another, "Did you?" and answered, "No not me, did you?" Mina just kept staring down, but she was having a hard time not laughing out loud. Dicey was sure Mina had written it about herself, but she didn't know why she was so sure. She just knew it.

And all the time this girl's listening and laughing, all the same. I'm watching her and I don't know what she's thinking, and then I'm thinking, Maybe I do. I guess by now you know who I'm talking about, you know it's me, Wilhemina Smiths.

The class burst out laughing, and praised Mina. Mina looked around and pretended to take a bow. Mr. Chappelle told her to stand up. As she did, she caught Dicey's eye. Dicey pursed her lips into a mute whistle, to try to say how impressed she was. Mr. Chappelle stepped forward and gave Mina her paper. Mina didn't even unfold it to see the grade. She just sat down again.

After a minute, the noise in the room, and the occasional laugh, died away.

"Now for a horse of another color," Mr. Chappelle announced. He began to read.

At the first words, Dicey recognized it as hers. She stared at Mr. Chappelle's pale, impassive face as he read about Momma.

Mrs. Liza lived away up north, away out on Cape Cod, away in a town right at the end of the Cape. Her cabin was outside of town, right at the edge of the ocean. The ocean rolled up toward her rickety cabin, like it wanted to swallow it up; but it never did. Maybe it didn't even want to. The wind was always blowing around the cabin, like it too wanted to have that little building gone.

Mrs. Liza had children, but she never had been married, and the man who was her children's father had long ago gone and left her. She worked nights when the children were little, waiting tables in a restaurant, serving drinks in a bar, night-clerking in a motel. She always worked hard and was always willing to take days nobody else wanted, Christmas and Fourth of July, Easter. When the children got older, she switched to a daytime job, checkout in a super-market. She hadn't had any training for the kind of job that paid well, so she was always thinking about money, hoping she would have enough. Every sweater she owned had holes in it.

She had reasons to turn into a mean woman, but Mrs. Liza just couldn't. She had a face made to smile, and her eyes always smiled with her mouth. She had long hair, the color of warm honey in the winter, the color of evening sunlight in the summer. She walked easy, high narrow shoulders, but loose, as if the joints of her body never got quite put together. She walked like a song sung without accompaniment.

Then slowly, so slowly she never really could find out
the place where it began, life turned sour on Mrs. Liza.
People said things. While she never heard them herself, her
children heard them and got older and understood what people
meant. Mrs. Liza loved her children, so that worried her.
Money worried at her the way waves worry at the shoreline,
always nibbling away at the soft sand. Her money seemed to
run out earlier each week.

Mrs. Liza stood at the door of her cabin and looked out
at the ocean. The ocean looked back at Mrs. Liza and rolled
on toward her. She could see no end to the ocean. The wind
that pulled at her hair was always blowing. She looked out at
her children playing on the beach and reminded herself to get
some tunafish for supper; but she forgot.

Her eyes stopped smiling first, and then her mouth.
The holes in her sweaters got bigger. Meanwhile, people
talked and she didn't know what to say so they could under-
stand. Meanwhile, quarters and dimes got lighter, smaller.
Meanwhile, her children were growing bigger and they
needed more food, more clothes. Meanwhile, nothing she did
seemed to make any difference.

So Mrs. Liza did about the only thing left to her to do.
She went away into the farthest place she could find. They cut
her hair short. She didn't notice that, lying there, nor when
they fed her or changed the sheets. Her eyes never moved, as
if what she was looking at was so far away small that if she
looked off for a second, it would be gone.

Mr. Chappelle put the paper down and looked up.
Dicey felt proud: it was just about as good as she'd thought
it was. It was really good. But everybody was absolutely
quiet. Didn't they think it was good, too? She waited
nervously. Maybe she just liked it because it was hers, the
way you liked anything you had made yourself. Maybe

Mr. Chappelle read it because it was so bad, to show the difference between hers and Mina's. Still nobody spoke. Mr. Chappelle was staring down at the paper. He was wearing a green tie.

Dicey didn't care if nobody liked it but her. She remembered how she had felt, writing it down. It was hard, and she kept scratching out sentences and beginning again. Yet it kind of came out, almost without her thinking of it, almost as if it had been already written inside her head, and she just had to find the door to open to let it out. She'd never felt that way about schoolwork before, and she wondered if she could do it again. She made her face quiet, not to show what she was thinking.

At last, Mina broke the silence. "That surely *is* a horse of another color," she said. There was laughter in her voice. "I guess it about beat me around the track — before I even left the starting gate." She looked around the class.

"Oh, yes, it's very well written," Mr. Chappelle agreed.

Dicey kept quiet.

"But who wrote it?" somebody asked, a boy. "And what happened at the end? It sounded like she died. But it didn't say she died."

The voices went on talking.

"It sounded like she was about to die."

"No, she was already dead."

"Where was she?"

"In jail? In a hospital? It said they fed her and changed the sheets."

"But what happened?"

"She couldn't support her family. She was poor, couldn't you tell? And it just got her down."

"Yeah, because she started out happy, didn't she?"

"Why didn't she get married?"

"The guy walked out, weren't you listening?"

"Maybe he didn't want to get married."

"Maybe he didn't want all those kids."

"But it takes two — you know what I mean. It wasn't just *her* fault."

"It wasn't fair what happened to her."

"Fair — what difference does fair make?"

"Did she go crazy? I would."

"And it's a mental hospital at the end? But it sounded like a jail picture, at the end."

"Who wrote it, Mr. Chappelle, tell us. You're the one who knows."

They stopped for his answer: "I do, and I don't," he said.

Dicey bit her lip. Now what did that mean?

"It's like one of the stories in our book," somebody said.

"What do you mean?" Mr. Chappelle asked quickly. "Did you read it in our text?"

How could she have? Dicey thought impatiently.

"No, I mean — it doesn't sound like one of us wrote it. It doesn't sound like anything I could write. I never knew anybody like Mrs. Liza. And even if I did, I couldn't — say it like that. Tell us, did *you* write it?"

Mr. Chappelle came around to the front of the desk. He leaned back against it, half-sitting on it. "No, I didn't. Dicey Tillerman did. Stand up, Dicey."

Dicey stood up. She stood up straight and didn't even lean her hand on her desk. Everybody stared at her. "I shoulda guessed," Mina said. She smiled across the room at Dicey, congratulating.

"What *did* happen to her at the end?" somebody asked, but Mr. Chappelle cut off the question.

"Do you have anything to say?" he asked Dicey. She kept her mouth shut, and her face closed off. She knew now what he was thinking.

"No? But I'm afraid I do. I'm very much afraid I have a great deal to say. I'm not one of your great brains, but I've taught this course long enough to be able to tell the kind of work students can do."

Dicey felt frozen. He wasn't looking at her, but she was looking at him, at his pale mouth out of which words marched slowly.

"Now I can't say what book this came out of — if it came out of a book. I can't even say for sure that it did come out of a book. Maybe somebody else helped Dicey write it."

He gave her time to say something there, but he didn't look at her. Dicey didn't say a word. In the first place, her tongue felt like it was frozen solid, and her head was a block of ice, and all the blood in her body had chilled and congealed.[1] In the second place, he had more to say. She could guess what that was.

"But even if I can't prove plagiarism,[2] I can still smell it. Besides, there was a restriction on this assignment. It was supposed to be about someone you knew. A real person. On those grounds alone, the essay fails."

Dicey should have known. She should have known this would happen, and everyone would believe him. The silence in the room told her what everyone was thinking. She was the only one standing up, for everyone to look at.

"What I primarily resent is the deceitfulness of it, the cheap trickery, the lies," Mr. Chappelle declared.

"That's not true."

---

[1] **congealed** (kən jēld′): thickened.
[2] **plagiarism** (plā′jə rĭz′əm): copying or using another's work or ideas without giving credit to the other.

Dicey turned to see who had spoken. She thought she could hear her neck bones crackling, like ice, when she turned her head.

Mina was standing up. She looked around the room, her eyes dark as coffee and puzzled. "How can you believe that?" she demanded of Mr. Chappelle.

"Come now, Wilhemina," he said.

"*I* don't believe it," she declared. Her voice sounded certain.

Mr. Chappelle looked around the classroom. Dicey could have laughed. He didn't quite dare order Mina to sit down, because people listened to her and liked her.

"Dicey wouldn't do that," Mina went on. "She doesn't care enough about what we think to cheat on something."

How did Mina know that? Dicey wondered. She wondered it deep behind her icy face.

"Someone like Dicey — she's too smart to worry about her grades; she doesn't have to worry. And if she cared what we thought" — her hand sketched a circle including all the students — "she'd act different. Don't you think?"

People rustled in their seats. They could think whatever they wanted. Now Dicey understood the C+ in English.

The bell rang, ending class, but Mina spoke before anybody could move to leave. "Stay here, I'll prove it."

"How can you prove it?" Mr. Chappelle asked. He had moved back behind his desk. "I've got these essays to hand out."

"Wait," Mina said.

They could stay or go for all Dicey cared.

"I can prove it," Mina repeated. "Dicey?" She looked across the room at Dicey. Her eyes were filled with sympathy. Dicey didn't need anybody's pity. But behind the liquid darkness of Mina's eyes, Dicey saw mischief. Mina knew she was right, and she was enjoying herself.

"Dicey? Is this someone you know?"

"Yes," Dicey said. She was talking just to Mina.

"Did you write it yourself?"

"Yes," Dicey said.

"What does that prove?" Mr. Chappelle muttered.

"Do you want to hear Dicey lie?" Mina asked him. "Dicey, is this someone you're related to?"

Dicey lifted her chin. She didn't answer. There was no way anybody could make her answer. In her mind, she made a picture: the little boat, she'd have painted it white by then, or maybe yellow — it was out on the Bay beyond Gram's dock and the wind pulled at the sails. Dicey could feel the smooth tiller under her hand, she could feel the way the wooden hull flowed through the water.

"Dicey," Mina asked, with no expression in her voice, "what are you thinking about?"

"About sailing," Dicey answered. "About a boat and how it feels when you're sailing it." Those might be the last words she spoke in that class, and why should she bother to make them a lie.

Then people did get up and go. They didn't look at Dicey, but they looked at Mr. Chappelle as they walked past his desk and picked out their papers.

Dicey was almost at the door when he stopped her and gave the paper to her. "I'm sorry," he said. "I'll change the grade — to an A+ — and I'll change the mid-semester grade too, of course."

Dicey didn't say anything. She didn't care what he said.

"It's my mistake and I'm really very sorry," he said again. "I'm giving you an A for the marking period, of course."

It didn't make any difference to Dicey what he said.

She sat through horrible home ec without any trouble at all. On the outside, she was paring carrots and slicing them thin to boil them at the stoves. She didn't eat any, just scraped them into the garbage. She went to work, without even noticing if Jeff was outside playing his guitar. She did her work hard and fast and answered Millie's questions without thinking. She rode home through a wind like a knife blade, but it didn't make her cold. She put her bike in the barn and leaned her free hand against the boat for a minute before going on into the house. Gram was in the kitchen. Maybeth and James worked in the living room by the fire. Dicey put her books up in her bedroom and then came back downstairs. She peeled some potatoes for Gram, then cut them up into chunks for hash browns. Sammy came through, rubbing his hands and puffing out cold air. Dicey stood at the wooden countertop, slicing the potatoes first, then cutting across the slices, then cutting again perpendicularly. Slice after slice.

Gram was shaking chicken pieces in a brown paper bag. Dicey could hear the sound it made, like somebody brushing out a rhythm on drums. "How was school today?" Gram asked.

"Fine," Dicey said. She cut slowly, carefully, making her squares as even as possible.

"How's Millie?" Gram asked. There was a kind of sharpness in her voice, and alertness, but Dicey didn't turn around to read the expression on her face. She heard the chicken pieces shaking, in flour, salt, and pepper.

"Fine."

Gram was staring at her. She could feel it.

"You never said," Gram said without breaking the rhythm of the shaking, "if you got your English grade changed."

"Well," Dicey said. Then she couldn't think of how to finish the sentence.

"Well?" Gram asked after a while. "Was it a mistake? Were you right?"

Dicey picked up the last potato. She cut it into neat slices. She lay the slices down flat in front of her. "Yeah, it was a mistake. Boy was it a mistake." She felt pretty calm again, cold and still.

"What happened?" Gram asked. For a second, Dicey was irritated. It wasn't like Gram to insist on a subject Dicey didn't want to talk about. Usually, Gram understood and stopped asking questions.

"We had an essay to write," Dicey explained. She felt like she was talking to the potato, because that was what she looked at. Behind her, Gram moved around the kitchen, getting things ready. "A character sketch, about a real person and conflict. I wrote one, and thought it was pretty good. He handed them back today. He thought I'd copied mine. Or something. He thought the person wasn't real. He thought I'd taken it out of a book." She slowed her hands down. When she finished with this potato, what was she going to do about what to look at?

Gram's voice came from behind her. "It must have been pretty good, if he thought it came out of a book."

Dicey turned around. Gram was looking at her. "Yeah," Dicey said, hearing how fierce her own voice sounded, "it was."

"Did you tell him?" Gram asked.

Dicey shook her head.

"You mean he thinks you cheated?"

Dicey shook her head again.

"Exactly what happened?" Gram asked, sounding ready to get angry.

"He read a couple of the papers out loud, to everyone. Mine was one. Then he said, he thought I'd cheated but he couldn't prove it. But he said I hadn't done the assignment, because it was supposed to be a real person. So he was flunking it."

"In front of the whole class?" Gram demanded.

"Yeah."

Gram's mouth moved and her eyes burned. That made Dicey feel warm, down deep in her stomach. Gram was angry for Dicey's sake. "Can I read it?" Gram asked.

"Sure."

"Now?"

"OK."

"Will you get it, girl? I've got fat heating."

So Dicey went upstairs to get her essay. She started the potatoes while Gram sat at the table and read. She placed the cubes of potato neatly in the hot bacon fat and turned the gas down to medium once she heard the fat start to sizzle under the layer of potatoes. She checked the lard in the other frying pan, to see if it was smoking hot yet. She got down a jar of tomatoes that Gram had put up that summer. Every now and then she glanced over to see what Gram was doing. Gram read the essay through once, and then again, and then again.

"Well," Gram said at last, "I can see why he thought it came out of a book. I like it, Dicey. I like it very much. Your poor Momma. He couldn't know she was real. It *is* hard to believe. Are you going to tell him?"

Dicey shook her head. "Anyway, he knows," she told Gram. "He said he'll change the grade — as if that mattered – and on the report card too."

"Tell me what happened, Dicey," Gram said.

"Well, there's this girl in our class — we worked together on a science project, and she's about the most popular girl I guess. Mina. He was yelling at me for cheating, and she said she didn't believe it." As she recalled it, Dicey saw the picture she and Mina must have made and she started to smile. "I was standing up, I was the only one. And she stood up too, and she's — she's tall and strong-looking. And her voice — I don't know how to tell you, like an actress."

Gram nodded, listening.

"She said she didn't think I'd cheat or lie. Because I didn't care enough about what people thought. Well, she's right." Dicey grinned now. "Then she said she could prove it. So she asked me a couple of questions — she ought to be a lawyer, really. The bell rang and she told everybody to stay put and they did. Anyway, she proved it, I guess, because before I left he told me about the grades and he said he was sorry."

Gram was laughing. "I wish I'd been there," she said. "I wish I'd seen this. I like the sound of this girl. She your friend?"

"No, not really. I mean — no, not really."

"Hunh," Gram said, getting up from the table and going to the stove. She started putting pieces of chicken into the fat. Dicey stepped back. "Must have been hard on you, though," Gram remarked.

"It doesn't matter," Dicey said.

Then Gram started laughing again. "That teacher sure had his hands full, didn't he, between you and this Mina character. I bet he was sorry the day he assigned that essay." And Dicey joined in now that she could see the scene as if it was part of a movie.

361

Responding to Dicey's Song

Thinking and Discussing

Gram asks Dicey if Mina is her friend, and Dicey answers, "No, not really. I mean — no, not really." Do you think Mina is Dicey's friend? Explain your answer.

Dicey's essay describes Momma, but what traits does it also reveal about Dicey? What does Dicey's decision not to defend herself in class reveal about her character?

What do readers learn about Mina from her essay and from the way she defends Dicey?

Choosing a Creative Response

Advising Dicey Imagine you are Dicey's friend. If Dicey comes to you for advice on how to deal with the events in English class, what suggestions might you give her? Jot down some notes about what you would say to Dicey.

Writing Dicey's Diary Write a diary entry that Dicey might have written the day Mr. Chappelle returned her essay. The entry should reflect Dicey's feelings as well as record the events of the day.

Creating Your Own Activity
Plan and complete your own activity in response to *Dicey's Song.*

Exploring Language

Rich language in *Dicey's Song* helps readers to see the characters and the setting vividly. For example, the author writes that "the sun shone with a diamond hardness." About Dicey she writes, "her tongue felt like it was frozen solid, and her head was a block of ice. . . ." Find other examples of rich, descriptive language in the selection, or write some of your own to share with your group.

Thinking and Writing

Mr. Chappelle asks the students in his English class to write a description of a real person who faces a conflict. Think of someone you have read about or heard about who faced a conflict, and write about that person. Use Mina's and Dicey's essays as examples.

Jeremiah's Song

By
Walter
Dean
Myers

Illustrated by Jim Baldwin

I knowed my cousin Ellie was gonna be mad when Macon Smith come around to the house. She didn't have no use for Macon even when things was going right, and when Grandpa Jeremiah was fixing to die I just knowed she wasn't gonna be liking him hanging around. Grandpa Jeremiah raised Ellie after her folks died and they used to be real close. Then she got to go on to college and when she come back the first year she was different. She didn't want to hear all them stories he used to tell her anymore. Ellie said the stories wasn't true, and that's why she didn't want to hear them.

I didn't know if they was true or not. Tell the truth I didn't think much on it either way, but I liked to hear them stories. Grandpa Jeremiah said they wasn't stories anyway, they was songs.

"They the songs of my people," he used to say.

I didn't see how they was songs, not regular songs anyway. Every little thing we did down in Curry seemed to matter to Ellie that first summer she come home from college. You couldn't do nothin' that was gonna please her. She didn't even come to church much. 'Course she come on Sunday or everybody would have had a regular fit, but she didn't come on Thursday nights and she didn't come on Saturday even though she used to sing in the gospel choir.

"I guess they teachin' her somethin' worthwhile up there at Greensboro," Grandpa Jeremiah said to Sister Todd. "I sure don't see what it is, though."

"You ain't never had no book learning, Jeremiah," Sister Todd shot back. She wiped at where a trickle of sweat made a little path through the white dusting powder

she put on her chest to keep cool. "Them old ways you got ain't got nothing for these young folks."

"I guess you right," Grandpa Jeremiah said.

He said it but I could see he didn't like it none. He was a big man with a big head and had most all his hair even if it was white. All that summer, instead of sitting on the porch telling stories like he used to when I was real little, he would sit out there by himself while Ellie stayed in the house and watched the television or read a book. Sometimes I would think about asking him to tell me one of them stories he used to tell but they was too scary. . . .

It was right after Ellie went back to school that Grandpa Jeremiah had him a stroke and Macon started coming around. I think his mama probably made him come at first, but you could see he liked it. Macon had always been around, sitting over near the stuck window at church or going on the blueberry truck when we went picking down at Mister Gregory's place. For a long time he was just another kid, even though he was older'n me, but then, all of a sudden, he growed something fierce. I used to be up to his shoulder one time and then, before I could turn around good, I was only up to his shirt pocket. He changed too. When he used to just hang around with the other boys and play ball or shoot at birds he would laugh a lot. He didn't laugh so much anymore and I figured he was just about grown. When Grandpa got sick he used to come around and help out with things around the house that was too hard for me to do. I mean, I could have done all the chores, but it would just take me longer.

When the work for the day was finished and the sows[1] fed, Grandpa would kind of ease into one of his stories and Macon, he would sit and listen to them and be

---

[1] **sows** (souz): grown female pigs.

real interested. I didn't mind listening to the stories when Grandpa told them to Macon because he would be telling them in the middle of the afternoon and they would be past my mind by the time I had to go to bed.

Macon had an old guitar he used to mess with, too. He wasn't too bad on it, and sometimes Grandpa would tell him to play us a tune. He could play something he called "the Delta Blues" real good, but when Sister Todd or somebody from the church come around he'd play "Precious Lord" or "Just a Closer Walk With Thee."

Grandpa Jeremiah had been feeling poorly from that stroke, and one of his legs got a little drag to it. Just about the time Ellie come from school the next summer he was real sick. He was breathing loud so you could hear it even in the next room and he would stay in bed a lot even when there was something that needed doing or fixing.

"I don't think he's going to make it much longer," Dr. Crawford said. "The only thing I can do is to give him something for the pain."

"Are you sure of your diagnosis?" Ellie asked. She was sitting around the table with Sister Todd, Deacon Turner, and his little skinny yellow wife.

Dr. Crawford looked at Ellie like he was surprised to hear her talking. "Yes, I'm sure," he said. "He had tests a few weeks ago and his condition was bad then."

"How much time he got?" Sister Todd asked.

"Maybe a week or two at best," Dr. Crawford said.

When he said that, Deacon Turner's wife started crying and goin' on and I give her a hard look but she just went on. I was the one who loved Grandpa Jeremiah the most and she didn't hardly even know him so I didn't see why she was crying.

Everybody started tiptoeing around the house after that. They would go in and ask Grandpa Jeremiah if he was comfortable and stuff like that or take him some food or a cold glass of lemonade. Sister Todd come over and stayed with us. Mostly what she did is make supper and do a lot of praying, which was good because I figured that maybe God would do something to make Grandpa Jeremiah well. When she wasn't doing that she was piecing on a fancy quilt she was making for some white people in Wilmington.

Ellie, she went around asking everybody how they felt about Dr. Crawford and then she went into town and asked about the tests and things. Sister Jenkins asked her if she thought she knowed more than Dr. Crawford, and Ellie rolled her eyes at her, but Sister Jenkins was reading out her Bible and didn't make no notice of it.

Then Macon come over.

He had been away on what he called "a little piece of a job" and hadn't heard how bad off Grandpa Jeremiah was. When he come over he talked to Ellie and she told him what was going on and then he got him a soft drink from the refrigerator and sat out on the porch and before you know it he was crying.

You could look at his face and tell the difference between him sweating and the tears. The sweat was close against his skin and shiny and the tears come down fatter and more sparkly.

Macon sat on the porch, without saying a word, until the sun went down and the crickets started chirping and carrying on. Then he went in to where Grandpa Jeremiah was and stayed in there for a long time.

Sister Todd was saying that Grandpa Jeremiah needed his rest and Ellie went in to see what Macon was doing. Then she come out real mad.

"He got Grandpa telling those old stories again," Ellie said. "I told him Grandpa needed his rest and for him not to be staying all night."

He did leave soon, but bright and early the next morning Macon was back again. This time he brought his guitar with him and he went on in to Grandpa Jeremiah's room. I went in, too.

Grandpa Jeremiah's room smelled terrible. It was all closed up so no drafts could get on him and the whole room was smelled down with disinfect and medicine. Grandpa Jeremiah lay propped up on the bed and he was so gray he looked scary. His hair wasn't combed down and his head on the pillow with his white hair sticking out was enough to send me flying if Macon hadn't been there. He was skinny, too. He looked like his skin got loose on his bones, and when he lifted his arms, it hung down like he was just wearing it instead of it being a part of him.

Macon sat slant-shouldered with his guitar across his lap. He was messin' with the guitar, not making any music, but just going over the strings as Grandpa talked.

"Old Carrie went around out back to where they kept the pigs penned up and she felt a cold wind across her face. . . ." Grandpa Jeremiah was telling the story about how a old woman out-tricked the Devil and got her son back. I had heard the story before, and I knew it was pretty scary. "When she felt the cold breeze she didn't blink nary an eye, but looked straight ahead. . . ."

All the time Grandpa Jeremiah was talking I could see Macon fingering his guitar. I tried to imagine what it would be like if he was actually plucking the strings. I tried to fix my mind on that because I didn't like the way the story went with the old woman wrestling with the Devil.

We sat there for nearly all the afternoon until Ellie and Sister Todd come in and said that supper was ready.

Me and Macon went out and ate some collard greens, ham hocks, and rice. Then Macon he went back in and listened to some more of Grandpa's stories until it was time for him to go home. I wasn't about to go in there and listen to no stories at night.

Dr. Crawford come around a few days later and said that Grandpa Jeremiah was doing a little better.

"You think the Good Lord gonna pull him through?" Sister Todd asked.

"I don't tell the Good Lord what He should or should not be doing," Dr. Crawford said, looking over at Sister Todd and at Ellie. "I just said that *my* patient seems to be doing okay for his condition."

"He been telling Macon all his stories," I said.

"Macon doesn't seem to understand that Grandpa Jeremiah needs his strength," Ellie said. "Now that he's improving, we don't want him to have a setback."

"No use in stopping him from telling his stories," Dr. Crawford said. "If it makes him feel good it's as good as any medicine I can give him."

I saw that this didn't set with Ellie, and when Dr. Crawford had left I asked her why.

"Dr. Crawford means well," she said, "but we have to get away from the kind of life that keeps us in the past."

She didn't say why we should be trying to get away from the stories and I really didn't care too much. All I knew was that when Macon was sitting in the room with Grandpa Jeremiah I wasn't nearly as scared as I used to be when it was just me and Ellie listening. I told that to Macon.

"You getting to be a big man, that's all," he said.

That was true. Me and Macon was getting to be good friends, too. I didn't even mind so much when he started being friends with Ellie later. It seemed kind of natural, almost like Macon was supposed to be there with us instead of just visiting.

Grandpa wasn't getting no better, but he wasn't getting no worse, either.

"You liking Macon now?" I asked Ellie when we got to the middle of July. She was dishing out a plate of smothered chops for him and I hadn't even heard him ask for anything to eat.

"Macon's funny," Ellie said, not answering my question. "He's in there listening to all of those old stories like he's really interested in them. It's almost as if he and Grandpa Jeremiah are talking about something more than the stories, a secret language."

I didn't think I was supposed to say anything about that to Macon, but once, when Ellie, Sister Todd, and Macon were out on the porch shelling butter beans after Grandpa got tired and was resting, I went into his room and told him what Ellie had said.

"She said that?" Grandpa Jeremiah's face was skinny and old looking but his eyes looked like a baby's, they was so bright.

"Right there in the kitchen is where she said it," I said. "And I don't know what it mean but I was wondering about it."

"I didn't think she had any feeling for them stories," Grandpa Jeremiah said. "If she think we talking secrets, maybe she don't."

"I think she getting a feeling for Macon," I said.

"That's okay, too," Grandpa Jeremiah said. "They both young."

"Yeah, but them stories you be telling, Grandpa, they about old people who lived a long time ago," I said.

"Well, those the folks you got to know about," Grandpa Jeremiah said. "You think on what those folks been through, and what they was feeling, and you add it up with what you been through and what you been feeling, then you got you something."

"What you got Grandpa?"

"You got you a bridge," Grandpa said. "And a meaning. Then when things get so hard you about to break, you can sneak across that bridge and see some folks who went before you and see how they didn't break. Some got bent and some got twisted and a few fell along the way, but they didn't break."

"Am I going to break, Grandpa?"

"You? As strong as you is?" Grandpa Jeremiah pushed himself up on his elbow and give me a look. "No way you going to break, boy. You gonna be strong as they come. One day you gonna tell all them stories I told you to your young'uns and they'll be as strong as you."

"Suppose I ain't got no stories, can I make some up?"

"Sure you can, boy. You make 'em up and twist 'em around. Don't make no mind. Long as you got 'em."

"Is that what Macon is doing?" I asked. "Making up stories to play on his guitar?"

"He'll do with 'em what he see fit, I suppose," Grandpa Jeremiah said. "Can't ask more than that from a man."

It rained the first three days of August. It wasn't a hard rain but it rained anyway. The mailman said it was good for the crops over East but I didn't care about that so I didn't pay him no mind. What I did mind was when it rain like that the field mice come in and get in things like the flour bin and I always got the blame for leaving it open.

When the rain stopped I was pretty glad. Macon come over and sat with Grandpa and had something to eat with us. Sister Todd come over, too.

"How Grandpa doing?" Sister Todd asked. "They been asking about him in the church."

"He's doing all right," Ellie said.

"He's kind of quiet today," Macon said. "He was just talking about how the hogs needed breeding."

"He must have run out of stories to tell," Sister Todd said. "He'll be repeating on himself like my father used to do. That's the way I *hear* old folks get."

Everybody laughed at that because Sister Todd was pretty old, too. Maybe we was all happy because the sun was out after so much rain. When Sister Todd went in to take Grandpa Jeremiah a plate of potato salad with no mayonnaise like he liked it, she told him about how people was asking for him and he told her to tell them he was doing okay and to remember him in their prayers.

Sister Todd came over the next afternoon, too, with some rhubarb pie with cheese on it, which is my favorite pie. When she took a piece into Grandpa Jeremiah's room she come right out again and told Ellie to go fetch the Bible.

It was a hot day when they had the funeral. Mostly everybody was there. The church was hot as anything, even though they had the window open. Some yellowjacks flew in and buzzed around Sister Todd's niece and then around Deacon Turner's wife and settled right on her hat and stayed there until we all stood and sang "Soon-a Will Be Done."

At the graveyard Macon played "Precious Lord" and I cried hard even though I told myself that I wasn't going to cry the way Ellie and Sister Todd was, but it was such a

374

sad thing when we left and Grandpa Jeremiah was still out to the grave that I couldn't help it.

During the funeral and all, Macon kind of told everybody where to go and where to sit and which of the three cars to ride in. After it was over he come by the house and sat on the front porch and played on his guitar. Ellie was standing leaning against the rail and she was crying but it wasn't a hard crying. It was a soft crying, the kind that last inside of you for a long time.

Macon was playing a tune I hadn't heard before. I thought it might have been what he was working at when Grandpa Jeremiah was telling him those stories and I watched his fingers but I couldn't tell if it was or not. It wasn't nothing special, that tune Macon was playing, maybe halfway between them Delta blues he would do when Sister Todd wasn't around and something you would play at church. It was something different and something the same at the same time. I watched his fingers go over that guitar and figured I could learn that tune one day if I had a mind to.

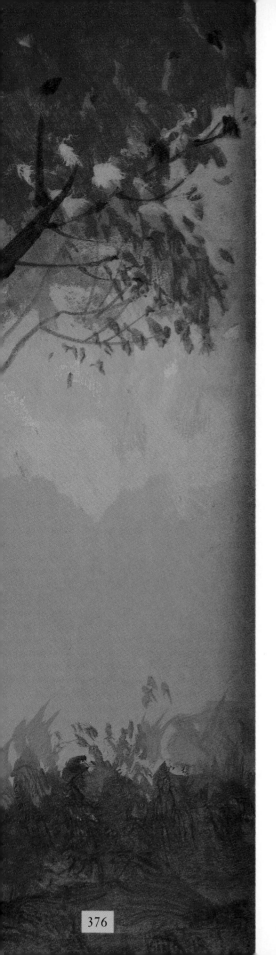

Responding to Jeremiah's Song

Thinking and Discussing

Jeremiah's song is made from stories he tells of his people and their past. What do Jeremiah's stories symbolize, or represent, to the people who hear them?

What role does Macon play in the selection? How does he fit in between the past and the present? Explain your answer.

From whose point of view is the selection narrated? What do we know about the narrator from clues the author gives?

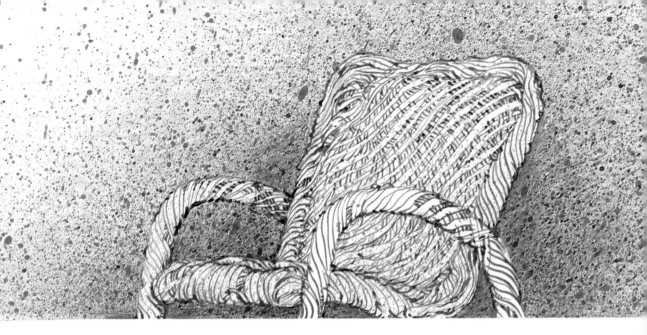

Choosing a Creative Response

Passing on Stories As Grandpa Jeremiah knows, stories of the past can often serve as bridges between generations. Have you heard a story from an adult that has served as a kind of bridge between you and that person? Have you had experiences that can serve as a bridge between you and a younger friend? Think of an example, and tell it to your group.

Writing Macon's Song Suppose that Macon is writing a song about Grandpa Jeremiah and has asked for the narrator's help. How might the two of them tell Grandpa Jeremiah's story? What might Macon say about

Grandpa Jeremiah meant to him? What might the narrator say? Make up two verses, one for Macon and one for the narrator. Copy the verses neatly and illustrate them if you wish.

Interviewing Your Elders
Interview senior members of your community. Find out about the ways in which they share their knowledge and experience with younger people. If possible tape your interview, and play it for your group.

Creating Your Own Activity
Plan and complete your own activity in response to "Jeremiah's Song."

Thinking About Realism

Evaluating Realism

Realistic fiction often deals with serious problems. However, realism does more than simply describe unpleasant situations. The selections in "Choices" also offer suggestions and hope for coping with problems the characters face.

With your group, identify the real-life problem treated in each selection. Also identify the ways in which the author shows the characters facing the problem. Then discuss whether you think that type of approach would be effective not just in realistic fiction, but in real life as well.

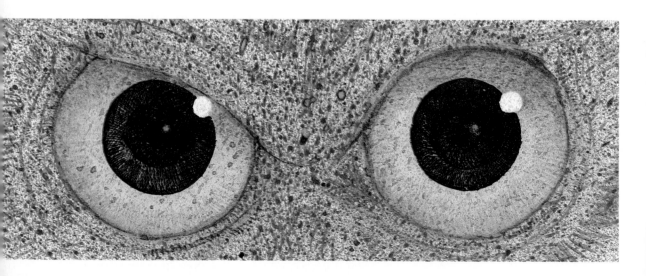

Talking About Literature

Literature does many things: it helps people think, feel, and change. Hold a symposium — a conference for discussing a topic — to find out how the selections in "Choices" affect members of your class. In your group, talk about these questions:

- Which selection is most thought-provoking? Why?
- Which selection prompts the strongest emotions? Describe those feelings.
- Which selection is most likely to change people's lives? What forms might the changes take?

Then select one or two group members to share your group's thoughts with the rest of your class at the symposium.

Choosing Theme Music

Imagine that one of the selections in "Choices" is going to be produced as a play in your community, and you will select the music for the production. What theme music would you choose to capture the mood of the selection? Jot down notes, and share them with your group. If possible, play a recording of the music for your classmates.

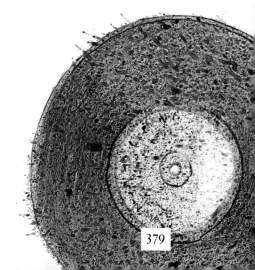

Jaap ter Haar *was born in 1922 in Hilversum, Netherlands. A professional writer since 1955, he has written fiction, nonfiction, picture books, and plays. Many of his works for young people have been translated into other languages.* Boris *is among his most popular works. In 1966 it won the City of Rotterdam Award for best book of the year.*

Ter Haar has been praised for the "compassion, vigor, and factual accuracy" of his work. He still lives in Hilversum.

Ossie Davis *was born in 1917 in Cogdell, Georgia. He became interested in the theater after becoming involved in set production and construction at Howard University. While in the army, he began writing and producing his own stage works to entertain military personnel. Later he wrote and acted in numerous plays and movies. He has also written television scripts. His play for young people,* Escape to Freedom, *was first produced in New York in 1976, and was published in 1978.*

Cynthia Voigt *was born in 1942 in Massachusetts. In ninth grade, she decided that she wanted to become a writer. After graduating from college, she moved to New York City where she worked for an advertising agency. In 1982 and 1983,* Tell Me If the Lovers Are Losers *and* The Callender Papers *were published. In 1983, Voigt won the Newbery Medal for* Dicey's Song. *The book was also selected as an American Library Association Best Children's Book.*

Walter Dean Myers *was born in 1937 in Martinsburg, West Virginia, and grew up in New York City's Harlem district.*

Myers's contribution to literature for young people is widely recognized. Where Does the Day Go? *won the Council on Interracial Books for Children Award.* It Ain't All for Nothin' *and* Hoops *won the American Library Association "Best Book for Young Adults" citations.* Motown and Didi: A Love Story *won the Coretta Scott King Award. Myers lives in New Jersey.*

More Choices

***People to Remember:
Biography and Realistic Fiction***
(Houghton, 1993)

This collection of realistic fiction and biography presents an array of lively people making choices that affect their own lives and, in some cases, the lives of those who read about them.

After the Dancing Days
by Margaret I. Rostkowski
(Harper, 1986)

When her father, a doctor, comes home from World War I, Annie is drawn to the veterans' hospital where he works. Although her mother disapproves, Annie finds new friends and challenges there. She also begins to understand heroism and the effects of war.

M. C. Higgins, the Great
by Virginia Hamilton (Macmillan, 1974)

Because his family lives just below a strip mine in the Appalachian Hills, M.C. dreams of moving away from the danger. He cannot accept his situation until two strangers come into his life.

Kim/Kimi

by Hadley Irwin

(Houghton, 1991; Macmillan, 1987)
In her Iowa town, Kim is
"different" because she looks
Japanese. Even though she
has a happy home with her
mother and her stepfather,
she longs to know more
about her Japanese
American father, who died.
Finally Kim travels to
California to learn about
her father's culture.

Daphne's Book

by Mary Downing Hahn (Clarion, 1983)
Jessica is assigned to work with class
misfit Daphne on their seventh grade Write-a-
Book project. Jessica loses her misgivings once the
two girls get to know one another. Protecting
Daphne's home life becomes very important to Jessica.

Harriet Tubman: Conductor on the Underground Railroad

by Ann Petry (Crowell, 1955)
This biography tells the dramatic
story of a slave who escaped the harsh
treatment of her masters and then
helped other slaves reach freedom.
Harriet Tubman's courage served her
through years of hardship and risk.

FANTASY

BOOK 6

HALL
OF
MIRRORS

*Fantasyland isn't some
faraway special place.
It's right around you,
right now.*

Laurence Yep

Hall of Mirrors

The Strange Illness of Mr. Arthur Cook

by Philippa Pearce

Illustrated by Joan Hall

O n a cold, shiny day at the end of winter the Cook family
went to look at the house they were likely to buy. Mr. and
Mrs. Cook had viewed it several times before, and had
discussed it thoroughly; this was a first visit for their
children, Judy and Mike.

Also with the Cooks was Mr. Biley, of the real-estate agent's firm
of Ketch, Robb and Biley in Walchester.

"Why's *he* come?" whispered Judy. (And, although the Cooks
were not to know this, Mr. Biley did not usually accompany clients in
order to clinch deals.)

Her parents shushed Judy.

They had driven a little way out of Walchester into the country.
The car now turned down a lane which, perhaps fifty years before, had
been hardly more than a farm-track. Now there were several houses
along it. The lane came to a dead end at a house with a *For Sale* notice at
its front gate. On the gate itself was the name of the house: Southcroft.

"There it is!" said Mr. Arthur Cook to his two children.

"And very nice, too!" Mr. Biley said enthusiastically.

But, in fact, the house was not particularly nice. In size it was small
to medium; brick-built, slate-roofed; exactly rectangular; and rather

bleak-looking. It stood in the middle of a large garden, also exactly rectangular and rather bleak-looking.

Mike, who tended to like most things that happened to him, said, "Seems O.K." He was gazing round not only at the house and its garden, but at the quiet lane — ideal for his bike — and at the surrounding countryside. It would be all far, far better than where they were living now, in Walchester.

Judy, who was older than Mike, and the only one in the family with a sharply pointed, inquisitive nose, said nothing — yet. She looked round alertly, intently.

"Nice big garden for kids to play in," Mr. Biley pointed out.

"I might even grow a few vegetables," said Mr. Cook.

"Oh, Arthur!" his wife said, laughing.

"Well," Mr. Cook said defensively, "I haven't had much chance up to now, have I?" In Walchester the Cooks had only a paved backyard. But, anyway, Mr. Cook, whose job was fixing television aerials onto people's roofs, had always said that in his spare time he wanted to be indoors in an easy chair.

"Anyway," said Mr. Biley, as they went in by the front gate, "you've lovely soil here. Still in good tilth."[1]

"Tilth?" said Mr. Cook.

"That's it," said Mr. Biley.

They reached the front door. Mr. Biley unlocked it, and they all trooped in.

Southcroft had probably been built some time between the two wars. There was nothing antique about it, nor anything of special interest at all. On the other hand, it all appeared to be in good order, even to the house's having been fairly recently redecorated.

---

[1]**tilth** (tĭlth): the condition of the soil when prepared for planting.

The Cooks went everywhere, looked everywhere, their footsteps echoing uncomfortably in empty rooms. They reassembled in the sitting-room, which had French windows letting on to the garden at the back. Tactfully Mr. Biley withdrew into the garden to leave the family to private talk.

"Well, there you are," said Mr. Cook. "Just our size of house. Not remarkable in any way, but snug, I fancy."

"Remarkable in one way, Arthur," said his wife. "Remarkably cheap."

"A snip," agreed Mr. Cook.

"Why's it so cheap?" asked Judy.

"You ask too many questions beginning with *why*," said her father, but good-humoredly.

It was true, however, that there seemed no particular reason for the house's being so cheap as it was. Odd, perhaps.

"Can't we go into the garden now?" asked Mike.

Mike and Judy went out, and Mr. Biley came in again.

There wasn't much for the children to see in the garden. Close to the house grew unkempt grass, with a big old apple tree — the only tree in the garden — which Mike began to climb very thoroughly. The rest of the garden had all been under cultivation at one time, but now it was neglected, a mass of last season's dead weeds. There were some straggly bushes — raspberry canes, perhaps. There had once been a green-house: only the brick foundations were left. There was a garden shed, and behind it a mass of stuff which Judy left Mike to investigate. She wanted to get back to the adult conversation.

By the time Judy rejoined the party indoors there was no doubt about it: the Cooks were buying the house. Mr. Biley was extremely pleased, Judy noticed. He caught Judy staring at him and jollily, but very unwisely, said, "Well, young lady?"

Judy, invited thus to join in the conversation, had a great many questions to ask. She knew she wouldn't be allowed to ask them all, and she began almost at random: "Who used to live here?"

"A family called Cribble," said Mr. Biley. "A very *nice* family called Cribble."

"Cribble," Judy repeated to herself, storing the piece of information away. "And why —"

At that moment Mike walked in again from the garden. "There's lots of stuff behind the shed," he said. "Rolls and rolls of chicken wire, in an awful mess, and wood — posts and slats and stuff."

"Easily cleared," said Mr. Biley. "The previous owners were going to have bred dogs, I believe. They would have erected sheds, enclosures, runs — all that kind of thing."

"Why did the Cribbles give up the idea?" asked Judy.

Mr. Biley looked uneasy. "Not the Cribbles," he said, "the Johnsons. The family here before the Cribbles."

"Why did the Johnsons give up the idea, then?" asked Judy. "I mean, when they'd got all the stuff for it?"

"They —" Mr. Biley appeared to think deeply, if only momentarily. "They had to move rather unexpectedly."

"Why?"

"Family reasons, perhaps?" said Mrs. Cook quickly. She knew some people found Judy tiresome.

"Family reasons, no doubt," Mr. Biley agreed.

Judy said thoughtfully to herself: "The Johnsons didn't stay long enough to start dog-breeding, and they went in such a hurry that they left their stuff behind. The Cribbles came, but they didn't stay long enough to have time to clear away all the Johnsons' stuff. I wonder why *they* left . . ."

Nobody could say that Judy was asking Mr. Biley a question, but he answered her all the same. "My dear young lady," he said, in a manner so polite as to be also quite rude, "I do not know why. Nor is it my business." He sounded as if he did not think it was Judy's either. He turned his back on her and began talking loudly about house-purchase to Mr. Cook.

Judy was not put out. She had investigated mysteries and secrets before this and she knew that patience was all important.

The Cooks bought Southcroft and moved in almost at once. Spring came late that year, and in the continuing cold weather the house proved as snug as one could wish. When the frosts were over, the family did some work outside, getting rid of all the dog-breeding junk: they made a splendid bonfire of the wood, and put the wire out for the garbage men. Mr. Cook took a long look at the weeds beginning to sprout everywhere, and groaned. He bought a garden fork and a spade and hoe and rake and put them into the shed.

In their different ways the Cooks were satisfied with the move. The new house was still convenient for Mr. Cook's work. Mrs. Cook found that the neighbors kept themselves to themselves more than she would have liked, but she got a part-time job in a shop in the village, and *that* was all right. Mike made new friends in the new school, and they went riding round the countryside on their bikes. Judy was slower at making friends, partly because she was absorbed in her own affairs, particularly in investigation. In this she was disappointed for a time. She could find out so little about the Cribbles and the Johnsons: why they had stayed so briefly at Southcroft, why they had moved in so much haste. The Cribbles now lived the other side of Walchester, rather smartly, in a house with a large garden which they had had expensively landscaped. (Perhaps the size of the garden at Southcroft was what had attracted them

to the house in the first place. In the village people said that the Cribbles had already engaged landscape-garden specialists for Southcroft, when they suddenly decided to leave.) As for the Johnsons, Judy discovered that they had moved right away, to Yorkshire, to do their dog-breeding. Before the Cribbles and the Johnsons, an old couple called Baxter had lived in the house for many years, until one had died and the other moved away.

The Cooks had really settled in. Spring brought sunshine and longer days; and it also brought the first symptoms of Mr. Cook's strange illness.

At first the trouble seemed to be his eyesight. He complained of a kind of brownish fog between himself and the television screen. He couldn't see clearly enough to enjoy the programs. He thought he noticed that this fogginess was worse when he was doing daylight viewing, at the weekends or in the early evening. He tried to deal with this by drawing the curtains in the room where the set was on, but the fogginess persisted.

Mr. Cook went to the optician to see whether he needed glasses. The optician applied all the usual tests, and said that Mr. Cook's vision seemed excellent. Mr. Cook said it wasn't — or, at least, sometimes wasn't. The optician said that eyesight could be affected by a person's state of general health, and suggested that, if the trouble continued, Mr. Cook should consult a doctor.

Mr. Cook was annoyed at the time he had wasted at the optician's, and went home to try to enjoy his favorite Saturday afternoon program. Not only did he suffer from increased fogginess of vision, but — perhaps as a result, perhaps not — he developed a splitting headache. In the end he switched the set off and went outside and savagely dug in the garden, uprooting ground elder, nettle, twitch and a great number of other weed species. By tea-time he had cleared a large patch, in which Judy at once sowed radishes and mustard and cress.

At the end of an afternoon's digging, the headache had gone. Mr. Cook was also able to watch the late night movie on television without discomfort. But his Saturday as a whole had been ruined; and when he went to bed, his sleep was troubled by strange dreams, and on Sunday morning he woke at first light. This had become the pattern of his sleeping recently: haunted dreams and early wakings. On this particular occasion, as often before, he couldn't get to sleep again; and he spent the rest of Sunday — a breezy, sunny day — moving restlessly about indoors from Sunday paper to television set, saying he felt awful.

Mrs. Cook said that perhaps he ought to see a doctor, as the optician had advised; Mr. Cook shouted at her that he wouldn't.

But, as spring turned to summer, it became clear that something would have to be done. Mr. Cook's condition was worsening. He gave up trying to watch television. Regularly he got up at sunrise because he couldn't sleep longer and couldn't even rest in bed. (Sometimes he went out and dug in the garden; and, when he did so, the exertion or the fresh air seemed to make him feel better, at least for the time being.) He lost his appetite; and he was always irritable with his children. He grumbled at Mike for being out so much on his bicycle, and he grumbled at Judy for being at home. Her investigations no longer amused him at all. Judy had pointed out that his illness seemed to vary with the weather: fine days made it worse. She wondered why. Her father said he'd give her *why*, if she weren't careful.

At last Mrs. Cook burst out that she could stand this no longer: "Arthur, you *must* go to the doctor." As though he had only been waiting for someone to insist, Mr. Cook agreed.

The doctor listened carefully to Mr. Cook's account of his symptoms and examined him thoroughly. He asked whether he smoked and whether he ate enough roughage. Reassured on both these points, the doctor said he thought Mr. Cook's condition might be the result of nervous tension. "Anything worrying you?" asked the doctor.

"Of course, there is!" exploded Mr. Cook. "I'm ill, aren't I? I'm worried sick about that!"

The doctor asked if there was anything else that Mr. Cook worried about: His wife? His children? His job?

"I lie awake in the morning and worry about them all," said Mr. Cook. "And about that huge garden in that awful state . . ."

"What garden?"

"Our garden. It's huge and it's been let go wild and I ought to get it in order, I suppose, and — oh, I don't know! I'm no gardener."

"Perhaps you shouldn't have a garden that size," suggested the doctor. "Perhaps you should consider moving into a house with no garden, or at least a really manageable one. Somewhere, say, with just a patio, in Walchester."

"That's what we moved *from*," said Mr. Cook. "Less than six months ago."

"Oh, dear!" said the doctor. He called Mrs. Cook into the surgery[2] and suggested that her husband might be suffering from overwork. Mr. Cook was struck by the idea; Mrs. Cook less so. The doctor suggested a week off, to see what *that* would do.

That week marked the climax of Mr. Cook's illness; it drove Mrs. Cook nearly out of her wits, and Judy to urgent inquiries.

The week came at the very beginning of June, an ideal month in which to try to recover from overwork. Judy and Mike were at school all day, so that everything was quiet at home for their father. The sun shone, and Mr. Cook planned to sit outside in a deckchair and catch up on lost sleep. Then, when the children came home, he would go to bed early with the portable television set. (He assumed that rest would be dealing with fogginess of vision.)

Things did not work out like that at all. During that week Mr. Cook was seized with a terrible restlessness. It seemed impossible for him to achieve any repose at all. He tried only once to watch television;

---

[2]**surgery** (sûr′jə rē): a doctor's office.

and Judy noticed that thereafter he seemed almost — yes, he seemed afraid. He was a shadow of his former self when, at the end of the week, he went back to work.

After he had left the house that morning, Mrs. Cook spoke her fears: "It'll be the hospital next, I know. And once they begin injecting and cutting up — Oh, why did we ever come to live here!"

"You think it's something to do with the house?" asked Judy. Mike had already set off to school; she lingered.

"Well, your dad was perfectly all right before. I'd say there was something wrong with the drains here, but there's no smell; and, anyway, why should only he fall ill?"

"There is something wrong with the house," said Judy. "I couldn't ask the Johnsons about it, so I asked the Cribbles."

"The Cribbles! That we bought the house from?"

"Yes. They live the other side of Walchester. I went there —"

"Oh, Judy!" said her mother. "You'll get yourself into trouble with your questions, one of these days."

"No, I shan't," said Judy (and she never did). "I went to ask them about this house. I rang at the front door, and Mrs. Cribble answered it. At least, I think it must have been her. She was quite nice. I told her my name, but I don't think she connected me with buying the house from them. Then I asked her about the house, whether *they* had noticed anything."

"And what did she say?"

"She didn't say anything. She slammed the door in my face."

"Oh, Judy!" cried Mrs. Cook, and burst into tears.

Her mother's tears decided Judy: she would beard[3] Mr. Biley himself, of Ketch, Robb and Biley. She was not so innocent as to suppose he would grant her, a child, an official interview. But if she could

---

[3]**beard** (bîrd): to face someone boldly.

buttonhole[4] him somewhere, she might get from him at least one useful piece of information.

After school that day, Judy presented herself at the offices of Ketch, Robb and Biley in Walchester. She had her deception ready. "Has my father been in to see Mr. Biley yet?" she asked. That sounded respectable. The receptionist said that Mr. Biley was talking with a client at present, and that she really couldn't say —

"I'll wait," said Judy, like a good girl.

Judy waited. She was prepared to wait until the offices shut at half past five, when Mr. Biley would surely leave to go home; but much earlier than that, Mr. Biley came downstairs with someone who was evidently rather an important client. Mr. Biley escorted him to the door, chatting in the jovial way that Judy remembered so well. They said good-bye at the door, and parted, and Mr. Biley started back by the way he had come.

Judy caught up with him, laid a hand on his arm: "Mr. Biley — please!"

Mr. Biley turned. He did not recognize Judy. He smiled. "Yes, young lady?"

"We bought Southcroft from the Cribbles," she began.

Mr. Biley's smile vanished instantly. He said, "I should make clear at once that Ketch, Robb and Biley will not, under any circumstances, handle that property again."

"Why?" asked Judy. She couldn't help asking.

"The sale of the same property three times in eighteen months may bring income to us, but it does not bring reputation. So I wish you good day."

Judy said, "*Please*, I only need to ask you one thing, really." She gripped the cloth of his sleeve. The receptionist had looked up to see what

---

[4]**buttonhole** (bŭt′n hōl′): to stop someone and make him listen.

400

was going on, and Mr. Biley was aware of that. "Well? Be quick," he said.

"Before the Cribbles and the Johnsons, there were the Baxters: when old Mr. Baxter died, where did Mrs. Baxter move to?"

"Into Senior House, Waddington Road." He removed Judy's fingers from his coat sleeve. "Remember to tell your father *not* to call in Ketch, Robb and Biley for the resale of the property. Good-bye."

It was getting late, but Judy thought she should finish the job. She found a telephone booth and the right money and rang her mother to say she was calling on Mrs. Baxter in the Old People's apartments in Waddington Road. She was glad that her telephone-time ran out before her mother could say much in reply.

Then she set off for Waddington Road.

By the time she reached the apartments, Judy felt tired, thirsty, hungry. There was no problem about seeing Mrs. Baxter. The porter told her the number of Mrs. Baxter's apartment, and said Mrs. Baxter would probably be starting her tea. The residents had just finished seeing a film on mountaineering in the Alps, and — as he put it — would be brewing up late.

Judy found the door and knocked. A delicious smell of hot-buttered toast seemed to be coming through the keyhole. A thin little voice told her to come in. And there sat Mrs. Baxter behind a tea-pot with a cosy on it, in the act of spreading honey on a piece of buttered toast.

"Oh," said Judy, faintly.

Mrs. Baxter was delighted to have a visitor. "Sit down, dear, and I'll get another cup and saucer and plate."

She was such a nice little old woman, with gingery-grey hair — she wore a gingery dress almost to match — and rather dark pop-eyes. She seemed active, but a bit slow. When she got up in a slow, plump way to get the extra china, Judy was reminded of a hamster she had once had, called Pickles.

Mrs. Baxter got the china and some biscuits[5] and poured out another cup of tea. All this without asking Judy her name or her business.

"Sugar?" asked Mrs. Baxter.

---

[5]**biscuits** (bĭs′kĭts): cookies.

"Yes, please," said Judy. "I'm Judy Cook, Mrs. Baxter."

"Oh, yes? I'll have to get the tin of sugar. I don't take sugar myself, you know."

She waddled over to some shelves. She had her back to Judy, but Judy could see the little hamster-hands reaching up to a tin marked *Sugar*.

"Mrs. Baxter, we live in the house you used to live in: Southcroft."

The hamster-hands never reached the sugar tin, but stayed up in the air for as long as it might have taken Judy to count ten. It was as though the name Southcroft had turned the little hamster-woman to stone.

Then the hands came down slowly, and Mrs. Baxter waddled back to the tea-table. She did not look at Judy; her face was expressionless.

"Have a biscuit?" she said to Judy.

Judy took one. "Mrs. Baxter, I've come to ask you about Southcroft."

"Don't forget your cup of tea, dear."

"No, I won't. Mrs. Baxter, I must ask you several things —"

"Just a minute, dear."

"Yes?"

"Perhaps you take sugar in your tea?"

"Yes, I do, but it doesn't matter. I'd rather you'd let me ask you —"

"But it does matter," said Mrs. Baxter firmly. "And I shall get the sugar for you. I don't take it myself, you know."

Judy had had dreams when she had tried to do something and could not because things — the same things — happened over and over again to prevent her. Now she watched Mrs. Baxter waddle over to the shelves, watched the little hamster-hands reach up to the sugar tin and — this time — bring it down and bring it back to the tea-table. Judy sugared her tea, and took another biscuit, and began eating and drinking. She was trying to steady herself and fortify herself for what she now realized was going to be very, very difficult. Mrs. Baxter had begun telling her about mountaineering in the Alps. The little voice went on and on, until Judy thought it must wear out.

It paused.

Judy said swiftly, "Tell me about Southcroft, please. What was it like to live in when you were there? Why is it so awful now?"

"No, dear," said Mrs. Baxter hurriedly. "I'd rather go on telling you about the Matterhorn."

"I want to know about Southcroft," cried Judy.

"No," said Mrs. Baxter. "I never talk about it. Never. I'll go on about the Matterhorn."

"Please. You must tell me about Southcroft." Judy was insisting, but she knew she was being beaten by the soft little old woman. She found she was beginning to cry. "Please, Mrs. Baxter. My dad's ill with living there."

"Oh, no," cried the little hamster-woman. "Oh, no, he couldn't be!"

"He is," said Judy, "and you won't help!" Stumblingly she began to get up.

"Won't you stay, dear, and hear about the Matterhorn?"

"No!" Judy tried to put her cup back on the dainty tea-table, but couldn't see properly for her tears. China fell, broke, as she turned from the table. She found the handle of the door and let herself out.

"Oh dear, oh dear, oh dear!" the little voice behind her was crying, but whether it was about the broken china or something else it was impossible to say.

Judy ran down the long passages and past the porter, who stared at her tear-wet face. When she got outside, she ran and ran, and then walked and walked. She knew she could have caught a bus home, but she didn't want to. She walked all the way, arriving nearly at dusk, to find her mother waiting anxiously for her. But, instead of questioning

Judy at once, Mrs. Cook drew her into the kitchen, where they were alone. Mike was in the sitting-room, watching a noisy television program.

Mrs. Cook said, "Your dad telephoned from Walchester soon after you did. He said he wasn't feeling very well, so he's spending the night with your Aunt Edie."

They stared at each other. Mr. Cook detested his sister Edie. "He'd do anything rather than come here," said Judy. "He's afraid."

Mrs. Cook nodded.

"Mum, we'll just have to move from here, for Dad's sake."

"I don't know that we can, Judy. Selling one house and buying another is very expensive; moving is expensive."

"But if we stay here . . ."

Mrs. Cook hesitated; then, "Judy, what you were doing this afternoon — your calling on old Mrs. Baxter — was it any use, any help?"

"No."

Mrs. Cook groaned aloud.

Judy's visit to Mrs. Baxter had not led to the answering of any questions; but there was an outcome.

The next day, in the afternoon, Judy and Mike had come home from school and were in the kitchen with their mother. It was a gloomy tea. There was no doubt at all that their father would come home this time — after all, here were his wife and his children that he loved — but the homecoming seemed likely to be a grim and hopeless one.

From the kitchen they heard the click of the front gate. This was far too early to be Mr. Cook himself, and, besides, there'd been no sound of a car. Mike, nearest to the window, looked out. "No one we know," he reported. "An old lady." He laughed to himself. "She looks like a hamster."

Judy was at the front door and opening it before Mrs. Baxter had had time to ring. She brought her in and introduced her to the others, and Mrs. Cook brewed fresh tea while the children made her comfortable in the sitting-room. Besides her handbag, Mrs. Baxter was carrying a dumpy zip-up case which seemed heavy; she kept it by her. She was tired. "Buses!" she murmured.

Mrs. Cook brought her a cup of tea.

"Mrs. Baxter doesn't take sugar, Mum," said Judy.

They all sat round Mrs. Baxter, trying not to stare at her, waiting for her to speak. She sipped her tea without looking at them.

"Your husband's not very well, I hear," she said at last to Mrs. Cook. "No."

"Not home from work yet?"

"Not yet."

Mrs. Baxter was obviously relieved. She looked at them all now. "And this is the rest of the family . . ." She smiled timidly at Mike: "You're the baby of the family?"

Mike said, "I'm younger than Judy. Mum, if it's O.K., I think I'll go out on my bike with Charlie Feather." He took something to eat and went.

Mrs. Baxter said, "We never had children."

"A pity," said Mrs. Cook.

"Yes. Everything would be different, if it had been different." Mrs. Baxter paused. "Do you know, I've never been back to this house — not even to the village — since Mr. Baxter died."

"It was very sad for you," said Mrs. Cook, not knowing what else to say.

"It's been a terrible *worry*," said Mrs. Baxter, as though sadness was not the thing that mattered. Again she paused. Judy could see that she was nerving herself to say something important. She had been brave and resolute to come all this way at all.

Mrs. Cook could also see what Judy saw. "You must be tired out," she said.

But Judy said gently, "Why've you come?"

Mrs. Baxter tried to speak, couldn't. Instead she opened the zip-up bag and dragged out of it a large, heavy book: *The Vegetable and Fruit Grower's Encyclopaedia and Vade-Mecum.* She pushed it into Mrs. Cook's lap. "It was Mr. Baxter's," she said. "Give it to your husband. Tell him to use it and work hard in the garden, and I think things will right themselves in time. You need to humor him."

Mrs. Cook was bewildered. She seized upon the last remark: "I humor him as much as I can, as it is. He's been so unwell."

Mrs. Baxter tittered. "Good gracious, I didn't mean *your* husband: I meant mine. Humor Mr. Baxter."

"But — but he's dead and gone!"

Mrs. Baxter's eyes filled with tears. "That's just it: he isn't. Not both. He's dead, but not gone. He never meant to go. I knew what he intended; I knew the wickedness of it. I told him — I begged him on his deathbed; but he wouldn't listen. You know that bit of the burial service: 'We brought nothing into this world, and it is certain that we can carry nothing out'? Well, there was something he'd dearly have liked to have taken out: he couldn't, so he stayed in this world with it: his garden. We were both good church-goers, but I believe he set his vegetable garden before his God. I know that he set it before me." She wept afresh.

"Oh, dear, Mrs. Baxter!" said Mrs. Cook, much distressed.

"When he was dying," said Mrs. Baxter, after she had blown her nose, "I could see there was something he wanted to say. I'd been reading the Twenty-third Psalm to him — you know, about the Valley of the Shadow of Death. He was trying to speak. I leant right over him and he managed to whisper his very last words. He said, 'Are the runner beans up yet?' Then he died."

Nobody spoke. Mrs. Baxter recovered herself and went on.

"I knew — I *knew* he wouldn't leave that garden, after he'd died. I just hoped the next owners would look after it as lovingly as he'd done, and then in time he'd be content to go. That's what I hoped and prayed. But the first lot of people were going to cover it with dog-kennels, and I heard that the second lot were going to lay it out with artificial streams and weeping willows and things. Well, he made their lives a misery, and they left. And now your husband . . ."

"He's just never liked gardening," said Mrs. Cook.

The two women stared at each other bleakly.

"Why can't Dad be allowed to watch TV?" asked Judy. Then, answering herself: "Oh, I see: he ought to be working in the garden every spare minute in daylight and fine weather."

"Mr. Baxter quite enjoyed some of the gardening programs, sometimes," Mrs. Baxter said defensively.

There was a long silence.

"It's lovely soil," said Mrs. Baxter persuasively. "Easy to work. Grows anything. That's why we came to live here, really. All my married life, I never had to buy a single vegetable. Fruit, too — raspberries, strawberries, gooseberries, all colors of currants. So much of everything, for just the two of us, that we had to give a lot of stuff away. We didn't grow plums or pears or apples — except for the Bramleys — because Mr. Baxter wouldn't have trees shading the garden. But all those vegetables — you'd find it a great saving, with a family."

"It seems hard on my husband," said Mrs. Cook.

"It's hard on mine," said Mrs. Baxter. "Look at him!" Startled, Mrs. Cook and Judy looked where Mrs. Baxter was looking, through the French windows and down the length of the garden. The sun fell on the weedy earth of the garden; on nothing else.

Mrs. Cook turned her gaze back into the room, but Judy went on looking, staring until her eyes blurred and her vision was fogged with a kind of brown fogginess that was in the garden. Then suddenly she was afraid.

"But *look!*" said Mrs. Baxter, and took Judy's hand in her own little paw that had grown soft and smooth from leisure in Senior House:

"*Look!*" Judy looked where she pointed, and the brown fogginess seemed to concentrate itself and shape itself, and there dimly was the shape of an old man dressed in brown from his brown boots to his battered brown hat, with a piece of string tied around the middle of the old brown waterproof he was wearing. He stood in an attitude of dejection at the bottom of the garden, looking at the weeds.

Then Mrs. Baxter let go of Judy's hand, and Judy saw him no more.

"That was his garden mac," said Mrs. Baxter. "He would wear it. When all the buttonholes had gone, as well as the buttons, and I wouldn't repair it any more, then he belted it on with string."

"He looked so miserable," said Judy. She had been feeling sorry for her father; now she began to feel sorry for Mr. Baxter.

"Yes," said Mrs. Baxter. "He'd like to go, I've no doubt of it; but he can't leave the garden in that state." She sighed. She gathered up her handbag and the other empty bag.

"Don't go!" cried Mrs. Cook and Judy together.

"What more can I do? I've told you; I've advised you. For *his* sake, too, I've begged you. No, I can't do more."

She would not stay. She waddled out of the house and down the front path, and at the front gate met Mr. Cook. He had just got out of the car. She gave him a scared little bob of a "good-day," and scuttled past him and away.

Mr. Cook came in wearily; his face was greyish. "Who was that old dear?" he asked. But he did not really want to know.

His wife said to him, "Arthur, Judy is going to get your tea — Won't you, love? — while I explain a lot of things. Come and sit down and listen."

Mrs. Cook talked and Mr. Cook listened, and gradually his face began to change: something lifted from it, leaving it clear, almost happy, for the first time for many weeks. He was still listening when Judy brought his tea. At the end of Mrs. Cook's explanation, Judy added hers: she told her father what — *whom* — she had seen in the garden, when Mrs. Baxter had held her hand. Mr. Cook began to laugh. "You

saw him, Judy? An old man all in brown with a piece of string tied round his middle — oh, Judy, my girl! When I began really seeing him, only the other day, I was sure I was going off my rocker! I was scared! I thought I was seeing things that no one else could see — things that weren't there at all! And you've seen him too, and he's just old man Baxter!" And Mr. Cook laughed so much that he cried, and in the end he put his head down among the tea-things and sobbed and sobbed.

It was going to be all right, after all.

In Mr. Baxter's old-fashioned mind, the man of the family was the one to do all the gardening. That was why, in what Judy considered a very unfair way, he had made a dead set at[6] her father. But now all Mr. Cook's family rallied to him. Even Mike, when the need was explained, left his bicycle for a while. They all helped in the garden. They dug and weeded and made bonfires of the worst weeds and began to build a compost heap of harmless garden rubbish. They planted seeds if it were not too late in the season, and bought plants when it was. Mr. Cook followed the advice of the *Encyclopaedia*, and occasionally had excellent ideas of his own. When Judy asked him where he got them, he looked puzzled at himself and said he did not know. But she could guess.

Every spare moment that was daylight and fine, Mr. Cook worked in the garden; and his illness was cured. His appetite came back; he slept like a top; and he would have enjoyed television again except that, in the middle of programs, he so often fell asleep from healthy exhaustion.

Well over a year later, on a holiday jaunt in Walchester, Judy was passing one of the cinemas. An audience mainly of Senior Citizens was coming out from an afternoon showing of *Deadly Amazon*. Judy felt a touch on her arm, soft yet insistent, like the voice that spoke, Mrs. Baxter's: "My dear, how — how is he?"

"Oh, Mrs. Baxter, he's much, much better! Oh, thank you! He's really all right. My mum says my dad's as well as she's ever known him."

---

[6]**make a dead set at:** to aim yourself directly at someone.

"No, dear, I didn't mean your father. How is *he* — Mr. Baxter?"

Judy said, "We think he's gone. Dad hasn't seen the foggiest wisp of him for months; and Dad says it doesn't *feel* as if he's there any more. You see, Dad's got the garden going wonderfully now. We've had early potatoes and beans and peas — oh, and raspberries — and Dad plans to grow asparagus —"

"Ah," said Mrs. Baxter. "No wonder Mr. Baxter's gone. Gone off pleased, no doubt. That *is* nice. I don't think you need worry about his coming back. He has enough sense not to. It won't be long before your father can safely give up gardening, if he likes."

"I'll tell him what you say," Judy said doubtfully.

But, of course, it was too late. Once a gardener, always a gardener. "I'll never give up now," Mr. Cook said. "I'll be a gardener until my dying day."

"But not after that, Arthur," said his wife. "Please."

the
end

Responding to "The Strange Illness of Mr. Arthur Cook"

Thinking and Discussing

Which of Mr. Cook's symptoms suggest that his illness was caused by something outside reality?

How do the different members of the Cook family feel about Mr. Baxter? Why does each person feel that way?

Think about Mr. Cook at the beginning and at the end of the story. In what way does he change and why?

Choosing a Creative Response

Tracing Judy's Investigation When Judy begins to suspect that something about the house is making her father ill, she carries out a well-ordered investigation to find out the cause. Make a list or chart of the steps she takes and the clues she obtains at each step. Where and when do you think she first suspects that the cause is something beyond everyday reality? You may want to sketch a map or diagram of her travels with an X to mark that place.

Describing a Family Effort Describe a situation in which a family works together to accomplish a goal, as Mr. Cook's family helps him to regain his health. Explain why help is needed, and describe the contribution each family member makes. Evaluate whether the family's effort is successful.

Creating Your Own Activity Plan and complete your own activity in response to "The Strange Illness of Mr. Arthur Cook."

Thinking and Writing

Write a letter to Mr. Cook's doctor from Judy, telling about the strange pattern of Mr. Cook's illness and dreams. Ask for the doctor's help in solving the mystery.

Discovery consists of
seeing what everybody has
seen and thinking what
nobody has thought.

Albert Szent-Györgyi

The False Mirror by René Magritte, 1928, oil on canvas

Writing AN ANALYSIS

What would you do if you were to encounter a ghost in your garden? What would happen if you were to find a pair of magical glasses? What would you do if you were able to travel through time?

As you read the stories in "Hall of Mirrors," note the story elements that are based on fantasy. Think about what would happen if one or more of those elements could exist in real life. Then write an analysis that points out and explains the changes that would occur in the world as we know it if fantasy were to become reality.

In your analysis, use sound reasoning to explain the effects of introducing one or more fantasy elements into the real world. Present logical arguments to support your ideas about the people and places that might be affected.

Begin writing whenever you are ready. If the stories give you another writing idea, try that one instead.

1. Prewriting

Before you begin writing, choose the fantastic story elements that you think are most fascinating — perhaps things you *wish* would come true. Consider the effects on you, your family, your neighborhood, your town, and the world. Jot down your ideas.

2. Write a First Draft

As you begin writing, think carefully about your audience and your purpose for writing. Analyze the situation you are presenting, and organize your ideas clearly.

3. *Revise*

Read your analysis to a partner. Identify ways in which it can be improved. Have you looked at the situation from all angles? Are your thoughts well organized? Make any necessary changes.

4. *Proofread*

Check your analysis for correct spelling, capitalization, and punctuation.

5. *Publish*

Make a neat copy of your analysis. You may wish to add illustrations that show fantasy becoming reality. Share your analysis with your classmates.

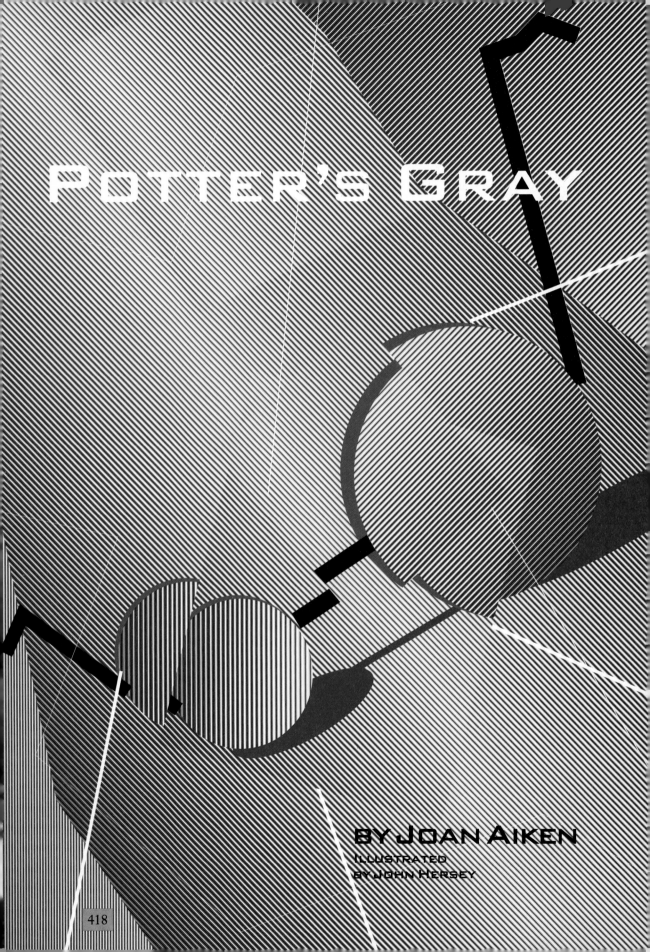

POTTER'S GRAY

BY JOAN AIKEN

ILLUSTRATED
BY JOHN HERSEY

They were hurrying through the cold, windy streets of Paris to the Louvre[1] Museum — young Grig Rainborrow, and the au pair[2] girl, Anna. They visited the Louvre two or three times every week. Grig would far rather have gone to one of the parks, or walked along by the river, but Anna had an arrangement to meet her boyfriend, Eugène, in the Louvre; so that was where they went.

Alongside one of the big main galleries, where hung huge pictures of battles and shipwrecks and coronations, there ran a linked series of much smaller rooms containing smaller pictures. Here visitors seldom troubled to go; often the little, rather dark rooms would be empty and quiet for a half hour at a time. Anna and Eugène liked to sit side by side, holding hands, on a couple of stiff upright metal chairs, while Grig had leave to roam at will through the nest of little rooms; though Anna tended to get fidgety if he wandered too far away, and would call him back in a cross voice, "Grig! Grig, where are you? Where have you got to? Come back here now!" She worried about kidnapers, because of the importance of Grig's father, Sir Mark. Grig would then trail back reluctantly, and Eugène would grin at him, a wide, unkind grin, and say, *"Venez vite, petit mouton!"*[3] Grig did not like being called a sheep, and he detested Eugène, who had large untrustworthy mocking black eyes, like olives; they were set so far apart in his face that they seemed able to see around the back of his head. He had a wide, oddly shaped mouth; his curling lips were thick and strongly curved like the crusts of farmhouse bread, and his mouth was always twisting about; it never kept still. Grig had once made some drawings of Eugène's mouth, but they looked so nasty that he tore them up before Anna could see them; he thought they might make her angry.

---

[1]**Louvre:** the former residence of the kings of France, now a famous museum of fine arts.
[2]**au pair:** a mother's helper.
[3]**"Venez vite, petit mouton!":** "Hurry up, little sheep!"

"Hurry up!" said Anna, jerking at Grig's hand. "We're going to be late. Eugène will be waiting; he'll be annoyed." Grig did not see why it would hurt Eugène to wait a few minutes, he never seemed to have anything to do but meet Anna in the Louvre museum. That was where they had met in the first place.

Standing waiting to cross the Rue de Rivoli at a traffic light, Grig was sorry that he lacked the courage to say, "Why do we have to meet hateful Eugène almost every day?"

But he knew that his courage was not up to that. Anna could be quite fierce. She had intense blue eyes the color of marbles, but they weren't very good for observing. Grig noticed a million more things than Anna did, he was always saying, "Look, Anna —" And she would say, "Oh, never mind that! Come along!" But the stare of her eyes was so piercing when she lost her temper, they were like two gimlets boring right through him, and she had such a way of hissing, "You *stupid* child!" making him feel pulpy, breathless, and flattened, that he did not say what he felt about Eugène. He kept quiet and waited for the lights to change, while French traffic poured furiously past in a torrent of steel, rubber, and glass.

"Come on! There's a gap — we can go," said Anna, and jerked at Grig's hand again.

They hurled themselves out, in company with a French girl who had a small child in a stroller and, bounding on the end of his lead, a large Alsatian dog that the girl could only just control. As they crossed, the stroller veered one way, the dog tugged the other — it seemed

amazing that the trio had survived among the traffic up to this day. A tall thin white-haired man in pink-tinted glasses observed their plight, and turned to give the girl a helping hand with her wayward stroller; a sharp gust of wind blew just at that moment, the dog tugged, the stroller swerved crazily, and the pink-tinted glasses were jerked off the man's face to spin away into the middle of the road, just as a new wave of traffic surged forward.

With a cry of anguish, the white-haired man tilted the stroller over the curb, hurriedly passing its handle into the mother's grasp, and then turned back to retrieve his glasses. Too late — and a terrible

mistake: a motorcyclist, twisting aside to avoid him, collided with a taxi, and a Citroën[4] following too close behind the cycle struck the elderly man on the shoulder and flung him onto the sidewalk, where he lay on his face without moving.

If he had been wearing his glasses at that moment, they would have been smashed, Grig thought.

The mother with the stroller let out a horrified wail, *"Oh, oh, c'est le vieux Professeur Bercy!"*[5] and she ran to kneel by him, while, out in the road, all was confusion, with brakes squawking and horns braying, and a general tangle and snarl of traffic coming too suddenly to a stop.

Police, blowing their whistles, were on the spot in no time — there are always plenty of police near the Louvre.

"Come along, Grig!" snapped Anna. "We don't want to get mixed up in all this, your father wouldn't be a bit pleased —" for Sir Mark, Grig's father, was the British Ambassador in Paris. But it wasn't easy to get away; already the police were swarming around, asking everybody there if they had seen the accident.

"Oh, I do *hope* the poor man is not badly hurt!" cried the distraught young mother. "It is Professor Bercy, the physicist — I have often seen his face in the papers and on TV — It was so kind of him to

---

[4]**Citroën:** a French car.
[5]**"C'est le vieux Professeur Bercy!":** "It's old Professor Bercy."

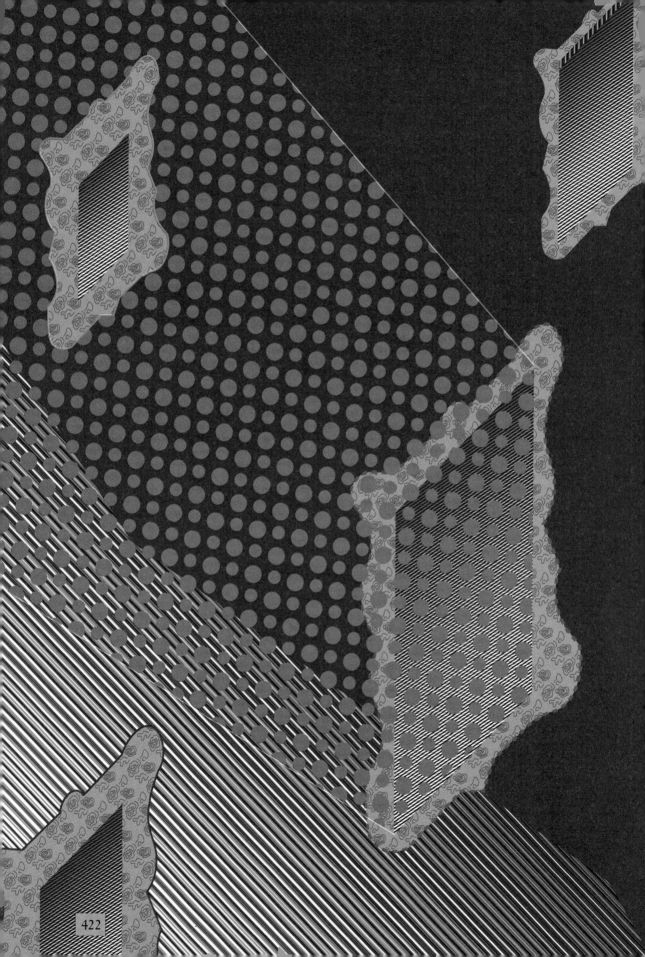

take my baby carriage — oh, it will be terrible if he is badly injured, and all because he stopped to help me —"

A gendarme[6] was talking to Anna, and, while she snappishly but accurately gave an account of what had happened, Grig slipped out into the street and picked up the professor's glasses, which he had noticed lying — astonishingly, quite unharmed — about six feet out from the edge of the road, among a glittering sprinkle of somebody's smashed windshield.

"*Grig! Will* you come out of there!" yelled Anna, turning from the cop to see where he had got to, and she yanked his arm and hustled him away in the direction of the Louvre entrance, across the big quadrangle, before he could do anything about giving the pink-tinted glasses to one of the policemen.

"But I've got these —"

"Oh, who cares? The man's probably dead, he won't want them again. If he hears that you got mixed up in a street accident your father will be hopping mad. And Eugène will be upset — he'll be wondering where we've got to."

It seemed to Grig that the last of these three statements was the real reason why Anna didn't want to hang around at the scene of the accident. He pulled back from her grasp and twisted his head round to see if an ambulance had arrived yet; yes, there it went, shooting across the end of the square with flashing lights. So at least the poor man would soon be in the hospital.

Well, it was true that if he was unconscious — and he had looked dreadfully limp — he wouldn't be needing his glasses right away.

Maybe he only wore them outdoors.

I'll ask mother to see that he gets them, Grig decided. She'll be able to find out which hospital he has gone to, and make sure that the glasses are taken to him. Mother was fine at things like that; she always knew what must be done, and who was the best person to do it. She understood what was important. And — Grig thought — the glasses

---

[6]**gendarme:** a police officer.

must be *very* important to Professor Bercy, or he would hardly have risked his life in the traffic to try to recover them. Could they be his only pair? Surely not. If he was such an important scientist, you'd think he'd have dozens of pairs!

The glasses were now in Grig's jacket pocket, safely cradled in his left hand; the right hand was still in the iron grip of Anna, who was hauling him along as if the Deluge[7] had begun and they were the last two passengers for the Ark.

Eugène was there before them, waiting in the usual room; but, surprisingly, he didn't seem annoyed at their lateness, just listened to Anna's breathless explanation with his wide frog-smile, said it was quite a little excitement they'd had, and did the man bleed a lot? Then, even

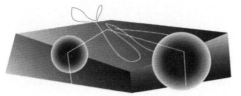

more surprisingly, he produced a small patissier's[8] cardboard carton, tied with shiny string, and said to Grig,

"Here, *mon mouton*, this is for you. For your *petit manger*. A cake."

Grig generally brought an apple to the Louvre. Indeed, he had one today, in his right-hand pocket. Eugène called the apple Grig's *petit manger* — his little snack. While Anna and Eugène sat and talked, Grig was in the habit of eating his apple slowly and inconspicuously, as he walked around looking at the pictures.

"Go on," repeated Eugène. "The cake's for you."

Grig did not want to appear rude or doubtful or suspicious at this unexpected gift; but just the same he *was* suspicious. Eugène had never before showed any friendly feelings; the things he said to Grig were generally sharp or spiteful or teasing; why, today, should he have brought this piece of patisserie — rather expensive it looked, too, done up so carefully with a gold name on the side of the box. Eugène was

---

[7]**Deluge** (dĕl'yōoj): the great Flood referred to in the Bible.
[8]**patissier's:** belonging to a baker of cakes and other pastries.

always shabby, in worn jeans and a rubbed black-leather jacket, and his sneakers looked as if they let in the water. Why should he suddenly bring out such an offering?

"Say thank you!" snapped Anna. "It's very kind of Eugène to have brought you a cake!"

"Thank you," said Grig. He added doubtfully, "But I don't think people are allowed to eat in here."

"Oh, don't be silly. Who's going to see? Anyway, you always eat your apple — here, I'll undo the string."

It was tied in a hopelessly tight, hard knot — Anna nibbled through it with her strong white teeth, and Eugène made some low-voiced remark, in French too quick for Grig to catch, which made her flush and laugh, though she looked rather cross. Once the string was undone, the little waxed box opened out like a lily to disclose a gooey glistening brown cake in a fluted paper cup.

"Aren't you lucky; it's a rum baba," said Anna.

As it happened, a rum baba was Grig's least favorite kind of cake: too syrupy, too squashy, too scented. He wasn't greatly surprised, or disappointed; he would have expected Eugène to have a nasty taste in cakes, or anything else. He thanked Eugène again, with great politeness, then strolled away from the pair at a slow, casual pace, looking at the pictures on the walls as he went.

"Eat that up fast, now, or it'll drip syrup all over everywhere," Anna called after him sharply, and then she began talking to Eugène, telling him some long story, gabbling it out, while he listened without seeming to take in much of what she said, his eyes roving after Grig,

who wandered gently into the next room, and then into the one after that, wondering, as he went, if it would be possible to slip the pastry into a litter bin without being noticed.

"Don't go too far now —" he could hear Anna's voice, fainter in the distance behind him.

As usual, there weren't any other people in the suite of small dark

rooms. Grig supposed that the pictures here were not thought to be very important, though some of them were his particular favorites.

There was one of an astronomer with a globe; Grig always liked to look at that; and another of a woman making lace on a pillow; she wore a yellow dress, and had a contented, absorbed expression that reminded Grig of his mother while she was working on her embroidery. There was a picture that he liked of a bowl and a silver mug, with some apples; and another of a china jug with bunches of grapes and a cut-up pomegranate that he deeply admired. Grig intended to be a painter himself by and by; he always stood before this picture for a long, long time, wondering how many years it took to learn to paint like that — so that you could actually see the bloom on the grapes and the shine on the pearl handle of the knife, and the glisten on the red seeds of the pomegranate. Then there was a picture of a boy about Grig's age, sitting at a desk, playing with a spinning top. The boy was really a bit old to be playing with a childish toy such as a top; you could see that he had just come across it, maybe among some forgotten things at the back of his desk, and had taken it out to give it a spin because he was bored and had nothing better to do just then; he was watching it thoughtfully, consideringly, in fact he had the same intent expression as that on the face of the woman working at the lace on her pillow. Perhaps, thought Grig, that boy grew up to be some kind of scientist or mathematician (he must have lived long ago, for he wore an old-fashioned satin jacket) and at the sight of the spinning top, some interesting idea about speed or circles or patterns or time had come into his head. The boy with the top was one of Grig's favorite pictures, and he always stood in front of it for quite a while.

Then he was about to move on to his very favorite of all, when his attention was caught by an old lady, who had been walking through the rooms in the contrary direction. She paused beside Grig and glanced out through the window into the big central courtyard. What she saw there seemed to surprise her very much and arouse her disapproval too. She let out several exclamations — *"Oh, la la! Tiens! Quel horreur!"*[9] — put on a pair of long-distance glasses to take a better look at what was going on outside, stared frowningly for a moment or two more, then muttered some grumbling comment to herself, in which Grig caught several references to Napoleon III; then, shaking her head in a condemning manner, she went stomping on her way. After waiting until she was out of sight, Grig put a knee on the leather window seat and hoisted himself up to look out, in order to see what was happening outside that aroused such feelings of outrage in the old girl.

What he saw in the quadrangle made him surprised that he had not noticed it as they made their way in; but he remembered that then he had been looking back for the ambulance, and worrying about Professor Bercy's glasses; that must have been why he did not take in the oddness of the scene.

A wooden barricade had been built around the central part of the quadrangle, and it seemed that digging was going on inside this fence, a big excavator with its grabbing jaw could be seen swinging its head back and forth, dumping soil and rubble in a truck that stood by the paling.

Then, outside the barrier — and this was probably what had shocked the old lady — three fullsize chestnut trees lay, crated up, on huge towing trucks, the sort that usually carry heavy machinery, or sardinelike batches of new cars. The trees all had their leaves on, and

---

[9]**"Oh, la la! Tiens! Quel horreur!":** "Oh! Look at that! What a shame!"

their roots too; the roots had been carefully bundled up in great cylindrical containers made from wooden slats — like flower tubs, only a million times bigger, Grig thought. It appeared that the trees had been dug up from the central area and were being taken away, perhaps to be replanted somewhere else, just like geraniums or begonias in the public gardens. What on earth could Napoleon III have to do with it? Grig wondered, thinking of the old lady. Had he planted the trees, perhaps? They looked as if they could easily be over a hundred years old. Napoleon III had done a lot to beautify Paris, Grig knew. Perhaps among the roots of the trees, now parceled up like bean sprouts, there might be coins, francs and centimes from 1850, or medals or jewels, or all kinds of other relics. I'd love to have a closer look at them, thought Grig, and his left hand happened to touch Professor Bercy's sunglasses in his jacket pocket at the moment this thought came to him; he absentmindedly pulled out the glasses and perched them on his nose.

They fitted him quite well. He could feel that the earpieces were made out of some light, strong, springy material that clung, of its own accord, not uncomfortably, to the sides of his head. The lenses, squarish in shape, were very large; in fact they almost entirely covered

his face, so that he could see nothing except through their slightly pinkish screen. For a moment they misted over, after he had put them on; then they began to clear, and he looked through them, out of the window and into the courtyard.

For years and years and years afterward, Grig went over and over that scene in his memory, trying to recall every last detail of it. When he had grown up, and become a painter, he painted it many times — the whole scene, or bits of it, small fragments, different figures from it — over and over and over again. "Ah, that's a Rainborrow," people would say, walking into a gallery, from thirty, forty feet away, "You can always tell a Rainborrow."

What did he see? He would have found it almost impossible to give a description in words. "*Layers,*" he thought. "It's like seeing all the layers together. Different levels. People now — and people *then*. People when? People right on back to the beginning. How many

thousands of years people must have been doing things on this bit of ground! And, there they all are!"

As well as the people *then*, he could see the people *now*; several students, a boy riding a bicycle, a policeman, and the three great chestnut trees, tied on their trucks like invalids on stretchers. And, sure enough, in among the roots of the trees, Grig could catch a glimpse of all kinds of objects, knobby and dusty, solid and sparkling; perhaps that was what Professor Bercy had been coming to look at? The glasses must have had a fairly strong magnifying power, as well as this other mysterious ability they had, to show the layers of time lying one behind another.

What else could they show?

Grig turned, carefully, for he felt a little dizzy, to look inward at the room behind him. The first thing that caught his gaze, as he turned, was Eugène's gift, the rum baba, which he still clutched awkwardly in his right hand. Through Professor Bercy's pink-tinted glasses the cake looked even nastier than it had when seen by the naked eye. It was darker in color — the dark blood-brown, oozy and horrible; embedded in the middle of it he now saw two pills, one pink, one yellow. The pills hadn't been visible before, but through the pink lenses Grig could see them quite distinctly; sunk in the wet mass of dough they were becoming a bit mushy at the edges, beginning to wilt into the surrounding cake.

Why should Eugène want to give him cake with pills in it? What in the world was he up to? With a jerk of disgust, Grig dropped the little patisserie box on the floor. Nobody else was in the room. With his heel, he slid box and cake out of view under the window seat, then wiped his fingers — the syrup had already started to ooze through the carton — wiped his fingers vigorously, again and again, on a tissue. He glanced behind him to make sure that his action had not been seen by Anna or Eugène — but no, thank goodness, they were still safely out of sight, several rooms away.

Turning in the opposite direction, Grig walked quickly into the next room, where his favorite picture of all hung.

This was a painting of a horse, by an artist called Potter. Grig always thought of it as Potter's Gray. The picture was not at all large: perhaps one foot by eighteen inches, if as much; and the horse was not particularly handsome, rather the contrary. It was a gray, with some blobby dark dappled spots. Grig could hardly have said why he liked it so much. He was sure that the painter must have been very fond of the horse. Perhaps it belonged to him. Perhaps he called it Gray, and always gave it an apple or a carrot before sitting down with his easel and his tubes or pots of paint. The picture was over three hundred years old; a label said that Potter had been a Dutchman who lived from 1625 to 1654. He was only twenty-nine when he died, not old. Mother, who knew all sorts of things, once told Grig that Potter died of tuberculosis, which could have been cured these days. Grig thought that very sad. If Potter had lived now, he could have painted many more pictures of horses, instead of having his life cut off in the middle.

Anyway, this Gray was as good a horse as you could wish to meet, and, on each visit to the Louvre, Grig always walked to where his portrait hung, on the left of the doorway, between door and window, and — after first checking to make certain no one else was in the room — stood staring until his whole mind was filled with pleasure, with the whole essence of the horse; then he would pull the apple out of his pocket, take a bite of it himself, hold the rest up on the palm of his hand as you should when feeding a horse, and say, "Have a bite, Gray."

He did so now. But this time, something happened that had never happened before.

Gray put a gentle, silvery muzzle with soft nostrils sprouting white hairs out of the picture *and took the apple from Grig's hand.*

Then he withdrew his head into the frame and ate the apple with evident satisfaction.

Grig gasped. He couldn't help it — he was so pleased that he felt warm tears spring into his eyes. Blinking them away, he looked rapidly around the small gallery — and saw, without any particular surprise, that every picture was alive, living its life in its own way as it must have done when the artist painted it: a fly was buzzing over the grapes that lay beside the china jug, some men were hauling down the sail of a ship, the woman, winding the bobbins of her lace pillow, carefully finished off one and began another. Then she looked up and gave Grig an absent-minded smile.

There were other people in the room too, outside the pictures, walking about — people in all kinds of different clothes. Grig wished, from the bottom of his heart, that he could hear what they were saying, wished he could speak to them and ask questions — but Professor Bercy's glasses were only for seeing, they couldn't help him to hear. You'd want headphones too, Grig thought, straining his ears nonetheless to try and catch the swish of a dress, the crunch of Gray finishing the apple — but all he heard was the angry note of Anna's voice, "*Grig!* Where in the *world* have you *got* to?" and the clack of her wooden-soled shoes on the polished gallery floor as she came hurrying in search of him. Grig couldn't resist glancing back at Potter's horse — but the apple was all finished, not a sign of it remained — then he felt Anna's fingers close on his wrist like pincers, and she was hurrying him toward the exit, angrily gabbling into his ear. "What in heaven's name have you

been *doing* with yourself all this time? Can't you see it's started to rain and we'll be late, we'll have to take a taxi —"

All this time she was hurrying Grig through one gallery after another, and Eugène was walking beside them, looking a little amused, and calmly indifferent to Anna's scolding of her charge.

Grig himself was still dizzy, shaken, confused, and distracted. Firstly, he would have liked to stop and stare with minute attention at each of the huge canvases they were now passing in the main galleries. Because — just *look* at what was happening in that coronation scene with Emperor Napoleon putting the crown on his queen's head, and the Pope behind him — and those people struggling to keep on the

raft which was heaving about among huge waves — but some of them were dead, you could see — and the lady lying twiddling her fingers on a sofa — and the man on a horse — they were all alive, it was like looking through a series of windows at what was going on beyond the glass.

But also, Grig was absolutely horrified at what he saw when he looked across Anna at Eugène; the sight of Eugène's face was so extremely frightening that Grig's eyes instantly flicked away from it each time; but then he felt compelled to look back in order to convince himself of what he had seen.

All the *workings* were visible: inside the skull the brain — inside the brain, memory, feelings, hopes and plans. The memories were all dreadful ones, the hopes and plans were all wicked. It was like, from the height of a satellite, watching a great storm rage across a whole continent; you could see the whirl of cloud, the flash of lightning; you could guess at uprooted trees, flooded rivers, and smashed buildings. You could see that Eugène planned to do an enormous amount of damage; and it was plain that, here and now, he hated Grig and had a plan about him; what kind of a plan Grig didn't exactly know, but little details of it that came to him in flashes made him shudder.

"Come on, hurry up," said Anna, buttoning her raincoat, when they reached the entrance lobby. "Button your jacket, put your scarf around. Eugène's getting a taxi, and he'll drop us at the embassy and go on —"

"*No!*" said Grig. He didn't intend going with Eugène in any taxi. And he knew well that Eugène had no plans at all to drop them at the embassy.

"What do you mean, *no*?" said Anna furiously. "What in the world are you *talking* about? Don't act like a baby. You'll do as I say, or else —"

"*No,*" repeated Grig doggedly, and yanked at the wrist which she still grasped in an unshakable grip. He looked at Anna and saw that she was not wicked like Eugène, but stupid all through, solid like a block of marble or plaster. It would be useless to argue with her and say, "Eugène is bad. He has some awful plan. Why did he put pills in that cake?"

Grig was still terribly confused and distracted by the complicated sights, the layers and layers of different happenings that were taking place all around him. But at last he realized what he must do. With his free hand he pulled the pink-tinted glasses off his face, and said, "Please, Anna. Put these on for a moment."

"Oh, don't be so *silly*! Why in the world should I? Where ever did you *get* those glasses?" She had forgotten all about the accident, and Professor Bercy. "What is this, anyway, some kind of silly joke?"

"Please put them on, Anna. If you don't —" What could he do, what could he possibly do? Then, with a gulp of relief, he remembered some practical advice that his mother had once given him. "It sounds babyish," she had said, "but if ever you are in a tight corner, *yell*. It at-tracts attention; people will come running, and that will give you time to think, so never mind that you may feel a fool, just do it, just yell."

"If you don't put them on," said Grig, "I shall scream so loud that people will think I've gone mad. I mean it, Anna."

"I think you already *have* gone mad," she said, but she looked at him, saw that he did mean it, and put on the glasses. At that moment Eugène came back through the glass entrance door, his black leather jacket shiny with rain, and on his face a big false smile. Without the glasses, Grig could no longer see the evil workings of Eugène's brain — which was in every way a relief — but just the same, he knew exactly how false that smile was.

"Okay," said Eugène, "*venez vite, tous les deux —*"[10] and then Anna, looking at him, started to scream. Her scream was far, far louder than any yell that Grig could have raised, he had no need even to open his mouth. The smile dropped from Eugène's face like paper off a wet window, he stared at Anna first with shock, then with rage. "*Come* on, girl, what *is* this?" he said, trying to grab her hand, but she twisted away from him, still shrieking like a machine that has blown off its safety valve. "No — no — no — get away — get away — you're *horrible —*"

By this time, as Mother had prophesied, people were running toward them; people were staring and exclaiming and pushing close, trying to discover what was the matter with Anna. Now Eugène's nerve suddenly broke. He let out a couple of wicked, hissing swearwords, turned on his heel, went out the glass doors, and vanished from view. At the same moment Anna, furiously dragging the tinted glasses from her face, flung them on the stone floor as if they were poisoned, trampled them into fragments, and burst into hysterical sobs.

"Would you please telephone my father?" Grig said to a uniformed woman who seemed like someone in a position of authority. "I think my *gouvernante*[11] has been taken ill. My father is the British Ambassador," and he gave her the embassy number.

So they went home in a taxi after all.

"Please, can you take me to see Professor Bercy in the hospital?"

---

[10]**"Venez vite, tous les deux —":** "Hurry up, both of you!"

[11]**gouvernante:** a governess.

Grig asked his mother, the next day, when Anna was under sedatives and the care of a doctor, and a new au pair girl was being advertised for, and in the meantime Lady Julia Rainborrow was leaving her ambassadorial duties to take her son for an airing.

But she said, "Darling, no; I'm afraid I can't. It was on the news this morning. He died last night in the hospital; he never recovered consciousness."

"Oh," said Grig. "Oh."

He had dreaded having to tell Professor Bercy that his glasses had been smashed; but this was far worse.

I wonder if they *were* his only pair? Grig thought, plodding along the street beside Lady Julia. Or if other people — the other scientists who worked with him — knew about them too?

"Where would you like to go?" Grig's mother asked him. "It's not a very nice day — I'm afraid it looks like rain again."

"Can we go to the Louvre?"

"Are you sure you want to go there?" she said doubtfully.

"Yes, I would like to," said Grig, and so they walked in the direction of the Louvre, finding it hard to talk to each other, Grig very unhappy about Professor Bercy, dead before he had finished his life's work — and what work! — while Lady Julia worried about Grig. But what can you do? You can't look after somebody twenty-four hours a day. Ambassadors' sons have to take their chances, like everybody else.

Going quickly through the suite of dark little galleries, Grig came to the picture of Potter's Gray. He stood and stared at the dappled horse, very lovingly, very intently, and thought: Yesterday I gave you an apple, and you put out your head and took it from my hand, and I stroked your nose. I shall come back tomorrow, and next week, and the week after, and that will never, never happen again. But it *did* happen, and I remember it.

Do you remember it, Gray?

He thought that the gray horse looked at him very kindly.

Responding to "Potter's Gray"

Thinking and Discussing

After the glasses change the way Grig sees things, he grows up to be a famous painter. How does the author use the glasses as a way of saying something about how people see things?

Why do Anna and Grig have such different reactions when they wear the glasses?

Choosing a Creative Response

Describing a Scene Grig's favorite picture is "Potter's Gray." Tell about your favorite painting or a scene from real life as if you were looking at it through Professor Bercy's glasses.

Continuing the Story Grig feels unhappy that Professor Bercy will not be able to finish his work. Write a description of what you think Professor Bercy's next invention might have been, and how he might have used the glasses in the development of that invention. How else might the professor have used the glasses in a positive way?

Creating Your Own Activity Plan and complete your own activity in response to "Potter's Gray."

Exploring Language

Artists use color to paint pictures. Writers use words. What words in the description of Gray eating the apple made you feel it was really happening? What additional words might you have used to describe the horse?

Horse in a Meadow by Paulus Potter

Even without Grig's special glasses, a viewer might be astonished by how real Paulus Potter's painted animals seem. Potter is not widely known now, but in his own time (1625–1654) he was considered one of the greatest Dutch painters of animals. His gift can be seen in *Horse in a Meadow*, painted in 1653. The horse that Grig called Potter's Gray is painted lovingly in great detail. Bathed in a golden light, it dominates the gentle Dutch landscape. Potter's Gray appears to be an admirable horse.

The Lace-Maker by Jan Vermeer

One of Grig's favorite paintings in the Louvre is *The Lace-Maker*, painted by the Dutch artist Jan Vermeer around 1664. Vermeer's finest paintings show ordinary people doing daily tasks such as making lace, reading letters, or pouring water. Like Grig, you might feel that you could gaze forever at these peaceful scenes. Why? Because Vermeer designed his paintings very carefully. Nothing seems to be out of place or out of balance. Cool blues and yellows create glowing sunlight in the paintings.

The Parrot

by Vivien Alcock

Illustrated by Maria Stroster

t was one of those hazy October mornings, when the weather may do anything, and you don't know what to wear. When I was halfway down Sebastian Street, the sun came out. I was too hot in my jacket, but couldn't be bothered to take it off. I already had enough to carry with my schoolbooks.

I don't know what made me look up. I don't often look up when I'm walking. I either look around to see if there's someone I know, or at the pavement before my feet, in case anyone has dropped some money.

I wasn't thinking of anything in particular. I can't remember hearing any odd sound. But something made me look up, sharply — and there it was. A gray, hunched bird, sitting in a tree, just above the high stone wall. It looked wet. Mist seemed to cling about it; and drops of water, like glass berries, hung on the branch beneath its claws. It looked as if it had been out in the rain all night, or maybe fallen into a bucket of water. The sunlight avoided it, as if it were a shadow.

It was a gray parrot, old, bedraggled, a most wretched bird. Even the rosy feathers on its tail looked cold, like a red nose in a winter face. Its eye was round, rain-colored, and fixed on me with a gloomy stare. As I stopped, it came hopping along the branch toward me, putting its head on one side in an anxious, ingratiating way, as if it wanted comfort, a friendly hand. . . .

Not my hand. I wasn't going to touch it. I stood, with my fists in my pockets and my heart banging loose in my chest. In spite of the sunlight and my new jacket, I began to shiver.

You'll think I was stupid to be scared of a parrot. All right! you'll say, maybe it *is* unusual to see a parrot loose in an English autumn when the nights are cold, but that's no reason to shake in your shoes like a thief. But you see, for a moment,

I thought I knew that parrot. Only it wasn't possible! The parrot I had known must be dead. Dead and stiff on some lonely Devon hill.

When I was small, we lived in Devon, next door to a very old lady who had a parrot, a gray parrot with a rosy tail. Polly, she called him. Every year she went to visit her sister for a week, and as her sister did not like parrots, she asked my parents if we could look after him. In return, she offered to look after our cat, three gerbils, one hamster and a moth-eaten goldfish, when we went on holiday. If this seems an unequal bargain, with us getting the better part, then all I can say is — you didn't know that parrot.

He shrieked all day, a harsh, strange cry that frightened our cat and set our teeth on edge. He screamed as I sat puzzling over my sums, so that I could not hear myself count. He woke Bobby in his crib, drowned out the TV, made the neighbors complain. And if we put the cloth over his cage to silence him, we would sit there feeling guilty, thinking of the bird cramped in his unnatural night.

"Poor thing. He seems very unhappy," my mother said. "He's probably missing Miss Brown. I expect he will settle down in a day or two."

After three days, he was quieter. I think he had screamed himself hoarse. There would be hours when he was silent, sitting hunched up in his gray wings, like an invalid in a shawl. I felt sorry for him. I came up to his cage, and he sidled along his perch to meet me, putting his head on one side and fixing me with his pearl-button eye.

"Pretty Polly. Pretty Polly," he said hopefully, and ducked his head down as if he wanted to be stroked. I put my finger through the bars of his cage . . . Crack! That iron beak had got it! I still have the scar. I'm lucky, I suppose, to have kept the finger that goes with it.

After that, we could not like Polly. We were kind to him, feeding him well, giving him the tidbits he loved, grapes and pieces of banana; and keeping his cage clean. But we never liked him. And when the old lady died, and her sister came to her house to clear up, *she* did not want the parrot either.

She came smiling over the fence when Bobby and I were playing in the garden, and said, "I know my sister would have liked you to have Polly."

We looked at each other. Bobby put his finger in his mouth and his chin began to wobble. I said, "Oh, thank you, but — we've already got a lot of pets. Too many, Mom says. I don't think she'd let us have a parrot."

"I'm sure if you ask her nicely, she will. After all, you and Polly are old friends, aren't you? He'll feel quite at home."

We did not want Polly to feel at home in our house. We were frightened of him. But we were small, then, and shy of grown-ups; so when she said, "Run along and ask her, dears" — we went.

My mother was in the kitchen.

"She wants us to have old Miss Brown's Polly," I said.

"*'She'* is the cat's mother. If you mean Mrs. Jenkins, say so," said my mother improvingly. Then she took in what I had said. "No! Not that bird! Not ever again. I'm sorry, Anna, but that's final, so it's no use nagging and whining. . . ."

"I'll tell her," I said.

My mother looked surprised, not having expected such an easy victory. Not knowing we were on her side.

 We ran back into the garden.

"Sorry. Mom says we can't have him," we said, trying to hide our relief.

"I don't know what to do," said Mrs. Jenkins, "I can't have him in my apartment. Pets are not allowed. He'll have to be put down."[1]

---

[1]**put down:** to have a veterinarian put an animal to sleep.

445

As she said this, she looked at us slyly. Knowing children have kind hearts, she thought this would be enough to move us.

It did. It moved us to shame and guilt, so that when my father came home, I said, "Dad, Polly's going to be put down if we don't have him."

"Don't you believe it," said my father, "She's just trying it on. I'm not having a caged bird as a pet. It's cruel to keep them confined. There ought to be a law against it. Birds need to fly."

"I'll tell her myself in the morning that we can't have him," said my mother. "It's not as if she'll have any difficulty getting rid of him. She could always sell him to the pet shop. Parrots fetch quite a lot of money."

But in the morning, Bobby had a sore throat and spots, and Mom had to wait in for the doctor. So I went around to Mrs. Jenkins. Nobody had asked me to, but I was still young enough to like running errands; it made me feel important. Like a little parrot, I repeated what my father had said, that it was cruel to keep birds in cages. She looked offended. I told her my mother had said she could sell it for a lot of money. Now she looked interested. Then I spoiled it. "At least five pounds!" I invented, hoping to impress her. Five pounds was my idea of a fortune then. It wasn't hers. I often

wish I hadn't said that. Perhaps if she'd known how much parrots were really worth, she might have tried to sell him and things would have been different. . . .

"You won't have poor Polly put down, will you?" I said, "Promise?"

I suppose she kept her promise — in a way. That afternoon, when I was at school, she took his cage out into the garden and set him free. Mrs. King, who lived on the other side, watched from a bedroom window, and told us about it later. The parrot kept flying at the windows, trying to get in, she said, but Mrs. Jenkins had shut them all and put his cage in the garden shed. And when he perched in the apple tree, she came out with a broom and shooed him away, until at last he flew off into the huge, empty sky. I suppose she meant to be kind. But it was October then, as it is now, and although the sun was shining, the nights were cold.

My father was furious when he learned what she had done. I heard him talk to my mother about it; they did not know I was listening behind the door. The woman was a fool, he said. It would have been far kinder to have had the poor bird put to sleep. It had no chance of surviving the coming winter. No chance at all.

I cried that night, lying awake and warm beneath my blankets, thinking of the poor, cold bird flying over the dark, windy hills, trying in vain to escape the winter. And I felt guilty, knowing I had not begged and pleaded and whined for him, as I might have done for a new doll.

So you see now why I was startled — oh, to tell the truth, frightened — to see a gray parrot, sitting there like a ghost out of my past, staring at me with eyes as cold and pale as winter. But I was older now and sensible, though I say it myself. I knew it could not really be Polly. He could not have survived the bitter frosts of six long winters, nor flown two hundred miles to find us here in our London suburbs. There were other parrots, after all. The big pet shop in Camden Town sells blue macaws, white cockatoos, all sorts of parrots. Regents Park Zoo is not far away. Some other parrot must have escaped its cage.

I ought to tell someone, I thought. It'll die if it's not caught; the nights are cold now. I hesitated. I would be late for school if I didn't hurry. But I couldn't help that. I didn't want *this* parrot on my conscience.

I went back to the nearest house and knocked on the door. At first, no one came.

I knocked again. A woman appeared, still in her dressing-gown. I could hear a baby crying in the house behind her. What did I want? A parrot in her garden? She knew nothing about it and cared less. "Try the corner shop," she suggested, as she shut the door, "They know everyone."

I thought this was a good idea. I knew the woman there; it was where I bought my candy. She was kind and liked animals. I started walking quickly, glancing up as I came to the tree on which the parrot had been sitting. It was still there.

"Don't worry," I said foolishly, "I'm getting help."

Then it spoke. Its voice was harsh, grating, as if its tongue were made of iron that had begun to rust.

"Go back!" it said, "Go back! Go back!"

I stopped — tried to go on but could not. I told myself that parrots only copy the noise words make. It was not really talking to me. But there was something so urgent, so foreboding[2] in its voice, something so horribly familiar about its pale, sad eye, that I felt as if one of its scaly claws had clutched my heart. I thought — oh, it's stupid, I know — but I really thought it was Polly come back, out of his grave.

---

[2]**foreboding** (fôr **bō′**dĭng): an uneasy feeling that something bad is going to happen.

"What — P-Polly, is it you?" I stammered.

"Go back!" it said again, "Go back! Go back!"

I looked around. There was no one in sight. A car passed, but its windows were steamed up. I could not see the driver. The way I felt at that moment, there might not have been one. Everything seemed strange. The sunlight fell coldly on the pavement, throwing shadows, sharp as knives. The leaves on the tree seemed to rattle together, as if they were fighting, pushing each other off the twigs into the gutter below. Winter was coming. I felt I could hear its heavy tread.

"I'm sorry, Polly," I said. "Honest, I cried when I heard what that horrid woman had done. I didn't want you to die. I couldn't have known, could I?"

I looked at it pleadingly, but all it said was "Go back! Go back! Go back!"

Was it warning me? Would something terrible happen if I went on? Its eye seemed transparent as glass, and yet . . . I had never known what it thought of me. It did not wag its tail like a dog, or purr like a cat when it was pleased. True, it had bitten my finger once, which did not look like affection; but perhaps it had thought it was food, some small pink banana it was being offered for its tea? Perhaps the poor feathered ghost, for ghost I

thought it was, was sorry it had hurt me and was trying to make amends[3] by saving me from some horrible fate.

 Or did it hate me? Had it always hated me for not loving it, blamed me for its sad end? Was it sending me back to be run over as I crossed the road, was a bomb going to blow up in the mailbox as I crossed, or a slate fall off the roof onto my head? You see the fix I was in?

I dithered on the paving stone like someone on a shrinking island, unable to decide which way to escape. The sense of doom was so strong. To remain where I was might not be safe. Even now a thunderbolt might be descending on my head. I looked up hastily, but the sky was empty, a dead, colorless sky like the parrot's eyes.

"Go back!" the bird shrieked insistently. "Go back! Go back!"

Back where? My mother was at home. It was the thought of her, plump and warm and smiling, that decided me. I started running back down the road, hearing behind me a harsh shriek and a flapping of gray wings.

I was careful, even then, frightened as I was. I looked both ways before I crossed the road. I made a wide circle around the mailbox. I raced

---

[3]**make amends** (māk ə **mĕndz′**): to make up for having insulted or injured someone.

down the path to our kitchen door so fast that no falling slate had a chance to hit me. The door was unlocked. I pushed it open so hard that it banged against the wall. Then I heard a great crash upstairs that set the teacups dancing on the dresser. And my mother screamed.

I have never run upstairs so fast. She was in Bobby's room, lying on the floor beside a fallen stepladder. And there was scarlet everywhere, on her dress, on the carpet . . . so much that I thought at first it must be paint. Then I saw her hand was clasping her arm, with blood pumping up between the fingers . . .

Her voice was faint. I had to bend down to hear it.

"Quick! Get Mrs. Jessop!" she said.

They told me later I *was* quick. They said I must have flashed next door like lightning. Dad says I'm a heroine, and Mom might have bled to death but for me. She had been changing a light bulb and had fallen off the ladder onto the glass lampshade, which she had thoughtlessly left lying on the floor. Mrs. Jessop, who had been to First Aid classes all last winter, had known what to do, and did it; while I dialed 999. It was something I had longed to do, but I was too upset to enjoy it.

After the ambulance had taken Mom to hospital, I told Mrs. Jessop about the parrot. Oh, not that I thought it was a ghost, just that I had seen one loose. She said, "Poor thing," but she was too full of what had happened to take much notice.

"Wasn't it lucky I took those First Aid classes!" she kept saying.

All that evening, Bobby and I went up and down the street, knocking on doors. But no one had seen a parrot. No one knew anyone who might have lost one. Nobody claimed it. We went to the police station and told the desk sergeant, and he promised they would look out for it.

"I shouldn't worry," he said. "Parrots are clever birds. When it feels cold, it'll soon find its own way home."

Perhaps it did. I never saw it again.

I've often thought about that parrot. I don't believe in ghosts. I'm twelve now and quite sensible. At least most of the time. I know it must have been some other parrot. London is a big place, and you don't always know the people living a street or two away. I like to think it belongs to an old lady, who loves it, and lets it fly about the gardens on sunny days. I can almost hear her, when the parrot returns, shooing it gently toward its open cage, calling out, "Go back! Go back! Go back!"

It is only sometimes, when winter is coming and the nights are cold, that I wonder . . . When my mother came back from hospital, with seven stitches in her arm and a huge bandage, I asked her:

"What made you fall off the ladder?"

"I don't know, darling," she said, "Just carelessness, I expect."

"It couldn't have been a sudden noise, startling you?"

"A noise? No, I can't remember. What sort of noise?"

The noise of the kitchen door banging against the wall, when she thought she was alone in the house; the noise of my unexpected return. I think this, but I don't say it aloud.

So you see, if it was Polly come back, I still don't know what he intended. I like to think he was being kind, to make up for my bitten finger, and has now flown off happily to some bright jungle in the sky. But I can't be sure. What do you think?

Responding to "The Parrot"

Thinking and Discussing

What is there about the author's description of the parrot in the tree that makes the reader question whether the parrot is real or not?

If the parrot is trying to communicate with Anna, why is Anna unable to decide whether it wants to help her or harm her? What do *you* think the parrot intends?

Choosing a Creative Response

Acting Out a Trial One reason Anna mistrusts the parrot is that she feels guilty about the way she treated Polly in the past. Do you think that Anna is guilty of mistreating Polly? Write down points that could be used for and against Anna in a courtroom trial. Then work with classmates to play the roles of Anna, the defense lawyer, and the prosecutor in a mock trial.

Planning a Movie If you were going to make a movie of "The Parrot," how would you do it? Think about the mood and setting of the story as well as the characters and the action. Would you use real actors, puppets, or a technique such as animation? Present your ideas to your classmates.

Creating Your Own Activity Plan and complete your own activity in response to "The Parrot."

Thinking and Writing

The ending of "The Parrot" is indefinite — Anna and the reader are not sure what caused the accident or what the parrot really was. Write a different ending to the story that gives a solution to the mystery.

*Imagination is
more important
than knowledge.*

Albert Einstein

Your Mind
Is a
Mirror

by Joan Aiken

Illustrated by Theo Rudnak

 A keen wind scoured the deck of the ferry ship *Colossos*, probing between the slats of the wooden seats on the upper section, making the passengers huddle together, pull on cardigans if they had them, or go below for cups of hot coffee. Mist was beginning to veil the Turkish coast on the left-hand side, and blur the shapes of the islands to the right. Another hour must pass before the ship docked in Rhodes. Sam and Linnet wrapped their bare legs in their swimming towels, but a damp swimming towel is very poor protection against a cold searching wind. They had begged for a last swim and Ma had said, "Oh, very well! Meet us at the dock, and promise you won't be a minute later than half past twelve. But that means you'll have to wear beach clothes on the boat, because your other clothes will be packed."

"Doesn't matter," Sam had said. "It'll be hot."

But it wasn't hot; the weather had turned misty and windy. "Most unlike the Aegean at this time of year," other passengers were grumbling. The Palmers' luggage was at the very bottom of a huge heap of bags and crates on the lower deck; impossible to dig down to their rucksacks and get out warmer clothes. All their books were packed, too; there was nothing to do but sit and shiver, for the boat was jam-packed with tourists, mainly Swedes and Germans; you couldn't even walk about to keep yourself warm, because there wasn't a foot of spare deck space. Sam did his best to doze a bit; he had woken very early and listened to the crowing of roosters near and far, anxious not to miss a minute of their last day on Kerimos. But it was too cold on the boat for proper sleeping; he had a brief, sad dream about his dear French teacher who had died, Madame Bonamy.

When he shook himself awake, Father was sitting staring ahead in silence, as usual, and Ma was murmuring something to Linnet in a low anxious voice.

In several ways it had been a miserable holiday. The tiny Greek island was beautiful, of course; the little Greek house with its bare painted floors, basic wooden furniture, and garden full of roses and lemons, had been perfect; the swimming in a clear green sea, the cliffs covered with rockroses, the village that was all steps up and steps down, dazzling white houses, ancient crumbling churches, and flowers everywhere — every detail of that had been marvellous, wonderful, but Father had spoiled it. Silent, grim, day after day, he had sat in one place, generally the darkest corner of the darkest room indoors, unless Ma had urged him to go out, when he had shrugged and slouched out to the garden as if it did not matter to him where he moved his load of misery. On excursions, or when they ate dinner out at one of the tavernas[1] on the quayside,[2] he had accompanied his wife and children like an angry, speechless ghost. Why should he object if we are enjoying ourselves? thought Sam resentfully. We aren't doing *him* any harm.

Possibly Father didn't really notice whether they were enjoying themselves or not; he never looked at the other three members of his family, just stared off into the distance like an Easter Island statue on the side of a hill. His wife and children shared plain, nondescript looks: Sam and Linnet had straight brown hair, snub noses, freckles, and greyish brown eyes; Ma had a pleasant friendly face, but it was always worried nowadays which made it almost ugly; she didn't bother about clothes or make-up much any more, and her hair was badly in need of a perm, it looked like a piece of knitting that had gone wrong. Father had always been the handsome member of the family, with his classically straight forehead and nose, all in one line, his bright brown hair and beard, now just touched with grey, and bright dark twinkling grey eyes. But now his eyes had ceased to twinkle; they stared into the distance, hour after hour, day after day, as if nothing nearby had the power to please them. Once, his conversation had been full of jokes and interesting information; now, often, a whole day would pass without his speaking at all except to say "I don't mind."

---

[1]**tavernas:** small, informal restaurants or inns.
[2]**quayside (kē′sīd):** the side of a stone wharf or **quay** (kē) where ships are loaded and unloaded.

460

"Would you rather have a boiled egg or scrambled, Jonathan?" Ma would ask at breakfast.

"Do you want to watch BBC or ITV?"

"Shall we go to Brighton to see Fanny, or for a walk on the Heath?"

"I don't mind."

In the end, Ma hadn't even bothered to consult him about the holiday on Kerimos; she sold some shares Granny had left her, bought the tickets, rented the house, and packed Father's bag for him. He hadn't raised any objections. But for all the good that sun and sea and Greek air had done him, he might as well have stayed at home in Camden Town.

"You do realise he's sick, don't you?" Ma had said anxiously to Sam.

"How do you mean, sick? Has he got a pain, is something wrong with him?"

Sickness to Sam meant medicine, hospitals, bandages, injections.

"His mind is sick. He's depressed, because he was let go, because he can't get a teaching job anywhere. And he's such a good teacher —"

Sam couldn't see it. Lots of the boys at school had unemployed parents, who grumbled and moaned, of course, worried about money, were hopeful of jobs or disappointed when the hopes came to nothing; but in between times they seemed reasonably cheerful, mowed their lawns, took the family to the movies once in a while, didn't retreat into this marble staring world of silence. Why did Jonathan Palmer have to be different?

An extra-keen gust of wind worked its way under Sam's thin T-shirt and he shivered.

"Brr, I'm freezing!"

"So am I," sighed Linnet.

Their father's indifferent gaze passed right over them, as if they had spoken in Hindustani, but Ma said, "Here, you two, here's a couple of hundred drachmae.[3] You'd better go and buy yourselves a coffee. And bring some back for me and Father. I'll stay here. . . ."

"I wonder if she thinks he might jump over the side," murmured Linnet, shivering as they stood in line at the coffee counter.

Sam muttered, "I hate Dad. I really hate him. I almost wish he would jump over the side."

"Oh, Sam. You know it's just that he's ill. And think how hard it must have been for him losing his job, when Ma's still teaching at the same school. He just isn't himself. Remember! He never used to be like this."

"Well, why can't he go back to the way he used to be?" Sam said disbelievingly.

"People can't get better just by wanting to."

"Well then he ought to go to a shrink."

"Costs money. And the Health Service shrinks have waiting-lists as long as the Milky Way." Linnet paid for the coffee and looked frustratedly at the huge pile of baggage. "I do wish we could get our books out and read."

Sam fingered the beach satchel under his arm. As well as damp swimming trunks, flippers, and snorkel mask, it contained a guilty secret.

Several times, swimming from the tiny town beach, they had noticed a Greek family group who attracted Sam's attention because they seemed in every way the converse of the Palmers. There were two lively handsome dark brothers, older; two small pretty sisters, younger; there was a fat cheerful aunt, a plump smiling mother, and above all, there was a talkative, ebullient[4] father who seemed the king-pin of the whole tribe, affectionate with the girls, companionable and teasing with the boys, bounding in and out of the water, rushing away to the quay and returning with almond cakes, ice-creams, and fruit; sweeping the

---

[3]**drachmae (drăk′mē):** Greek coins.
[4]**ebullient (ĭ bŭl′yənt):** bubbling with enthusiasm or high spirits.

family off to eat lunch at quayside tavernas, and all the time making jokes, laughing, hugging his wife, complimenting his sister-in-law, carrying the smaller girl piggyback up the rocky path. If only Father could be like that! Had he ever been?

Sam could hardly remember the days before Jonathan Palmer's illness; the mist of unhappiness that surrounded him seemed to block out any view of the past.

On this final morning the Greek father had produced from his pocket a little book, a glossy paperback, from which he proceeded to read aloud, amid bursts of general hilarity. At every paragraph, almost every sentence he read, his wife, children, and sister-in-law collapsed and beat their chests in hiccups of laughter. Sam could feel a smile break out over his own face at the sight and sound of so much happy humour. Then, gaily, impulsively, forgetting the book, leaving their swimming things scattered on the sand, they had all gone bounding off to the nearest quayside cafe for coffee and cakes. Linnet was still in the sea, making the most of her last swim, nobody else on the beach was anywhere near; Sam had walked casually past, casually dropped his towel, and picked up towel and book together. Why? He hardly knew himself. Perhaps the book was a kind of token, a talisman, a spell, a magic text that would bring fun and good humour back into his own family if he read it aloud?

There had been no chance to look inside the book since he picked it up; Linnet had dashed out of the sea, they had dressed and sprinted round to the berth where the *Colossos* waited at her moorings. But now Sam could feel the paperback, a small, encouraging rectangular shape, wrapped in a plastic bag between his trunks and towel. He would study it tonight when they were back at home, though now it seemed almost impossible to believe that by bedtime they would be in their own house, in Camden Town, the island of Kerimos, with its white houses and turquoise sea, nothing but a bright memory.

Home, when they reached it, smelt shut-in and stuffy; Ma went round at once throwing open windows. Father sat down, just as he was, without even pulling off his windcheater, in a chair by the fireplace, and stared, unseeing, at the unlit gas fire. Home smelt of all the sorrow that had ever happened there. . . .

But here was fat Simon, Sam's cat, a plump sharply striped young tabby, half frantic with pent-up affection, wanting to be picked up, rolling on his back to have his stomach rubbed, leaping 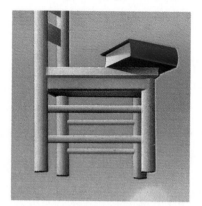 onto Sam's lap at every possible and impossible moment, miaowing and purring nonstop and simultaneously to indicate his displeasure at having been left to the care of neighbours for two solid weeks.

"I don't believe a word of what you say!" Sam told him. "*You* aren't starved, fat cat Simon — you're even fatter than you were when we left. You should see some of those skinny Greek cats, you spoilt thing."

The island had been full of cats, healthy and active but thin as diagrams; they waited hungrily and acrimoniously for fishbones around every quayside cafe.

Sam raced up to his room with Simon wailing two steps behind him, flung his rucksack on the bed, then pulled the stolen book from his beach satchel and eagerly opened it.

The disappointment was shattering; there were no pictures in the book, and (as he might have considered if he had given it a moment's thought) the text was all in Greek, in Greek characters; he could read no more than a word here and there, *kai* for "and," *alla* for "but." He had committed theft, he had stolen a book, the book that had given them all such joy, and it was no use to him, no use at all. Guilt began to rise up in him like bubbles in jam that has started to ferment and go bad. He felt sick with dismay and horror at what he had done.

"Sam, you're tired out," said Ma, looking at him acutely when he came downstairs with a load of dirty clothes for the machine. "Off you go, straight to bed. It's too late for supper. Lin's gone up already."

465

Father had not gone to bed. He sat on, staring at the dead fire; he often sat that way all night.

"Good night, Father," Sam called, but did not expect, or receive, any answer.

Sam dragged himself up the stairs to bed, feeling as if he had travelled three times, on hands and knees, round the world. His only comfort (but that was a substantial one, he must admit) was fat cat Simon, lovingly shoving himself as close to Sam's chin as he could squeeze.

Sam fell asleep and began to dream instantly.

There was Madame Bonamy, half stern, half smiling, as she often had been, her white wild hair standing up in a corona all round her head, elegantly tilted on its long neck, her deep-set dark eyes watchful on either side of an aquiline nose, her mouth set in a firm line.

Madame Bonamy had been quite young, in her thirties; illness, not age, had turned her hair white. Her skin was smooth but completely colourless; that, and the fine thistledown white hair, had given her the look of a ghost long before she became one. She did not behave like a ghost,

 then or in Sam's dreams. As a teacher she had been very funny, used to tell zany, crazy stories, and dry, ironic ones which packed a terrific punch, so it was worth listening to them carefully. Her students always came out top in French exams. For several years she had been a great friend of the Palmers'. Jonathan and his wife both taught at the same school, where Sam and Linnet were pupils, and Madame Bonamy often came to their house for meals, or joined them on family excursions, before she went into hospital for the last time and died.

"Why do people have to get ill? Why do they have to lose their jobs?" Sam asked her now, in his dream.

But Madame Bonamy did not answer his question. She had something of her own to say.

466

"Ah, Sam, why, why did you do it? *Non, non, non, ce n'est pas gentil!*[5] That was a wrong thing to do, you know well. You must give it back. You should not have taken it."

"Give it *back*?" he said, appalled. "But — how can I? That family are on a Greek island — on Kerimos — six hours' journey from here. How can I possibly take it back? I don't know their name — I can't even post it to them. They probably didn't live on the island — they were on holiday too. . . ."

"Sam, Sam, why did you take it?"

He tried to explain. "It was such a funny book — it was making them all laugh so much — I thought — I thought perhaps it might make Father laugh, if it was so funny. *You* ought to understand that," he told her.

"Ah, I see." She reflected in silence for a moment. Then she told Sam, "Well, it is still possible for you to return it. That will mean going into the past."

"Into the past? How in the world can I do that?"

"You must go back precisely to the point at which you took the book. Not a moment sooner, not a moment later. Put the book down on the beach where you picked it up."

"How can I get there?"

"You go backwards," explained Madame Bonamy. "That is not difficult. Write with this diamond pencil on the looking-glass. Write very small. First, place the book under the glass — so."

Sam, who had got out of bed, took the diamond pencil from her and stood before the mirror on the dressing-table. Simon the cat, uncurling himself, yawning, stretching, followed Sam.

"What shall I write?"

"You must write in backwards writing, beginning at the bottom right-hand corner. Each word back to front. Each sentence back to front. You must write everything that you did, every single thing that you have done today, backwards, beginning at the last minute before you got into bed."

---

[5]**"Non, non, non, ce n'est pas gentil!"**: "No, really, that wasn't very kind."

"I see." Sam thought for a minute, then lifted his hand towards the glass.

"*Attendez un moment,*"[6] said Madame Bonamy. "This is important. As soon as you have replaced the book on the beach, *come straight back;* it is possible to come back very fast, as if you were quickly rewinding a tape. Do not linger for a single instant."

"Why not?"

"To go back, just for an instant like that, does not part the strands of time," said Madame Bonamy. "But if you stayed even a few moments longer, you would begin making differences, having effects on future events. Also, you might get lost."

The very thought made him shiver.

Quickly he began to write on the glass.

"Let me think then . . . I brushed my teeth; I took off my clothes; I came upstairs; I said goodnight to Father; I took the clothes down to Ma; I looked at the book; I put my rucksack down on my bed; I fed Simon; I helped get the bags out of the taxi . . ."

Minute by minute he navigated back through the long day, and each minute in its turn was recorded in tiny, spidery silver writing from right to left across the face of the mirror. At last Sam came to the point of recording: "I stooped and picked up the book and the towel both together."

And *there he was*, back on the cool, sunny beach, clouds already beginning faintly to mist over the sun, stooping down with the glossy paperback in his hand.

He laid it neatly where it had been before, and straightened, looking about him, with an immense lightening of the heart.

One thing at least had been put right; one thing need trouble him no longer.

But then, with a shock of utter dismay, he felt fat Simon rubbing possessively against his leg. Fat cat Simon, who had no right in the world to be there on a Greek beach on the island of Kerimos!

---

[6]**"Attendez un moment!":** "Wait a minute!"

And next minute one of the quayside cats, a thin, raggedy black tom, howled out such a frightful piece of insulting cat language from the concrete steps close by, where they were building a new cafe, that fat Simon, insulted beyond bearing, shot after the black cat in a flash, there was a flurry, a scurry, black and tabby fur flew about, and both cats vanished, yowling and spitting, under a half-built boat.

"*Simon!* Come back here!" shouted Sam in horror, and darted up the steps after his cat. But, hunt though he might all over the quay, his cat was nowhere to be found. There were dozens and dozens of crannies and corners where the two cats might have retired to carry on their dispute: up alleyways, under stalls, under boats, in crowded little food shops, or under the tablecloths and benches of tavernas. The search almost at once began to seem utterly hopeless.

And all the time he could hear the voice of Madame Bonamy saying, *come straight back.* He knew he should not be there, that Simon should not be there. He did not dare speak to anybody, ask if they had seen his cat. Was he already parting the strands of time, by searching and calling?

Oh, if only Madame Bonamy were there!

I mustn't stay here in Kerimos by myself, he thought wretchedly. But to leave Simon here — how could he do that? What could he do?

Then a hopeful idea slid into his mind. Wild, maybe, but hopeful. If it were possible to go back earlier still — go back to a time *before* the Kerimos holiday — before Simon was lost . . .

But how to do that, without the diamond, without the mirror?

Standing in miserable indecision, looking across the brilliant blue water of the harbour at the white houses on the far side, Sam heard the echo of another voice, remembered from long ago.

"Your mind is a mirror; your mind is a mirror reflecting the world, showing you the image of the world around you, and all you have ever seen in it."

Who had said that?

Never mind who said it, *it was true*! My mind is a mirror, Sam thought; I can write on it. I have to remember all that has happened to me, from taking the book, back and back and farther back, like unwinding a tape . . .

And, thinking hard, thinking for his very life, he began to remember.

Minute by minute he travelled back, and as he grew more expert at remembering, the minutes zipped by faster and faster, while he guided himself through the past with the skill of a skater or a wind-surfer, steering towards marker buoys, watching out for mileposts as they flashed up and past him. There was the time Linnet broke her leg; the time the chimney blew off in a gale; the time he lost his watch; the time they had the French boy, Pierre, to stay; the time Granny came for Christmas; the time he and Linnet had measles — stop! *That* had been when Dad gave him Simon as a kitten to cheer up a miserable convales-cence,[7] when his ears ached, and his glands were all swelled up, and Linnet went back to school and he was still stuck in bed.

Stop! he ordered the minutes, and they whirled to a flashing con-clusion and left him in his own bed, in his own room in Camden Town, and there was Father, as he used to be, undoing a square cat-basket with holes in the sides to reveal a roly-poly grey-and-black-striped kitten, who displayed no sort of anxiety or homesickness but leapt confidently straight onto Sam's bed, and burrowed and trod himself a comfortable nest under the feather quilt.

"Measles medicine," said Sam's father, smiling, "to help you pass the time till you're allowed to read again."

"Oh, Dad!"

Being deprived of books had been the worst part of measles.

"It's so boring lying in bed doing nothing," Sam had complained, and Dad said — yes, yes, it was Dad who had said it — "Your mind is a mirror, reflecting the world. Look into your mind and you can find any image that it has ever held. You can always find something there to think about, to entertain yourself."

---

[7]**convalescence** (kŏn′və lĕs′əns): gradual return to health after illness or injury.

Dad had said it.

"Can I come up?" called a familiar voice from downstairs. "*Est-ce qu'on peut entrer?*"[8] and Madame Bonamy came into the bedroom carrying a pile of books. "Yes, yes, I know that you are not permitted to read, Sam, but I have come to read *to* you, so pay attention. Mary gives permission for this visit. *Allô*, Jonathan, *mon vieux*,[9] have you heard the story about the horseman and the oysters?"

And in no time she and Sam's father were swapping lunatic tales and laughing their heads off, and Sam showed Madame Bonamy his new kitten, burrowed under the quilt, and Ma had come up with a pot of tea and cups and a big mug of orange juice for Sam; it had been a memorably happy afternoon.

"Madame Bonamy," said Sam swiftly when there was a break in the talk, "I have to ask you something. I'm all tangled up in time, things just couldn't be worse or more complicated. Simon is going to be lost on Kerimos — how will I ever get him back?"

He would have liked to ask about Father, too — how to unlock him, how to get him out of the marble prison — but how could that be done with Dad right in the room there, and Ma pouring tea? As it was, Sam's parents gave him puzzled looks, and Ma said, "Are you running a temperature again, Sam? Going to be lost on Kerimos, whatever are you talking about?"

But Madame Bonamy appeared to understand Sam and she answered, "Cats are not subject to time quite as humans are, Sam, so perhaps you need not despair. Also there is a lucky charm with cats that I have sometimes used. When you walk up the hill on your way to school, count the cats in the front gardens as you go by —"

"Oh yes, I've often done that! If you get as far as nine, it's a lucky day."

"So; no need to instruct you, I see," she said, smiling. "You have discovered for yourself how to undo the time chain."

---

[8] **"Est-ce qu'on peut entrer?":** "Is it all right if I come in?"
[9] **"Allô, Jonathan, mon vieux":** "Hello, Jonathan, old friend."

Then she read aloud a French play to Sam, and his parents, though protesting that they ought to be correcting exam books, had stayed and taken parts; everyone had laughed at their bad pronunciation, and Madame Bonamy carefully tore a slip of paper from her notebook and inscribed a Z on it. "For the worst French accent in the country," she said, giving it to Jonathan Palmer. "Well," he objected, "I teach physics, not French, what do you expect?" But Madame Bonamy said she knew the rudiments of physics as well as French; one ought to extend the range of one's knowledge as wide as possible, she said. "It is never too late to learn."

Then she had left, calling from the stairs that she would let herself out and hoped to see Sam in class again next week. Sam wondered at the time why his mother gave Madame Bonamy such a loving, intent look; full of admiration yet sorrowful too, like that of an older sister who knows the troubles the younger one will have to meet. Later, Sam thought he understood that look.

Was that the last time Madame Bonamy had come to the house? It had been a long, long time ago.

Thinking these thoughts, Sam became aware that he was sitting up in bed, that he was awake, at home in Camden Town, and that the night was nearly over, the grey light of dawn filtering in at the windows.

Good heavens. Had he dreamed the whole thing? Madame Bonamy, and her advice, and the journey back in time to Kerimos, the journey even farther back in time, to this very room?

Which layer of time was he occupying now?

Rather tremulous, feeling hollow and strange, as if his legs had been walking hundreds of miles while he was asleep, Sam got out of bed and tiptoed across to the dressing-table, to the mirror. Nothing was written on its surface: no faint, spidery, silvery backwards handwriting — there was nothing to be seen but his own anxious face, pale and smudge-eyed, staring back at him from the glass.

But the book that had lain under the mirror was gone.

And, search as he might through his scattered belongings, and all over the room, Sam could not find it.

Fat cat Simon was gone too. Which was worrying: dreadfully worrying. True, the window was open, and Simon often did go out, via the branches of a plum tree, towards the end of the night, on his own concerns; but how to be sure of that? Suppose he was still left behind, fighting the wild black cat on Kerimos?

But — wait a minute, wait a minute — what had Madame Bonamy said about that? About cats?

Hastily, but trying to be as quiet as a ghost because it was still very, very early — yesterday at this time he would have been listening to the crowing of Greek roosters — no town traffic was abroad yet, no trains passing, no milk bottles clattering — Sam scrambled into his clothes and stole downstairs. He simply had to be sure about Simon, he could not bear another minute's uncertainty.

On his way to the front door he stopped, with a gulp that seemed to shift his heart on its foundations, at the sight of his father, Jonathan, still sitting, wide awake, silent and staring, in the front room, as he must have sat all night long.

"Oh — hallo, Dad," Sam gasped in a whisper, but trying to make his voice sound as ordinary as possible. "I — I got up early. I'm just — just going out to look for Simon."

His father's eyes moved in their sockets and regarded Sam; they held a vaguely puzzled expression.

"Dad," burst out Sam irrepressibly, "do you remember once saying that your mind is a mirror? That you can look into it and see anything in the world, anything in the past? Do you remember that?"

Jonathan's eyes seemed to become even more puzzled; then there emerged a soft sound from him as if he were trying out his throat, preparing to speak.

"Do you remember, Dad," Sam went on in a rush, "do you remember an afternoon when Madame Bonamy came and read a French play to me, and gave you a Z mark for your bad pronunciation? It was the day you brought me Simon."

Slowly, as if movements were not something he was used to, Jonathan pulled out a wallet from his breast pocket and began awkwardly and hesitantly thumbing through its contents. At last, from the very back, he pulled out a grimy slip of paper, on which was inscribed in ink a large flourishing capital Z.

He held out the paper; the eyes of father and son met over it, and both smiled, just a little.

Then Jonathan spoke, in a rusty whisper.

"Where — er — where did you say that you were going?"

"Out to look for Simon. He's missing. I shan't be gone long, I hope," Sam asserted stoutly, trying to sound confident and cheerful. "When I come back I'll put on the kettle for a cup of tea."

And he walked out into the cool grey city dawn. Far off he could hear the voice of industry beginning to stir and rumble. But here, in this elderly residential neighbourhood, all was quiet.

Cats were out in gardens, though; Sam saw the marmalade tom across the street, and the slinky grey from next door, and the dirty black-and-white in the garden two houses along.

He moved on very slowly, with his hands clenched in his pockets. It wouldn't do to go too fast, he wanted to give the cats time to come out into the front gardens. Let there be nine of them, he thought. And, Shall I ever find that book again? Or has it really vanished? Did I really see Madame Bonamy? Or was she just a dream? Can Mother and Father miss her as much as I do?

While he walked on up the hill — methodically noting the tortoiseshell at Number 19 and the Siamese at Number 12 — two thoughts floated to the top of his mind and stayed there.

Perhaps Simon will be the ninth cat. And, perhaps Father will have put on the kettle by the time I get back.

Responding to "Your Mind Is a Mirror"

Thinking and Discussing

Think about Sam's experiences in the story. Which events can Sam be sure really happened? How does he know?

Which events might Sam have only imagined or dreamed? What is the evidence that they *might* have happened? What further evidence would Sam need to prove to himself that these events *did* happen?

Madame Bonamy tells Sam that he can move back in time by listing his experiences — in reverse order — writing backwards on a mirror. Why might the author have chosen this device? Do you think it is effective? Why or why not? What other ways might an author use to show a character moving backward in time?

Choosing a Creative Response

Designing a Book Jacket Designers of book jackets use color and symbols to suggest the mood and tone of the story. Think of a design for a book jacket for "Your Mind Is a Mirror." Make notes that would tell an artist how to carry out your design. You might want to include a sketch and some color samples.

Creating Your Own Activity Plan and complete your own activity in response to "Your Mind Is a Mirror."

Thinking and Writing

At the end of the story, Sam hopes that he will find Simon and that his father will be better by the time Sam gets home. Do you think either or both of these things will happen? Why or why not? Write a brief statement of your predictions and your reasons for them.

Thinking About Fantasy

Conducting a Survey Some of the selections in "Hall of Mirrors" ended with a return to everyday reality, while others were left open-ended. Which kind of story do you prefer? Conduct a survey of your classmates, and make a graph of your findings. You may want to include other classes in your survey. Do different groups vary in their preferences?

Inventing a Fantasy Game Plan a computer fantasy game. Describe the setting, the characters, the problem to be solved, the rules, and the other details of the game.

Creating a Poster Think about the four selections in "Hall of Mirrors." Then design and illustrate a poster for a fantasy book display that will include the titles of these stories and other similar stories. Try to show the characteristics of the stories that make them appealing. You may wish to read some of the stories aloud and record them on tape. Then play them for the class's enjoyment when you present your poster.

About the Authors

Joan Aiken, the daughter of Conrad Aiken, a well-known American poet, was born in 1924 in Sussex, England. From early childhood, she loved to write, and she has never stopped writing.

Aiken has become well known for her suspense novels for young people. The stories in *Up the Chimney Down*, from which "Potter's Gray" was taken, cross and recross the line between reality and fantasy so cleverly that the author makes the unreal seem possible. Her novels include *Black Hearts in Battersea*, *Nightbirds on Nantucket*, and the award-winning *The Wolves of Willoughby Chase*.

Vivien Alcock was born in 1924 in Worthing, England, and now lives in London. Since 1980, she has written several ghost stories for young people, including *The Haunting of Cassie Palmer*, *The Stonewalkers*, *The Sylvia Game*, and *Travelers by Night*. Alcock says, "Although I have a liking for dramatic and sometimes fantastic plots, I try to make my characters as real as possible, and their relationships true . . . I find I tend to write about children who are facing some great change or difficulty in their lives, and who learn to grow through it to a greater understanding of themselves and other people."

Philippa Pearce was born in the riverside village of Great Shelford in Cambridgeshire, England. Many of her books, including *The Minnow Leads to Treasure* and the award-winning *Tom's Midnight Garden*, are set in her childhood home, village, and countryside. Settings are important in Philippa Pearce's stories. "That often comes to me before anything else," she says. Among her notable books are *A Dog So Small*, *The Way to Sattin Shore*, *The Battle of Bubble and Squeak*, *Who's Afraid? and Other Strange Stories*, and *The Shadow-Cage*. In this last story collection, which includes "The Strange Illness of Mr. Arthur Cook," the author finds unexpected meaning and humor in everyday events.

Stories to Dream On

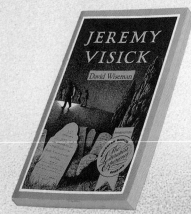

Jeremy Visick by David Wiseman
(Houghton, 1981)

Matthew is drawn back in time to
help a boy who was lost in an 1852 mining
disaster in his own small town of
Cornwall, England.

More Stories to Dream On (Houghton, 1993)

This collection of fantasy stories will take
you from the ball field to the edges of the world
as you know it. Read about strange and impossible events that occur in a variety of settings.

Tom's Midnight Garden by Philippa Pearce (Lippincott, 1958)

Tom is bored by a visit with his aunt until he discovers the
garden that exists only when the grandfather
clock strikes thirteen. Entering the garden
at night, he meets fascinating people who
used to live in the house, especially a
mysterious girl named Hattie. His school
vacation is almost over; Tom doesn't
know how he can stand to leave the
Midnight Garden and Hattie.

The Widow and the Parrot
by Virginia Woolf (Harcourt, 1988)

Poor Mrs. Gage is delighted when her stingy brother dies and she inherits a house and some money, but unfortunately the house is shabby and run-down, the money is nowhere in sight, and the only thing of any possible value is a scruffy parrot. Mrs. Gage shouldn't count on finding her brother's money anytime soon.

The Transfigured Hart
by Jane Yolen (Crowell, 1975)

Richard and Heather have a strange experience in common. They've both sighted the same magnificent white animal in the woods. Could it be the fabled unicorn, or is it just an albino deer, as the hunters claim? Together, Richard and Heather try to protect the freedom of the rare beast.

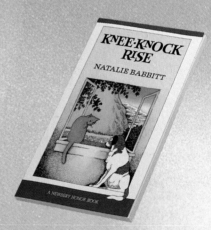

Kneeknock Rise
by Natalie Babbitt (Farrar, 1970)

What a nice thing for a town — a Megrimum camped out on a nearby hill! Never mind the terrifying sounds coming from the hill known for good reasons as Kneeknock Rise. Egan can get rid of the noisy Megrimum, but the towns-people aren't sure they want to lose their town's claim to fame.

SCIENCE

BOOK 7

ANIMAL BEHAVIOR
AND COMMUNICATION

Animal Communication

SPECIAL
ASSIGNMENT

Join our investigative team and unravel the mysteries of animal communication. Travel with scientists as they observe animals in the wild. Experiment in the laboratory. Gather evidence and develop your own theories about animal language. Help the Scientific Investigators' Society find the answers!

WANTED

SCIENCE DETECTIVES

QUALIFICATIONS: an open mind, fact-gathering ability, curiosity, thoroughness

ORGANIZATION: Scientific Investigators' Society

ASSIGNMENT: to explore the question: **Can Animals Talk?**

Animal Communication

SPECIAL ASSIGNMENT

ANIMAL BEHAVIOR

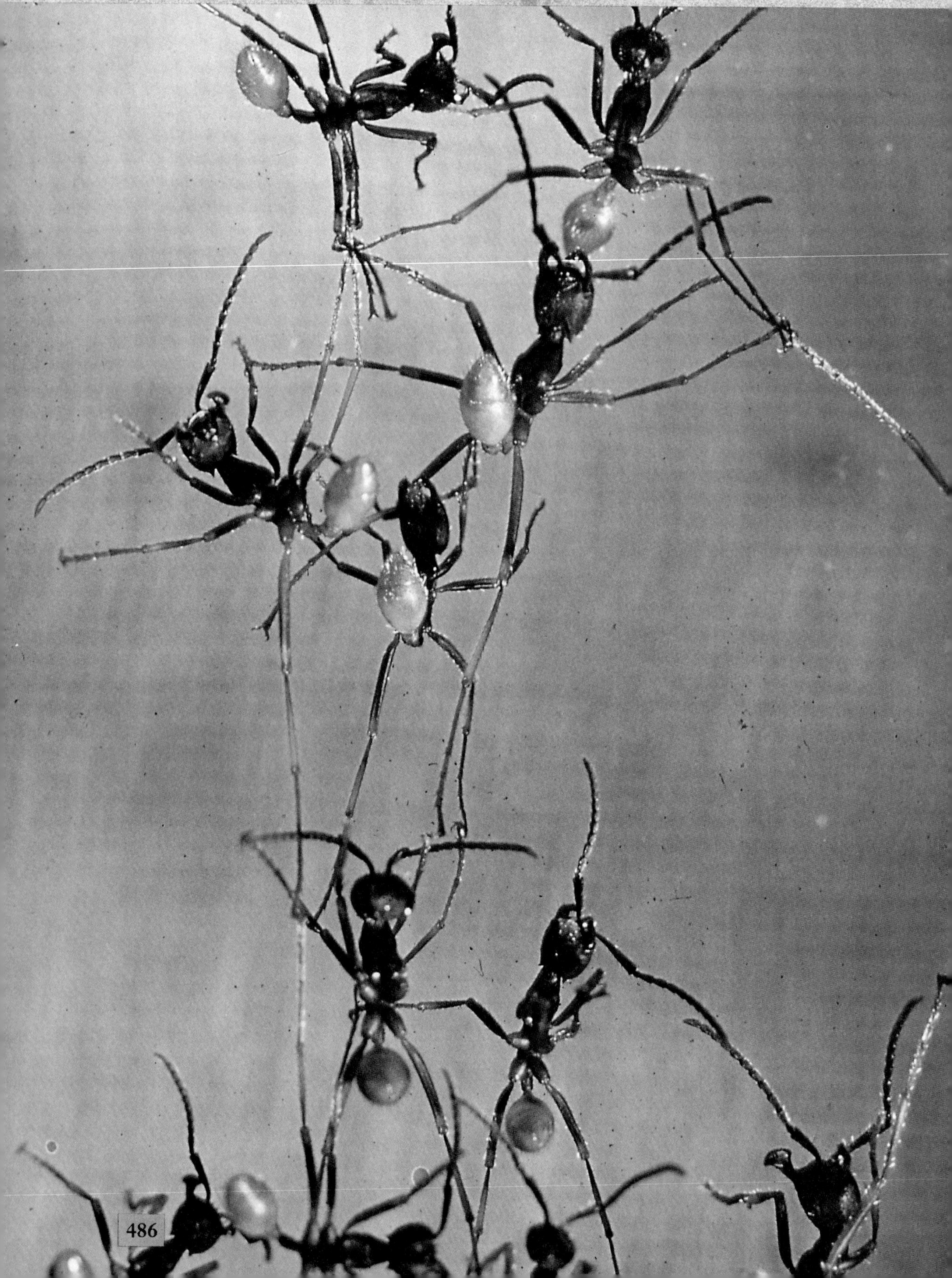

1 Behavior & Learning

▸ **Focus:** What are the basic elements of animal behavior?

- stimulus
- response
- conditioning
- trial and error

▸ **Key Terms:**
- inborn behavior
- learned behavior
- reasoning

Have you ever disturbed an anthill? How did the ants react to the sudden change in their environment? By looking closely, perhaps you noticed many ants dragging eggs and pupae (young ants) into tunnels. Their actions served a purpose, to protect their young.

The ants reacted predictably to the attack on their nest. Other creatures would have reacted too, though in different ways. Ant, squirrel, elephant, human — each organism's reaction to its environment is called its behavior. Eating, sleeping, and home-building are common animal behaviors.

Perhaps you wonder why ants — and other members of the animal kingdom — behave as they do. So do many scientists! In fact, their curiosity has led them to search for answers to questions, including the following:

- What kinds of behaviors do animals show?
- How does living in groups affect animal behavior?
- How do animals communicate? For what purposes?

At the heart of these and other questions lies the desire to understand the reasons for animal behavior. Using evidence from careful research, scientists have developed theories to explain why organisms act as they do. In this chapter you will learn more about what these scientists have concluded.

Ants climbing a
vertical surface

487

Behavior — Its Basic Parts

Most scientists agree that behavior results from something that happens in an animal's environment, something called a **stimulus**. When you disturbed the anthill, you changed the ants' environment. In turn, that stimulus caused a reaction, or **response**, from the ants. They gathered their young and fled. A stimulus in an animal's environment causes it to respond.

Animals respond differently to a similar stimulus. When threatened, a turtle pulls its head into its shell. A bee stings its enemy. A rabbit freezes and then scampers away. These are just a few ways that animals respond to danger. What other kinds of behaviors do animals use to protect themselves?

Kinds of Behavior

Scientists are curious about *how* an animal knows which response to a stimulus is the right one. What influences how an animal reacts to its environment? To answer this question, researchers describe two general categories of behavior.

Inborn Behavior A newly hatched fish knows how to swim. It does not need to think about forcing water through its gills to breathe. The fish was equipped at birth with many preset responses to its environment.

Most organisms are born with general behavior patterns that help them stay alive. Such **inborn behavior** is not learned; instead it comes naturally when triggered by a stimulus. Thus, hornets know the set of steps needed to make a paper nest. Likewise, bats are "preprogrammed" to use high squeals and echoes to locate food and to navigate.

Bats using radar to find food

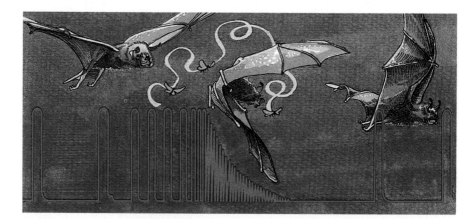

A hooded skunk

Some inborn behaviors are fairly simple, while others are far more complicated. For example, if you touch something hot (stimulus), you quickly pull your hand away (response), usually before the problem registers in your mind. This reflex, or involuntary action, happens automatically. What reflex occurs if someone's fingers snap near your eyes?

Instinct, a far more complicated form of inborn behavior, requires a complex set of responses. Often a series of actions or steps are followed, as in the case of a hungry archerfish. When a fly buzzes in the air above it, instinct causes the fish to draw water into its mouth. Then it squirts a jet of water at the insect, which is knocked into the pond for the fish to eat. Instinctive behaviors such as mating, migrating, and nest-building permit members of a species to survive. Inborn behaviors, however, do not account for all animal activities.

Learned Behavior A coyote pup corners a skunk, which instinctively protects itself by spraying the pup with a foul-smelling liquid. The next time the pup comes across a skunk, it turns and runs. The pup has learned from earlier experience to leave skunks alone!

Many creatures are capable of such **learned behavior.** They use memories of earlier experiences to change their responses to new ones. Rats can be trained to find their way through mazes. In the wild, many animals teach their offspring how to hunt and live together in groups. Animals such as oxen, elephants, and horses have been trained by people to perform hard labor.

How do animals learn new behaviors, especially ones that differ greatly from their natural activities in the wild? Scientists interested in the learning process have identified various methods, including the following:

Conditioning In the late 1800's a Russian scientist named Ivan Pavlov observed that food (the stimulus) made a hungry dog's mouth water (response). In an experiment, he added a second stimulus — the ringing of a bell — each time the dog was fed. After several weeks, Pavlov could make the dog's mouth water just by ringing the bell. Pavlov concluded that the dog had learned to associate the ringing bell with feeding. Called **conditioning**, this type of learned behavior results when one stimulus (the bell) becomes *associated* with another (food).

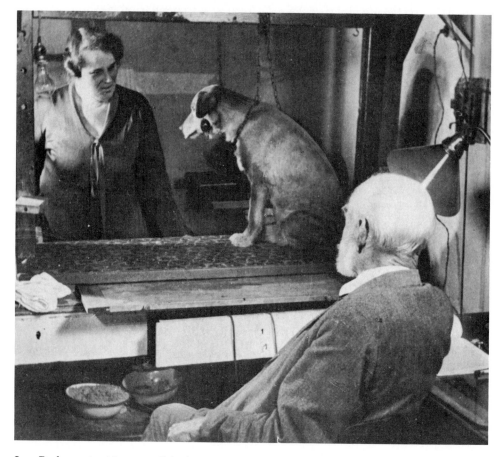

Ivan Pavlov supervising a conditioning experiment on a dog

Trial and Error   In another classical experiment, a food pellet slid into a feeding tray each time a rat stepped on a green lever. Nothing happened when the rat stepped on a blue or red lever. By doing the task over and over, the rat learned which lever rewarded it with food. This **trial and error** method of learning rewards a desired behavior.

Insight Learning   In a series of experiments, scientists tested the problem-solving abilities of chimpanzees by hanging bananas from the ceiling. To get their reward, the chimps piled up boxes, used a pole for a ladder, and in one case, jumped on an experimenter's shoulders. The chimps knew from earlier experiences that they could use something (or someone) to help them reach the banana. This kind of behavior, called **insight learning,** requires animals to use memories of past experiences to solve new problems. Dolphins, apes, and other animals with higher levels of intelligence are also believed to use simple insight.

Possibly the greatest difference between the two kinds of behavior is that inborn behaviors tend to be set, rigid patterns while learned behaviors reflect the ability to change. Inborn behaviors may occur even when they are not appropriate — as when an archerfish shoots at a block of wood. On the other hand, learned behaviors show an ability to vary responses to fit new situations. If a wild chimpanzee breaks its stick while fishing in a termite hole, it may remove the broken end or choose another stick to use! Many animal activities combine inborn and learned responses into complex sets of behavior.

Review
1) What is behavior?
2) Compare inborn behavior to learned behavior.
3) In what ways can animals learn new behaviors in the wild? In what ways can people train animals to learn new behaviors?

Animal Communication

▶ Focus: How do animals communicate with one another?

▶ Key Terms:
- social behavior
- social order
- division of work
- language

Herds of buffalo, schools of tuna, ant colonies, wolf packs — many animals band together with others of their own kind.

By living and working in a group, social animals benefit from being together. The group provides more protection for its members, and a variety of mates. It may also supply food, shelter, and other basic needs, thus bettering the animals' chances to survive.

Social Behavior

Social animals interact with other group members as they go about their daily activities. The various interactions, called **social behavior**, are the animals' responses to group living.

An orangutan imitating human facial expressions

In wolf packs and other animal communities, a few members become leaders. Leaders are often given the best food or other privileges, but they are also expected to keep the group from danger. Some groups also rank followers in their order of importance and treat one another accordingly. This respect for the **social order** reduces the tension and fighting among group members.

In another form of social behavior, **division of work**, group members carry out different tasks. Members of ant, wasp, and other insect colonies are highly specialized. In an ants' nest, for instance, each member has one set job, often for life. The queen lays eggs that produce new ants. Certain workers care for the queen and her young, while others gather food. Still others build, enlarge, repair, and protect the nest. In some species special soldier ants with powerful heads and jaws serve to protect the colony. This cooperative approach benefits the entire group.

Communication

A dog growls, shows its teeth, and lays back its ears. The hair on its neck rises, and it stands stiff-legged in front of you. This dog is communicating a threat. No words are needed — with its threatening behavior, the dog sends out the message, "Steer clear of me!"

Communication occurs when animals send and receive signals that are meant to alter the behavior of others. This information exchange helps animals protect themselves from danger, attract mates, find food, and so survive.

The communicating behaviors of animals take many forms. The actions of a threatened dog differ from those of an ape, which screams, sways back and forth, and throws leaves or even rocks. A rattlesnake may shake the rattles on its tail to warn off attackers. No matter what the behavior, however, animals are able to convey messages to their own kind — and to other species as well.

Bull elk fighting

Animals communicate with one another by using sounds and body movements. They also send messages with odors, coloration, touch, or a combination of senses. Ants, for instance, leave chemical "scent" trails for other workers to follow. Many fish change or deepen their colors as they prepare to fight or attract mates. In chimpanzee communities, huffing noises are used as greetings or to calm and reassure individual members.

Greeting a friend, talking on the phone, writing a letter or report — you constantly use a form of communication known as **language**. In this complex learned behavior, you use sounds and symbols (like the ones on this page) to communicate thoughts and feelings.

How does human language differ from other forms of animal communication? Do some animals use languages of their own, or is language an ability limited to humans? Researchers are focusing on these kinds of questions, with interesting results. Consider the following findings:

- Dolphins have been known to signal one another when hurt, in danger, or in need of help. Researchers have studied dolphins to find out whether the noises they make are random sounds or deliberate sounds that symbolize specific meanings. In one experiment, two captive dolphins in different pools whistled and clicked to one another through an underwater "telephone." Later, when the noises made by one dolphin were played back to the other, it responded with clicks and whistles similar to the ones in the original "conversation."

A researcher conducting communication exercises with dolphins

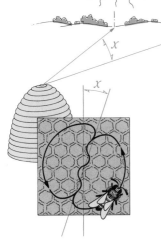

A honeybee, her leg sacs filled with pollen, "dancing" to tell other bees where to find the flowers she has just located

• When a honeybee hive lacks a particular food or other badly needed material, workers fly away to search for it. A worker that finds a supply of the item returns to the hive and begins to dance in a circle or a figure-eight pattern, alerting the other bees to its find. By waggling its body and moving in a certain direction, the worker describes the distance and direction the others need to travel. The amount of energy used by the dancer communicates the desirability of the item. The dancer uses symbolic movements to pass along information to its fellow workers.

• Several apes have been taught a simple sign language. Surprisingly, some have performed beyond expectation by using words they knew to name new items. *Celery* was called *pipe food*; *cucumber* became *banana which is green*; and *watermelon* was named both *candy drink* and *drink fruit*.

Not all scientists agree on how this and other evidence should be interpreted. Some argue that these behaviors are only instinctive or that they do not reflect the true nature of human language. Others insist that, in time, and with enough observation, particular signals will be matched with particular responses. They are convinced that certain species *do* show an ability to use language.

While recent research into animal communication has caused controversy, it has also challenged previously held theories and revealed gaps in current knowledge. Even the definition of *language* is being re-examined. Ultimately, scientists will raise more questions and begin new research to explore the mysteries that surround animal communication and other behavior.

Three sea lions greeting one another

Review
1) How does living in groups help certain animals to survive?
2) Name five different ways in which animals may communicate.
3) How is language different from other forms of communication?

THE SCIENTIST AT WORK

In July of 1960, Jane Goodall came to Africa to study chimpanzees in their natural habitat. For the next four months she searched the area for chimpanzees, hoping to learn more about their behavior. One day she saw a chimpanzee poke a thick grass stalk into a termite hole, remove it, and lick the insects off it. The chimp was using a tool! Was this "fishing" for termites something unusual, or did chimps do it on a regular basis?

Goodall's sighting was the first-ever observation of this chimpanzee activity in the wild. Based on years of subsequent observations, Goodall went on to conclude that chimpanzees could indeed make and use simple tools. And this was just one of many conclusions drawn about a chimpanzee community during more than twenty-five years of continuous study.

In most laboratory experiments, conditions are carefully controlled. This means that, for example, to study how sugar affects the behavior of mice, scientists must be sure that no other factors influence their subjects' behavior. But field studies cannot be controlled in this way. Goodall's research had to be done in the African wilderness under less than ideal conditions. In order for her field study to be useful to other scientists, she wanted her work to reflect accurate, real-life chimpanzee behavior. She therefore relied on certain scientific methods, principles basic to science research.

Observation To collect accurate data, Goodall set up an elaborate observation system. Daily observation was necessary, and each of her helpers was armed — with binoculars, a watch, several charts and checklists for recording behaviors, and often, a camera. *Where did the chimps go and what did they eat? Who were their "family" and "friends"? Their "enemies"?* These were just a few of the questions to be answered.

497

Repetition Goodall and her assistants were careful not to make generalizations about chimpanzee behavior through observing one or two actions. Often, individual chimpanzees were followed for days at a time to get an accurate picture of certain kinds of behavior. Observers set out to record facts — only what they saw and heard. Over the years, the information grew, so that detailed records of chimpanzee behavior are now available.

Inferring From Evidence By studying the information in her records and comparing them with records from other study sites, Goodall has been able to infer, or conclude from evidence, the causes of many chimpanzee behaviors. For instance, the apes' communication behavior is better understood now.

Chimpanzees use a variety of sounds, facial expressions, and body movements to communicate their emotions and other details to one another. By noting the response of other chimpanzees to certain calls, Goodall was able to figure out the general meaning of many chimpanzee vocalizations. Should a chimp be surprised, puzzled, or slightly anxious about an unknown rustling or a small creature, it often makes a *huu* sound. In response, other nearby chimps will move closer to study the object that caught the caller's attention. The *cough-threat*, a soft, grunting bark, is used only by chimpanzees of high social rank to send a mild warning to those lower in the social order. The call signals the sender's mild annoyance at what it believes the lower-ranking animal is about to do.

Jane Goodall's research has provided new insights into chimpanzee behavior. Other dedicated scientists are doing equally remarkable work. Together, their contributions add to the growing store of knowledge about animal behavior.

Responding to "Animal Behavior"

Thinking and Discussing

In what ways is communication among dogs, among insects, and among apes similar? In what ways is communication different for each species?

How does the text define social behavior? In explaining social behavior, what other terms does the text introduce? What do these terms mean?

Scientist Jane Goodall reached many conclusions about chimpanzees. What were some of her conclusions? Describe the careful process she followed in her research. Do you think the results of her study are reliable? Why, or why not?

Applying Science Concepts

Illustrating Behavior Working with your group, make a poster showing one of the methods of learning new behaviors — conditioning, trial and error, and reasoning — discussed in the selection. On poster paper, use watercolors, crayons, or markers to illustrate the behavior of the animal described in the passage you select. Your illustration can be one picture, or it can be made up of several pictures that show the progression of the events. Display your poster in the classroom.

Writing A REPORT OF INFORMATION

Scientists learn much about animals simply by observing them. The information gathered from their observations is often organized in reports. In reports of information, scientists present facts and ideas clearly so that others may appreciate and understand their research.

Write a report of information on something you can observe in nature. You may choose to study the behavior of a favorite pet, the plant growth in a park or garden, or the changes in the night sky. Pay attention to the way the authors of the articles here have presented their information about animal behavior. Start writing whenever you feel ready. If the selections give you another writing idea, write about that one instead.

1. _Prewriting_ Before you begin writing, choose something that you want to observe for at least a few days. Keep accurate notes of your observations. Make data sheets that list descriptions of your subject and the date and time of each observation. Be sure that you can draw reasonable conclusions from observations of repeated patterns. What conclusions can you draw from your data? How will you present your information?

2. _Write a First Draft_ Write a first draft based on your data. Think about your audience and your purpose for writing. Do you want to write a narrative or a more straightforward presentation of information? Will charts, graphs, and photographs help you make your points?

3. *Revise* Read your first draft and make any necessary changes. Does your study detail observable patterns? Have you given evidence to support your conclusions? Read your report to a classmate to make sure it is informative and interesting.

4. *Proofread* Check your report for correct spelling, capitalization, and punctuation.

5. *Publish* Make a neat copy of your scientific report. Share your findings with your classmates on a day of scientific discovery.

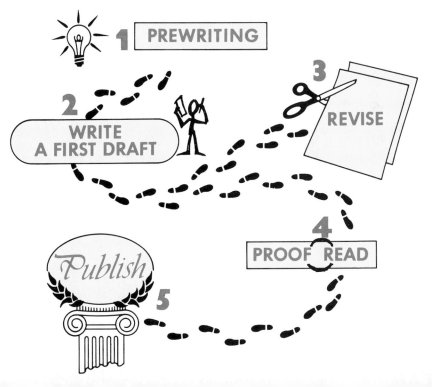

1 PREWRITING

2 WRITE A FIRST DRAFT

3 REVISE

4 PROOF READ

5 Publish

Keeping in Touch

If you are lucky enough to see wolf tracks in the wild, you will probably not see the footprints of a single animal. Wolves travel in groups; they hunt in groups, and they perform almost all the other activities of their lives in the company of fellow wolves. This is one of the most important facts that modern science has learned about wolves and one of the things that most clearly explains their way of life.

The *pack*, the basic unit of wolf social life, is usually a family group. It is made up of animals related to each other by blood and family ties of affection and mutual aid. The core of a pack is a mated pair of wolves — an adult male and female that have bred and produced young. The other members of the pack are their offspring: young wolves ranging in age from pups to two- and three-year-olds. Most packs have 6 or 7 members, although some may include as many as 15 to 25 wolves.

An adult wolf watching over young members of the pack while other adults hunt for food

Like members of all families, the individual wolves in a pack play different roles in relation to the others in the group. Just as in a human family, the parent wolves are the leaders of the pack. Scientists refer to them as the *alpha male* and *alpha female* to indicate their superior position within the *dominance hierarchy*, or pack social structure. (Alpha is the first letter in the Greek alphabet.)

The alpha male and female are the oldest members of the pack and the ones with the most experience in hunting, defending territory, and other important group activities. The other pack members respect their positions and follow their leadership in almost all things. The alpha wolves are usually the ones to make decisions for the pack, for instance, when the group should go out to hunt or move from one place to another.

The other pack members all have positions in the hierarchy inferior to those of the alpha male and female. The young adult wolves, who are the grown-up offspring of the alpha pair, have their own special roles under the leadership of their parents. Some of them are able to "boss

Two-week-old wolf pups in the security of the den

Wolf pack members nuzzling each other in a typical display of pack unity and affection

505

around," or dominate, their sisters and brothers because they have established themselves as superior in some way. This superiority might be physical — larger size or greater strength — but it can also be based on personality. *Dominant* wolves in the pack usually have more aggressive and forceful personalities than their relatives of the same age.

The juveniles and pups — wolves under two years old — do not occupy permanent positions within the pack hierarchy. They all take orders from their parents and older brothers and sisters, but their relationships with each other change frequently. During their play and other activities, they are constantly testing one another to find out who will eventually be "top wolf" in their age group.

Relationships among creatures that live close together in groups are often very complicated, and this is true of the ties that connect the members of a wolf pack. Scientific studies of captive wolves and wolf packs in the wild have shown that many complex rules of behavior seem to govern the way that the animals relate to each other. The methods that wolves use to communicate with fellow pack members are also quite elaborate.

When wolf pups are born into a pack, one of the most important things they must learn is the "language" of the group, the method by which pack members keep in touch with each other, sharing information and communicating their feelings. Scientists have discovered that wolves have a very complicated system of communication, quite different from the language of humans but used in a similar way to convey meaning.

An efficient system of communication is vital to all animals that live in groups. In order for the members of a pack, a family, or a nation to cooperate and to live peacefully together, there must be a way for individuals to let others know what they are planning and feeling. Human societies use words, both spoken and written, as a means of communication among their members. A wolf pack communicates with sounds, but it also employs smells, movements, and body positions to convey information of various kinds.

Because rank and hierarchy are so important to the orderly functioning of a wolf pack, much of the communication among pack members is related to this aspect of their lives. Using movements and body

The Social Structure of a Wolf Pack

Alpha Pair
♂ ♀

Beta Male
(second-ranking male; sometimes
mates with alpha female)
♂

Young Subordinates
(often dominated by
"little alphas")
♂ ♀

Juveniles and Pups
♂ ♀

"Scapegoat"
(lives on fringes of pack;
may be mistreated by
other members)
♂ ♀

♂ Male
♀ Female

A wolf howling
to locate its
pack members

positions, the leaders of the pack continually remind the other wolves of their dominant roles in the group. In return, the subordinate wolves communicate their respect and affection for — and sometimes their fear of — the pack leaders.

One of the clearest symbols of a wolf's rank in a pack is the position of its tail. Unlike the tails of many breeds of dogs, a wolf's long, bushy tail normally hangs down rather than curling up over its back. The alpha wolves in a pack, however, usually hold their tails high in the air instead of letting them droop.

In any pack, the wolf carrying its tail high like a hairy banner will almost always be the alpha male. The alpha female also holds her tail

A low-ranking pack member, its tail tucked between its legs, approaching an alpha wolf

high, although usually not as high as that of her mate. Wolves occupying positions below the pack leaders keep their tails correspondingly low, especially in any confrontation with the alpha pair. The lowest-ranking members of the pack tuck their tails between their legs to express their inferiority to the wolves above them in the hierarchy.

The positions of other body parts are also used as a means of communicating status in the pack. An alpha wolf usually keeps its ears standing up, while low-ranking pack members lay their ears back. They also keep their fur flat, in contrast to the fluffed-out fur of the pack leaders.

There are some occasions in the life of the pack that call for more specific expressions of the relationships among the pack members. When a low-ranking wolf approaches one of the pack leaders, it keeps its body low to the ground, with its fur and ears flattened. From this position, it reaches up with its muzzle and gently licks or nips the muzzle of the alpha wolf. Sometimes all the pack members gather around the alpha male and greet him in this manner, often when he returns to the pack after being away for a while.

Scientists call this behavior *active submission* and see it as a method whereby the pack members express friendly feelings toward the leaders and respect for their authority.

Sometimes the interaction between the dominant wolves and the rest of the pack is not so friendly. If an alpha feels that a pack member is resisting its authority, it may take strong measures to bring the rebellious wolf back in line. Often a stern and unwavering stare is enough to convince the rebel that it should submit itself to the pack leader. Like dogs and many other animals, wolves avoid looking each other directly in the eye unless they are trying to exert their authority.

An even stronger message of authority is given when a dominant wolf growls and bares its teeth at an inferior or crouches as if to spring on the offender. When a subordinate wolf is threatened in this way, it usually makes a gesture of *passive submission* by lying on the ground and exposing its side or belly to the threatener. This movement, which is also performed by pups, seems to convey a message of helplessness and dependence — "I'm harmless, please don't hurt me." Satisfied by this admission of inferiority, the dominant wolf accepts the rebel's "apology," and peace is restored in the pack.

The main purpose of all the communications expressing rank and relationships within the pack is to keep peace. Pack members rarely fight with each other because they have so many other ways of settling their differences and establishing their proper positions in the group. Physical conflict, which would be destructive to the well-being of the pack, is avoided by the use of a language of gestures and symbolic actions.

Of course, not all the communications that take place in a pack have to do with such serious subjects. Frequently, the message that one pack member wants to convey to another is, "Let's play!"

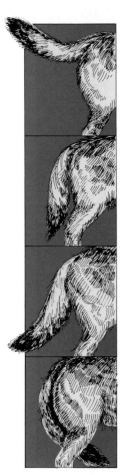

Four stages of tail talk, the positions signaling (from top to bottom) dominance, relaxation, the possible beginning of a threat, and submission

Adult wolves, like pups, enjoy chasing, wrestling, and tumbling on the ground. When a wolf is looking for a playmate, it may approach another wolf, bow down low with its front legs flat on the ground, and wag its tail vigorously. If the invitation is not accepted, it will be repeated and sometimes alternated with leaping about in a zig-zag fashion. (Many dogs make almost exactly the same movements when they are in a playful mood.) If the other wolf is willing to play, the two will engage in mock fights or take turns chasing each other until both are worn out and ready to rest.

Invitations to play and messages about social status in the pack are usually conveyed by means of movements and postures, but wolves also

use sounds to communicate with each other. The animals are capable of making several kinds of sounds, including the threatening growl or snarl and the whimper used in communications between pups and adults. The most famous wolf sound is, of course, the howl, and it is a very important part of wolf language.

When people think about howling, they usually imagine a mournful, lonely sound made by a wolf sitting all alone on a hilltop in the moonlight. Like most human images of wolves, however, this one is not very accurate. Wolves howl at any time, not just at night, and they often howl together, not alone.

Group or chorus howling is another means by which the members of a wolf pack reaffirm their ties with each other and their closeness as a group. One wolf — often the alpha male — will point its nose at the sky, open its mouth, and start to howl. Immediately the other members of the pack rush to stand beside him, shoulder to shoulder, and join their voices to his. The whole group seems to be excited and happy, tails wagging and bodies wiggling. Each wolf howls on its own note so that a grand chorus of slightly different sounds is produced.

Chorus howling often takes place before a wolf pack goes out to hunt. This ceremony of togetherness may encourage the pack members to cooperate with each other in the difficult job of finding and bringing down prey. At the end of a successful hunt, the pack may also celebrate with a group howl. While wolves are on the track of prey, they are usually silent.

There are occasions when a wolf will howl by itself. This may happen when an animal is separated from the pack and is trying to locate its companions. Pack members seem to recognize each other's voices and will keep responding to the howl of their wandering relative until the group is reunited.

Because howling is a sound that carries over a considerable distance, it is very useful in communications among separated members of a pack. Howling is also used when members of different packs have to get in touch with each other to relay information about their location and their intentions.

Responding to "Keeping in Touch"

Thinking and Discussing

How do the authors define the terms *rank* and *hierarchy*? How important are rank and hierarchy to wolf society?

How do wolves communicate with one another? How do these ways of communicating relate to the pack's social organization?

In addition to the printed text, how does "Keeping in Touch" provide information about wolves? Do these aids provide information similar to what is in the text? What information do they provide that is not in the text?

Applying Science Concepts

Charting Animal Groups Find out what other animals live in groups. Pick one that interests you. Make a chart that shows its social organization. What types of animals live in the group? What special place does each have? What role does each play? What methods of communication are important to the group? Write short captions for your drawings. Display your chart for the class.

Writing an Essay Before reading "Keeping in Touch," did you have any misconceptions, or mistaken ideas or beliefs, concerning wolves? Write a brief essay detailing the difference between the mistaken ideas you had about wolves and the accurate information you have learned from the selection. Give the essay a title. Read it before the class if you wish.

In 1947, biologist Farley Mowat accepted a job studying wolves in their natural habitat in the Canadian wilderness. Mowat, with the help of Mike, a native trapper, and Ootek, Mike's Eskimo cousin, spent months observing wolves in the barren lands of northern Canada. He became especially familiar with one wolf pack, naming the father George, the mother Angeline, and a third pack member Uncle Albert. The Canadian government, sponsor of the study, assumed that Mowat's findings would confirm a long-held belief: Wolves were responsible for killing off large numbers of caribou, and should therefore be slaughtered. Instead, Mowat found that wolves ate only the sick and weak caribou, thereby actually strengthening the herds. Mowat's study was one of the first to present an in-depth, sympathetic picture of the wolf.

NEVER

by Farley Mowat   Illustrated by Robert Roth

CRY WOLF

My real education in lupine linguistics[1] began a few days after Ootek's arrival. The two of us had been observing the wolf den for several hours without seeing anything of note. It was a dead-calm day, so that the flies had reached plague proportions, and Angeline and the pups had retired to the den to escape while both males, exhausted after a hunt which had lasted into mid-morning, were sleeping nearby. I was getting bored and sleepy myself when Ootek suddenly cupped his hands to his ears and began to listen intently.

I could hear nothing, and I had no idea what had caught his attention until he said: "Listen, the wolves are talking!" and pointed toward a range of hills some five miles to the north of us.[2]

I listened, but if a wolf was broadcasting from those hills he was not on my wavelength. I heard nothing except the baleful buzzing of mosquitoes; but George, who had been sleeping on the crest of the esker, suddenly sat up, cocked his ears forward and pointed his long muzzle toward the north. After a minute or two he threw back his head and howled; a long, quavering howl which started low and ended on the highest note my ears would register.

Ootek grabbed my arm and broke into a delighted grin.

"Caribou are coming; the wolf says so!"

I got the gist of this, but not much more than the gist, and it was not until we returned to the cabin and I again had Mike's services as an interpreter that I learned the full story.

According to Ootek, a wolf living in the next territory to the north had not only informed our wolves that the long-awaited caribou had started to move south, but had even indicated where they were at the moment. To make the story even more improbable, this wolf had not actually seen the caribou himself, but had simply been passing on a report received from a still more distant wolf. George, having heard and understood, had then passed on the good news in his turn.

---

[1]**lupine linguistics** (lōō′pĭn′ lĭng gwĭs′tĭks): the science of wolf language.

[2]During the two-year period that I knew Ootek, his English improved considerably, and I learned quite a bit of Eskimo, so that we were able to converse freely. I have therefore converted our earlier conversations, which tended to be complicated, into a form more understandable to the reader. (Author's note)

514

I am incredulous by nature and by training, and I made no secret of my amusement at the naiveté of Ootek's attempt to impress me with this fantastic yarn. But if I was incredulous, Mike was not. Without more ado he began packing up for a hunting trip.

I was not surprised at his anxiety to kill a deer, for I had learned one truth by now, that he, as well as every other human being on the Barrens,[3] was a meat eater who lived almost exclusively on caribou when they were available; but I *was* amazed that he should be willing to make a two- or three-day hike over the tundra on evidence as wild as that which Ootek offered. I said as much, but Mike went taciturn and left without another word.

Three days later, when I saw him again, he offered me a haunch of venison and a pot of caribou tongues. He also told me he had found the caribou exactly where Ootek, interpreting the wolf message, had said they would be — on the shores of a lake called Kooiak some forty miles northeast of the cabin.

I knew this *had* to be coincidence. But being curious as to how far Mike would go, to pull my leg, I feigned conversion and asked him to tell me more about Ootek's uncanny skill.

Mike obliged. He explained that the wolves not only possessed the ability to communicate over great distances but, so he insisted, could "talk" almost as well as we could. He admitted that he himself could neither hear all the sounds they made, nor understand most of them, but he said some Eskimos, and Ootek in particular, could hear and understand so well that they could quite literally converse with wolves.

I mulled this information over for a while and concluded that anything this pair told me from then on would have to be recorded with a heavy sprinkling of question marks.

However, the niggling idea kept recurring that there just *might* be something in it all, so I asked Mike to tell Ootek to keep track of

---

[3]**Barrens**: the Keewatin Barren Lands of northern Canada.

what our wolves said in future, and, through Mike, to keep me informed.

The next time we encountered Mike I recalled him to his promise and he began to interrogate Ootek.

"Yesterday," he told me, "Ootek says that wolf you call George, he send a message to his wife. Ootek hear it good. He tell his wife the hunting is pretty bad and he going to stay out longer. Maybe not get home until the middle of the day."

I remembered that Ootek could not have known at what time the male wolves returned home, for he was then fast asleep *inside* the tent. And 12:17 is close enough to the middle of the day for any practical purpose.

For two more days my skepticism ruled — until the afternoon when once again George appeared on the crest and cocked his ears toward the north. Whatever he heard, if he heard anything, did not seem to interest him much this time, for he did not howl, but went off to the den to sniff noses with Angeline.

Ootek, on the other hand, was definitely interested. Excitement filled his face. He fairly gabbled at me, but I caught only a few words. *Inuit* (Eskimos) and *kiyai* (come) were repeated several times, as he tried passionately to make me understand. When I still looked dense he gave me an exasperated glance and, without so much as a by-your-leave, headed off across the tundra in a direction which would have taken him to the northwest of Mike's cabin.

I was a little annoyed by his cavalier departure, but I soon forgot about it, for it was now late afternoon and all the wolves were becoming restless as the time approached for the males to set off on the evening hunt.

There was a definite ritual about these preparations. George usually began them by making a visit to the den. If Angeline and the pups were inside, his visit brought them out. If they were already outside, Angeline's behavior changed from that of domestic boredom to one of excitement. She would begin to romp; leaping in front of George, charging him with her shoulder, and embracing him with her forelegs.

George seemed at his most amiable during these playful moments, and would sometimes respond by engaging in a mock battle with his mate. From where I sat these battles looked rather ferocious, but the steadily wagging tails of both wolves showed it was all well meant.

No doubt alerted by the sounds of play, Uncle Albert would appear on the scene and join the group. He often chose to sleep away the daylight hours some distance from the den site, perhaps in order to reduce the possibility of being dragooned[4] into the role of babysitter at too frequent intervals.

With his arrival, all three adult wolves would stand in a circle, sniff noses, wag their tails hard, and make noises. "Make noises" is not very descriptive, but it is the best I can do. I was too far off to hear more than the louder sounds, and these appeared to be more like grunts than anything else. Their meaning was obscure to me, but they were certainly connected with a general feeling of good will, anticipation and high spirits.

After anywhere from twenty minutes to an hour of conviviality (in which the pups took part, getting under everyone's feet and nipping promiscuously at any adult tail they might encounter) the three adults would adjourn to the crest of the den, usually led by Angeline. Once more they would form a circle and then, lifting their heads high, would "sing" for a few minutes.

This was one of the high points of their day, and it was certainly *the* high point of mine. The first few times the three wolves sang, the old ingrained fear set my back hairs tingling, and I cannot claim to having really enjoyed the chorus. However, with the passage of sufficient time I not only came to enjoy it, but to anticipate it with acute pleasure. And yet I find it almost impossible to describe, for the only terms at my disposal are those relating to human music and these are inadequate if not actually misleading. The best I can do is to say that this full-throated and great-hearted chorus moved me as I have very occasionally been moved by the bowel-shaking throb and thunder of a superb organ played by a man who had transcended his mere manhood.

---

[4]**dragooned** (drə g$\overline{oo}$nd′): forced.

The impassionata never lasted long enough for me. In three or four minutes it would come to an end and the circle would break up; once more with much tail wagging, nose sniffing and general evidence of good will and high content. Then, reluctantly, Angeline would move toward the den, often looking back to watch as George and Albert trotted off along one of the hunting trails. She made it clear that she wished desperately to join them; but in the end she would rejoin the pups instead, and once more submit to their ebullient demands, either for dinner or for play.

On this particular night the male wolves made a break from their usual routine. Instead of taking one of the trails leading north, or northwest, they headed off toward the east, in the opposite direction from Mike's cabin and me.

I thought no more about this variation until sometime later when a human shout made me turn around. Ootek had returned — but he was not alone. With him were three bashful friends, all grinning, and all shy at this first meeting with the strange *kablunak* who was interested in wolves.

The arrival of such a mob made further observations that night likely to be unproductive, so I joined the four Eskimos in the trek to the cabin. Mike was home, and greeted the new visitors as old friends. Eventually I found a chance to ask him a few questions.

Yes, he told me, Ootek had indeed known that these men were on their way, and would soon arrive.

How did he know?

A foolish question. He knew because he had heard the wolf on the Five Mile Hills reporting the passage of the Eskimos through his territory. He had tried to tell me about it; but then, when I failed to understand, he had felt obliged to leave me in order to intercept and greet his friends.

And that was that.

Responding to "Never Cry Wolf"

Thinking and Discussing

What is the author's purpose in writing this account? How does this differ from the author's purpose in "Animal Behavior"? How is *Never Cry Wolf* like a fictional story? Why do you think its author chose a narrative style? How else might a science writer present this information?

How does the author react at first to Ootek's claim that "the wolves are talking"? Does his opinion change as he tells his story? Do you believe Ootek? Why, or why not?

How well do the author and Ootek understand each other? How well do Ootek and the wolves understand each other? Do you think it strange that Ootek and the wolves might have a stronger bond than Ootek and the author? Explain your answer.

A Native American wolf headdress

Applying Science Concepts

Researching Animal Sounds People often try to explain the reasons for dramatic animal noises. Often, what people imagine has nothing to do with scientific fact. Think of some dramatic animal noises such as the howl of a wolf. You might want to consider an elephant's trumpet, a peacock's yell, a whale's song, a rooster's crow — or many other noises. Are there common myths about any of them? What do you think are the reasons each animal makes this sound? Do research to learn what scientists know about these noises. Display your findings on a poster labeled "Fact and Fiction."

DOLPHINS

.... *our friends from the sea*

from
Animal Communication by Jacci Cole

On the coast of Western Australia in Shark Bay there is a beach known as Monkey Mia. For over twenty-five years people have been coming to this beach to swim and to play with the dolphins. Fishermen tell the story of a dolphin named Old Charley. He would appear at the same time every morning while the men were catching their baitfish for the day. Old Charley would help the fishermen by rounding up small bony herring and yellow tails and herding them toward the boats. Later, when the fishermen returned to shore, they would give their extra fish to Old Charley and his friends. No one knows why the dolphin did this. He was able to catch plenty of fish on his own. He didn't need the fishermen's handouts. The fishermen think he did it because he liked helping them and because he liked their company.

A Mysterious Attraction

Charley is gone, but other dolphins come to shore now and frolic in the shallow water with the swimmers. World traveler and writer Elizabeth Gawain has observed this many times. She says dolphins love to have their backs rubbed just like cats. "They seem especially attracted to small children and in order to reach them one dolphin (named Holey-fin) will enter into water so shallow that her belly rubs bottom."

Some people think the dolphins are only interested in getting something to eat. But Gawain doesn't think so. "They do accept almost any small fish . . . but they do not always swallow it. . . . I have seen little boys duck underwater to gather these discarded fish and hand them out once again to eager dolphins, that only drop them in the water once more. . . . Clearly it is a game" for the dolphins.

Why are these wild dolphins so friendly with people? For centuries people who have encountered dolphins have wondered this. The ancient Greeks believed dolphins were repentant pirates who had died and then returned in a fishlike form. Some, such as animal scientist Dr. John Lilly, believe dolphins are friendly because they want to communicate with us. They say dolphins are very intelligent and have the ability to learn to speak.

Even Aristotle, the ancient philosopher, believed dolphins had the ability to speak. "The voice of the dolphin in air is like that of the human in that they can pronounce vowels and combinations of vowels, but have difficulties with the consonants," he wrote. Because dolphins communicate with each other underwater, Lilly speculates their sounds in the air are attempts to speak with people. Could dolphins speak to us? Do they "speak" to each other?

Dolphin Communication

Sealife researcher Jacques Cousteau doesn't know if dolphins are able to speak with people, but he believes dolphins communicate with each other and that they probably tell each other important things. "We know that dolphins 'speak' to one another," he says, "and that they send out calls and warning signals."

Aboard his boat the *Calypso*, Cousteau and his crew followed a group of dolphins, hoping to capture one. They wanted to study one for a few days before returning it to the sea. They lowered a huge net and were able to capture a dolphin. It swam around and around in the net crying and whistling to the other dolphins who hovered nearby. The dolphins came to the net and exchanged clicks and whistles with the captured dolphin. Cousteau felt the dolphins were trying to comfort their captured friend. Days later, when they freed the dolphin, the others came and touched and rubbed their friend and the ocean was alive with their "talking." Cousteau said that they appeared to be very happy to have their friend with them again!

On another occasion, Cousteau and his crew watched and listened while one dolphin chattered to a nearby group of dolphins. Immediately the group disappeared. Within moments a pod of killer whales was sighted. The dolphin had warned the others that danger was nearby. Was his warning conscious, intelligent communication, or was it merely instinct at work?

Dolphin Language

Dolphins make a wide variety of sounds including clickings, grindings, clappings, squeaks, chirps, and whistles. Because dolphins have no vocal chords scientists are puzzled about how they produce these tones — and why.

Cousteau states that dolphins use their sounds for two different reasons. One, as has been shown earlier, is to communicate with other dolphins. The other reason, Cousteau says, is for the dolphins' echolocation system: The echoes from the dolphins' sounds help them discover the shapes of obstacles. Their echoes help them know where they are in murky

A silver coin of ancient Greece showing the goddess Arethusa surrounded by dolphins

water. These sounds also help them find food at night by means of reflected sound waves.

Dolphin researchers David and Melba Caldwell disagree. "From the outset," they counter, "we want to make it clear we do not believe that dolphins 'talk.'" The Caldwells argue that the possibility of communication between dolphins has received a lot of attention in the media, but there has not yet been enough study. They say there is not enough evidence to support the claims made for dolphin communication.

The Caldwells have done their research mostly with bottle-nosed dolphins. When recording dolphin sounds, they have found that dolphins made some sounds for special reasons. "It is likely," they say, "that at least some of these vocalizations are emitted [sent out] in social situations [while swimming or playing] and therefore have some communicative function." But they firmly add that "other sounds are not" social. Possibly they are the clicks and moans dolphins use to echolocate.

They say there is no "complicated language from dolphins' whistle contours." In other words, dolphins' whistles carry no messages. However, the Caldwells have discovered that each dolphin has its own distinctive whistle, which they have termed its "signature" whistle. The signature whistle tells the other dolphins which animal is whistling.

Dolphins and Human Language

Dr. John Lilly firmly believes dolphins can talk, and he goes further. "Eventually it may be possible for humans to speak with another species," he claims. He adds that dolphins are the prime candidate for communication between people and animals. They have a brain equal to ours in size and complexity, and they have a potential for learning comparable to our own. "I have come to this conclusion," he says, "after careful consideration of evidence gained through my research experiments with dolphins."

In the 1950's, in his early work with dolphins, Lilly routinely recorded everything

Researchers David and Melba Caldwell displaying sonograms of dolphin sounds

A diver recording dolphin sounds

that occurred during the experiments. When the tapes were replayed he noted that the dolphins had been making deliberate sounds in the air. Normally, dolphins vocalize only underwater. When the tapes were slowed, the dolphins' noises sounded like human speech. The dolphins seem to be trying to mimic the sounds of their trainers. Lilly says this observation was the key to all his work that followed.

In Lilly's later experiments he attempted to teach dolphins to understand and respond to English through continual repetition, saying the same phrases over and over. One dolphin named Elvar was considered quite capable of producing sounds like those of human speech. However, he was emitting these sounds in frequencies too high for the human

525

ear to hear unaided. Again, after the tapes were slowed down, the resemblances to human speech were heard.

After Lilly worked persistently with this dolphin, it progressed from making babbling noises to those of understandable words: Lilly states, "In September [1961] we decided he was ready for Step 2, the formation of understandable words. A typical

Dolphins finding their way by
using their echolocation systems

experience is that of the 10th of September. . . . He learned the words 'stop it' and the words 'bye-bye.' Another example from the 23rd of October was 'more Elvar.' "

David and Melba Caldwell contest Lilly's claims. They argue that "the large, well-developed brain of cetaceans [dolphins and whales] is almost surely related more to the acoustic system (probably echolocation in particular) than to the high degree of 'intelligence' often ascribed to these mammals." They aren't convinced that a large brain necessarily equals intelligence.

To many scientists, intelligence and the ability to communicate are related. An animal shouldn't have one without the other. Researcher Robert McNally explains it this way: "Our common sense understanding of intelligence has something very much to do with communication. When we say that a particular animal is intelligent, we mean much the same as 'This animal communicates in a sophisticated and varied way.' "

McNally believes the argument about intelligence and brain size is based mainly on human experience. Humans have large brains and a sophisticated means of communication — language. Therefore, some people say, other animals that have large brains should also be intelligent and should have some sophisticated ways to communicate. McNally says John Lilly's ideas about dolphin intelligence follow this logic — dolphins have large brains, so they must be intelligent and have a language.

However, McNally says, it's a nice thought but it hasn't been proven. "Unfortunately, Lilly's sole demonstration of [dolphin] language is the vocal reprogramming . . . which delivers much less than it advertises." (Lilly attempted by continuous repetition to "brainwash" or to "reprogram" the dolphins into speaking English.) McNally adds, however, that Lilly's ideas, "however poorly presented and supported, are unsettling." It is still possible that, using better techniques, scientists of the future may prove that Lilly's startling ideas are right.

McNally does not entirely dismiss the idea that cetaceans can communicate intelligently. He believes that dolphins and whales are not used enough as experimental animals. Thus, there is not enough information to answer questions about their intelligence and methods of communication. Perhaps as scientists discover more about dolphins, the ideas of

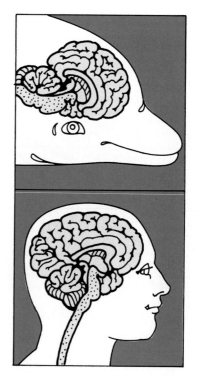

A comparison showing that the dolphin brain is the same size as the human brain

their intelligence and possible language will seem less strange.

Do Dolphins Understand?

Skeptics of dolphins' language ability also believe that scientists may misinterpret experimental results. They believe dolphins can pick up unintentional cues from people or other dolphins. "Experiments did not prove that dolphins have any language ability," the Caldwells state, "but rather only that dolphins tend to respond to another's whistle and that they can be conditioned or taught to respond to sound cues that are sometimes subtle."

Robert McNally gives an example of cue conditioning. In his book *So Remorseless a Havoc*, he describes an experiment conducted by Jarvis Bastian, a psychologist from the University of California at Davis. The experiment's purpose was to see if one dolphin could send information to another. Two dolphins were put in a tank of water and were separated by a curtain so they could not see each other. The researchers put two paddles on the side containing the dolphin named Buzz. With Doris, the other dolphin, they put

a flashing light. McNally states, "For both dolphins to earn a food reward from the automatic fish feeder, Buzz had to push the correct paddle. But only Doris knew, from either a flashing light or a steady light on her side of the tank, which paddle was correct. For her to get a fish, she had to tell Buzz which paddle to push."

When Jarvis Bastian started the experiment, he believed that dolphins did not have a language. But "it surprised him to no end that in little time Buzz was picking the correct paddle nine times out of ten."

Exactly how did those dolphins communicate? It took the experimenters a long time to connect Doris's sounds to Buzz's

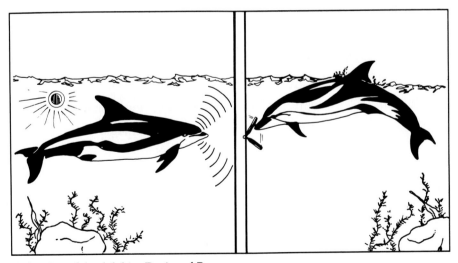

A drawing of the dolphins Doris and Buzz during the communication experiment

A scientist conducting intelligence tests on two dolphins that are operating an underwater computerized keyboard

choice. Doris, they finally found, made a short series of clicks when the light was steady, but when the light flashed she would keep quiet.

The researchers then questioned whether Doris's clicks were voluntary (that is, if she were making the clicks as an intelligent effort to communicate with Buzz) or if they were somehow associated with the lights. So they put together another group of experiments. They found that Doris clicked even when she knew that Buzz was not in the tank. They concluded, McNally says, that "Doris had learned unconsciously and quite by chance to make certain sounds in response to the light, and Buzz had learned by trial and error what the sounds meant." Behaviorists call this adventitious [accidental] conditioning. It is not communication.

Does this mean that dolphins don't communicate intelligently at all? Or do they, as John Lilly believes, communicate in a way that we don't yet understand?

Deeper Mysteries

There is much about dolphins we do not yet know. The one point scientists do agree on is that decades may pass before we find the answers. Perhaps then we will know if dolphins and people will be able to communicate with each other. Perhaps we will teach them our language, or they will teach us theirs.

These animals remind us that our planet is inhabited by creatures as remarkable as ourselves. And it may be that as we find out more about them, we will find out they are even more remarkable than we previously believed.

Responding to "Dolphins: Our Friends from the Sea"

Thinking and Discussing

How do the Caldwells and Dr. Lilly differ in their ideas about animal communication? How did Dr. Lilly test his ideas? Why did the Caldwells disagree with him? Do you agree with either position? Why?

What does researcher Robert McNally say about the relationship between intelligence and the ability to communicate? How does he distinguish between *communication* and *language*? Do you believe that "smarter" animals communicate in ways that are "better"? Explain your answer.

Applying Science Concepts

Evaluating Scientific Theories When a scientist develops a theory, he or she must back it up with supporting evidence. What theories have been proposed about dolphin language? What evidence exists to support each one? Write a brief paragraph about each theory, collecting the paragraphs in a report titled "Dolphin Language: Theory and Evidence."

Defining Cetaceans What is a *cetacean*? Find out, and write your definition on a large sheet of paper. Below your definition, describe several different kinds of cetaceans. You may choose to illustrate your descriptions.

The Dolphin Fresco from ancient Greece

For centuries, people have longed to speak with the ape. Psychologists Allen and Beatrice Gardner were the first to succeed: They taught a chimp named Washoe to converse in American Sign Language (Ameslan), a human gesture language. Ameslan, used in the United States by thousands of deaf people, utilizes hand signs instead of words.

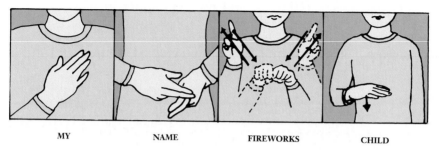

MY   NAME   FIREWORKS   CHILD

Then in 1972, psychology student Penny Patterson decided to try to teach Ameslan to a gorilla. At the San Francisco Zoo, she befriended a baby gorilla. Born on the Fourth of July, the ape was named Hanabi-Ko, which is Japanese for "Fireworks child." In 1974, Patterson persuaded the zoo to let her move the ape, whom everyone called Koko, to a trailer on the grounds of Stanford University, so she could continue her study.

Project Koko, which Patterson hopes to eventually move to a wide open, tropical space in Hawaii, continues to this day.

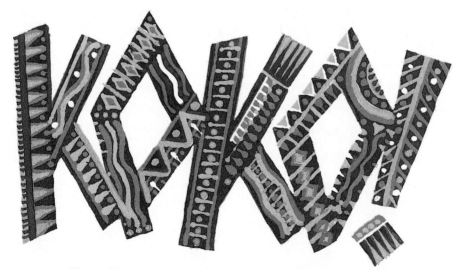

From *Thinking Gorillas* by Bettyann Kevles

Illustrated by Robert Roth

533

Penny Patterson had become interested in apes and languages after hearing the Gardners, who were visiting Stanford, describe Washoe. Patterson wanted to repeat their experiment using a gorilla, and at the beginning she followed the Gardners' examples.

The Gardners had tried different ways of teaching Washoe hand signs before they settled on the way that worked best. They call it *molding*, and it is a way of actually taking the ape's hand and bending the fingers into the right form, molding them.

Patterson did the same with Koko. She shaped Koko's hand until Koko got the sign right, although at first she had to ward off Koko's attempts to bite her. Gradually the young gorilla stopped resisting, and soon she could learn a "molded" sign in just a few minutes. But unlike the Gardners, Patterson also spoke to Koko in English at the same time. Koko's experiment is different, then, from Washoe's or from the way deaf children learn. Koko actually learned two languages at once: sign language, in which she could respond as well as receive messages, and English, in which for a long time she could only receive.

From time to time Patterson gives Koko a standard intelligence test, one that has been especially designed for preschool children who cannot read. But Patterson had to change some of the answers to make it suit a gorilla. Koko was shown five pictures — ice cream, an apple, a block, a shoe, and a flower. Then she was asked to point out which ones are edible. Koko chose the flower and the apple. Patterson considers that the right answer because gorillas do eat flowers.

An IQ score is a general measure of an individual's ability to answer questions in comparison with most people's ability to answer these questions. Children are scored by comparing the number of correct answers they get with the average number of correct answers that children the same age score. If someone is five years old and can answer the questions most ten-year-olds can, then that person has a mental age of ten. An IQ is the mental age, divided by the real age, and then multiplied by 100. If a five-year-old can answer all the questions exactly as most five-year-olds can, then that person's IQ is 5, divided by 5, times 100, or 100. 100 is the average IQ.

Koko falls a few months behind the mental age of a human child taking the same tests. Koko's IQ is therefore between 70 and 90. This is below average, but not very far below. Many people who lead normal lives score less than "average" on IQ tests. This means that if Koko were human, she would be able to get along in the world as well as quite a few of the people in it.

Koko making the sign for *lipstick*

But, Patterson points out, Koko is not human, and she excels in skills that human children cannot do as well. Koko can swing from a bar and climb a tree better than any child her age.

Patterson also tests Koko on her vocabulary. She uses the same system the Gardners used. Koko has to use a sign voluntarily for at least fifteen days in a month for that sign to qualify as learned vocabulary. According to this standard, Koko knew 375 qualified words when she was seven, but she is still learning new signs all the time.

Patterson estimates that Koko knows another 300 words which have not qualified yet, but which are nonetheless part of Koko's working vocabulary.

Koko learned most of these signs through molding. But she has picked up other signs by making them up and by "eavesdropping." She explained to Patterson in February 1978 that she could "sign." Patterson had never taught her the gesture for *sign*. She traced the use of the gesture back to Koko's observing Patterson use it in conversation with one of Koko's deaf tutors. Koko had apparently seen it, understood what it meant, and incorporated it into her own vocabulary.

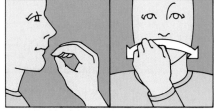

EAT FLOWER

Koko's signs are not as clear as a human's because her hands are not as flexible as ours. But what she says is indisputable. Koko has confirmed, in Ameslan, what other psychologists have discovered through different kinds of experiments. Koko knows that a picture of an object is not the same as that object, but is a symbol. She has two words for *flower* in her vocabulary: one for a real flower and one for a picture of a flower. When a visitor arrived wearing a flowered skirt, Koko told her in signs that she eats flowers, but not pictures of flowers.

And when she went to Patterson's off-campus apartment to see herself on television, Koko recognized herself and said so. When she was given a drink from a mug with King Kong's picture on it, she signed that she knew that the picture was a picture of Koko.

Koko has already shown that she has a range of ability far beyond what anyone expected. She can start conversations and does not simply wait to be asked questions. In fact, Koko seems to be able to express herself as well as most human children. She can string signs together into sentences when she wants to share experiences, such as "Listen bird." She can demand what she wants, such as refusing a meal of rice bread and pointing, instead, towards the refrigerator and signing "Bottle, there, apple."

She could explain her mood when her tutor finally moved out of the trailer by saying, "Yes, sad cry, morning." But she can also tell her "Me feel fine."

Koko has shown that she can think abstractly, a skill once thought confined to humans. When she was caught chewing on the sponge with which she had cleaned up a spill – and sponge-chewing is something she is not supposed to do — Patterson confronted her with the remaining sponge and asked Koko what it

YES

SAD

CRY

MORNING

was. Koko answered "Trouble!" Or when she was caught biting the lead point off her pencil, another forbidden act, Koko pointed to her mouth and signed "teeth," meaning that her teeth were responsible, not Koko.

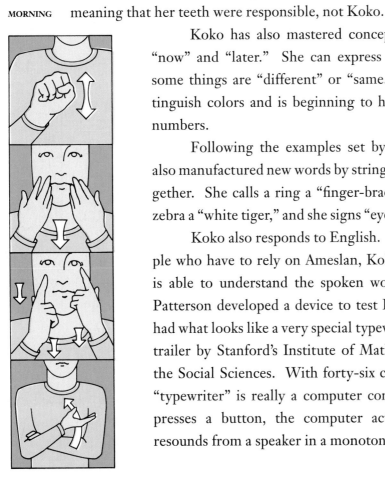

Koko has also mastered concepts of time, such as "now" and "later." She can express the knowledge that some things are "different" or "same." And she can distinguish colors and is beginning to have a small grasp of numbers.

Following the examples set by Washoe, Koko has also manufactured new words by stringing familiar signs together. She calls a ring a "finger-bracelet," a picture of a zebra a "white tiger," and she signs "eye-hat" to mean mask.

Koko also responds to English. For unlike deaf people who have to rely on Ameslan, Koko can hear, and she is able to understand the spoken words. In June 1977, Patterson developed a device to test Koko's English. She had what looks like a very special typewriter installed in the trailer by Stanford's Institute of Mathematical Studies in the Social Sciences. With forty-six color-coded keys, the "typewriter" is really a computer console. When Koko presses a button, the computer activates a voice that resounds from a speaker in a monotone.

If Patterson asks Koko what she wants to eat, Koko may sign "catchup" to put on her mashed potatoes. Or she may go to the typewriter and punch the *A* so that the voice says "apple." She may even respond in a phrase, as she did when Patterson offered her a navy bean. Koko rejected it, explaining her action by going to the computer and punching the words "like not."

With two languages, a gesture language and a machine-operated oral language, Koko can express herself well. In the trailer she may prefer the novelty of the computer. Outside she has to depend on her hands. She seems to choose the one she wants to use arbitrarily, but she never mixes them up.

Both of her languages depend on the use of her hands, but she is clever with them. Koko can type with one and sign with the other, for she is ambidextrous as well as bilingual.

Yet even with two languages at her command, Koko is still a gorilla, with gorilla ways. She hates loud noises and seems impervious to pain. She play-bites as all gorillas do, and when she is very excited, she bites hard. As a small animal she went through a stage of biting the people who came to tutor her. But Patterson stopped that habit before it grew by applying a mild electric shock. Like most wild gorillas, Koko likes to sleep in a nest and makes her own by gathering towels around her on the floor. Like all small gorillas, she loves to play "tickle chase," only Koko *asks* to be tickled.

Patterson's accomplishment with Koko is fascinating. Still unexplained, however, is why such intelligent animals did not develop language on their own. There are people who believe that there cannot be thought without language. This implies that Patterson gave Koko more than words. It would mean that when Patterson gave Koko words, she also gave her the power to think.

Others disagree. They do not link thinking with having a formal language. They argue that the great apes have always been able to communicate with each other through their sounds and gestures. By teaching them our symbols, we have only agreed upon a common vocabulary.

Koko signing tickle

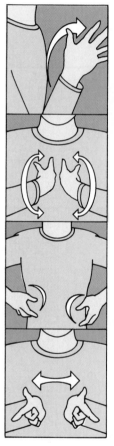

FINE

ANIMAL

MONKEY

LARGE

538

Responding to "Koko"

Thinking and Discussing

What did Penny Patterson want to prove about Koko? How did she go about this task?

What tests did Patterson use to support her work with Koko? What do the results indicate about gorillas?

How did Koko show that she could initiate communication? What new words did she make up? Why are these factors important to the research?

Applying Science Concepts

Experimenting with Sign Language With a partner, experiment with learning American Sign Language (Ameslan), or develop your own sign language. Decide which partner will research Ameslan or make up new signs. Then that partner can try to teach a specific number of signs to the other partner. Be sure no spoken words are used in the sign language lessons! How will you show your partner what each sign means? How many signs can you learn? Evaluate your results.

Studying Wild Gorillas How do gorillas live in the wild? Find out more about these animals. Where do they live? What do they eat? Are they social animals? How do they communicate with each other? Write a short report, or design a captioned-drawing or photo display to present your findings.

Thinking About Science

Conducting a Talk Show With a group, imagine that you are part of a television talk show. Have students play the parts of the experts: Mowat, Cousteau, one of the Caldwells, Patterson, or another person referred to in "Animal Communication." Choose someone to be the talk show host. Each scientist should give a three-minute talk stating his or her opinion on the question "Can Animals Talk?" To prepare, you may want to consider the following points:

- What does it mean to "talk"?
- What is *communication*?
- What is *language*, and do animals use it?
- What has research revealed?

After each person has had a chance to make a contribution, the question should be opened up for discussion. The host may call on members of the group audience to challenge the experts, or call on the experts for comment.

Speaking in Body Language Communication is much more than the spoken word — even for people! We use gestures, postures, and other subtle signals that convey information. Find out just how much we communicate without words by doing the following exercise in body language. In front of a partner or a group, act out the following scene: You have some news to tell a friend. It may be good news, exciting news, sad news, or even news concerning an emergency. First, walk up to the friend's door, then knock. Do not use words. Can others guess what news you have to tell, simply from the way you act? Take turns acting this scene — or a scene of your own.

Creating a Communication Mural

With a partner or a group, create a chalkboard mural that shows the many different forms of animal communication: coloration, touch, sounds, and body movements. Write the four categories across the top of the chalkboard. Each student can pick an animal. Briefly research how your animal communicates. Draw a picture of your animal under each of its appropriate categories. Write a caption for each picture.

Animal Communication

SPECIAL ASSIGNMENT

About the Authors

Alice Aamodt works as a volunteer at the Science Museum of Minnesota. It was through helping produce an exhibit called "Wolves and Humans: Coexistence, Competition, and Conflict" that Aamodt developed her knowledge and appreciation of wolves. She is now working on an exhibit on hunting in human societies.

Jacci Cole currently lives in Oregon with her husband and three children. Cole and her husband operate a freelance editing business. Favorite spare-time activities include reading, camping, painting, and mushroom hunting.

Sylvia A. Johnson was born in Indianapolis, Indiana. She has worked as an editor, but is best known for her contributions to the Natural Science Books series published by Lerner Books. Titles by Johnson include *Penguins*, *Beetles*, *Crabs*, *Mushrooms*, *Mosses*, and *Rice*; these and other contributions earned her awards from the New York Academy of Sciences and the National Science Teachers Association. Johnson also produced six books in Lerner's Wildlife Library series, among them *Animals of the Deserts*, *Animals of the Mountains*, and *Animals of the Polar Regions*.

 Bettyann Kevles was born in New York City in 1938. She has received degrees from Vassar College and Columbia University, and worked as an editor/writer and then as a history teacher before becoming a full-time free-lance writer. Kevles's first book is *Watching the Wild Apes*, for which she received the best older juvenile award from the New York Academy of Sciences in 1977, and the *Boston Globe–Horn Book* best nonfiction award in 1978. Kevles says, "Until completing the *Wild Apes*, most of my writing has been fictional, and a lot of it was science fiction, mostly short stories. My research [on apes] has proven to me that finding out what is really happening is as exciting as fantasy." Her most recent book is *Females of the Species* (1986), which discusses many species of animals. Kevles lives with her family in Pasadena, California.

 Farley Mowat was born in Ontario, Canada, in 1921. As a young boy he became interested in bird watching and also enjoyed nature photography. There were always many pets in the Mowat household, including crows, magpies, gophers, owls (whose story is told in *Owls in the Family*), squirrels, and dogs (including Mutt of *The Dog Who Wouldn't Be* fame).

Following his discharge from the Canadian Army in 1946, Mowat took part in an expedition to the Barren Lands of northern Canada. His assignment as a government field biologist was to study the area's wolves and their diet. Mowat later wrote about this experience in *Never Cry Wolf*. Other books in which Mowat has expressed his concern for wild animals and for Native American people include *People of the Deer*, *The Grey Seas Under*, and *The Desperate People*.

THE SEA WORLD BOOK OF
DOLPHINS
BY RANDALL R. REEVES AND
STEPHEN LEATHERWOOD

My Life
With The Chimpanzees
by Jane Goodall
The Fascinating Story of One of the World's
Most Celebrated Naturalists

BLACK BEAR
The Spirit of the Wilderness
Ford

HARPER
TROPHY $3.95 US
                                          $4.95 CDN

JEAN CRAIGHEAD GEORGE
Julie of the Wolves
Winner of the Newbery Medal

544

Further Investigations

My Life with the Chimpanzees by Jane Goodall
(Minstrel, 1988)

    Jane Goodall, a renowned naturalist, tells about the events that led her to Africa and her many years of researching a group of wild chimpanzees.

Julie of the Wolves by Jean Craighead George (Harper, 1972)

    Miyax, an Inuit girl, runs from her home toward San Francisco to meet a pen pal who calls her Julie. When Miyax gets lost in the Arctic, she must depend on a family of wolves to survive.

Black Bear: The Spirit of the Wilderness by Barbara Ford
(Houghton, 1981)

    In this absorbing account, readers learn about an animal that has roamed the woodlands of North America for thousands of years and its relationship with human beings.

Can Bears Predict Earthquakes? Unsolved Mysteries of Animal Behavior by Russell Freedman (Prentice, 1982)

    This book contains insights into eight questions about unusual animal behavior, exploring the nature of dolphin intelligence, bird navigation, and other mysteries.

The Sea World Book of Dolphins by Randall R. Reeves and Stephen Leatherwood (Harcourt, 1987)

    In this well-illustrated book, two dolphin-research scientists share what they have learned from working with remarkable dolphins in captivity.

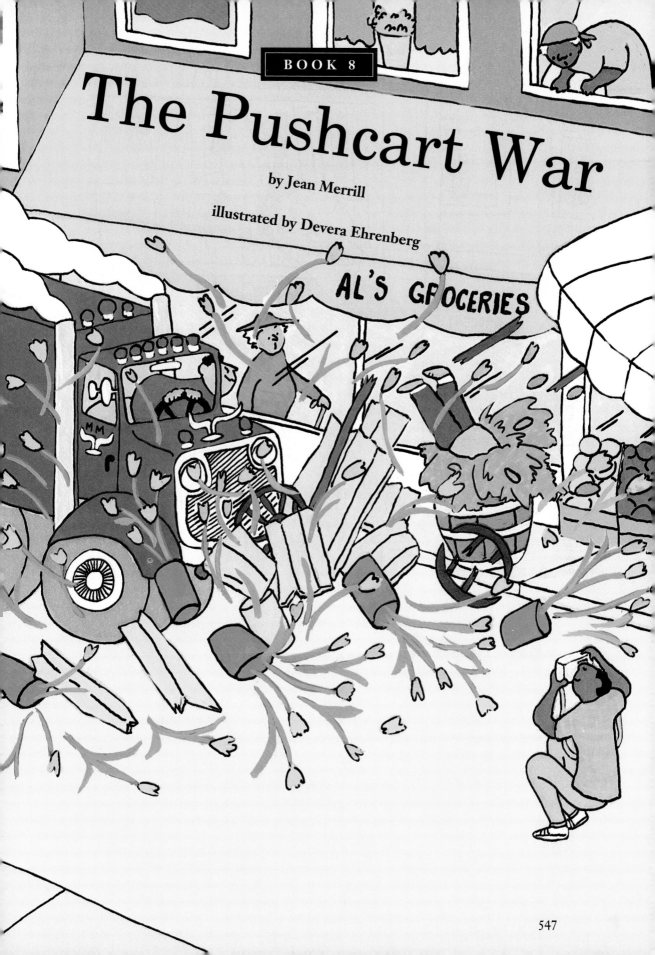

BOOK 8

The Pushcart War

by Jean Merrill

illustrated by Devera Ehrenberg

AL'S GROCERIES

FOREWORD

by Professor Lyman Cumberly of New York University,
   author of *The Large Object Theory of History*

As the author says in her introduction, it is very important to the peace of the world that we understand how wars begin. Unfortunately, most of our modern wars are too big for the average person even to begin to understand. They take place on five continents at once. (One has to study geography for twenty years just to locate the battlefields.) They involve hundreds of armies, thousands of officers, millions of soldiers, and the weapons are so complicated that even the generals do not understand how they work.

The extraordinary thing about the Pushcart War is that a child of six will grasp at once precisely how the weapons worked. The Pushcart War is the only recent war of which this can be said.

The result is that we have been having more and more wars simply because the whole procedure is so complicated that peace-loving people give up trying to understand what is going on. This account of the Pushcart War should help to remedy this distressing situation. For big wars are caused by the same sort of problems that led to the Pushcart War.

Not that the Pushcart War was a small war. However, it *was* confined to the streets of one city, and it lasted only four months. During those four months, of course, the fate of one of the great cities of the world hung in the balance.

The author of this book is to be commended for her zeal in tracking down much behind-the-scenes material never before published. I, myself, had never heard the amusing story of Frank the Flower's crocheted target, or the story behind Maxie Hammerman's capture of the bulletproof Italian car, a feat that demonstrates conclusively the brilliance of Maxie's strategy throughout the war.

Neither, I am ashamed to say, did I ever know the meaning of the inscription under General Anna's statue in Tompkins Square Park, although it is a park in which I spent many happy hours working on my *Large Object Theory of History*. (The author does not mention, I believe, that Tompkins Square Park was the battleground of another famous American war — but, of course, there are very few places left that have not been battlefields.)

I am sorry to say that I think the author may be mistaken about the number of pile driving firms in New York City at the time of the Pushcart War. She gives it as forty-three, although the *Pile Drivers' Annual* for that year lists fifty-three. A minor error in an otherwise impressive effort.

New York University
December 2, 1996

INTRODUCTION

As it has been only ten years since the Pushcart War, I was surprised when one of my nephews a few months ago looked puzzled at the mention of a Mighty Mammoth. Then I realized that he had probably never seen a Mighty Mammoth. (He was only two at the time of the war and, moreover, was living in Iceland where his father had been sent on a government assignment.)

That a twelve-year-old boy might never have seen a Mighty Mammoth was understandable. What astonished me was that he had never even *heard* of one. But I have since discovered that there has never been a history of the Pushcart War written for young people.

Professor Lyman Cumberly's book, *The Large Object Theory of History*, drawn mainly from his observations of the Pushcart War, is a brilliant work. However, it is written primarily for college students.

I have always believed that we cannot have peace in the world until *all of us* understand how wars start. And so I have tried to set down the main events of the Pushcart War in such a way that readers of all ages may profit from whatever lessons it offers.

Although I was living in New York at the time of the war and saw the streets of New York overrun with Mighty Mammoths and Leaping Lemas, I did not then know any of the participants personally — except Buddy Wisser.

I did contribute in a small way to the decisive battle described in Chapter XXXIV but, like most New Yorkers, was asleep in the early days of the war as to what was at issue — until Buddy Wisser alerted us all with his 160-by-160-foot enlargement of Marvin Seeley's photograph of the Daffodil Massacre.

Needless to say, Buddy Wisser has been a great help to me in the writing of this book. Buddy, before he became editor of one of New York's largest daily newspapers, had been sports editor of my high school newspaper, and at the time of the Pushcart War, Buddy and I still ran into each other occasionally at Yankee Stadium.

It is to Buddy that I am indebted for the story behind the story of Marvin Seeley's picture. And it was through Buddy, of course, that I was able to meet many of the brave men and women who fought in the Pushcart War.

In addition to Buddy Wisser, I would like to express my appreciation to Maxie Hammerman for the many hours he spent answering my questions about his recollections of the war. Thanks, too, to Joey Kafflis for his permission to quote excerpts from his diary and to the New York Public Library's Rare Document Division for letting me see "The Portlette Papers."

Jean F. Merrill
Washington, Vt.
October 14, 1996

CHAPTER I

How It Began: The Daffodil Massacre

The Pushcart War started on the afternoon of March 15, 1986, when a truck ran down a pushcart belonging to a flower peddler.   Daffodils were scattered all over the street.   The pushcart was flattened, and the owner of the pushcart was pitched headfirst into a pickle barrel.

The owner of the cart was Morris the Florist.   The driver of the truck was Mack, who at that time was employed by Mammoth Moving.   Mack's full name was Albert P. Mack, but in most accounts of the Pushcart War, he is referred to simply as Mack.

It was near the corner of Sixth Avenue and 17th Street in New York City that the trouble occurred.   Mack was trying to park his truck.   He had a load of piano stools to deliver, and the space in which he was hoping to park was not quite big enough.

When Mack saw that he could not get his truck into the space by the curb, he yelled at Morris the Florist to move his pushcart.   Morris' cart was parked just ahead of Mack.

Morris had been parked in this spot for half an hour, and he was doing a good business.   So he paid no attention to Mack.

Mack pounded on his horn.

Morris looked up then.   "Why should I move?" Morris asked.   "I'm in business here."

Maybe if Mack had spoken courteously to Morris, Morris would have tried to push his cart forward a few feet.   But Morris did not like being yelled at. He was a proud man.   Besides, he had a customer.

So when Mack yelled again, "Move!" Morris merely shrugged.

"Move yourself," he said, and went on talking with his customer.

"Look, I got to unload ninety dozen piano stools before five o'clock," Mack said.

"I got to sell two dozen bunches of daffodils," Morris replied.   "Tomorrow they won't be so fresh."

"In about two minutes they won't be so fresh," Mack said.

As several students of history have pointed out, Mack *could* have simply nudged Morris' cart a bit with the fender of his truck.   The truck was so much bigger than the pushcart that the slightest push would have rolled it forward. Not that Morris would have liked being pushed. Still, that was what truck drivers generally did when smaller vehicles were in their way.

But Mack was annoyed. Like most truck drivers of the time, he was used to having his own way. Mammoth Moving was one of the biggest trucking firms in the city, and Mack did not like a pushcart peddler arguing with him.

When Mack saw that Morris was not going to move, he backed up his truck. Morris heard him gunning his engine, but did not look around. He supposed Mack was going to drive on down the block. But instead of that, Mack drove straight into the back of Morris' pushcart. Daffodils were flung for a hundred feet and Morris himself, as we have said, was knocked into a pickle barrel. This was the event that we now know as the Daffodil Massacre.

These facts about the Daffodil Massacre are known because a boy, who had just been given a camera for his birthday, happened to be standing by the pickle barrel. His name was Marvin Seeley.

CHAPTER II

The Blow-up of Marvin Seeley's Picture

Marvin Seeley had been trying, on the afternoon of March 15th, to take a picture of a pickle barrel which stood in front of a grocery store on 17th Street. Marvin had been annoyed to have a man go flying into the barrel at the very instant he snapped the picture. However, when the picture was developed, the daffodils came out so nicely that Marvin sent the picture to a magazine that was having a contest.

Although the magazine preferred pictures of plain pickle barrels to pictures of accidents, the picture won an Honorable Mention and was printed in the magazine where a newspaper editor's wife, named Emily Wisser, happened to see it. Emily, who was fond of flowers, cut out the picture for a scrapbook she kept.

Later, when everyone began arguing about how the Pushcart War had started, Emily remembered Marvin Seeley's picture and showed it to her husband. Emily's husband, Buddy Wisser, had always laughed at his wife's scrapbooks, but for once he was very interested. As editor of one of the city's largest papers, he could not afford to laugh off a good story.

From Marvin Seeley's picture, Buddy Wisser was able to track down a good many facts. For one thing, he was able to identify the owner of the pushcart as Morris the Florist (although you cannot see Morris' face in the picture, as his head is well down in the pickle barrel).

Mack's face, however, is clearly visible, as is the name of the trucking company. Mack is leaning from his cab window and scowling, and MAMMOTH MOVING is printed in large letters on the side of the truck.

Mammoth was a well-known trucking firm. The firm owned seventy-two trucks at the time. Its slogan was: "If It Is a Big Job, Why Not Make It a MAMMOTH Job?"

Mammoth trucks came in three sizes. There were the Number One's, or "Baby Mammoths," as the drivers called them. There were the Number Two's, or "Mama Mammoths," and there were the Number Three's, the "Mighty Mammoths." It was a Mighty Mammoth that ran down Morris the Florist.

There was a lot of argument about the size of Mack's truck until Buddy Wisser decided to have Marvin Seeley's picture enlarged. Buddy Wisser had the picture blown up until Mack's face was life-size, and when Mack's face was life-size, the pickle barrel and the daffodils and the truck were all life-size, too. Then all Buddy Wisser had to do was to take a tape measure and measure the truck.

Not that this was easy. The enlarged picture was so large that Buddy Wisser had to go to a park near his office and lay the picture on the ground in order to measure the truck. It was a Mighty Mammoth, all right.

It was this big picture that also gave Buddy Wisser the clue he needed to identify the owner of the pushcart. In the lower left-hand corner of the picture, Buddy observed several splintered bits of the pushcart. On one of these fragments, he made out the letters "ORRIS," and on another — "ORIST."

Buddy Wisser's enlargement of Marvin Seeley's picture now hangs in the Museum of the City of New York. The Museum preserved the picture, partly because its size makes it a curiosity, and partly because it is a historical document. It is the best proof we have of how the Pushcart War actually began.

CHAPTER III

More About Morris the Florist & A Little About Frank the Flower and Maxie Hammerman, the Pushcart King

At the time of the Pushcart War, Morris the Florist had been in the flower line for forty-three years. He was a soft-spoken man, and his only claim to fame before the war was that it was impossible to buy a dozen flowers from him.

If a customer asked Morris for a dozen tulips — or daffodils or mixed snapdragons — Morris always wrapped up thirteen flowers. The one extra was at no cost. "So it shouldn't be a small dozen," Morris said.

Morris sold his flowers from a pushcart which he pushed between Sixth and Seventh Avenues from 14th Street to 23rd Street. He never went above 23rd. It was not that he didn't like it farther uptown, but above 23rd was Frank the Flower's territory.

Frank the Flower and Morris the Florist were not close friends before the Pushcart War, but they respected each other. Frank was the first to chip in to help buy Morris a new pushcart after Mack ran him down.

Anyone who knew Morris in those days found it hard to imagine him provoking a war. It would be closer to the truth to say that for a long time there had been trouble coming, and that Morris the Florist just happened to be standing on the corner of Sixth Avenue and 17th Street the afternoon it came.

For a long time New York had been one of the largest cities in the world. New Yorkers had long been proud that their streets were busier and noisier and more crowded than anyone else's.

Visitors to New York would say, "It's nice, but it's so crowded."

To which New Yorkers would reply cheerfully, "Yes, it's about the most crowded city in the world." And the city had kept on growing.

Every year there were more automobiles. More taxis. More buses. More trucks. Especially more trucks. By the summer of the Pushcart War, there were more trucks in New York than anyplace in the world.

There were also some five hundred pushcarts, though few people had any idea that there were more than a hundred or so. Probably only Maxie Hammerman really knew how many pushcarts there were.

Maxie knew, because Maxie or Maxie's father or Maxie's grandfather had built most of the pushcarts in New York. Maxie had a shop where he built and repaired pushcarts. It was the same shop in which his father and grandfather had started building pushcarts.

Maxie Hammerman knew the license number of almost every pushcart licensed to do business in New York. If you said to Maxie, "Morris the Florist," Maxie would come right back at you, "X-105," which was Morris' license number.

Also, Maxie was very nice about giving business advice. If a peddler came to Maxie and asked him to build a pushcart for a fresh-vegetable line, Maxie would think the matter over and then he would ask the peddler where he planned to push the cart.

If the peddler said, "East of Tompkins Square, north to 14th and south to Delancey," Maxie would run over his license list in his head and say, "Already there are thirteen carts in the fresh-vegetable line in that territory. Maybe you could push some other line?"

Maxie's advice was usually very sound, and he was known to his friends and to the peddlers who bought their carts from him as the Pushcart King. Very few people except Maxie's friends and the pushcart peddlers even knew there was a pushcart king.

CHAPTER IV

The Summer Before the War

Certainly there had been trouble coming. Anyone who had had any experience of wars would have seen it coming long before the afternoon that Mack ran down Morris the Florist.

There had been general grumbling. New York had become so crowded with cars and taxis and buses and trucks that traffic was very slow.

At first, everyone blamed everyone else. People who drove their own cars grumbled about people who rode in taxis. If there were no taxis, said the automobile owners, there would be room to drive in the streets.

Taxi drivers, on the other hand, complained about people who drove their own cars. If private cars were kept off the streets, people could get where they wanted to go in a hurry, the taxi drivers claimed.

The bus drivers suggested that both the taxis and the private cars should get off the streets. And the people who liked to walk found fault with everything on wheels.

But what irritated *everyone* were the trucks. There were so many of them, and they were so big that they did not have to get out of the way for anyone.

Most of the businesses in the city hired trucks to carry their goods from one place to another. To get an idea of how many trucks there were on the streets at the time, one may turn to the telephone book for that year.

In the classified section, for instance, if one opens to the "P" listings, a few of the products one will find advertised there are:

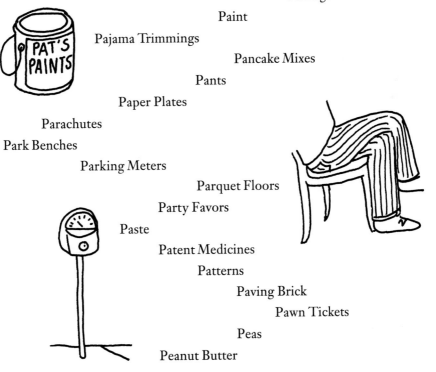

Package Handles

Paint

Pajama Trimmings

Pancake Mixes

Pants

Paper Plates

Parachutes

Park Benches

Parking Meters

Parquet Floors

Party Favors

Paste

Patent Medicines

Patterns

Paving Brick

Pawn Tickets

Peas

Peanut Butter

Pearls

Pecans

Pencils

Pen Knives

Penicillin

Pennants

Pens

Pepper

Perambulators

Percales

Perfumes

Periodicals

Permanent Wave Machines

Pet Shop Supplies

Petroleum

Pewter

Pharmaceuticals

Phonographs

Photographic Supplies

Piano Stools

Piccolos

Pickle Barrels

Picnic Tables

Picture Frames

Picture Post Cards

Picture Windows

Pies

Pigskins

Pile Drivers

Pillows

Pins

Pipe

Pipe Organs

Pistol Belts

Piston Rings

Pizza Pie Supplies

Place Cards

Planetariums

Plant Foods

Plaques

Plaster of Paris

Plastics

Plate Glass

Platforms

Platinum

Playground Equipment

Playing Cards

Playsuits

Playthings

Pleating Machine Parts

Plexiglass

Pliers

Plows

Plugs

Plumbago

Plushes

Plywood

Pocketbooks

Podiums

Poker Chips

Poisons

Poles

Police Badges

Polish

Polo Mallets

Pompoms

Ponchos

Pony Carts

Pool Tables

Popcorn Machines

Porch Furniture

Postage Stamp Affixers

Posters

Potatoes

Potato Peelers

Pot Holders

Potted Plants

Pottery

Poultry

Powder Puffs

Precious Stones

Precision Castings

Premium Goods

Preserves

Pressing Machines

Pressure Cookers

Pretzels

Price Tags

Printing Presses

Propellers

Projectors

Prunes

Public Address Systems

Publications

Pulleys

Pulpits

Pumice

Pumps

Punch Bowls

Puppets

Purses

Pushcart Parts

Putty

Puzzles

One must keep in mind that the products mentioned above are only a *few* of the things listed under the letter "P". Consider, too, that the phone book lists not only pile drivers, for example, but forty-three *different* firms in the pile-driving business (not to mention the *7234!* different firms in the plastics business). Then, if one remembers that *each* of those forty-three firms employed on the average of seventeen and a half trucks a day, one will begin to get an idea of the number of trucks that there must have been in New York just before the Pushcart War.

The worst of it was that during the period that more and more trucks had been appearing in the city streets, the trucks had been getting bigger and bigger. The truck drivers had it all figured out.

At least, that is what Professor Lyman Cumberly, of New York University, said when he was writing about the Pushcart War some years later. Professor Cumberly's notion was that the truck drivers had gotten together and figured out that in crowded traffic conditions, the only way to get where you wanted to go was to be *so* big that you didn't have to get out of the way for anybody. This is known as the Large Object Theory of History.

CHAPTER V

Wenda Gambling Sees the Danger Signs

It is a matter of historical record that the average truck in New York City at the time of the Pushcart War was so big that no one driving behind it could see around it to check the names of the streets he was passing. Wenda Gambling, a well-known movie star, on her way to 96th Street to visit her ninety-year-old grandmother, once got stuck behind a gasoline truck.

For all her experience in the movies, Wenda was a timid driver and was afraid the truck would explode if she tried to pass it. It had big red DANGER signs painted all over it, Wenda recalls.

Since Wenda did not dare pass the truck, and since she could not see any street signs, she not only went past 96th Street, but was at Bear Mountain, some fifty miles beyond the city limits, before she had any idea where she was. By then, of course, she was so frightened that she had to spend the night in a log cabin in Harriman State Park.

A search party did not find her until 6:30 the following morning. She had not had anything to eat but some dry oatmeal that someone had left in the cabin.

This kind of thing kept happening. Wenda's case is remembered, because Wenda's activities were always reported in the headlines. But other people ran into similar troubles.

More and more the truck drivers crowded other drivers to the sides of the street. They hogged the best parking places. Or, if there were no parking places, and a truck driver felt like having a cup of coffee, he simply stopped his truck in the middle of the street and left it there, blocking the traffic for miles behind him.

The heavier the traffic, the ruder the truck drivers became. At busy intersections, they never let anyone else turn first. If anyone tried to, a truck driver had only to gun his engine and keep on coming. Few automobile drivers cared to argue with a twelve-ton truck, even when they were in the right.

Even the taxi drivers began to lose their confidence. For a long time the taxis had been considered a match for the trucks because of the daring, speed, and skill of their drivers. When the taxi drivers grew cautious, many people were alarmed.

CHAPTER VI

The Peanut Butter Speech

One of the first people to speak out against the growing danger was a man named Archie Love. Archie Love was running for Mayor at the time, and he promised to reduce the number of trucks in the streets.

It looked briefly as if Archie Love might be elected on the strength of this promise alone. But that was before Archie's opponent, Emmett P. Cudd (who was already Mayor and did not want to lose his job), made his famous "Peanut Butter Speech" in Union Square.

Mayor Cudd repeated the Peanut Butter Speech ninety times in one week. It went more or less as follows:

"Friends and New Yorkers: New York is one of the biggest cities in the U.S.A. We are proud of that fact.

"What makes a city big? Big business, naturally.

"And what is the difference between big business and small business? It is this: If you order fourteen cartons of peanut butter, you are running a small business. If you order four hundred cartons of peanut butter, you are running a big business.

"Fourteen cartons of peanut butter, you can get delivered in a station wagon. But for four hundred cartons of peanut butter, you need a truck. And you need a *big* truck. Big trucks mean progress.

"My opponent, Archie Love, is against trucks. He is, therefore, against progress. Maybe he is even against peanut butter."

Naturally, all the truck drivers voted to re-elect Mayor Cudd, and so did a lot of other people. Very few people wanted to be against progress. No one wanted to be against peanut butter. And *everyone* wanted to be proud of their city, because they always had been. Thus, Archie Love did not get elected, and the trucks kept getting bigger.

As the trucks increased in size, traffic — as Archie Love had predicted — grew steadily worse until, in the spring before the Pushcart War, the city was one big traffic jam most of the time. One day it took a taxi four hours to drive five blocks.

The passenger in the taxi was Professor Lyman Cumberly, who did not complain because he was working on his Large Object Theory of History and found the situation interesting from a scientific point of view. During this ride, Professor Cumberly fell into conversation with an impatient young man from Seattle who was trapped in an adjoining taxi.

The young man was shocked that so many New Yorkers accepted the terrible conditions in their streets without protest, and Professor Cumberly recalls that the visitor had very definite ideas what should be done about the trucks. In fact, encouraged by Professor Cumberly's interest, the young man flew back to Seattle and wrote a book.

The book, called *The Enemy in the Streets*, was a fearless attack on the trucks. However, as the author was unknown, the book did not receive much notice at the time it was published. It is remembered today largely because the author is now President of the United States.

CHAPTER VII

The Words That Triggered the War
(Wenda Gambling's Innocent Remark)

What finally brought matters to a head was a television program called "The Day the Traffic Stopped." The day before the program, the traffic *had* stopped entirely, and one of the television stations had hurriedly called in a panel of experts to explain why.

The members of the panel were:

Robert Alexander Wrightson — Traffic Commissioner of New York

Alexander P. Wolfson — head of Wolfson & Wolfson, specialists in traffic coordination

Dr. Wolfe Alexander — a traffic psychologist

Wenda Gambling — a well-known movie star

Wenda Gambling was hardly an expert on traffic. But as the three other panel members were elderly men (one stout, one bald, and one near-sighted), the moderator of the program felt that the panel would be more interesting to the audience if Wenda were at the table.

In introducing Wenda, the moderator of the program said, "As we all know, Miss Gambling's new movie, *The Streets of New York*, is being shot on the streets of New York, and as the streets of New York are the subject of our discussion tonight, it is very appropriate that she should be here."

Wenda tactfully left most of the talking to the experts. Each of the three men had a different theory as to why the traffic had stopped.

Robert Alexander Wrightson said that there was no cause for alarm, that the whole thing was a simple matter of what he liked to call "the density of moving objects."

Alexander P. Wolfson disagreed. He said the problem involved nothing more than "a predictable increase in the number of unmoving objects."

Dr. Wolfe Alexander said that it did not matter whether the objects were moving or unmoving as the whole thing could be easily solved by "a more thorough conditioning of drivers to hopeless situations."

"And what do you think, Miss Gambling?" asked the moderator, as the three experts began to argue with each other.

"I don't know what they are talking about," said Wenda Gambling.

"Well," said the moderator, who was not quite sure himself, "I believe our subject this evening was traffic."

"Oh," said Wenda Gambling. "Well, I think that there are too many trucks and that the trucks are too big."

Since most of the television audience had been watching Wenda Gambling rather than the experts — and since everyone watching *did* know what Wenda was talking about — this one remark received more attention than anything else that was said on the program. Before the program was off the air, over five thousand viewers had called the station to say that they agreed with Wenda Gambling.

Professor Lyman Cumberly has suggested that except for Wenda Gambling's innocent remark, there might never have been a Pushcart War. Instead, says Professor Cumberly, the trucks would have simply gone on taking over the city, crowding out the taxis, buses, cars — and finally the people themselves. No one would have challenged them until it was too late.

It would, Professor Cumberly believes, have been the end of life in New York as we know it. But once Wenda Gambling had stated the danger for all to hear, war was inevitable.

CHAPTER VIII

The Secret Meeting & The Declaration of War
(Excerpts from the Diary of Joey Kafflis)

The truck drivers themselves were the first to grasp the meaning of the widespread response to Wenda Gambling's remark. The day after the television program, representatives of all the trucking firms in the city held a secret meeting.

The meeting was organized by "The Three," as the owners of the three largest trucking firms in the city were called. The Three were Moe Mammoth (of Mammoth Moving) — or "Big Moe," as his drivers called him, Walter Sweet, of Tiger Trucking (who preferred to be known as "The Tiger") and Louie Livergreen of LEMA (Lower Eastside Moving Association).

The plotting of the Pushcart War and the truckers' strategy throughout was, for the most part, the work of The Three.[1] Big Moe generally served as spokesman for The Three, and it was Big Moe who presided over the secret meeting.

The meeting was held in an underground garage owned by Mammoth Moving. It was at this meeting that a young truck driver named Joey Kafflis had the nerve to stand up and say, "People are right. Traffic is lousy, and there *are* too many trucks."

Joey, who worked for Tiger Trucking, was fired shortly after this meeting. Fortunately, Joey kept a diary. The diary was something that he had started to pass the time when his truck was stalled in a traffic jam. It is from this diary that we have a first-hand account of what happened at the first secret meeting and in the days that followed.

Here are some excerpts from Joey Kafflis' diary, dated the day after the secret meeting:

February 15. Columbus Avenue and 66th Street en route to 9th and 86th with two dozen pipe organs. 11:15 A.M.

It looks like a long tie-up ahead, so I may as well put down a few more facts about the meeting last night. After I have said, "Traffic is lousy," there is a big silence. Everybody looks at me very surprised, and several guys look as if I have hurt their feelings.

Then Big Moe, who is running the meeting, gets up and growls. By that I mean that he clears his throat in a particular way Big Moe has of clearing his throat. It is as if you were racing your engine a little bit to test whether you have the power and the engine is warmed up.

---

[1]"The Three" were originally known as "The Big Three," but this caused some confusion as the leaders of three important nations of the time were also called The Big Three, and after a city newspaper ran a headline announcing BIG THREE CARVE UP CHINA (over a story about Mammoth, LEMA, and Tiger Trucking buying out the China Carting & Storage Co.), there was some international trouble in the course of which Moscow was bombed by an Indo-Chinese pilot. After that the city papers referred to the three big trucking firms simply as The Three.

"Now maybe traffic is not so good," Big Moe says. For a minute I think he is going to agree with me. But instead he glares at me and says — and he is nicely warmed up by now — "*I* say, Mr. Kafflis, that is all a question of who is to blame for the traffic situation. Why pick on the poor trucks?"

When Big Moe says "poor trucks," I laugh out loud. But nobody hears me, because everybody is cheering for Big Moe. . . .

12:15 P.M. Columbus Avenue and 69th Street.

I thought I was going to make 86th Street by lunch time, but there is still trouble up ahead. So I will continue.

After Big Moe says "poor trucks," a trucker named Little Miltie stands up. Little Miltie says, "I agree with Big Moe. Why blame the poor trucks? If you ask me, it is all those pushcarts that are blocking the streets."

Nobody likes this Little Miltie too much, as he is known as a very mean driver. By that I mean that Little Miltie would crowd out another truck as soon as he would a taxi. But for once Little Miltie gets a big hand, and about ten different truck drivers then begin to tell how slow the push- carts are, and how pushcarts are always sitting by the curb where a trucker wants to park, and how pushcarts should not be allowed to take up space in a modern city like New York.

Once more I have to laugh, and this time everyone hears me. So I explain, "Come on — how much room do a few pushcarts take?" Because I personally do not mind the pushcarts.

When I am stuck in traffic like today (like almost any day, for that matter), a pushcart will come along and sell me a sausage roll, which passes the time. You get the best sausage rolls around Thompson Street. Sixty-ninth, where I am now, is not too good for sausage rolls.

It looks like something is moving up ahead, so I will put this away until another time.

Columbus Avenue and 75th Street. 4:05 P.M.

Now there is a trailer truck backed up to the curb at 76th. It is sticking halfway out into the street. The taxi driver ahead of me says that they are unloading permanent wave machines, and that it will be a half-hour tie-up, at least. So I may as well finish writing about the secret meeting while it is still fresh in my mind. I left off with how I was speaking up for the pushcarts.

"Come on," I say, "how much room do a few pushcarts take?" I address my question to a driver named Mack.

"You could line up two dozen pushcarts along the curb before those carts would take up one-half the space of a truck like a Mighty Mammoth," I point out to Mack. Mack drives a Mighty Mammoth.

"Or, a Ten-Ton Tiger," I say, putting myself in the same spot. When I mention a Ten-Ton Tiger, Big Moe looks at my boss. My boss is Mr. Walter Sweet, who is sitting right beside Big Moe, as he is one of The Three.

Big Moe asks Walter Sweet, "Does this boy drive for Tiger Trucking?" — a silly question, as I have as much as said I drive a Ten-Ton Tiger. And the boss has to admit I do.

I am sorry if I have embarrassed the boss. Mr. Walter Sweet has a kind heart for the most part.

"Do you have anything more to say, Mr. Kafflis?" Big Moe asks me. And he asks me in such a tone of voice that I know he is telling me he could be helpful in helping me to lose my job with Tiger Trucking.

However, I am not afraid of Big Moe. It occurred to me a long time ago that there are so many reasons you could lose a job that if you started to worry about them all, you would be afraid to say anything. And for anyone who has a lot to say, as I do, this would be a hardship.

However, I shut up for the simple reason that I do not have anything else to say at the moment. It is such a nutty argument about the pushcarts.

The next speaker at the meeting is Louie Livergreen. Louie owns all those Leaping Lemas on the Lower East Side and has pretty well cut everybody else out of business down there.

Now Louie speaks in a very smooth way. He is not a pleasant-looking man, but he speaks in a smooth voice. I have noticed that each of The Three speaks in a different way.

Big Moe speaks in a loud voice — "a voice like a truck driver," my sister once said, which I felt was an insulting remark. But many people think of truck drivers in this way.

The Tiger, on the other hand, has a low voice. And Louie Livergreen, on the third hand, speaks — as I mentioned — in a smooth voice.

Of The Three, it is Louie Livergreen that I would be afraid of, and I think that is because his voice is as smooth as a good grade of motor oil, whether he is saying something perfectly pleasant or something terrible. If somebody says something terrible in a pleasant tone of voice, I get very nervous. I would feel better if they yelled.

Well, as I said, Louie Livergreen starts to talk to the drivers in that smooth voice. "Our boys are telling us that the pushcarts are ruining the city," Louie says.

"And believe me, I am glad that you have been so frank about the trouble. Mr. Mammoth and Mr. Sweet and myself are not out in the trucks so much ourselves, and we have to rely on our boys to give us the facts.

"And now that we have got the facts," says Louie, "it is very clear what we have got to do."

Louie explains that what we have got to do is to educate the public. "When people complain about the traffic," he says, "we have got to tell the people who is to blame. Otherwise, they will be blaming the trucks."

From the tone of his voice and the respectful way the truck drivers are listening to him, Louie could be delivering a sermon in a church, which is not exactly the case.

"I know what you boys are up against," Louie goes on to say. "I operate on the East Side where most of the pushcarts also operate. And I know these people. They are behind the times and a danger to the rest of us, and they have got to go."

Louie gets a big hand at this point, but he is not finished. "I will tell you something else," he says. "And it is not something I am proud of. My own father was a pushcart peddler, and if I had not had the guts to get out and fight for myself, no matter who was in my way, I might be pushing a pushcart myself.

"Instead," Louie points out, "I have built up the firm of LEMA and put one hundred Leaping Lemas on the streets every day of the year, rain or shine. And that I am proud of!"

Louie gets a big hand again. Not from me, though. While I agree that one hundred trucks is something to be proud of, I do not see why a man wants to talk as Louie is talking about his father — who maybe did not have such an easy time, and rain or shine, is out in the streets with a pushcart. Whereas Louie — if it rains — can send out one hundred drivers.

Louie has a few other remarks. Mainly this one: "I think you boys know that the Lower Eastside Moving Association has been working on a Master Plan for the streets of New York, a plan that will greatly improve the situation for truck drivers. I have discussed this plan with Mr. Moe Mammoth and Mr. Walter Sweet, and the plan is moving forward nicely. But before it can go into effect, we have got to solve the pushcart problem."

I have not heard about this Master Plan of Louie Livergreen's before, but all around me drivers are nodding as if it is a fine idea.

I ask several of the boys about it, and they say it is probably the usual thing — to make things better for the truckers in the streets and maybe more money for the drivers.

I don't know about the Master Plan, but it seems to me that the idea of the meeting is that The Three are declaring war on the pushcarts.

Well, I must sign off now, as the taxi driver ahead is signaling that they have got those permanent wave machines off the trailer. Unfortunately, I see that it is 5:30, so I will have to take the pipe organs back to the warehouse and try to get to 86th Street tomorrow.[2] Really, traffic *is* lousy."

---

[2]Joey Kafflis never did get to deliver the pipe organs that he was transporting on February 15. The following day he was fired, and the rest of his diary is concerned with a potato farm on eastern Long Island that he acquired shortly thereafter.

CHAPTER IX

The Secret Campaign Against the Pushcarts

The Pushcart War is generally divided into two major campaigns. The first of these is referred to as the Secret Campaign. For although we now have the evidence of the Kafflis diary that The Three *had* declared war on the pushcarts at the secret meeting, this declaration was not at the time made public. This gave the trucks an enormous advantage in the beginning.

The pushcart peddlers themselves did not know for over a month that the truckers had declared war on them. All they knew was that suddenly the truck drivers were nudging their pushcarts out of the way more and more often, and that they were nudging harder and harder.

In one week alone, more than one hundred carts were brought into Maxie Hammerman's for repairs. Maxie repaired broken slatting, broken spokes, broken handles, and bent axles. Many of the pushcarts had to be entirely rebuilt, and Maxie did not have time to build any new carts. Also, the number of serious accidents involving pushcarts increased, and several peddlers needed hospital treatment for broken legs or crushed ribs.

At first, the pushcart peddlers thought that all these troubles were simply a case of the already terrible traffic conditions getting rapidly worse. Then they began to hear puzzling remarks from people standing on street corners. Whenever someone complained about the traffic, there was always someone else on hand to say, "I hear it is the pushcarts that are to blame."

People always said, "I *hear.*" Where they had heard, nobody was sure.

A great many of the rumors probably came from readers of a weekly newspaper called *The Ears & Eyes of the Lower East Side.* This paper was published as a community service by LEMA (Lower Eastside Moving Association). *The Ears & Eyes* was given away free to grocery stores to pass on to their customers. It was also sent free to members of the City Council and other important people.

In *The Ears & Eyes*, there was a regular column by a man who signed himself "The Community Reporter." The Community Reporter wrote a great many columns just before the war about what he called "The Pushcart Menace."

The Community Reporter reported that "people" wanted to get rid of the pushcarts in order to make the streets of the city safer and more attractive. He said that "people" said that the pushcarts were "unsound and unsanitary."

The Community Reporter was always telling people about what "people" wanted. Before he began writing about The Pushcart Menace, he wrote about trees. He said that "people" also wanted to get rid of the trees planted along the sidewalks of the city so that the streets could be wider and more attractive. He said that trees were unsanitary, too, because leaves were always falling on the sidewalk.

The Community Reporter said that people thought the streets should be wider and more attractive, even if it meant getting rid of the sidewalks and some of the houses and schools and churches and small candy stores. Many of these were unsound and unsanitary anyway, he said.

However, in the spring before the war, it was mainly the pushcarts that the Community Reporter wrote about. He made it sound as if pushcarts were even more unsound and unsanitary than trees, houses, schools, churches, and candy stores.

It is uncertain how many people read *The Ears & Eyes*. (Some grocers said that they had trouble giving it away, as most of their customers did not mind a few leaves falling off trees.) But enough people did see the Community Reporter's column for one of the more respectable daily papers to announce a series entitled: "Pushcarts — Are They a Menace to Our Streets?"

As part of this series, a reporter interviewed Moe Mammoth. This was the day after a Mama Mammoth had upset three vegetable carts on Avenue C.

"That poor Mama," said Big Moe. "Tomatoes all over the street, and twenty pushcart peddlers yelling at the truck driver, and picking up broken tomatoes and throwing them at him. What kind of working conditions are those?"

"Are you saying the pushcarts *are* a menace?" asked the reporter.

"The facts speak for themselves," said Big Moe. "As a public service, Mr. Louie Livergreen, of the Lower Eastside Moving Association — which has one hundred trucks out on the streets every day — has made a count of the number of accidents involving pushcarts in the last month.

"In the last month alone," Big Moe said, "Mr. Livergreen tells me there have been one hundred and forty-one *more* pushcart accidents than in the month before.

"My own drivers," Big Moe added, "have orders to report every push-cart accident they see, and they say that they are held up by pushcarts several times a day."

"And you think that these accidents are tying up the traffic?" asked the reporter.

"That is what my drivers say," said Big Moe. "Of course, we all know the pushcarts are not designed for modern traffic conditions."

When Maxie Hammerman read that last remark, he was so angry that he threw a hammer through his own shop window. "Not *designed!*" he roared at Frank the Flower, who had stopped by Maxie's shop to have a few bolts tightened on his cart.

"Someone is saying that a pushcart is not *designed*? A pushcart is *perfectly* designed," Maxie said, glowering at his broken window.

"Look now," he said, slapping the side of Frank the Flower's cart. "Look how compact. So it shouldn't take up too much space in a crowded street."

"I am not complaining," said Frank the Flower.

"*Designed*," growled Maxie Hammerman, normally a pleasant-tempered man. He was really very insulted.

"Designed," Maxie went on, "— what I would like to get my hands on designing is Mr. Moe Mammoth. I give you my word, when I'm finished, he will be designed very much smaller."

Maxie Hammerman was not the only one to take offense at Big Moe's remarks. All the pushcart peddlers were angry at Big Moe's blaming the accidents on them.

"Because the pushcarts are *in* the accidents, does it mean we *caused* them?" asked Eddie Moroney, whose cart was not only well-designed, but beautifully lettered — "Coal & Ice — Home Delivered." (Eddie Moroney had lettered circus carts and posters before he went into business for himself.)

"Since when did a pushcart hit a truck?" Eddie demanded.

"Believe me, it would give me pleasure," said Frank the Flower.

"What I don't like is 'unsanitary,'" said Old Anna, who sold apples and pears of the best quality outside hospitals and museums.

"What is this *unsanitary* I am hearing about?" Old Anna demanded. "My cart is as clean as a teacup I would drink from. How can I be unsanitary in front of hospitals? What do they mean 'unsanitary'?"

"Plastic bags, maybe," said Frank the Flower. "In the supermarkets, they put the apples and pears in plastic bags."

"Plastic!" said Old Anna. "So you can't examine the fruit. That is why they have plastic bags."

"But people think it is more sanitary," said Frank the Flower.

"Sanitary!" said Old Anna. "Who sees whether the man who puts the fruit in the plastic bags has washed his hands?"

"Every customer can see for himself that my hands are clean," said Old Anna. "You put apples in a plastic bag in the back room of a store — and who *knows*?

"Also," said Old Anna, "I have noticed that apples in a plastic bag are two pounds for twenty-nine cents. In a paper bag, such as I use, they are three pounds for twenty-nine.

"You ask me what is the menace," said Old Anna. "And I will tell you. It is *plastic bags*!"

CHAPTER X

The Meeting at Maxie Hammerman's: The Pushcarts Decide to Fight

Looking back on the Pushcart War, it seems possible that the trucks might have gone on slowly breaking up the pushcarts in what looked like accidents, if it had not been for Mack's brutal attack on Morris the Florist. But the day after Mack hit Morris, the pushcart peddlers held a meeting at Maxie Hammerman's shop. It was at this meeting that the peddlers decided to fight back.

The meeting had been called to take up a collection to buy Morris the Florist a new cart. Peddlers from all over the city were there.

Every kind of pushcart business was represented — hot dogs and sauerkraut, roast chestnuts, old clothes, ice and coal, ices and ice cream sticks, fruit and vegetables, used cartons, shoe laces and combs, pretzels, dancing dolls, and nylon stockings, to mention only a few. Most of the peddlers who became well-known to the public during the Pushcart War were present at this meeting.

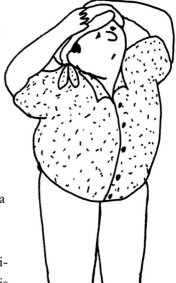

Old Anna ("Apples and Pears") was there. So was Mr. Jerusalem ("All Kinds Junk — Bought & Sold"). Harry the Hot Dog ("Harry's Hots & Homemade Sauerkraut") was there. Carlos ("Cartons Flattened and Removed") was there. Eddie Moroney ("Coal & Ice — Home Delivered" — lettered in three colors) was there. Papa Peretz ("Pretzels — 6 for 25¢") was there.

Frank the Flower, of course, was there. He was the first to speak. It was Frank the Flower's idea to take up a collection to buy Morris a new cart.

"As you can see from the bandage on his head, my friend Morris has had a terrible experience," said Frank the Flower. "Worse yet, his cart is ruined."

"It is a fact," said Maxie Hammerman. "I could not put that cart together in one hundred years."

"What I wish to point out," said Frank the Flower, "is this: Today it is Morris they are putting out of business. Tomorrow it may be you or me. I think we should every one of us give ten cents — maybe fifteen — so that Morris can buy a new cart. If it happened to us, Morris would do the same."

"Believe me, I would," said Morris. "But I pray it shouldn't happen to anyone else."

Mr. Jerusalem ("All Kinds Junk — Bought & Sold") stood up. "The ten cents we will give," he said. "Or fifteen. No question. What I want to know is why they are breaking us up. All of a sudden — accidents."

"*Accidents!*" said Old Anna. "Is it an accident that Morris the Florist has had? Accidents on purpose, that is what is happening."

"All right — on purpose," Mr. Jerusalem agreed. "But *why?*" he demanded.

"They are telling everybody we are in the way," said Papa Peretz ("Pretzels — 6 for 25¢"). "I hear it on 14th Street. I hear it on 23rd. Even on Delancey Street I hear it. Everywhere, they are saying that we are in the way."

"*Way!*" said Old Anna. "Whose way am I in? I am quiet about my business. I don't take up much space. For forty-five years I sell my apples in front of hospitals, museums, and the best downtown offices. My customers ask about my health — my family. It is the first time I hear that I am in the way. *Whose* way?"

Maxie Hammerman got up then. "I will explain," said Maxie, who had been doing some serious thinking since the day he threw his hammer through his own shop window.

"Conditions are very bad in the streets," Maxie said. "People are getting mad at the trucks. They should have got mad a long time ago. But everybody was scared. Who wants to argue with a truck?

"However, there comes a time," Maxie said. "People begin to complain, and the trucks do not want the blame for tying up the streets. So they have to find somebody else to blame.

"Who shall they blame?" Maxie asked. "Taxis? No, there are too many taxis. Cars? No, too many cars. The trucks do not want to fight the cars and the taxis. That would make too many *more* people mad at them. But pushcarts — how many are there?"

"There are hundreds of pushcarts," said Harry the Hot Dog ("Harry's Hots & Homemade Sauerkraut").

"Five hundred and nine, to be exact," said Maxie Hammerman. "More than most people think, because pushcarts stay in their own neighborhoods. They are not rushing all over the city to make the traffic worse. Stop a man on the street and ask him how many pushcarts has he seen today. He will tell you, 'Three — maybe four' — although there are five hundred and nine carts licensed to do business in this city.

"However," Maxie added. "Even five hundred and nine is a small number beside taxis and cars."

"I don't understand," said Papa Peretz. "They could kill us all, and the traffic would still be terrible."

"So then they will have to find someone else to blame," said Maxie Hammerman. "Motorcycles, maybe. Or grocery carts, such as the ladies take to the supermarket. Then people will see how silly it is."

"By then," said Old Anna, "we will all be dead."

"That is correct," said Maxie Hammerman. "We will all be dead. Unless —" Maxie picked up a hammer and held it as if he were about to hit something a quick hard blow.

"Unless what?" said Frank the Flower, seizing Maxie's arm, in case he should be about to throw the hammer through his window again.

"Unless we fight back," said Maxie Hammerman, pulling his arm free and whamming the hammer down on the table in front of him. "I say the pushcarts have got to fight."

"Of course, we have got to fight," said Old Anna.

"Fight the trucks?" said Papa Peretz. "How can the pushcarts fight the trucks?"

"Maybe you'd rather be dead?" said Old Anna.

"Naturally, we wouldn't," said Harry the Hot Dog. "But how can we fight the trucks?"

"Listen to me, Harry," said Old Anna. "*First*, you decide to fight. Then you ask me how."

"All right," said Harry the Hot Dog. "Fight! So now I ask you — how?"

"Yes, General Anna, we are listening," said Eddie Moroney, bowing to Old Anna. (This is how Old Anna came to be known as General Anna. Eddie Moroney called her General at the meeting at Maxie Hammerman's shop, and the name seemed to suit her.)

When it came to a vote, all the pushcart peddlers were with General Anna. They realized that they had to stick together. And they had to fight.

"But how?" Harry the Hot Dog asked again. "You want me to sell poison hot dogs to all the truck drivers maybe?"

General Anna shook her head. "It's okay by me you should poison the truck drivers. Only you might get the poison dogs mixed up with the regular, and then you'll be giving the poison to a good customer."

"We need a secret weapon," said Papa Peretz. "Like a big bomb."

"For carrying around bombs, you get arrested," said General Anna.

To everyone's surprise, it was Carlos ("Cartons Flattened and Removed") who had the best idea. Carlos had never spoken out in a meeting before.

CHAPTER XI

The Secret Weapon

Carlos was known to the pushcart peddlers as the most skillful carton-flattener in the Lower East Side section of New York City. Carlos' business was to go around to small stores that had clean cardboard cartons which they wished to be rid of. With two or three deft motions, Carlos would flatten the cartons and carefully stack them on his pushcart. Carlos was the only flattener in the business who could stack to a height of twelve feet without the cartons slipping off.

When he had a load, Carlos would deliver the cartons to another small business that needed a few cartons. This was a very practical business as Carlos did not have to pay out any money for the goods he sold. The storekeepers were glad to get rid of the cartons. Carlos' only expense was for his pushcart.

One reason Carlos never said much was that he spoke only in Spanish — except to give the price of a load of cartons. That he could do in English. He could also follow the main idea of a conversation in English. But to reply to a complicated matter, he preferred to speak in Spanish.

Carlos' idea at the meeting at Maxie Hammerman's was too complicated for him to explain in English. Maxie Hammerman had to explain it for him. Maxie Hammerman spoke Spanish and twelve other languages. He had to, being the Pushcart King.

"Carlos wishes to say," Maxie Hammerman began, "that the problem is to make people see who *is* blocking the streets."

"Certainly," said Harry the Hot Dog. "But how?"

"Carlos has described to me a very clever pea shooter that his youngest boy has made," said Maxie Hammerman. "Carlos says that the pea shooter shoots not just ordinary peas, but peas with a pin stuck in them."

"Children!" said Papa Peretz. "You have to watch them every minute. For example, my grandson —"

"Wait, Papa Peretz," said Maxie Hammerman, "we are coming to the point. The point is that Carlos has told his boy that he must never use such a pea shooter to shoot at people as it would not be so nice to put a pin in someone's arm."

"That's what I mean," said Papa Peretz.

"Wait," said Maxie Hammerman. "Carlos' little boy replies, 'Then what good is the shooter?' Carlos does not know how to answer, and he feels bad because the shooter is very cleverly made, and it is a shame if the boy cannot use it at all.

"Then *suddenly*," said Maxie Hammerman, "when Papa Peretz says at this meeting that we need a secret weapon, Carlos is happy. He sees what the shooter is good for."

"To put pins in the truck drivers?" said Harry the Hot Dog.

Carlos shook his head.

"No," Maxie Hammerman explained. "It is Carlos' belief that even truck drivers are people. He has told his little boy that he must never shoot at people, and he does not wish to set a bad example."

"Then what good *is* the pea shooter?" asked Frank the Flower.

Carlos spoke very excitedly to Maxie Hammerman in Spanish.

"Aha," said Maxie Hammerman. "Carlos says we will not, of course, shoot at the truck drivers. What we will shoot at is the truck tires. He says we will kill the truck tires."

"*Bang!*" said Carlos, pointing at an imaginary truck tire. "Bang, bang!" It was a word he had learned from his boy.

"Then *goma vacia*!" Carlos said.

"*Goma vacia*," Maxie Hammerman explained, meant in Spanish 'flat tire.'

"*Si,*" Carlos nodded, blowing his breath out and sinking to the floor as if he were a truck tire going flat.

Morris the Florist took off his hat. "Such an idea!" he said. "For such an idea Carlos could be President of the U.S.A."

"*President!*" said Papa Peretz. "How can the President speak Spanish?"

"Never mind the President," said Harry the Hot Dog. "It is a good idea."

"*Good?*" said General Anna. "It is beautiful. I see the picture. The question is: *Who* is blocking the traffic? All right. We kill the truck tires, and suddenly everywhere in the streets — *big, dead trucks*! They can't move. They are blocking everything. People look around. In every block they see six, seven, *eight* dead trucks. People will *see* who is blocking the traffic."

"Of course," said Mr. Jerusalem, "it is not such a nice thing to do."

"Not *nice*!" said Morris the Florist. "Compared to smashing a man's cart so badly that it can never be fixed, it is a *very* nice thing to do."

"No matter how nice," said Eddie Moroney, "we should not let the truck drivers see us doing it. There could be a difference of opinion."

"Naturally," said Papa Peretz. "It should be a surprise attack. We will keep the pea shooters in our pockets. We wait until the truck driver looks the other way. Then, quick — *pffft*! Then *we* look the other way."

"Just so," said General Anna. "So it should look like an accidental flat tire."

"And all of a sudden there will be so many accidents," said Harry the Hot Dog.

"Yes," said Maxie Hammerman, figuring on a piece of paper. "If there are five hundred and nine pushcarts, and every man who has a pushcart —"

"And every lady," said General Anna.

"*And* every lady," agreed Maxie Hammerman. "If every pushcart peddler kills only six tires a day, that would be quite a few accidents."

"I am all for the accidents," said Frank the Flower, "but where can we get five hundred and nine pea shooters?"

"We will make them in my shop," said Maxie Hammerman. "Carlos' boy will show us how."

"Can we also make peas?" asked Papa Peretz.

"Peas, we can grow," said Eddie Moroney. "I have a window box, and already I have grown onions and beans good enough to eat."

"Good for you, Eddie Moroney," said General Anna. "But I am not going to wait for peas to grow in your window box. Much less to dry out. We must attack at once."

"We can buy the peas," said Harry the Hot Dog.

"Yes," said Maxie Hammerman. "I will order one ton of peas in the morning."

"And a ton of pins," said General Anna.

"A ton!" said Mr. Jerusalem. "But how much will so many pins cost? Even scrap metal junk by the ton — it adds up. I should know. Scrap metal is my line.

And one ton of new high-quality pins — who can afford? Not to mention one ton of peas, also an expense."

"Pin money we will need," Maxie Hammerman agreed. "And I will get it."

"From where?" asked Papa Peretz.

"I know a lady," said Maxie Hammerman. "She can afford to buy a few pins."

"A *few!*" said Mr. Jerusalem. "One ton is a few?"

"Who is the lady?" asked General Anna.

"By the name of Wenda Gambling," said Maxie Hammerman.

"From the movies?" said Harry the Hot Dog. "You would ask *her?*"

"Why not?" said Maxie Hammerman. "In my line I have to know a lot of people. Should I be the Pushcart King for nothing?"

"And you are sure this lady will give you the money for the pins?" said Mr. Jerusalem.

"I am confident," said Maxie Hammerman, tossing his hammer in the air. "I, myself," he said, catching the hammer, "heard her say that there were too many trucks."

Maxie Hammerman was right about Wenda Gambling. She meant it about the trucks, and she was very glad to buy a ton of pins and a ton of peas as well. Not only that, but she gave Maxie Hammerman five hundred autographed pictures of herself for the pushcart peddlers to paste on their carts if they wanted to. Most of them did. Even General Anna, who did not think much of the movies, took one.

"Never mind the movies," said General Anna. "The pins, I appreciate."

CHAPTER XII

The Pea Shooter Campaign — Phase I

It took a week for the pushcart peddlers to prepare for their attack. Maxie Hammerman kept his shop open twenty-four hours a day, and the peddlers in teams of twenty men took turns putting the pins in peas.

Carlos made all five hundred and nine shooters himself. He cut them from a roll of yellow plastic tubing that a storekeeper had given him for taking away his cartons for ten years at no charge.

At last, everything was ready. The attack was set for the morning of March 23rd. The evening before, the peddlers all reported to Maxie Hammerman's shop to collect their shooters and twenty-four rounds of ammunition each.

General Anna outlined the plan of battle. Everyone was to go to the location where he usually did business. He was to wait there until 10:00 A.M., when the morning traffic would be well under way. At 10:00 sharp, he was to fire at the tires of any trucks that came in range.

Frank the Flower had wanted Wenda Gambling to fire the opening shot from in front of the Empire State Building, but General Anna felt that this would attract too much attention.

"Where there is a movie star," said General Anna, "there is a crowd. We do not want the trucks to know what is hitting them."

So the Pea Shooter Campaign began in quite an ordinary way. Between 10:05 A.M. and 10:10 A.M. on March 23rd, ninety-seven truck drivers in different parts of the city discovered that they had flat tires. Not one of the drivers knew what had hit him.

Ninety-seven hits (out of some five hundred pea-pins that were fired in the opening attack) is, according to the Amateur Weapons Association, a very good average, especially as many of the peddlers had never handled a pea shooter before. And there were a few, like Mr. Jerusalem, who had grave doubts about the whole idea.

Mr. Jerusalem's heart was not in the attack. Though he had voted with the other peddlers to fight the trucks, fighting of any sort went against his nature. Mr. Jerusalem's performance on the first morning of the Pea Shooter Campaign is, therefore, of special interest.

At the time of the Pushcart War, Mr. Jerusalem was already an old man. No one knew exactly how old. He was held in great respect by the other pushcart peddlers, because his cart was not only his business, but it was also his home.

Unlike the other peddlers, Mr. Jerusalem did not have a room where he went to sleep or cook his meals. Instead he had a small frying pan, a cup, and a tin plate which he hung neatly from the underside of his cart. He had a charcoal burner built into one corner of the cart so that he could cook for himself whenever he felt like a hot meal.

Mr. Jerusalem's favorite joke was: "Some people go out to dinner on special occasions. I eat out all the time." This was true. Mr. Jerusalem was often to be seen sitting on a curb eating a plate of beans or turnips that he had cooked himself.

At night Mr. Jerusalem dropped canvas sheets over the sides of his cart so that there was a sort of tent underneath the cart. Then he would park the cart under a tree or in a vacant lot, crawl under the cart, roll up in a quilt, and go to sleep. In the summer he often did not bother with the canvas sheets, but slept alongside the cart so that he could see the stars. He was usually the first peddler on the streets in the morning.

Mr. Jerusalem had lived this way for fifty or sixty years, and he had never picked a fight with anyone. His motto was: "I live the way I want. You don't bother me. And I won't bother you."

Having lived by this motto for so long, Mr. Jerusalem was not happy about the Pea Shooter Campaign. To be sure, he had a great deal more at stake than the other peddlers. In his case, it was not only his business, but his home that was in danger as long as the trucks continued to attack the pushcarts. Still it went against his deepest convictions to cause another man trouble.

"There are not troubles enough in the world?" he had asked himself as he had worked alongside the other peddlers, putting pins in the peas. "Why should I make more?"

Mr. Jerusalem was still asking himself this question as he set off down Delancey Street on the morning of March 23rd. Like the other peddlers, Mr. Jerusalem was fully armed, although no one walking down the street would have noticed.

Anyone glancing at Mr. Jerusalem would have taken the yellow plastic straw sticking from his coat pocket for a yellow pencil. And no one would have taken any notice at all of the two dozen peas with a pin stuck carefully through the center of each, which Mr. Jerusalem had pinned to the sleeve of his jacket.

Or, even if someone had noticed, he would have supposed that Mr. Jerusalem had twenty-four tiny sleeve buttons on his jacket. Mr. Jerusalem's clothes never looked like anyone else's anyway. He picked them up here and there, secondhand, and he had his own style of wearing them.

"A sleeveful of ammunition!" Mr. Jerusalem muttered to himself, as he set off on the morning of March 23rd to pick up a secondhand popcorn machine that he had arranged to buy. "Who would believe it?

"A man my age — going to war!" Mr. Jerusalem shook his head sadly. "I can hardly believe it myself.

"Fighting in the streets!" he continued. "A man of peace for eighty years is walking fully armed down Delancey Street. A man who does not care for fighting.

"It is not only that I do not care for fighting," he went on.

"Naturally, I do not care for fighting," he admitted. "But it is also that fighting a ten-ton truck with a pea shooter is a little crazy. I do not think it will work.

"But what else can we do?" he asked himself.

He could not think of anything else. "So I will fight," he said. "If I have to," he added.

All the same Mr. Jerusalem was relieved when at 10:00 o'clock, the hour the attack was to begin, there was no truck parked within a hundred feet of his cart. Mr. Jerusalem did not think he could hit the tire of a moving truck.

"Would General Anna want me to waste the ammunition?" he asked himself. "Or Maxie Hammerman? Or Miss Wenda Gambling who has been so kind as to pay for one ton of pins? Not to mention peas."

When Mr. Jerusalem arrived at the candy store where he was to pick up the popcorn machine, he parked his cart. He was just starting into the store, when someone shouted at him.

Mr. Jerusalem looked around and saw a Leaping Lema. The driver of the Leaping Lema was trying to back into a space in front of Mr. Jerusalem's cart. The truck was loaded with new glass-and-chromium popcorn machines.

Now if there was any kind of truck that Mr. Jerusalem did not like, it was a Leaping Lema. The reason for this was that Mr. Jerusalem had known Louie Livergreen's father.

Louie's father had been, before his death, one of the most-respected pushcart peddlers in the secondhand-clothes line. Mr. Jerusalem had often made a cup of tea on his charcoal burner for Solomon Livergreen when he and Solomon were working on the same street.

Mr. Jerusalem should have been glad that Solomon's son was a big success — people said Louie Livergreen now owned one hundred big trucks. But Mr. Jerusalem held it against Louie Livergreen that from the day Louie had got his first truck, he had never come to see his father again. So every time Mr. Jerusalem saw a Leaping Lema on the streets, he thought, "They are breaking up family life."

As he watched the Leaping Lema backing into the curb on the first day of the Pea Shooter Campaign, Mr. Jerusalem wondered what his old friend Solomon Livergreen would have thought of the Pushcart War. Would Solomon, he wondered, have shot at a truck belonging to his own son, Louie Livergreen? And what would Solomon have wished his old friend Mr. Jerusalem to do?

"Shoot if you have to." That is what Solomon Livergreen would say, Mr. Jerusalem said to himself.

Mr. Jerusalem's conversation with Solomon Livergreen was interrupted by the driver of the Leaping Lema.

"Hey, Bud," shouted the driver. "Stop talking to yourself and move the baby buggy!" The driver was Little Miltie, a driver mentioned in the diary of Joey Kafflis.

Mr. Jerusalem frowned. It was bad enough that Little Miltie, a man one half the age of Mr. Jerusalem and not as tall, should call Mr. Jerusalem "Bud." But that Little Miltie should call Mr. Jerusalem's cart, which was also his home, a "baby buggy" — this was unnecessarily rude. However, Mr. Jerusalem answered courteously.

"I will only be a minute," he said.

"I can't wait a minute," said Little Miltie. "I got to deliver a popcorn machine."

"Well," said Mr. Jerusalem, "I have to pick up a popcorn machine. And until I pick up this secondhand popcorn machine, there will be no room in the store for a new machine such as you wish to deliver." And he turned to go about his business.

But as Mr. Jerusalem started into the candy store, Little Miltie raced his motor. Mr. Jerusalem hesitated. He remembered what had happened to Morris the Florist. He glanced over his shoulder.

"I'm backing up, Bud," Little Miltie said.

Mr. Jerusalem sighed and walked back to move his cart to the other side of the street.

Little Miltie grinned. "That's a good boy, Buster."

Mr. Jerusalem did not reply, but as Little Miltie was backing into the place Mr. Jerusalem had left, the old peddler took out his pea shooter. He looked at it doubtfully.

"A man my age — with a *pea shooter*!" he sighed. "Such a craziness on Delancey Street." However, he inserted one of the pea-pins, took careful aim — and fired.

For a moment nothing happened. Mr. Jerusalem felt foolish. "All right, I admit it," he said. "We are all crazy."

Mr. Jerusalem was about to drop his pea shooter in the gutter when he heard a slight hissing sound — the sound of air escaping from a tire.

"Or perhaps not so crazy," said Mr. Jerusalem.

He put the pea shooter back in his pocket and went to collect the popcorn machine. When he came out of the candy store, one of Little Miltie's rear tires was quite flat. Little Miltie was stamping up and down in the street and speaking even more rudely to the tire than he had spoken to Mr. Jerusalem.

"What is the matter?" asked Mr. Jerusalem. "The Leaping Lema is not leaping so good? A little trouble maybe?"

But Little Miltie was too angry to reply.

"Believe me, Solomon, I had to do it," Mr. Jerusalem said, as if to his old friend Solomon Livergreen.

"The fact is, Solomon," he continued, as he roped the popcorn machine onto his cart, "to cause a little trouble now and then is maybe good for a man.

"But, Solomon," he asked as he set off down Delancey Street, "who would have thought a man of my age would be such a good shot?"

"Naturally, it pays to use high-quality pins," he added.

Although Mr. Jerusalem knew where he could get a good price for the secondhand popcorn machine, he was now in no hurry to get there. He paused to look over every truck that had stopped for a traffic light or had pulled up to a curb to make a delivery.

Mr. Jerusalem chose his targets very carefully, and to his astonishment he hit four more trucks before he ran out of ammunition. At 2:30 in the afternoon, he headed back to Maxie Hammerman's for more pea-pins. He still had not got around to selling his popcorn machine.

CHAPTER XIII

Maxie Hammerman's Battle Plan & General Anna's Hester Street Strategy

Although Mr. Jerusalem was no more than half a mile from Maxie Hammerman's shop when he ran out of ammunition, it took him nearly three hours to get there. For by midafternoon, the city was a mess.

In the Delancey Street area, things were particularly bad. In every block Mr. Jerusalem saw two or three trucks stranded. Traffic was at a standstill, and people were shouting at the truck drivers for blocking the streets.

The truck drivers were furious. They were not used to being honked at and shouted at, and they had no idea what was happening to them.

The first few truckers who were hit thought that they had had the bad luck to pick up a splinter of glass or a nail. They telephoned for garage mechanics to come and help them change their flats, and went to have some coffee while they waited for the mechanics.

The truck drivers did not realize that their troubles were anything out of the ordinary until the mechanics began to sound irritated with them. Around

noon, the mechanics began to snap at the truck drivers who called for emergency service.

"Hold your horses, Buddy," more than one driver was told. "I got fourteen flats ahead of you, and you'll just have to wait until tomorrow." At that point, the truck drivers began to wonder.

Most of the stalled trucks were so big that a truck driver by himself could not possibly change a tire. So a driver had little choice but to sit with his truck and wait for help, getting crosser and crosser as the day wore on.

Mr. Jerusalem was impressed that the afternoon papers were already warning motorists that Delancey Street was a "disaster area" and that there were terrible tie-ups in other parts of the city. It was 5:30 before Mr. Jerusalem could get his cart through the tangled traffic to Maxie Hammerman's shop. In many streets, pushcarts were the only vehicles that were getting through at all.

By the time Mr. Jerusalem did get to Maxie's, Maxie had an enormous street map of New York City tacked on his wall. As the peddlers came in to report, Maxie had been sticking pea-pins in the streets where truck tires had been hit. These pea-pins had been painted a bright red, so that one could see at a glance how the battle was going.

There were a few gold pea-pins scattered among the red. Maxie explained that these were for the really big hits — such as trailer trucks or Mighty Mammoths or Ten-Ton Tigers.

"Or Leaping Lemas?" asked Mr. Jerusalem.

"If you got a Lema, I'll give you gold," said Maxie.

The map was already peppered with red and gold pea-pins. Mr. Jerusalem studied the map with pleasure. The battle looked very neat and well-organized on Maxie's map.

"On the streets," said Mr. Jerusalem, "it does not look so neat."

"That I know," said Maxie Hammerman as he stuck five pea-pins into the map for Mr. Jerusalem — four red and one gold. Although Maxie had not left his shop all day, he had the clearest picture of the battle because all the peddlers had been coming in to report to him.

"If there is, by chance, a street where the trucks have been getting through," said Maxie, "I can see it on the map. So whenever someone comes back to the shop for ammunition, I can advise him where it is most needed.

"So far, Harry the Hot Dog has the record," Maxie told Mr. Jerusalem. "He has killed twenty-three tires, and he has come in for ammunition twice."

"How wonderful to be young," said Mr. Jerusalem. "We should give him a medal."

"We will," said Maxie Hammerman. "The only thing that is worrying me," he added, "is General Anna."

"She has not been caught?" said Mr. Jerusalem.

"No, she has not been caught," Maxie said. "Though I do not know why. She cannot aim at all."

"It is hard for a lady," said Mr. Jerusalem.

"She comes to me in tears at twelve o'clock noon," Maxie said, "to tell me she has shot twenty-five pea-pins and has not hit one tire."

"Hitting is not important," said Mr. Jerusalem. "It is the spirit."

"I tried to tell her," said Maxie Hammerman. "But General Anna says, 'They call me General Anna. Should they call me General Anna *for nothing* ?' "

"It does not matter," said Mr. Jerusalem.

"Oho," said Maxie. "To General Anna, it matters. So, do you know what she is doing now?"

"What?" said Mr. Jerusalem.

"She is sticking in the pea-pins by hand," Maxie said.

"By *hand*!" said Mr. Jerusalem. "But anyone could see her do it."

"I told her," said Maxie Hammerman. "I told her — 'In broad daylight you are creeping up to a truck that is parked to deliver pajama trimmings on Hester Street! Are you crazy?'

"I tell her," Maxie explained, "that this is much too dangerous. Do you know what she says?"

"What?" said Mr. Jerusalem.

"She says, 'Don't worry. Who would suspect an old lady of putting a pea-pin in a tire? If anyone asks me why I am bending over in the street, I tell them that I am looking for a hat pin that I have dropped under the truck.' "

Mr. Jerusalem groaned. "We shouldn't let her do it."

"She has even had a policeman helping her look for a hat pin," said Maxie Hammerman.

"We must stop her," said Mr. Jerusalem.

"But she has killed fourteen tires," said Maxie Hammerman. "Since twelve o'clock noon."

"By *hand*?" said Mr. Jerusalem.

CHAPTER XIV

Some Theories As to the Cause of the Flat Tires: The Rotten-Rubber Theory,
The Scattered-Pea-Tack Theory,
and The Enemy-from-Outer-Space Theory

As the pushcart peddlers had hoped, the truck drivers had no idea what had hit them. There were clearly too many casualties in those first days of the Pea Shooter Campaign to be laid to bad luck. But the truckers did not know who to blame.

Big Moe, at first, blamed the tire company he traded with. He accused the firm of putting rotten rubber in their tires.

Big Moe's suggestion so offended the president of the tire company that he refused to sell Big Moe any more tires. This turned out to be very inconvenient. Big Moe was suddenly very much in need of extra tires, and other tire companies were so busy filling orders for their regular customers that they could not spare any tires for Big Moe.

It was curious, but for three days no one who changed a truck tire found the pea-pin that had done the damage. Either the pea-pins had worked themselves down between the deep grooves of the tires, or the pea had been broken off by the weight of the tire. It sometimes took five to ten minutes for the air to escape from a punctured tire. So drivers whose trucks were hit while moving often did not discover the damage until they stopped for a light half a mile from where they'd been hit.

Even those few mechanics who found pins in tires did not think them any odder at first than the nails or screws or bits of glass that they were always removing from tires. Finally, one sharp-eyed mechanic found a whole undamaged pea-pin, and when he extracted two more the same day, he began to be suspicious.

Once the mechanics knew what to look for, they pulled quite a few pea-pins from the truck tires. No one knew what the pea-pins were, of course, because no one had ever seen one before. The newspapers printed an enlarged drawing of one. They called it a "pea-tack."

It was supposed at first that a lot of pea-tacks had somehow been scattered through the city streets, possibly by a trucker hauling a load of pea-tacks. The police checked the "P" pages of the classified section of the telephone directory, but they could find no one in the pea-tack business.

Had the police looked under "Peas, Dried," they would have found Posey's Pea Co. ("By the Ounce, By the Pound, By the Ton"). And Mr. Posey might have told them that a lady named Wenda Gambling had ordered one ton of peas ten days before, and the police might have looked into that.

As it was, the police did not think of questioning Mr. Posey, and Mr. Posey did not think of telling the police about Wenda Gambling's order, because he did not make any connection between his peas and the pea-tacks the newspapers were talking about, as the peas he sold had no tacks in them.

On orders from Mayor Emmett P. Cudd ("Big Trucks Mean Progress"), the Police Commissioner sent out several patrols to sweep the streets, hoping to clean up the pea-tacks. The patrols found a few pea-pins that had missed their mark, but not enough to make it worth their while.

At the height of the mystery, a truck driver named Mack — the same Mack who had run down Morris the Florist — developed a theory that the pea-tacks were coming from Outer Space. An invisible enemy, Mack suggested, was circling the earth and spitefully bombarding it with pea-tacks. The fact that no one had ever seen a pea-tack before and that there were no pea-tacks listed in the New York telephone book gave some weight to the Outer Space Theory.

Mack's theory resulted in a number of truckers driving about the city with their heads out the window of their cabs. There was a rash of head-on collisions of trucks whose drivers were scanning the sky for pea-tacks.

The Outer Space Theory was the most frightening theory so far proposed, as it suggested the additional possibility that the pea-tacks might be radioactive. Tests, of course, were run on the pea-tacks that the mechanics had collected. None of these showed any radioactivity, and this calmed the general public, but the truck drivers remained uneasy.

Mack pointed out that the tests had been run on only a few pea-tacks, and that there was no proof at all that other pea-tacks might not be contaminated. Or, as a friend of Mack's suggested, that the radioactivity had not passed from the pea-tacks into the tires.

At this point, the morale of the truck drivers was very low, and many talked of quitting and going into some other line of work. The truck companies did everything they could to reassure their drivers. Several of the companies hired pea-tack spotters to ride on the hoods of the trucks.

The spotters were supposed to scan the skies and signal the drivers if they saw any pea-tacks in the air. Although the spotters signaled the drivers at frequent intervals, the signals all proved to be false alarms over a stray butterfly, or a scrap of paper that someone had dropped from an office window. No one ever produced a pea-tack that had come from Outer Space.

Finally it occurred to a newspaper reporter to ask Mack how he explained the fact that it was only *truck* tires that were getting hit. This was the first intelligent thinking that there had been on the problem, and it might have led to something had not a lady called a newspaper to say that it wasn't *true* that only truck tires were getting hit. She said that she had been painfully pricked by a pea-tack as she was crossing Second Avenue.

"Who missed?" demanded Maxie Hammerman when the newspapers reported this interesting development.

"I didn't miss," said Harry the Hot Dog. "She insulted my sauerkraut, and for once I couldn't resist."

"For once we understand," said General Anna. "But it shouldn't happen twice."

General Anna had to be firm with Harry the Hot Dog, as he was such a good shot that his friends were now calling him Harry the Hot Shot, which he did not mind at all. In fact, he was so pleased with himself that he would not have hesitated to shoot at Mayor Emmett P. Cudd himself, if anyone had dared him to.

"I am warning you, Harry the Hot Dog," said General Anna. "We are not shooting innocent people. That will only make trouble."

What most infuriated the truck drivers was that no one seemed to feel sorry for them. People would call out to a stalled driver, "What's the matter, Mister? A little trouble?" But they would smile as they asked the question, and no one ever offered to help a driver change a tire.

The truth was that it seemed to amuse people to see an enormous truck made helpless by a mere flat tire. Newspaper cartoonists kept drawing humorous pictures of the handicapped trucks, and one television comedian made himself famous overnight by his imitation of a truck in trouble.

Of course, there was great inconvenience to the city with trucks stalled everywhere. But the trucks had been inconveniencing the city for a long time, and the fact that the trucks themselves were the most inconvenienced by this new development seemed to cheer people, and they did not complain too much.

When the breakdowns began, the truck drivers had simply left their trucks in the middle of the streets until they could get mechanics to help them change the flat tires. But by the fourth day of the Pea Shooter Campaign, there were so many trucks disabled that the Traffic Commissioner issued an emergency order requiring that all vehicles with flat tires must be removed from the streets within one hour of the time the flat was reported. The penalty for leaving a truck in the middle of the street was $500.

As there were not enough tow trucks in the city to get all the stalled trucks off the streets, the truckers whose tires had not been hit had to stop their regular delivery work to tow their friends to garages. And from time to time one saw tow trucks with flat tires being towed by regular trucks.

When a truck carrying perishable goods — fruit or vegetables — broke down, the driver often had to hire half a dozen pushcarts to unload the truck and deliver the goods before they spoiled. This was very good business for the pushcarts.

"With the extra work," said Eddie Moroney, "we can — if necessary — buy more pins."

By the sixth day of the Pea Shooter Campaign, the number of trucks in the streets was reduced enough so that the traffic flowed at a brisk pace for the first time in ten years. There were occasional tie-ups caused by the pushcart peddlers shooting down more trucks, but the trucks were removed in a short time.

CHAPTER XV

The Arrest of Frank the Flower

On the ninth day of the Pea Shooter Campaign, Frank the Flower was arrested. A pea-tack spotter spotted him.

A few of the trucking companies had become dissatisfied with Mack's theory about the pea-tacks coming from Outer Space. These companies had removed their pea-tack spotters from the hoods of their trucks and stationed them on the tailgates of the trucks — or on the rear bumpers — with orders to watch for an enemy on the ground.

One of these spotters, riding on the tailgate of a moving van, saw Frank the Flower aiming at one of the rear tires of the van. At first he thought Frank was just moistening the tip of a yellow pencil. But when the van slowed down for a red light a few blocks later, the spotter heard air escaping from one of the truck's rear tires, and he remembered the look of concentration on Frank the Flower's face as he had put the "pencil" to his mouth.

While the driver got out to examine his punctured tire, the spotter ran back three blocks and was just in time to catch Frank the Flower sighting at another truck. The spotter did not actually see the pea-pin leave the shooter, but when the truck Frank the Flower had been aiming at limped to the curb with a flat tire before it reached the next corner, the spotter called a policeman and demanded that he search Frank the Flower.

When the policeman found the shooter in Frank the Flower's pocket and asked what it was, Frank said that it was a yellow plastic straw made for him by a good friend.

"In case I should order a bottle of cream soda and the restaurant should be out of straws," Frank explained.

"Cream soda?" said the policeman. He looked a little doubtful.

"My favorite drink," said Frank. "Some people don't mind drinking from a bottle," he added. "But I prefer to have a straw."

"My wife is like that," said the policeman, and he was about to give the shooter back to Frank the Flower when his eye fell on the half dozen pea-pins that Frank the Flower had stuck in his hatband.

Frank the Flower was about to suggest that they were imitation-pearl corsage pins that he gave out with special orders — in case a lady wanted to pin a bunch of flowers on her dress. But the spotter had already recognized them as the pea-tacks that the truckers had been finding in their tires.

Frank the Flower had no choice but to confess to shooting down the two trucks the spotter claimed he had shot down, especially after the spotter succeeded in finding the pea-pins in the tires.

The question arose then as to how many other trucks Frank the Flower might have shot down. Frank said he would have to think.

This was a difficult question for Frank. He had shot down either seventeen or eighteen trucks. But he could not be sure which.

On the second day of the Pea Shooter Campaign, one truck that was running through a red light had got away before Frank could tell whether he had scored a flat. And this one truck had been confusing his count ever since.

Some days Frank felt it was perfectly fair to count it. Other days he had to admit that he would be giving himself the benefit of the doubt.

Quite probably it *was* eighteen, he told himself, as the policeman waited for his answer. And while eighteen was not in the class with Harry the Hot Dog, it sounded suddenly like a very high score. Although Frank felt a certain pride in the matter, he did not want to be in any more trouble with the police than necessary. In which case, it would be better to say seventeen.

Frank considered the matter all the way to the police station. At the police station, the Police Commissioner himself took charge of the questioning.

"All right," said the Police Commissioner, when the officer who had arrested Frank had explained the problem. "How many?"

Frank the Flower wondered how long he would have to stay in jail if he did confess to eighteen.

"I'm waiting," said the Police Commissioner.

"Well," said Frank cautiously, "at least seventeen."

"At *least*," said the Police Commissioner. "And at most?"

"Maybe eighteen," Frank said uncertainly.

"*Maybe?*" said the Police Commissioner. "Now see here. There have been 18,991 flat tires reported in the last week, and I intend to find out who shot down every one of them. So how many *did* you shoot down? At most?"

It was at this moment that Frank the Flower became a hero. He looked the Police Commissioner in the eye. "Okay, I admit it," he said. "I shot them all."

"*All* of them!" said the Police Commissioner.

"All eighteen," Frank said. "All eighteen thousand, that is. I count by thousands."

"Eighteen *thousand*!" gasped the Police Commissioner.

Frank smiled apologetically. "Maybe a few more or less. I lose track."

"But eighteen thousand —" said the astonished Commissioner.

"All of them," Frank said firmly. "I shot them all."

"*All* 18,991!" said the Police Commissioner.

Frank the Flower nodded. When the Police Commissioner mentioned the large number of flat tires that had been reported, Frank suddenly realized that if he confessed to shooting down only seventeen or eighteen, the police would go on looking for whoever had shot down the rest. If that happened, all his friends might be arrested, too, and that would be the end of the Pea Shooter Campaign.

Frank decided that as long as he had already been arrested, he might as well take the blame for everything. It was better, he reasoned, that the police had caught him than Harry the Hot Dog, who was a better aim. Not that eighteen was anything to be ashamed of.

"*All* 18,991?" asked the Police Commissioner as if he had not heard correctly the first time.

"I lose track of the exact number," said Frank the Flower. Maxie Hammerman's map at last count had had over 20,000 pea-pins in it, but Frank the Flower did not like to tell the Police Commissioner that his count was off by a thousand or more. He felt sure that would annoy the Police Commissioner.

"I cannot be sure down to the last tire," said Frank the Flower. "But I have been at it several days now."

The Police Commissioner could hardly believe his luck in having got a full confession so easily. The truck drivers had been giving him a great deal of trouble with their complaints, and he was tired of the whole affair.

"But what did you do it for?" asked the Police Commissioner. "Have you got something against the trucks?"

Frank the Flower shrugged. "I am a crackpot," he said.

"I *thought* so," said the Police Commissioner. Being a sensible man himself, he took the view that only a crackpot could have done what Frank the Flower had confessed to doing.

Besides, Frank the Flower did not look to the Police Commissioner like a criminal type. This was mainly because of the hat Frank wore. It was an old felt hat with the crown cut out of it and small flowers of different colors — mostly bachelor buttons and jonquils — tucked in the hatband. (Frank the Flower put fresh flowers in the hatband every morning.)

Frank the Flower's hat was not really such an odd hat for someone in the flower line to wear. In a way, it was a kind of advertisement. However, the Police Commissioner had never seen a hat like this before.

The Police Commissioner felt that it definitely was *not* the kind of hat a true criminal type would wear. But he thought it might very well be the sort of hat that a crackpot would wear.

"But *18,991* tires!" said the Police Commissioner.

"It was nothing," said Frank the Flower modestly.

The Police Commissioner sat studying Frank the Flower for several minutes. Then he called the policeman who had arrested Frank. "You will have to lock this man up," he said. "But treat him gently. He is a harmless crackpot."

The Police Commissioner patted Frank kindly on the shoulder. He was much relieved to have solved the pea-tack problem.

Within half an hour, extras, announcing the arrest of Frank the Flower, were on the newsstands. "SPOTTER SPOTS PEA-TACKER," said one headline. "PEA-TACKER CAPTURED," said another. "TACK-MAN IS CRACKPOT," said a third. Under the headlines there were pictures of Frank the Flower.

When General Anna saw the headlines, she sent out word that all peddlers should report at once to Maxie Hammerman's. In the cellar of Maxie Hammerman's shop, the peddlers listened to the Police Commissioner on the radio.

The Police Commissioner was assuring the public that there was no further cause for alarm. The mystery of the punctured truck tires had been solved, he said. It had all been the work of a harmless crackpot.

The Police Commissioner's announcement brought tears to the eyes of some of Frank's friends. They realized that he was trying to protect them by taking all the blame himself.

"For such an idea, he should be President of the U.S.A.," said Morris the Florist.

"*President!*" said Papa Peretz. "How can the President be a crackpot? Not that I do not appreciate what Frank the Flower has done," he added.

"He is a hero," said General Anna. "May he live a hundred years."

"A hundred years?" said Mr. Jerusalem. "So he can spend them all in jail maybe. For so many truck tires, Frank the Flower could stay in jail for the rest of his life."

Mr. Jerusalem, who was used to sleeping under the stars, could not think of anything worse than being shut in a jail cell. He did not think it was right that Frank the Flower should take all the blame.

"We must all take our share," he said. "We must go to the Police Commissioner and explain."

"No," said General Anna. "If we all confess, the war is finished, and it is the trucks who have won. By taking the blame, Frank the Flower is telling us that he wishes us to carry on. How can we let him down when he is in so much trouble to help us?"

"No, we cannot let him down," said Harry the Hot Dog. "I, personally, will kill ten tires for Frank the Flower this afternoon."

"Wait," said Eddie Moroney. "As long as Frank the Flower is in jail, we cannot kill any more tires."

"Why not?" said Harry the Hot Dog. "You do not agree with General Anna that we must carry on?"

"I always agree with General Anna," said Eddie Moroney. "Of course, we must win the war. I am only pointing out that if there are any more flat tires, the Police Commissioner will not believe Frank the Flower's story that he himself has killed all those trucks. The police will look again. And now that they know what to look for, how long do you think it will be before they are arresting every pushcart peddler in the city?"

"Eddie Moroney is right," said General Anna. "Everybody will turn in his shooter and ammunition before leaving Maxie Hammerman's shop tonight."

"Everyone?" said Harry the Hot Dog. Harry the Hot Dog had had more fun shooting at truck tires than he had ever had before. He was proud of holding the record for the most tires killed, and he was even a little jealous that Frank the Flower (who had killed only seventeen or eighteen tires) should be getting *all* the credit in the newspapers.

"It is not the end of the war," said General Anna. "It is only the end of the Pea Shooter Campaign. We must find a new weapon."

<h1 style="text-align:center">CHAPTER XVI</h1>

Big Moe's Attack on the Police Commissioner

It was fortunate that General Anna had called in all the pea shooters on the day of Frank the Flower's arrest. For the day after Frank's arrest, the newspaper headlines read:

Big Moe said that the Police Commissioner was a fool to believe Frank the Flower's story. Big Moe pointed out that it was impossible for Frank the Flower to have been in all the places where the trucks had been shot down — even if he was a crackpot.

Big Moe gave as proof the fact that two Mammoth Moving trucks had been shot down on the first morning of the Pea Shooter Campaign. One of these trucks was shot down at 10:05 A.M. on 179th Street, and the other at 10:07 A.M. on 2nd Street.

"How could any man travel 177 blocks in two minutes?" Big Moe asked. "Especially in New York City traffic," he added.

Big Moe claimed that there was obviously a widespread conspiracy. He demanded that the Police Commissioner appoint a special Pea-Tack Squad to search for other "pea-tackers."

As setting up a Pea-Tack Squad would be admitting that he *had* been a big dope to believe Frank the Flower, the Police Commissioner told Big Moe to go sit on a pea-tack.

Big Moe did not take the Police Commissioner's advice. Instead, he called Mayor Emmett P. Cudd.

Mayor Emmett P. Cudd was very concerned about the trouble the trucks were having. After Mayor Cudd's famous Peanut Butter Speech, Big Moe had made the Mayor a present of 1,000 shares of stock in the Mammoth Moving Company as a token of appreciation of all Mayor Cudd was doing for big business.

The Tiger and Louis Livergreen naturally had not wished to be outdone by Big Moe. So they, too, had given Mayor Cudd tokens of their appreciation in the form of 1,000 shares in Tiger Trucking and the same number of shares in LEMA.

With all these tokens, the Mayor could not help having a real interest in the trucking business. As a result, Mayor Cudd and The Three were on the friendliest of terms. They played cards together every Friday night, and the Mayor was kept well informed about trucking problems.

"Your problems are my problems," he frequently said to The Three.

Therefore, when Big Moe called the Mayor to say, "Speaking as a friend, I think you ought to have the Police Commissioner appoint a Pea-Tack Squad to get to the bottom of this conspiracy," the Mayor took it as a friendly suggestion. He passed it on to the Police Commissioner.

The Police Commissioner did not take it as a friendly suggestion, but he had no choice. He organized a Pea-Tack Squad and ordered the Squad to comb the city for pea-tacks or pea-tackers.

However, thanks to General Anna's orders, there was nothing for the Squad to find. All the ammunition was locked in Maxie Hammerman's basement, and no trucks were shot down for three days.

"Well," people said, "never underestimate the power of a crackpot!"

There was even a little disappointment among the general public that the excitement was over. The mysterious attack on the trucks had become a popular topic of conversation, and there had been a good deal of friendly betting on the daily tire casualties.

There were two theories to account for the 177 blocks that so disturbed Big Moe. One was that Frank the Flower had had a helicopter. The second, and more widely-held explanation, was that Frank *had* shot down the truck on 2nd Street, but that the flat on 179th Street was caused by an ordinary nail.

The failure of the Pea-Tack Squad to find a widespread conspiracy made Big Moe look foolish, which cheered the Police Commissioner. The headlines now read: "POLICE COMMISSIONER SAYS BIG MOE HAS BIG IMAGINATION."

"I always thought Frank the Flower was an honest man," the Police Commissioner told reporters. "I can usually spot a crackpot when I see one."

But the Police Commissioner had cheered up a little too soon. The day after he spoke his mind, new outbreaks of flat tires were reported. The reports came from three different sections of the city.

CHAPTER XVII

The Pea Shooter Campaign — Phase II

The pushcart peddlers were as surprised as the Police Commissioner by the reports of new attacks on the trucks. General Anna summoned everyone to Maxie Hammerman's to find out whether any peddlers had not turned in their pea shooters as ordered.

Everyone had. Even Harry the Hot Dog, whom General Anna questioned privately, gave General Anna his word that — much as he had hated to do it — he had turned in his shooter and every pea-pin in his possession.

The mystery was solved when the Pea-Tack Squad caught several boys between the ages of eight and ten shooting down trucks near Manhattan Bridge. The boys were using shooters very much like Frank the Flower's and the police demanded to know where they had got them and whether they knew Frank the Flower.

The children said that they had never met Frank the Flower and that they had made the shooters themselves from the description of Frank the Flower's shooter in the newspapers. One of the boys had even made himself a hat like Frank the Flower's, though the flowers stuck in the hatband were made of paper.

The Pea-Tack Squad confiscated the shooters from the children and asked them to please not make any more. But by that time other children had had the same idea, and there were soon children all over the city making shooters and shooting at truck tires. Frank-the-Flower Clubs sprang up in several neighborhoods.

The Pea-Tack Squad no sooner caught one gang of children than they received a call about another. And since there were in the city many more children between the ages of eight and ten than there were pushcart peddlers, there were at the height of the children's campaign even more flat tires than there had been before Frank the Flower's arrest.

One day Big Moe reported that 36 out of his 72 trucks were laid up. The whole thing was a scandal, he said.

"Any minute," he warned, "these hoodlums will start shooting innocent people. Then perhaps the Police Commissioner will do something."

Curiously, the children never did start shooting at people — or cars — or taxis — or bicycles. There seemed to be a clear understanding among the children that this was a war against the trucks, and that it was more fun to keep it that way.

During this phase of the Pea Shooter Campaign, all of the Five & Ten's in the city did a brisk business in tacks and pins. (The children found that both worked equally well.) Grocery stores had a great many calls for dried peas, and florists reported a surprising increase in business from customers between the ages of eight and ten. Morris the Florist began making up small bunches of day-old flowers suitable for hatbands and selling them at a special low price to anyone under the age of ten.

It was natural that the truck drivers should have been unnerved by Phase One of the Pea Shooter Campaign, when they did not know who was shooting at them. However, they were even more unnerved by Phase Two, after it had been established that it was children who were doing the shooting.

As there were children all over the city, the truck drivers did not feel safe anywhere. If there was a child anywhere in sight, a truck driver hesitated to leave his truck to make a delivery or to have a cup of coffee. Most drivers thought twice about driving down a block where they could see children at play.

Although only a small number of the children in the city were involved in the shooting, it was almost impossible to judge from appearance alone which children might have pea shooters concealed in their jackets. One driver's suspicions got so out of hand that he had his own children searched for pea shooters every night before dinner.

When the children realized that the truck drivers were afraid of them, it was hard for them to resist teasing the drivers. Even those children so strictly brought up that they would not have thought of shooting at a truck tire, much less joining a Frank-the-Flower Club, got a good deal of satisfaction out of just hanging around parked trucks. Two or three children had only to stand on the sidewalk near a truck to give a truck driver the jitters.

"Don't trust *any* of them," Big Moe instructed his drivers. "If a kid gets within a hundred feet of your truck, clobber him." Clobbering, unfortunately, made enemies of even friendly, reliable children.

Matters went from bad to worse. Truckers, driving through blocks where children were playing, panicked and stepped on the gas and as a result were often arrested for speeding. When policemen halted a truck to write out a speeding ticket, the truck was what Frank-the-Flower fans called a "Sitting Truck," an easy shot. The truck drivers couldn't win.

The Frank-the-Flower Clubs had a whole language of their own. The expression, "Don't be a truck" replaced, among Frank-the-Flower fans, such earlier slang as "Don't be a dope, a jerk, a square." Although "Don't be a truck" is an expression that we all use today, it dates back to Phase Two of the Pea Shooter Campaign.

"You're a crackpot," as an expression of affection also originated with the Frank-the-Flower fans, who used the phrase to mean "You're a good guy, a prince, a buddy, a doll, a sweetheart." The use of this expression undoubtedly inspired the popular polka tune of the period, "Be My Little Crackpot."

The motto of the Frank-the-Flower Clubs was: "A Frank-the-Flower man is Respectful to Police Commissioners, Automobiles, Taxis, and Older People, and Death on Trucks. A Frank-the-Flower man is Loyal, Clean, and a Good Shot."

Members of the clubs greeted each other in a kind of code. "Hi ya, Bachelor" was a popular greeting. To which the proper reply was: "Hi ya, Button." Or, "Hi ya, Rose." To which: "Hi ya, Bud," was the answer.

Each club had its own variations:

"Hi ya, Sweet." "Hi ya, Pea."

"Hi ya, Chris." "Hi ya, Anthemum."

"Hi ya, Hi ya." "Hi ya, Cinth."

"Hi ya, Daff." "Did you say *Daff*?" "I said, Hi ya, Daff." "Oh! Hi ya, Dill."

The American Ambassador to Russia acquired a reputation for a quick wit when a sharp-tongued Russian diplomat addressed him at a party by his first name. To the diplomat's greeting, "Hi ya, John," the Ambassador responded without batting an eyelash, "Hi ya, Quill" — a nickname that stuck to the Russian for years.

The Ambassador's retort led to the President of the United States being asked at his next press conference whether his Ambassador was a member of a Frank-the-Flower Club. In defense of the Ambassador, the President simply grinned and replied, "Don't be a truck."

This response, although it lost the President the support of the trucking industry, greatly increased his popularity with both automobile drivers and pedestrians. While English teachers did not approve of the President speaking in such a slangy way, the majority of voters were impressed with the President's detailed knowledge of what was going on in every city of the country.

The general public had mixed feelings about the children's part in the Pushcart War. A few agreed with Big Moe that shooting at trucks was hoodlum behavior and should be severely punished. But the majority of people took the attitude that children had always had pea shooters, and that the pea-tack shooters were only a passing craze.

A respected child psychologist of the period said that in attacking the trucks, the children were expressing resentment of parents who pushed them around. "It is a classic case of the little guy against the big guy," said the psychologist. The psychologist's advice was that it was better on the whole for the children to be killing trucks than their parents. To forbid them to shoot at trucks, he suggested, might create worse problems. This made parents think twice about taking a firm stand about the trucks.

The pushcart peddlers did not know what to make of the children's campaign. It bothered Harry the Hot Dog that any eight-year-old could get away with flattening a truck while he had to stand idly by. He was much put out by a rumor that a nine-year-old boy in the East Harlem section of the city had killed almost as many trucks in one week as Harry had killed in the opening week of the Pea Shooter Campaign.

"Whose war is this, anyway?" Harry demanded.

"They are making a joke of it," he complained at a meeting that General Anna had called to discuss the situation.

"This war is a serious business," Harry said. "To pushcart peddlers, a matter of life and death. And these kids are making it like a big picnic. A big joke. They are laughing at us."

"Some joke!" said Morris the Florist. "Killing thousands of trucks. Let them joke, I say."

"Why is it a joke?" asked Papa Peretz. "Maybe they *seriously* don't like the trucks. A big truck hits a little kid. Is that a joke? I tell you, kids today are very smart."

"All those clubs!" Harry said. "They are making Frank the Flower look silly. They are even making fun of his hat."

Maxie Hammerman laughed. "For twenty years I have made fun of Frank the Flower's hat, and he does not care. He is proud of that hat."

"Also," said Morris the Florist, "the club members are writing letters to Frank the Flower in jail, and it is nice to get letters when you are confined."

CHAPTER XVIII

The Retreat of the Trucks & Rumors of a Build-Up on the Fashion Front

Although the children's Pea Shooter Campaign may have been, as many people said, a craze that would have died as suddenly as it had started, the truck drivers could not afford to wait and see. At the height of the children's campaign, the casualties were so heavy that the truck companies had to take their trucks off the streets.

The retreat of the trucks made it very pleasant for the people who wanted to drive around the city doing errands or a little sightseeing. It was delightful to see taxis zipping around corners again, making U-turns, and snaking in and out among the women drivers as gaily as they had in the days before the trucks had taken over the streets. Even the women drivers seemed to enjoy it. After years of battling with the trucks, dodging the taxis seemed like a game.

One sporting lady even blew a kiss to a taxi driver who clipped off her fender, and called out to him, "Well done!" (This so charmed the taxi driver, that he towed the lady to a garage, bought her a new fender, took her out to dinner, and married her.)

Indeed, everyone was in the best of spirits that first day that the trucks did not appear on the streets. It was like a holiday. The buses were loaded with ladies out shopping for new hats and perfume. Fathers took the afternoon off from their offices to take their children to the zoo. Teachers gave no homework. There were picnics in the parks, and the movie houses and bowling alleys were crowded.

All the pushcarts were back on the streets, and the pushcart peddlers did more business on that day than they had for nineteen years. The whole city was jubilant.

Except for the truck drivers, of course. The Three were quick to see that it would be dangerous to keep the trucks off the streets for more than a few days. Once people became accustomed to having the freedom of the streets again, they would object to the return of the trucks. The Three agreed that it was imperative to get the trucks back on the streets as fast as possible.

Big Moe called the Mayor and demanded that something be done to make the streets safe for trucks. "This is very bad for business," said Big Moe. "Another week of this, and I will be out of business."

Mayor Cudd was naturally sympathetic. He summoned the City Council, and the Council proposed to put a tax on tacks sold to anyone under the age of twenty-one. It was thought that if this tax were high enough (the Council set the rate at a dollar per pound of tacks), this would discourage children from buying tacks in any quantity.

This proposal, however, was not enough to satisfy the truck drivers. What guarantee was there, they demanded, when the newspapers published the proposals, that persons *over* twenty-one might not take it into their heads to shoot at truck tires? Frank the Flower, Big Moe pointed out to Mayor Cudd, was over twenty-one.

"But he is a crackpot," said the Mayor.

"Maybe," said Big Moe. "But listen to this. My wife tells me that a very fancy store on Fifth Avenue uptown put in its window two days ago a Frank-the-Flower hat for ladies, and the price of that hat is $29.95."

"Twenty-nine, ninety-five for a crackpot hat!" said Mayor Cudd.

"That is not the point," said Big Moe. "The point is that the store *already* cannot keep up with the orders for that $29.95 hat."

"What do you mean *already*?" asked Mayor Cudd.

"I mean already before today's paper in which I see a full-page advertisement for this hat," said Big Moe.

"Look in the paper," said Big Moe. "There is a big drawing of the hat, and it says underneath: *A Real Traffic Stopper!* It also says: *Do truck drivers whistle at you? This will really flatten them!*

"Also," said Big Moe, "I should warn you that a fashion magazine which my wife reads has on its cover this week the movie star, Wenda Gambling, in this same $29.95 Frank-the-Flower hat. And I would like to know what you will say when your wife asks you if she can have a $29.95 hat such as Wenda Gambling is wearing?"

"My wife does not ask my advice about hats," said Mayor Cudd.

"Naturally," said Big Moe. "That is the danger. Children are bad enough. But if the ladies get into this, we are finished."

The Mayor saw the danger. He called the City Council together again, and the Council amended the new tax ruling to cover the sales of tacks to persons of *all* ages.

CHAPTER XIX

The Tacks Tax & the British Ultimatum

The Tacks Tax, as all students of American history know, was the most unpopular tax in the history of New York City. It caused revolution in the city schools and almost brought England into the war.

The citizens of New York protested at once that the tax was undemocratic. They said it discriminated unfairly against the users of tacks as opposed to the users of screws, nails, bolts, and pins.

Users of screws, nails, bolts, and pins (and that took in nearly every household in the city) objected as strongly to the Tacks Tax as the tacks users. Their argument was that if the Mayor and the City Council could put a whopping tax on tacks, there was nothing to keep them from putting a whopping tax on screws, nails, bolts, and pins any time they chose.

The pushcart peddlers had no special interest in tacks, as they relied exclusively on pins for the manufacture of their ammunition. However, they supported the protest against the tax as a matter of principle.

Mr. Jerusalem risked arrest by giving away boxes of tacks to his customers, rather than charge the hated tax. He was picked up by the Pea-Tack Squad, but the Police Commissioner refused to jail him on the grounds that the Council ruling put a tax only on tacks that were *sold*. The Police Commissioner said that if Mr. Jerusalem wanted to go broke giving away tacks, that was his own business.

Teachers were among the hardest hit by the Tacks Tax, and they went on strike in protest. You could not have a bulletin board without tacks, they claimed. And you could not run a New York City classroom without a bulletin board, they said, or things got hopelessly out of hand.

Twelve thousand teachers carrying NO TACKS — NO TEACHERS signs picketed Mayor Cudd's office. And while they were picketing, the city schools had to be closed.

With the schools closed, children of school age were on the streets from morning to night, and the shooting of trucks increased accordingly. (As many of the children had been making their pea-tacks with pins all along — they couldn't see that it made any difference — the Tacks Tax did not bother them seriously.)

The strongest objection to the tax naturally came from England, who was at the time the world's largest producer of tacks. Most of the tacks used in New York City came from England.

England charged that the New York City Tacks Tax was designed to cut England out of the American tack market and was, in fact, a violation of Section 238 of the British-American International Tack Agreement. The British Ambassador protested in the strongest of terms to the President in Washington and suggested that his country might have to intervene directly in the fighting in New York if the Tacks Tax was not at once repealed.

The President acted promptly. He called Mayor Cudd to the White House and warned him that unless the tax law was repealed within twenty-four hours, he would have to send Federal troops to keep order in the city.

Mayor Cudd had to ask the City Council to repeal the tax he had asked them to pass the week before. The lifting of the tax was celebrated by the wildest spree of tack buying in the history of the city. (Over 800,000 pounds of tacks were sold on the first day of the repeal.) The Mayor, in alarm, hastily improvised the Pea Blockade in hopes of averting a mass outbreak of pea-shooting.

CHAPTER XX

The Pea Blockade

On the morning of May 11th, the Mayor issued an emergency order prohibiting the sale of dried peas in New York City until peace in the streets had been restored.

"No peace — no peas," said the Mayor in an address to the city, explaining the reasons for his action.

The City Council, the Mayor told the people, had contracted with Big Moe for nineteen Mighty Mammoths to blockade all bridges and tunnels leading into New York. Mammoth drivers had been instructed to search all incoming trucks for shipments of peas.

"And furthermore," announced the Mayor, "I have ordered the Pea-Tack Squad to close all pea-packaging plants in the city until further notice."

It was the Pea Blockade and the closing of all the pea-packaging plants that led to the discovery of the Pushcart Conspiracy, although the discovery was the purest sort of accident.

All of the pea-packagers in the city objected to the shutdown order. But the Pea-Tack Squad on the whole handled matters tactfully.

The Squad pointed out to the pea-packagers that: in the first place, the pea-packagers could not get any peas to package while the Pea Blockade was in effect, and that, in the second place, they could not get any trucks to deliver their packaged peas until there was order in the streets again. Since this was true, most of the packagers — some of them grumbling a little and some of them grumbling a lot — did as they were ordered. They dismissed their workers and locked up their plants.

On the whole, the Pea Blockade went smoothly until the Pea-Tack Squad arrived at Posey's plant. Mr. P. Posey, of Posey's Peas ("By the Ounce, By the Pound, By the Ton") did not give up so easily.

Although Mr. Posey had advertised his peas "By the Ounce, By the Pound, By the Ton" for thirty-one years, he had never had an order for a ton of peas until the spring of the Pushcart War. Most of his business was by the pound. Mr. Posey's biggest order in pre-war days had been a three-hundred-pound order from a church that was having a baked-pea barbecue.

Ever since the one-ton order, Mr. Posey had had big ideas. He was full of plans for expanding his business, and naturally he did not want to close down his plant just as his advertising was beginning to pay.

With the profits from his one-ton order, Mr. Posey had laid in a large supply of peas, enough to last through a long blockade. Moreover, he did not use trucks to deliver his packaged peas.

Mr. Posey was an old-fashioned pea merchant, and he had his peas delivered by pushcart. He had found that the pushcarts could get through the crowded streets more easily, and often faster, than the trucks. Also, their charges for delivery were less. The one-ton order had been delivered in twenty one-hundred-pound sacks by four pushcarts.

So, with a good supply of peas in his plant and no need for trucks to deliver them, Mr. Posey saw no reason at all for closing up his plant. Most of his business was with small restaurants that featured pea soup, and he could not see that pea soup had anything to do with the war in the streets.

"This is a peaceful pea plant," Mr. Posey said to Mrs. Posey, who helped him in the business. "And nobody is going to shut us down without a fight."

CHAPTER XXI

The Barricade at Posey's Plant

When the Pea-Tack Squad arrived at Posey's plant on the second morning of the Pea Blockade, they found the doors barricaded with one-hundred-pound sacks of dried peas.

"Open up," ordered the Chief of the Pea-Tack Squad, when six Squad men could not budge the door.

"Mayor's orders," he explained, when he saw Mr. Posey glaring down at him from a second-story window of the plant.

"I'm closed today," Mr. Posey called down, "for business reasons. Tell the Mayor."

"Well, open up because I have to close you up," said the Chief.

"I'm very busy right now," said Mr. Posey.

The Pea-Tack Squad finally had to call the Fire Department. Fire engines came roaring down the street, bringing with them a large crowd.

Two firemen took an axe to Posey's door. When Mr. Posey saw the firemen chopping through his door, he and his wife began bombarding the firemen and the Pea-Tack Squad from the second floor with ten-pound sacks of dried peas.

One fireman and two Squad men were knocked unconscious and another Squad man slipped on the dried peas that were rolling all over the sidewalk and broke his wrist.

When the firemen finally broke through the door and began hacking their way through the one-hundred-pound sacks of peas Mr. Posey had stacked against it, a torrent of peas poured into the street. Hundreds of children had gathered by now, and began excitedly stuffing their pockets with peas.

By the time the Squad men had fought their way through the barricade they were pretty mad. They seized Mr. Posey and his wife and tied them up — they had to, as the Poseys kept throwing sacks of peas at them. The Chief of the Pea-Tack Squad then demanded to know why Mr. Posey had barricaded his door.

Mr. Posey, who was close to tears by now, told the truth. He said that he had closed up his place of business because he did not want the Pea-Tack Squad closing it up.

Naturally, this was too simple an explanation to satisfy the Chief of the Pea-Tack Squad. "You manufacturing something illegal in here maybe?" he asked Mr. Posey. "Counterfeit money? Dynamite?"

"*Dynamite!*" said Mr. Posey scornfully. "If I had dynamite, would I be wasting perfectly good sacks of peas, throwing them from a second-story window?

"This is a one-hundred-percent-legal pea-packaging plant," said Mr. Posey, "and all I have in this place is peas and five, ten, twenty-five, and one-hundred-pound sacks for packaging them. If you untie me, I will show you what kind of business I run."

"We'll see for ourselves," said the Chief of the Pea-Tack Squad, and he ordered two of his men to search Mr. Posey's plant.

The Squad men searched the plant from top to bottom, and they did not find anything but peas in five, ten, twenty-five, and one-hundred-pound sacks. One of the men suggested to the Chief that the sacks of peas might be a hiding place for something else, such as smuggled diamonds.

"Diamonds!" said Mrs. Posey. "You think we are throwing diamonds out a second-story window? It's bad enough we should waste so many peas."

The Chief, however, took out a jackknife and ripped open a dozen one-hundred-pound sacks of peas. Dried peas cascaded all over the room, and the Pea-Tack Squad found itself up to its ankles in peas.

The Chief ordered the Squad to sift through the peas to make sure that there were no packets of diamonds or pearls or gold nuggets or maybe uranium concealed among the peas. The Squad man who had suggested the diamonds wished he had kept still.

When his men found nothing, the Chief only grew more suspicious. He asked to have Mr. Posey's business records brought to him.

It was only after the Chief had leafed carefully through Mr. Posey's books, which dated back thirty-one years, that the Chief began to feel a little ashamed. The books showed clearly that the only product Mr. Posey had sold during his long business career was dried peas.

Most of the orders, the Chief saw, were for ten and twenty-five-pound sacks. He realized then that Mr. Posey had to work very hard at his small business to make a living and that he had made a wreck of Mr. Posey's place of business for nothing.

The Chief was about to close the order books and to apologize to Mr. Posey for causing him so much trouble, when his eye fell on Wenda Gambling's order for one ton of peas. The Chief only noticed the entry because it was for such a large number of peas, as compared with Mr. Posey's usual orders.

"Not Wenda Gambling, *the movie star?*" said the Chief.

"Why not?" said Mrs. Posey. "Posey's Peas are a quality product."

"But what does a movie star want with a ton of peas?" asked the Chief.

"How do I know?" said Mr. Posey. "Should I ask a customer's private business? Maybe she is planting a pea farm for a hobby. Or maybe she is starting a pea soup plant."

"Or a pea shooter plant?" laughed the Chief.

"Why not?" said Mr. Posey.

"Why not," agreed the Chief. "Well, Mr. Posey, I think we have bothered you long enough." He untied Mr. Posey and his wife, and explained to Mr. Posey that even if he was running a one-hundred-percent-legal pea-packaging business, he would have to close his plant until the Pea Blockade was over.

"What difference does it make now?" said Mr. Posey. "I cannot clean up the mess you have made of my plant in less than a month."

"*Why not?*" shouted the Chief suddenly. "Why not? Why not?"

"Because it is a mess, that's why," yelled Mr. Posey.

"No, no, no, no," said the Chief. "Never mind the mess. I mean *why not* a pea shooter plant. For Wenda Gambling."

"What does Wenda Gambling want with a pea shooter plant?" asked Mr. Posey.

"Why not?" the Chief said again. "I mean, who knows. Do you have the bill for Miss Wenda Gambling's one ton of peas?"

"I have a carbon copy," said Mr. Posey.

"Let me see it," ordered the Chief.

The bill was made out to Miss Wenda Gambling at the Plaza Hotel. However, the Chief noticed that the one ton of peas had not been delivered to Wenda Gambling's apartment at the Plaza Hotel, but to Maxie Hammerman's shop.

The Chief pointed to Maxie's address. "Aha!" he said.

"Aha, what?" said Mr. Posey. He saw nothing odd about the order. He delivered peas to whatever address his customers requested.

"Maxie Hammerman, that's what," said the Chief.

"So?" said Mr. Posey. "Maybe they were a birthday present. Who is Maxie Hammerman?"

It happened that the Chief of the Pea-Tack Squad was one of the few people in New York City, outside of the pushcart peddlers and Maxie's personal friends, who knew who Maxie was.

"Maxie Hammerman," said the Chief thoughtfully, "is the Pushcart King."

CHAPTER XXII

The Raid on Maxie Hammerman's

Maxie Hammerman had no warning that the Pea-Tack Squad was going to raid his shop. The Squad, of course, found the shooters and all the ammunition that Maxie had stored in his cellar.

The Squad confiscated some five hundred pea shooters and half a ton of pea-tacks, and they arrested Maxie Hammerman. They could not arrest anyone else as they had no proof of anyone else being connected with the pea-tacks — except for Wenda Gambling, and she was in Africa for a week's vacation.

At the word of Maxie's arrest, alarm spread among the pushcart peddlers. Fifty or sixty of them met after dark in a vacant lot under Manhattan Bridge to discuss the situation. They all expected to be arrested momentarily.

"What is there to discuss?" asked Papa Peretz. "It was a good war while it lasted. But now it is only a matter of time."

General Anna, however, refused to panic.

"What kind of talk am I hearing?" she demanded. "There is a little capture of some pea shooters, and suddenly everybody is surrendering. This is an *army*? I should be general of such an army?"

"It is just that things do not look so good," said Morris the Florist.

"*Good!*" said General Anna scornfully. "Did you think a war was going to be like a picnic in the country? A nice time for everybody?"

"For weeks," General Anna pointed out, "we have been pushing back the trucks. Victory after victory. So now we have one little setback."

"*Little,*" said Mr. Jerusalem. "A five-hundred-pea-shooter raid is little?"

"Let them have the pea shooters," said General Anna. "At the moment we are not using them."

"But they have Maxie, too," Morris the Florist reminded General Anna.

"They also have Frank the Flower," said General Anna. "And Frank the Flower just sitting in jail is giving the trucks a great deal of trouble. A good man is a good man wherever he is sitting. And you can be sure that Maxie Hammerman is not sitting at Police Headquarters waiting to hear that we have surrendered."

"But what can we do?" asked Papa Peretz.

"In the first place, don't surrender," said General Anna. "In the second place, I will think of something."

General Anna paced up and down under the bridge for five or ten minutes, thinking to herself.

While General Anna was thinking, the confidence of the other peddlers began to return. Eddie Moroney and Carlos gathered up some scrap lumber and built a bonfire. Harry the Hot Dog pushed his cart alongside the fire and broke open several packages of hots to be toasted over the fire. Carlos began to sing a song in Spanish that he said his son had made up. It was called "The Boy Who Killed a Thousand Trucks." There were thirty-six verses, all in Spanish, and everyone joined in on the chorus which went: *"Bravo, bravo, bravo!"*

"Bravo!" said General Anna, as she joined the others around the campfire.

"Have you thought of something?" asked Papa Peretz.

"I am going to communicate with Maxie Hammerman," said General Anna.

"How?" asked Mr. Jerusalem.

"I will send him a message in an apple," said General Anna. "Lend me your knife, Eddie Moroney."

General Anna selected a large apple from her cart and with Eddie's knife, she carefully cut the core out of the apple. Then she wrote a short message on a piece of paper and stuffed the paper in the apple. She cut a half-inch off the core and pushed the core back into place.

"Like a cork in a bottle," said Papa Peretz. "But how will we get the apple to Maxie?"

"I will give it to the Police Commissioner to deliver," said General Anna. "Is there a law an old lady shouldn't send an apple to a friend who has the misfortune to be in jail?"

"What is the message to Maxie about?" asked Eddie Moroney.

"Strategy," said General Anna firmly, and she took the apple down to police headquarters herself.

The Police Commissioner was used to people sending messages to prisoners. He told General Anna that he would deliver the apple, but before he delivered it, he inspected it very carefully.

When the Police Commissioner discovered that the core of the apple was loose, he pulled it out and read the message. However, he could not see that it would do any harm to deliver it.

"Remove the message before you eat the apple," the Police Commissioner advised when he gave the apple to Maxie.

Maxie Hammerman smiled when he found the message in the apple. The message read: "Good Luck! How is the blister on your thumb? Your friend Anna."

Maxie wrote back: "Thanks! The blister is okay. Give my regards to everybody. Your friend Maxie Hammerman."

The Police Commissioner read the reply and said that he would see that it got to Maxie's friend Anna.

"What does Maxie say?" asked Papa Peretz when General Anna received the reply.

"He sends regards," said General Anna.

"Is that all?" said Morris the Florist.

"The rest is strategy," said General Anna, which was encouraging to everyone.

Meantime, Frank the Flower had his own strategy. As soon as he heard from the guards in the jail about the raid on Maxie's shop, he sent a message to the Police Commissioner. He informed the Commissioner that all the ammunition that the Pea-Tack Squad had confiscated belonged to him, and that his friend Maxie Hammerman had been letting him keep it in his cellar as a favor.

As soon as the Police Commissioner got Frank's message, he came down to Frank's jail cell to talk to Frank personally. Frank explained that he had been a good customer of Maxie's for many years.

"I have bought three pushcarts from Maxie Hammerman," said Frank the Flower, "and he makes all my repairs."

The Police Commissioner was inclined to believe Frank the Flower. It seemed reasonable to the Police Commissioner that a man who had shot down 18,991 trucks might have five hundred pea shooters hidden away somewhere. In addition, the Police Commissioner was not anxious to find a widespread conspiracy as that would make him look like a big dope all over again, and also would be a lot of trouble.

Unfortunately, the Pea-Tack Squad had found in Maxie's shop not only the ammunition Frank the Flower said belonged to him, but Maxie's big map with the red and gold pea-pins in it. The Police Commissioner had to admit that the map and certain notes that Maxie had made in the margins of the map did look suspicious.

The notes (Maxie's list of ace shots) read, "Harry the Hot Dog — 230; Eddie Moroney — 175; Morris the Florist — 175; General Anna — 160 (By Hand)."

The Police Commissioner could not make any sense out of the notes, but he guessed that they were a code that might explain the map. After studying the map for some time, he asked that Maxie Hammerman be brought to his office for questioning.

CHAPTER XXIII

The Questioning of Maxie Hammerman

The Police Commissioner questioned Maxie Hammerman in some detail. Maxie was very cooperative and did not refuse to answer any questions. The conversation, as recorded in the files of the New York City Police Department, went as follows:

Police Commissioner: Frank the Flower says that he is a friend of yours.

Maxie Hammerman: Why not? I got friends all over. As Pushcart King, I know everybody in the pushcart line.

P.C.: Why do they call you the Pushcart King?

M.H.: It is an honorary title. My father was Pushcart King, and I took over his business. My grandfather was also Pushcart King.

P.C.: Frank the Flower says that you have been storing a few items for him in your cellar.

M.H.: Why not? I like to do a favor for a friend if I can.

P.C.: Would you say that Frank the Flower is a crackpot?

M.H.: Why should I call a friend names? He has enough troubles.

P.C.: I have here what appears to be a map of the city of New York.

M.H.: Is it against the law to have a map of the city of New York?

P.C.: No. But I would like to know why you have such a map in your shop.

M.H.: Business reasons. It is a kind of business chart. As Pushcart King, I have to keep track of how business in the pushcart line is going.

P.C.: What are all those pea-tacks doing in the map?

M.H.: They are not pea-tacks. I have never seen a pea-tack in my life. Those are pea-pins in my map.

P.C.: Never mind what you call them. They are exactly like pea-tacks we have been finding in the truck tires and exactly like the pea-tacks you have been storing in your cellar for Frank the Flower.

M.H.: No, they are not. If you will examine them carefully, you will see that they are red, or once in a great while gold. Those you have found in the truck tires were white. At least, that is what I read in the newspapers.

P.C.: Red, gold, or white, what are they doing in that map?

M.H.: You have heard of "red-letter" days? Well, in my business I like to speak of "red-pin" days. It is the same idea. When a pushcart does a good business, I put a red pea-pin in the map where the business was good. If business is terrific, I put in a gold pea-pin. In this way, I know where in the city there has been the most activity.

P.C.: It is curious that the most activity on your map is in the same locations where the trucks have had the most flat tires.

M.H.: It stands to reason. When trucks break down, the traffic stops, so people cannot get to the stores uptown or downtown. When that happens, they buy from the pushcart closest at hand. Wherever there are flat tires, a pushcart does a good business.

P.C.: What does it mean at the bottom of the map where you have written in the margin: "Harry the Hot Dog — 230"?

M.H.: I am often writing notes to myself. That could be a note to remind me that I have promised Harry the Hot Dog that his cart, which he has perhaps left for repairs, will maybe be finished at 230 — that is to say, at 2:30 P.M.

P.C.: And "Eddie Moroney — 175"? Maybe 1:75 P.M. is when Eddie Moroney's cart will be fixed?

M.H.: Certainly not. There is no such time as 1:75 P.M., as you should know. So "175" is more likely to be a note to remind me that I have told Eddie Moroney that for $1.75, I will put two new wheel spokes in his cart.

P.C.: And "General Anna — 160 (By Hand)" — what does that mean?

M.H.: "By hand" is a peculiarity of General Anna. The note could be to remind me that I must fix Anna's cart by hand. Anna does not want any electric tools used on her cart. The cart was handmade in the first place by my father forty-two years ago, and Anna insists "only hand tools," such as the cart was built with in the first place. I can use a hammer, a saw, a screwdriver — as long as it is a hand tool. This is okay by me. I like working with my hands.

The Police Commissioner reported to Mayor Cudd that he had thoroughly questioned Maxie Hammerman and that he could find no reason to keep him under arrest.

CHAPTER XXIV

The Portlette Papers: The LEMA Master Plan
& The Plot to Capture Maxie Hammerman
(From the Shorthand Notes of Miriam Portlette)

The truck drivers, when they heard that Maxie Hammerman had been released, were furious. At a meeting of The Three on May 17th, Big Moe, The Tiger and Louie Livergreen decided to take matters into their own hands. This involved a plot to kidnap Maxie Hammerman.

This plot is known because a cleaning woman, a young lady named Miriam Portlette, was cleaning an office next to the LEMA office where The Three met to plot against Maxie. Miriam would have paid no attention to the discussion she heard through the open transom of Louie Livergreen's headquarters if it had not been that she was studying shorthand at an adult-education class on her nights off.

Miriam Portlette was studying shorthand in hopes of getting a better office job than the one she had. It was Miriam's ambition to have an office job with daytime hours so that she would not miss the evening television shows.

On the night that The Three met in Louie Livergreen's office, Miriam Portlette's shorthand assignment for the week was to take shorthand notes of a meeting. This assignment was a problem for Miriam. As she worked nights, she did not get to attend many meetings.

So when Miriam realized that some men were holding a meeting in the office next to the one that she was cleaning, she sat down on her mop bucket in the hall outside Louie Livergreen's office, and took down the whole meeting in shorthand notes on the backs of some order blanks that she had found in a wastebasket. The original copy of Miriam's notes (now known as "The Portlette Papers") is in the Rare Documents collection of the New York Public Library. A translation of the notes, by Miriam's shorthand teacher, reads as follows:

Shorthand notes of a meeting
by Miriam Portlette
Adult-Education Class 2-G
Seward Park High School

Dear Mr. Czerwinski:[1] Four men[2] are meeting together. Their names are Mr. Bigmo, Mr. Walter, Mr. Tiger, and Mr. Louie. I could not take shorthand notes of the very beginning of this meeting, as I had to look for some paper to make notes on. But the men were talking at first about ladies' hats and a movie star, and I do not think this was an important part of the meeting.

I think that the important part began when Mr. Louie said, "Let's get down to business." And, by then I had found some paper and a pencil.

THE MEETING

Mr. Louie: Let's get down to business. You called the meeting, Bigmo. What is the meeting about?

---

[1]Miriam Portlette's shorthand teacher.

[2]It is clear from Miss Portlette's mention a few words later of a Mr. Walter and a Mr. Tiger that there were only three men (The Three) at the meeting. The fact that Big Moe called Walter Sweet "Tiger," while Louie Livergreen called him "Walter" gave Miriam the impression that there were four men in the office.

Mr. Bigmo: It is about Maxie Hammerman. I don't care what the Police Commissioner says. There is obviously a pushcart experiment.[3]

Mr. Walter: It is logical. The pushcarts have the best reason to be fighting the trucks of anyone in the city. The Police Commissioner does not know that. But we do.

Mr. Bigmo: So we have got to expose the experiment.[4]

Mr. Louie: Why expose? Expose, and it may be exposed that the trucks started it all by hitting the pushcarts.

Mr. Bigmo: So what do you suggest, Louie?

Mr. Louie: Do we have a Master Plan — or do we not? I do not want to waste any more time on the pushcarts.

Mr. Bigmo: Certainly, we have a Master Plan. We are all in favor of the LEMA Master Plan. But to get rid of the pushcarts is the first part of the Master Plan. Until we get rid of the pushcarts, we cannot get the trucks on the streets to carry out the second part of the Master Plan.

Mr. Louie: The pushcarts are easy. Maxie Hammerman, it is clear, is the brains behind the pushcart experiment.[5] Get rid of Maxie Hammerman, and the rest of the peddlers will give up. I know pushcart peddlers. No fight. Would a man be in a small business like the pushcart business if he had any fighting spirit?

---

[3]"Pushcart experiment" is probably a mistake in the notes. Undoubtedly, Big Moe said "pushcart conspiracy." One must remember that Miriam Portlette had never taken shorthand notes before, and also that she was seated in the hall outside Louie Livergreen's office.

[4]See note above.

[5]See note above.

Mr. Tiger: Some people like a small business. They say you know the customers.

Mr. Louie: Customers! Who wants to know the customers? It is because they do not have the guts for a big business. And I guarantee — the push-cart peddlers would not be fighting without a very strong leader.

Mr. Bigmo: So we must get rid of Maxie Hammerman. As Louie says. But how?

Mr. Louie: We will kidnap him. Then we have a choice.

Mr. Bigmo: A choice?

Mr. Louie: A choice of how to get rid of him. We can torture him until he feels like giving the Police Commissioner a full confession that is guaranteed to get every pushcart peddler in the city locked up. Or, if he does not want to confess, he could just disappear, and we will knock off the rest of the pushcarts one by one.

Mr. Tiger: Do we have to kill off *all* the pushcarts? It is, after all, the cars and the taxis and the buses that are in our way. As you said, Louie, why waste time on the pushcarts?

Mr. Louie: We have to make an example of the pushcarts.

Mr. Tiger: An example?

Mr. Louie: Example, for example, for the cars and taxis. Example, for example, of what happens if a vehicle does not get out of the way of a truck. When we start on the cars, it is going to be tougher. The trucks are bigger, but there are four million cars in the city. And it will be very useful when we start on the cars, if all over the city people are whispering, "Remember what happened to the pushcarts?"

Mr. Bigmo: You understand, Tiger?

Mr. Louie: If we are going after four million cars, it is necessary that the cars should be scared when we start to hit them. They are a little bit afraid now. But not so afraid that they would give up without fighting.

Mr. Walter: To tell the truth, I am not so crazy about going after the cars.

Mr. Bigmo: But that is the idea of the Master Plan.

Mr. Louie: You have got to think ahead, Walter. There is not enough room for everybody in the streets. Why should people drive around the city for pleasure when they could take a bus? Get rid of the cars, and I can put two hundred Leaping Lemas on the streets. Get rid of the cars, and Big Moe can operate fifty more Mighty Mammoths and I don't know how many more Mama Mammoths and Baby Mammoths. And Tiger Trucking can put on the streets double the number of Ten-Ton Tigers you are now operating.

Mr. Tiger: Frankly, I got enough trucks now. It is just that traffic is so bad.

Mr. Bigmo: But that is the point, Tiger. Traffic is so bad that everybody will be wanting to get rid of the trucks if we do not get rid of them first.

Mr. Louie: You see, Walter, the Master Plan is in self-defense. We got no choice.

Mr. Walter: I suppose you are right, Louie. So the plan is we finish the pushcarts. Then the cars.

Mr. Bigmo: Then the taxis.

Mr. Louie: Then the small trucks.

Mr. Tiger: Trucks! But we are fighting to make the streets safe for the trucks.

Mr. Louie: For *big* trucks. Small trucks are as much a nuisance as cars and taxis. They are not efficient. One Leaping Lema can take the place of five small trucks. A small truck is as bad as a pushcart.

Mr. Bigmo: Louie is right, Walter. Don't cry over small trucks.

Mr. Walter: But we have not told the truck drivers that small trucks are a part of the Master Plan. Half the trucks in the city are small trucks. A lot of truckers will not go along with the fight if it is going to be their funeral in the end.

Mr. Bigmo: So who's telling them? Listen, Walter the Tiger, the three of us have been friends for a long time. But if you do not stop talking like a small businessman, I am going to say that two heads are better than three.

Mr. Louie: We all agreed to the Master Plan a long time ago. Before the secret meeting in Moe Mammoth's garage.

Mr. Tiger: But when you told us the plan, Louie, you did not mention the small trucks.

Mr. Louie: It occurred to me later. Anyway we do not get to the small trucks until we take care of the cars and taxis. And we cannot take care of them until we take care of Maxie Hammerman.

Mr. Walter: Who is going to kidnap Maxie?

Mr. Bigmo: We could each send half-a-dozen drivers.

Mr. Louie: No. The fewer people who know what has happened to Maxie Hammerman, the better. We will go ourselves.

Mr. Tiger: Just the three of us?

Mr. Bigmo: Three is not enough to take one man who is not expecting to be kidnapped?

Mr. Walter: When will we do it?

Mr. Louie: I am free next Friday night.

Mr. Bigmo: But that is the night we play cards with the Mayor.

Mr. Louie: Tell the Mayor we will have a late game.

Mr. Bigmo: All right. Now how shall we handle Maxie?

Mr. Louie: You want a Leaping Lema for the job?

Mr. Bigmo: No, Louie. We do not need a truck for a little trip like this. We will take my bulletproof Italian car.

The notes are signed:

> *Yours truly,*
> *Miriam Portlette*

P.S. (an explanation to her teacher): I did not stay to the end of the meeting as I had three more offices to mop, but I think it was almost over. *M. Portlette*

As far as Miriam Portlette was concerned, the meeting in Louie Livergreen's office was just a meeting. She did not know anything about the trucking business or the pushcart business. Nor had she heard that there was a war going on, because she did not read the newspapers and always missed the evening news on television, as she worked late.

Miriam simply copied down what The Three said at the meeting and turned in her notes to the teacher of her adult-education class. She had no idea that she had been present at a historic occasion.

The teacher of Miriam's adult-education class, however, did read the newspapers. And he listened to every news program on television.

In addition, Miriam's teacher lived next door to Eddie Moroney and went bowling with Eddie every Tuesday night. As a result, he was well informed about all the trouble that the pushcarts had been having with the trucks.

So when Miriam handed in her shorthand notes to be corrected, her teacher realized at once that they were important. He apparently copied them off — or at least those parts he could read — and he gave this copy of the notes to Eddie Moroney. Eddie, in turn, passed on the notes to Maxie Hammerman, and the notes undoubtedly saved Maxie's life.

CHAPTER XXV

The Three-Against-One Gamble
& The Capture of the Bulletproof Italian Car

Maxie Hammerman's handling of the plot to kidnap him was one of the more brilliant strategies of the Pushcart War. Eddie Moroney could not see the sense of it at first.

When Eddie gave Maxie Miriam Portlette's shorthand notes of the meeting of The Three, Eddie suggested that Maxie give them to a newspaper reporter.

"If the LEMA Master Plan is published in a newspaper," Eddie said, "then everyone will see what is happening."

Maxie laughed. "Who would believe it, Eddie? That three men have a plan to kill all the cars and taxis in New York City? Nobody wants to believe such a terrible thing. The Three would deny it, and the only thing that would happen is that I would disappear that much sooner."

"Maybe you are right," Eddie said. "But in any case you are not going to disappear next Friday night. Since we know about that part of the Master Plan, you can be a long way from the shop next Friday night."

"Certainly not," said Maxie.

"You do not believe the Master Plan yourself?" Eddie asked.

"Believe me, I believe it," said Maxie. "But this is what I believe also. I believe that the only way to win a war is to be on hand for the battle wherever it is going to be."

"On hand?" said Eddie.

"On hand in my shop," said Maxie, "when Big Moe in his bulletproof Italian car comes looking for me."

"Oh," said Eddie. "Well, if that is the idea, a number of people will be on hand. When The Three come looking for you on Friday night, there will be Harry the Hot Dog and Morris the Florist and Carlos and one or two others in the back room of your shop to greet them."

"No," said Maxie. "I will greet them by myself."

"But that will be a three-against-one fight," said Eddie.

"I am gambling," said Maxie, "that one head is sometimes better than three."

"Gambling is fine," said Eddie Moroney. "But we cannot afford to lose your head. Therefore I am coming on Friday night to watch you gamble. In case something should happen. Some little emergency."

"All right," said Maxie. "That would be a comfort to me. Especially as you have worked with a circus and can, no doubt, handle lions and tigers in an emergency."

"I only lettered the posters for the circus," said Eddie Moroney.

"Never mind," said Maxie. "That takes more brains."

"All the same," said Eddie Moroney, "I would just as soon we had one or two men besides myself on Friday night."

"I appreciate the advice," said Maxie. "However, for the time being, I do not want you to tell the other pushcart peddlers about the shorthand notes of Miriam Portlette. My only question is, can you play poker?"

Eddie said that he could.

"Good," said Maxie. "Come to my shop at seven o'clock on Friday night and bring a new deck of playing cards." That was all Maxie would tell Eddie Moroney about his plans.

Maxie then called the Police Commissioner. As he had parted from the Police Commissioner on friendly terms, Maxie suggested that the Commissioner drop around to his shop on Friday night for a friendly game of poker.

"I only play for money," said the Police Commissioner.

"I like to gamble myself," said Maxie Hammerman.

The Police Commissioner agreed to come then, especially as there were a few more questions he wanted to ask Maxie about Frank the Flower.

"To tell the truth, I have not had too much experience with crackpots," said the Police Commissioner, "but it does not seem to me that Frank is a hopeless case."

"Probably not," said Maxie. "And I will answer any questions I can."

So on Friday night, the evening The Three had set to kidnap Maxie Hammerman, Maxie was sitting down in the back room of his shop with his friend Eddie Moroney and the Police Commissioner for a friendly game of poker. The Police Commissioner had just drawn four aces when the door to the back room opened and in walked Big Moe and The Tiger and Louie Livergreen, all with their hands in their right overcoat pockets, from which Eddie Moroney guessed that they all carried guns.

The Three were so surprised to see the Police Commissioner that they could not decide whether to take their hands out of their pockets or not. The Police Commissioner, who never bothered with polite conversation with anyone who had a hand in his right overcoat pocket, jumped to his feet and pulled his own gun.

However, before the Police Commissioner could shoot, Maxie stepped in front of him and said, "Hello, Moe. Hello, Louie. Hello, Walter the Tiger. I have been expecting you."

As The Three had never set eyes on Maxie Hammerman in person before, and as he — to their knowledge — had never set eyes on them, Maxie's calling them by their first names scared even Louie Livergreen. And when Maxie held out his hand, Louie could not do anything but take his hand out of his pocket and shake Maxie's hand.

"Meet my friend the Police Commissioner," Maxie said. "Commissioner, these are my good friends who have just dropped in to play a little poker with us."

"Moe Mammoth is a friend of yours?" said the Police Commissioner. The Commissioner was still annoyed about Big Moe's calling him a big dope to the newspapers.

"A poker-playing friend," said Maxie. "We have differences of opinion, but we get together for a friendly game of poker."

"As you perhaps know," Maxie explained to the Police Commissioner, "Big Moe and The Tiger and Mr. Livergreen usually play a friendly game of cards with Mayor Emmett P. Cudd on Friday night. So we should be honored that they have come to play at my shop instead."

And before The Three knew what was happening, Eddie Moroney was politely helping them off with their overcoats which he hung up on the wall nearest Maxie Hammerman. The Police Commissioner started to put his gun back in his holster but, on second thought, laid it on the table beside him.

"There is just one little matter of business before we start our game," Maxie said as he shuffled the cards.

The Three exchanged nervous looks.

"What business is that?" Big Moe asked.

"Did you bring the bulletproof Italian car?" asked Maxie Hammerman.

At the mention of a bulletproof Italian car, the Police Commissioner put his hand on his gun.

"It is nothing to worry about," Maxie assured the Police Commissioner. "It is just that Big Moe has agreed to sell me his bulletproof Italian car, as he has no further need of it. Whereas, a man in my position cannot be too careful.

"You have the car outside?" Maxie asked.

"It's in front of the shop," Big Moe said warily.

"Good," said Maxie Hammerman. "Maybe I should have my friend the Police Commissioner fire one or two shots into the side to test whether it is really bulletproof. However, I trust you."

Maxie took a check from his pocket and laid it on the table. "I have here a check for $14.50 made out to Mr. Moe Mammoth for one bulletproof Italian car. Is that correct?"

"Big Moe is selling you a bulletproof car for $14.50?" said the Police Commissioner suspiciously.

"It's secondhand," said Maxie. "And we are friends." He passed the check across the table to Big Moe.

Big Moe looked at Louie Livergreen to see what he should do, but Louie was watching the Police Commissioner tapping the handle of his gun and offered no advice.

"Take it," whispered The Tiger.

So Big Moe picked up the check.

"If you will just give me a receipt," said Maxie Hammerman, "saying 'paid in full for one bulletproof Italian car, secondhand,' we can get on with the card game."

Eddie Moroney gave Big Moe a pen, and Big Moe wrote out the receipt.

"I hope everybody has had a good week's business," said Maxie, as he dealt the cards, "and can afford to make a few sporting bets, as I promised my friend the Police Commissioner a good game."

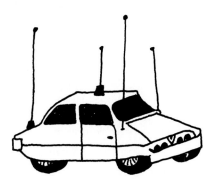

"I hope so, too," said the Police Commissioner, scowling at Big Moe. "I have never liked a man who talks like a big shot to the newspapers and then makes very small bets when he is at the poker table."

With the Police Commissioner's gun on the table and their overcoats on the wall beside Maxie Hammerman, The Three did not want to annoy the Police Commissioner by making any small bets. Fortunately, it was Friday night and The Three had in their pockets whatever amount of their profits they took home with them at the end of every week.

"Of course, it has been a bad week," said Big Moe, in case the Police Commissioner did not think the bets were big enough.

The Police Commissioner won the first three hands. His winnings were $237, most of which he won from The Three, as Eddie and Maxie did not bet much on the first three hands.

"For a big dope, you are a pretty good poker player," Maxie said to the Police Commissioner.

The Police Commissioner did not mind Maxie Hammerman calling him a big dope.

Eddie Moroney won the next hand and got $42 from Louie Livergreen. Louie had three queens and Eddie Moroney only had two jacks, but Eddie was so determined not to give in to Louie that Louie got nervous and threw in his hand.

Then Maxie Hammerman started winning. He won every one of the next ten hands, winning each time larger amounts, as The Three made bigger and bigger bets, hoping to stop Maxie. On the last hand alone, Maxie's winnings were $13,500, and altogether Maxie won over $60,000.

Big Moe lost the most money to Maxie. He even bet the $14.50 check Maxie had written him and lost that. The game had to stop then as none of The Three had any more money in their pockets.

"Now that is what I call a conspiracy," laughed the Police Commissioner, as he helped Maxie sort out the $60,000 into piles of ten, fifty, and hundred dollar bills. Big Moe was looking so foolish that the Police Commissioner did not begrudge Maxie a cent of his winnings.

"And," he said to Big Moe, "if you wish me to investigate this conspiracy, I will be glad to do so, as it would be worth my time to know how Maxie Hammerman won so much money on ten hands of poker."

The Police Commissioner then offered to take The Three home in a squad car as they did not have any money for bus fare. "If anyone sees you riding in the squad car," he said, "I will explain that you are not common criminals."

CHAPTER XXVI

Maxie Hammerman's War Chest: A Philosophy of War

Maxie Hammerman has sometimes been portrayed as a happy-go-lucky fighter whose victory over The Three on the night they came to kidnap him was a matter of pure luck. Maxie himself has always been modest about his part in the Pushcart War. From his own descriptions of the $60,000 card game, one might easily conclude that Maxie was simply a crazy gambler who was lucky enough to hold the right cards.

However, Eddie Moroney, who was there, guarantees that Maxie knew what he was doing at every step of the game. Eddie remembers a conversation with Maxie just after The Three had left with the Police Commissioner.

Eddie and Maxie were having a bottle of cream soda together, and Eddie said to Maxie, "I, also, would like to know, Maxie, how you won so much money on ten hands of poker, as I know you do not cheat at cards."

"It is simple," Maxie said. "I won all the money because Louie Livergreen — of whom The Tiger and Big Moe are a little afraid — because he is the one who makes all the plans — was afraid of me.

"Louie was afraid of me," Maxie explained, "because he knows I could have had the Police Commissioner shoot him on the spot for breaking into my shop.

But I did not. Instead, I pretended that Louie and Big Moe and The Tiger were my friends, by which Louie Livergreen knew that *I* was not afraid of him. And this scared Louie Livergreen. Because if I am not afraid of him, it means that either I am smarter than he is, or that I have made a plan which is even better, from my point of view, than to have the Police Commissioner shoot him.

"So," Maxie smiled, "Louie Livergreen's mind was not on the cards he was playing, and Big Moe and The Tiger could see that Louie Livergreen was nervous, which made them nervous, and they did not play their cards carefully.

"Also," said Maxie, "I played my cards very carefully."

"It was a good game," said Eddie. "But I still do not understand why you did not let the Police Commissioner shoot them. It would have been such a surprise to them."

"Yes," said Maxie, "but it would have been against my philosophy of war."

"In what way?" Eddie asked.

"In this way," said Maxie. "Louie Livergreen, you may recall, thought that if he kidnapped me, the pushcart peddlers would not fight."

"We would fight harder," said Eddie Moroney indignantly.

"Certainly," said Maxie Hammerman.

"In the same way," Maxie pointed out, "if we got rid of Big Moe and Louie and The Tiger, there would still be maybe a million truck drivers who hate the pushcarts. Also, there are three other men behind The Three who would be only too happy to see Big Moe and Louie and The Tiger disappear so that they could be the top three. I can name you twelve men who would fight with each other to be the top three.

"It is my idea," Maxie went on, "that if you are going to have enemies, it is better to have enemies you already know. It is easier to guess what they are going to do.

"Also," said Maxie, "it is better to have enemies who have learned to be a little afraid of you."

Maxie scooped up the $60,000 he had won and stuffed it into an old tool chest. Then he dipped his finger in a can of axle oil and lettered on the side of the box "WAR CHEST."

"What is that for?" asked Eddie Moroney.

"My philosophy of war," Maxie continued, "is that what you need to win a war is money.

Everybody is willing to fight for a good cause. Fine. But there comes a time when you run out of money for peas — for pins — for whatever you are using for ammunition at the moment. You cannot afford the repairs to your pushcart. Or for the doctor's bills when you get hurt in the fighting. Or, to feed the children because you cannot work a regular schedule. There comes a time.

"When that time comes," Maxie said, "we have this war chest. Anyone who cannot afford to pay me for repairs to his pushcart may take from this chest. No questions asked. As long as he is fighting, the money is there."

"You mean we are going to pay you to fix our carts with your own money which you won at poker?" said Eddie.

"Who knows it is my money?" asked Maxie. "Who needs to know? It is from contributions to our war effort."

"But who would contribute to us?" Eddie asked.

"Why not?" said Maxie. "I am the Pushcart King. Kings can get contributions."

"And a king, Eddie Moroney," Maxie said, looking very pleased with himself, "a king takes care of his people in time of war. You should know that."

Eddie Moroney pulled from his pocket the $42 he had won from Louie Livergreen and gave it to Maxie Hammerman. "It is a contribution," Eddie said.

"To the Pushcart King for the Pushcart War," he added.

CHAPTER XXVII

The Truck Drivers' Manifesto

After the failure of the plot to capture Maxie Hammerman, The Three were not anxious to tangle directly with Maxie again. They decided to attack in a different way.

They called a meeting of all the truck drivers in the city. At this meeting the drivers drew up a manifesto which they sent to Mayor Cudd. The manifesto claimed that Maxie Hammerman's map and the fact the ammunition had been found in his basement was clear evidence of a pushcart conspiracy.

The manifesto made four demands:

1.   That every pushcart peddler in the city be arrested;

2. That pushcarts be permanently banned from the streets as they were endangering the whole city;

3. That Maxie Hammerman be fined $60,000 and sentenced to 60 years in jail for organizing the Pushcart Conspiracy, and

4. That the Police Commissioner be fired, as there was reason to believe he was in on the whole conspiracy.

The truck drivers warned that if the Mayor did not act at once along the lines suggested, they would have no choice but to declare war on the pushcarts. Mayor Cudd called the Police Commissioner and read him the manifesto.

"Well, what do you want me to do?" asked the Commissioner. "If you fire me, I cannot arrest the peddlers."

The Mayor had not thought of that. "I think the truck drivers would settle for arresting the pushcart peddlers," he said. "At least, that is Point One of the manifesto."

"Well, I cannot arrest the pushcart peddlers in any case," said the Police Commissioner. "There are, according to Maxie Hammerman, over five hundred pushcart peddlers in this city, and we do not have that many empty cells in the jail.

"Moreover," said the Police Commissioner, "even if there *were* a pushcart conspiracy, it would be impossible to prove which trucks have been shot down by pushcart peddlers as a part of the conspiracy and which have been shot down by children purely in a spirit of fun.

"Do you want me to arrest all the children, too?" asked the Police Commissioner. "Including those whose fathers are truck drivers?"

"No, no," said the Mayor. "Just the pushcart peddlers."

"Well, I am not going to arrest *anybody* without proof," said the Police Commissioner, "including Maxie Hammerman, who is a gentleman, a good sport, and a good businessman. Once I start arresting people without proof, what is to stop me from arresting you?"

"*Me?*" said the Mayor nervously.

"But what can I do?" pleaded the Mayor. "Fifty thousand truck drivers have signed this manifesto. That is fifty thousand votes, you know."

"I suggest that you declare a truce until the question of a conspiracy can be fully investigated," said the Police Commissioner. "If any pushcart peddler violates the truce, I will arrest him — but not before."

CHAPTER XXVIII

The Truce

The period of the truce was a difficult time for the pushcart peddlers. They had won the first battle, but they had not won the war. The peddlers realized that within a week all the truck tires would have been repaired and that the trucks would be on the streets again in full force and more determined than ever to make trouble for the pushcarts.

This was exactly what happened. Within a week Maxie Hammerman's shop was filled with pushcarts needing repairs of all sorts. If it had not been for Maxie's war chest, many of the peddlers would have lost heart entirely.

One day General Anna had a wheel ripped off her cart by a truck crowding her into a curb. Maxie Hammerman said that Anna would need a new cart as there was damage to the axle that could not be repaired.

The pushcart peddlers held a meeting to discuss the truce. Morris the Florist pounded on a table. "When they hit a lady," he said, "it is too much! What kind of truce is that?"

"General Anna has had that cart for forty-two years," said Maxie Hammerman. "My father built it when I was just learning to use a hammer."

"Forty-two years, and I never had a day's trouble with it," said General Anna. "Maxie's father once said to me, 'When I build a cart, it could last a lifetime.' So maybe I should die now."

"Please don't, General Anna," said Papa Peretz.

"Naturally I won't," said General Anna. "I wouldn't give a truck the satisfaction. I was used to that cart. But never mind. Maxie Hammerman can build me another. What I want to know is: Why don't we fight back as before? Just selling apples and pears while a truck is cutting off my wheel, I don't like so much."

"I am perfectly willing to fight back," said Harry the Hot Dog.

" 'Willing' is not the question," said Maxie Hammerman. "If we break the truce, we are in serious trouble. The Police Commissioner has promised the Mayor that he will arrest anyone who breaks the truce."

"A truck is smashing my axle and it is a *truce?*" said General Anna.

"You are right," said Maxie Hammerman. "But how can you prove that it was not an accident? And any accidental damage we do the trucks now would be very risky. The truck drivers are looking for just one good excuse to make the Mayor put us off the streets entirely."

"Maxie is right," said Mr. Jerusalem. "We must not damage the trucks at this time. But I have an idea. We can make a peaceful protest."

"Peaceful!" said General Anna scornfully. "Peaceful like a broken axle?"

Mr. Jerusalem shook his head. "Like a Peace March," he said. "What I mean is this: the trucks want to run us down one at a time when nobody is looking. They hit General Anna, and everybody says it is an accident."

"That we already know," said Harry the Hot Dog.

"I am coming to something else," said Mr. Jerusalem. "Suppose a truck has to run down one hundred and seventy pushcarts at a time. Could that be an accident?"

"So we should all get killed?" said General Anna. "Is that what you are coming to?"

"For once, listen," said Mr. Jerusalem. "My idea is as follows: we choose three streets, three streets where there is always a lot of truck traffic. We divide into *three* teams — one hundred and seventy pushcarts to a team. Then we go marching down these three streets, one team down each street. We are lined up across the street, six or seven pushcarts in a row — like a parade."

"Or like an army," said General Anna. "An army of three divisions. Call it an army, and I like the idea. So continue," she added.

Mr. Jerusalem continued. "We have filled the streets where we are marching. No truck has room to pass us. A truck driver comes driving toward us. He says, 'Out of my way, Pushcarts.' But we keep marching forward. Very peaceful. Doing business as usual." Mr. Jerusalem paused to let everyone get the picture.

Papa Peretz looked doubtful. "And while we are doing business as usual, the truck keeps coming forward?"

"So he keeps coming," said Mr. Jerusalem. "Are we worried? No. To push us out of the way, that truck would have to run down six, twelve, eighteen, forty, maybe one hundred and seventy pushcarts to get through that street. Could that be an accident?" Mr. Jerusalem demanded.

"No," he replied triumphantly. "It could not! And so the truck drivers will have to bargain with us. They will have to guarantee no more hitting the pushcarts."

"*Bargain* with us," said Harry the Hot Dog. "They would rather run us down — six, twelve, eighteen, *forty* pushcarts. What do they care how many they hit?"

"Ah," said Mr. Jerusalem, "but if they *do* hit us, then everyone will *see* who is breaking the truce. Who could hit forty carts by accident? I say they will not dare."

"But if they do — ?" said Harry the Hot Dog.

Mr. Jerusalem shrugged. "Then six, twelve, eighteen, forty pushcarts will be smashed," he said. "Maybe we will all be killed. It is a war, isn't it?"

"A *Peace* March you are calling this!" said Harry the Hot Dog.

"Are *we* hitting anyone?" asked Mr. Jerusalem. "Are we breaking any law?"

"Yes," said Morris the Florist. "If the trucks are coming toward us and we are marching *toward* the trucks, and it is a one-way street, which it certainly will be, we will be going the *wrong* way down a one-way street — and *that* is against the law."

Mr. Jerusalem laughed. "A minor traffic violation," he said. "Nothing serious, like breaking a truce."

"Nothing serious," General Anna agreed. "In fact, it is a fine plan, and I am marching in the front line. You could hurry with the pushcart, Maxie?"

CHAPTER XXIX

The Peace March

Maxie Hammerman was able to finish General Anna's new pushcart in time for the Peace March by using, with General Anna's permission, his electric drill and power saw. It was true what Maxie Hammerman had told the Police Commissioner about General Anna's preferring the work on her cart to be done by hand.

"But we are at war," said General Anna. "It is more important that I should have the cart in time for the Peace March."

Maxie Hammerman said afterward that the greatest compliment anyone ever paid him was General Anna's remark when she saw her cart: "Even with electric tools, Maxie Hammerman can make a cart every bit as good as his father made by hand." Maxie was so proud of this compliment that he personally bought General Anna a cartful of the best-quality apples and pears, so that she would make the best appearance possible on the day of the Peace March.

As Mr. Jerusalem had suggested, the Peace Army was divided into three groups of about one hundred and seventy pushcarts each. Mr. Jerusalem was to lead the First Division down West Street. Harry the Hot Dog commanded the Second Division which was going to march down Broome Street. General Anna herself took charge of the Third Division which was to march down Greene Street.

General Anna gave orders that all divisions were to report to their stations at 7:30 on the morning of the Peace March so that they could get lined up before there was any amount of traffic in the streets. This meant that some of the peddlers had to set out before dawn to reach the street where their division was to march.

The Peace March was well organized. The peddlers had all dressed in their best clothes and many of the carts had been freshly painted for the occasion. A few peddlers in each division carried posters and some of the carts displayed banners.

The banners and posters had been lettered by Eddie Moroney. The lettering looked very professional because of Eddie's long experience in lettering circus carts and posters as a young man before he went into the pushcart line.

The banners all read: "PEACE MARCH," some in plain and some in circus-type lettering. The posters, however, said different things: "Be Fair to the Pushcarts" or "Don't Push the Pushcarts Around," or simply "Pushcarts for Peace."

Some of the posters were gaily decorated with birds and flowers and other designs Eddie Moroney felt were in keeping with a peace march. General Anna thought a lion or two would be very nice, as Eddie Moroney was known to be very good at drawing lions as well as at lettering. But Eddie said lions definitely were not in keeping with a peace march.

The Peace March was almost entirely peaceful. With the First and Second Divisions, everything went exactly as Mr. Jerusalem had predicted.

The truck drivers who found themselves confronted by the First and Second Divisions stopped their trucks. When the peddlers in the front lines refused to let the trucks through, and when the truck drivers saw that there were three or four solid blocks of pushcarts backing up the front lines, they realized that there was nothing they could do.

They agreed among themselves that they could not smash their way through a street full of pushcarts, even if they were angry enough to wish to. It was not that the trucks could not have broken a path through the carts. The difficulty was that while the drivers had been arguing with the peddlers about letting them pass, the banners and posters had attracted large numbers of people. If the drivers had challenged the Peace Army and anyone had been hurt, it would have been quite clear to the spectators that the truck drivers had rammed the carts intentionally.

It was annoying to the drivers to have to give in to the pushcart peddlers. But they had no choice. Traffic had piled up so rapidly behind them that they could not even turn around and drive off in the opposite direction.

So on both Broome and West Streets, the drivers were forced to agree, however bad-humoredly, to the condition named by Mr. Jerusalem and Harry the Hot Dog. This was simply a promise to ask The Three to meet with Maxie Hammerman and work out a peaceful settlement of the problems that had led to the Pushcart War.

One of the truck drivers warned Mr. Jerusalem that even if The Three did agree to talk with Maxie Hammerman that that was no guarantee that the push-carts would get what they wanted.

Mr. Jerusalem smiled. "Maybe not," he said. "But it is a beginning. To talk is better than to fight."

"Also," added Papa Peretz, "if the talk is not helpful, we can march again."

After the truck drivers had promised to ask The Three to meet with Maxie Hammerman, Papa Peretz gave each of them a bag of pretzels as a token of good will. At about the same time, over on Broome Street, Harry the Hot Dog was passing out free hot dogs.

Then Mr. Jerusalem and Harry the Hot Dog signalled their divisions that they were to turn their carts around and march peacefully down the block, clearing the street for the truck drivers. At the about-face signal from their leaders, all the peddlers swung their carts around.

As the pushcarts could not move very fast, the trucks had to creep along behind them for some blocks. Thus, it appeared to onlookers along the sidewalks as if the pushcarts of the First and Second Divisions were leading triumphal parades — which, in a way, they were. When people occasionally clapped their hands, Papa Peretz bowed to the right and left like the main actor in a play, which encouraged people to clap even harder and once or twice to break into cheers.

Down on Greene Street, however, the Third Division was running into trouble. The first truck to be challenged by the Third Division of the Peace Army was, unfortunately, driven by Albert P. Mack. Mack was driving the same Mighty Mammoth that had hit Morris the Florist's cart at the very beginning of the Pushcart War.

CHAPTER XXX

Mack's Attack

When Mack saw the army of pushcart peddlers in front of him, he thought at first he was having a bad dream. Mack had been having bad dreams about pushcarts ever since he had hit Morris the Florist.

Mack thought he must be dreaming now because he was on a one-way street. He knew *he* was going in the right direction, and he could see in his rear-view mirror at least six other trucks behind him. *Seven* trucks, Mack reasoned, could not be going the wrong way down a street they traveled every day.

Very much confused, Mack kept on going until he was within ten feet of the pushcarts. He did stop then, tramping on his brake so suddenly that the truck following him whammed him a terrific blow from behind.

There was a shattering of glass that sounded like a thousand punch bowls cracking up — which is exactly what it was — Mack was loaded with punch bowls that morning. Mack himself was flung against his steering wheel so hard that for a minute he was certain he had broken a rib. He gasped and blinked and peered groggily down at the pushcarts.

They were certainly no dream. They stretched in a solid mass as far as he could see. Mack was furious. He socked his horn, warning the Peace Army to move aside and let him through.

No one moved. General Anna, her new cart heaped high with the best-quality apples Maxie Hammerman had bought her, was in the very center of the front line. She simply stood there eating an apple as if she had all the time in the world.

Mack realized that the peddlers had not the least intention of letting him through. "What's the big idea?" he bellowed from his cab.

"Read for yourself," said General Anna, negligently tossing the apple core at one of Mack's front tires. "It says on the signs."

Mack could see the signs all right, but he was not interested in reading them.

"Get off the street!" he shouted. But none of the peddlers paid him the least attention. Some of them were doing a good business with people who had gathered to watch the Peace March.

Several other truck drivers, who had pulled up behind Mack, had climbed out of their cabs and come up to see what the trouble was. General Anna explained to them that the peddlers would let them through if the drivers promised to let the peddlers use the streets in peace.

"Why should we promise you anything?" demanded one of the drivers.

"Because if you do not, we will not let you pass," said General Anna. "Suit yourself."

"You trying to start a fight, lady?" asked one of the drivers.

"When there is a truce?" said General Anna, looking very shocked. "Certainly not. I am just going to stay here peacefully with my pushcart. My friends will do the same."

The drivers did not know what to do. They went back to consult with Mack who had refused even to get out of his truck to argue with the peddlers.

"I'm going through," Mack said.

"You can't, Mack," said one of the other drivers. "There are too many of them."

"There'll be fewer in a minute," said Mack, starting his engine.

"Wait, Mack, wait!" begged his friend. "You're crazy!"

Mack hesitated. He looked down at the Peace Army. Unluckily, his eye fell on Morris the Florist who was standing in the front line next to General Anna.

Mack had had a grudge against Morris ever since he had smashed Morris' cart, for he felt that Morris had put him in a bad light with his wife. Mack's wife had told him that driving a big truck did not give him the right to bully everyone else on the street.

So when Mack saw Morris in the front line with a new pushcart, the idea of the same pushcart peddler blocking his way a *second* time threw him into a rage. Without taking his eye off Morris, Mack revved his engine and let go his brake.

"Look out," he yelled. "I'm coming through!"

Two truck drivers jumped onto Mack's running board and grabbed his arm. Mack flung them off.

"They're obstructing the street," he growled. "Can't you see? It's illegal."

"But there are at least two hundred of them," said one of his friends. "Can't you *see* that?"

"I can see," Mack said and his voice grew frighteningly calm. "The thing is — this truck weighs twenty thousand pounds when it is empty — and it is now fully loaded."

Mack stepped on the accelerator. The two drivers who had tried to reason with him backed away, and Mack drove straight into the Peace Army.

There was a terrible splintering and cracking as pushcarts buckled and shattered and flew into the air. Onlookers screamed as slats, wheels, apples, used clothing, and dancing dolls rained down on them.

Fortunately, a pushcart axle, wrenched free by the collision of pushcarts and truck, was hurled, as if by design, straight through Mack's windshield. The axle missed Mack's head by less than an inch, but he lost control of the truck. The Mighty Mammoth swerved, plunged over the curb, sheared off a fire hydrant and crashed through a plate glass window into a cafeteria.

Miraculously, no one was killed. General Anna and Morris the Florist, who had been in the center of the line, directly in the path of the truck, had fallen to the ground so that the truck, although it shattered their carts, passed right over them.

Morris would have been killed if it had not been for General Anna. General Anna seized Morris by the hand and dragged him to the ground. Morris had been so stunned by the realization that he was about to be run down for the *second* time in three months by the *same* truck driver, that he had stood frozen with astonishment in the path of the truck. Only General Anna's quick thinking saved his life.

The peddlers directly behind Anna and Morris had a few seconds in which to run to the sides of the street, although they could not, of course, save their carts. About eighty carts were wrecked and a number of others were seriously damaged. There were a few broken arms and broken legs and any number of nasty cuts and bruises. But it could have been very much worse.

Forty thousand dollars' worth of damage was done to the cafeteria alone, and the proprietor estimated that several hundred people would have been killed if all his customers had not rushed out to the street minutes before the crash to hear Mack's argument with the Peace Army. Mack was immediately arrested for reckless driving, and there were plenty of witnesses eager to tell the police that Mack had run down the pushcarts on purpose.

Despite their losses, the pushcart peddlers were in good spirits. They felt certain that Mack's attack on the Third Division had demonstrated for once and for all who was to blame for the trouble in the streets. Eddie Moroney lifted General Anna onto his pushcart and personally pushed her all the way back to Maxie Hammerman's shop for a victory celebration. However, that celebration was never held.

CHAPTER XXXI

The Sneak Attack

By the time the battered but jubilant Third Division arrived at Maxie's shop, Mayor Cudd had begun the desperate sneak attack that was intended to wipe out the whole pushcart army at one blow.

The Third Division arrived at Maxie's to find their friends from the First and Second Divisions listening in shocked disbelief to a radio announcement by the Mayor. Mayor Cudd was announcing that he had suspended all pushcart licenses until further notice.

"An army is an army," Mayor Cudd was saying, "whether it calls itself a Peace Army or some other kind of army. And it is my view that the pushcart peddlers, in organizing an army, have violated the truce.

"They have provoked violence and bad feeling," said Mayor Cudd. "Not to mention the disruption of traffic on three streets of our city, and the destruction of public property."

"What are you talking about, you crazy Cudd?" shouted General Anna, seizing Maxie Hammerman's portable radio and shaking it in terrible anger.

"I am talking, of course, about the destruction of a fire hydrant on Greene Street," Mayor Cudd's voice continued.

"A hydrant was destroyed?" Maxie asked, as he had not heard all the details of Mack's attack on the Peace Army.

"By a truck, of course," said Morris the Florist. "The usual smashing."

"The Fire Commissioner is extremely upset," the Mayor went on. "Water is flooding Greene Street, and he has had five men there for an hour trying to seal off the water main."

"*The Fire Commissioner* is upset," General Anna screamed at the radio. "*That* is the worst thing that has happened today?" and she would have thrown the radio on the floor if Maxie Hammerman had not taken it firmly out of her hands and led her gently to a chair.

"And I am disturbed, too," the Mayor proceeded. "Therefore, I am not only temporarily suspending all pushcart licenses, but I am also recommending to the City Council when it meets next week that these licenses be permanently revoked."

The peddlers stared blankly at the radio as the Mayor went on to express his sympathy to Mack's family and to all truck drivers who had been inconvenienced by the Peace March. The Mayor expressed regret at Mack's arrest and said that he would do everything he could to see that he was released promptly.

Meantime, the Mayor said, he trusted that the citizens of the city appreciated the courage of this great driver's standing up to his traffic rights when he was so pitifully outnumbered. "Think of it," said the Mayor, "— one truck driver against hundreds of pushcarts!"

As for the promises extracted from the truckers by the First and Second Divisions, the Mayor said Mr. Mammoth had already assured him that he and Mr. Livergreen and Mr. Sweet had no intention of meeting with Maxie Hammerman. These law-abiding men, the Mayor explained, could hardly be expected to honor a promise made as a result of a Peace March that was a clear violation of a sacred truce.

At this point Mr. Jerusalem rose and, without a word, picked up one of Maxie's hammers and smashed the radio to bits.

The rest of the peddlers were too stunned to even discuss the incredible turn of events. Maxie urged everyone to return home as quietly and quickly as possible, and to get his cart off the street, for the Mayor's action had put them all in danger of arrest at any moment.

As Mr. Jerusalem had no place to put his cart but on the street, Maxie insisted that he spend the night at the Hammerman shop. It was the first time in seventy years that Mr. Jerusalem had slept indoors, and it made him feel like an old man.

CHAPTER XXXII

Frank the Flower's Crocheted Target

The Three left Mayor Cudd's headquarters on the night of the Peace March confident that the Pushcart War was as good as won. The Mayor's broadcast, they felt sure, would break the back of any further resistance on the part of the pushcart peddlers.

In fact, The Three left Mayor Cudd's to map their plans for Operation Krushkar (the code name for the autumn automobile offensive that was scheduled as the second stage of the LEMA Master Plan). The Three could hardly have foreseen at this point the possible significance of a psychological victory that Frank the Flower was to score over Albert P. Mack during the time the latter was held prisoner. But the resulting damage to Mack's morale — and to their own, when they heard it — may have had a critical effect on the events of the next few weeks.

On being arrested, Mack had been locked in a cell directly across from Frank the Flower's. This, in itself, had enraged Mack. While he was glad to see that Frank the Flower was still in jail, it angered him that Frank should have the similar pleasure of seeing him in jail.

From the moment he was locked up, Mack had been throwing temper tantrums, kicking at the walls of the cell, bellowing into the corridor, insulting the guards, and in general making a nuisance of himself. When the Police Commissioner was summoned to see what the guards were complaining about, Mack kicked him in the shins.

The Police Commissioner decided that Mack was definitely a criminal type. And when Mayor Cudd, as he had promised, personally requested that Mack be released, the Police Commissioner refused.

Mayor Cudd maintained that as he had declared the Peace March illegal, the Police Commissioner had no legal grounds for holding Mack for reckless driving.

The Police Commissioner replied that reckless driving was the least of it, as there were now more serious charges against Mack. The owner of the cafeteria that Mack had driven into claimed that, whether Mack was guilty of driving recklessly or not, he *was* guilty of trespassing on private property, and he refused to withdraw his charges.

"He is also guilty of kicking a police officer," said the Police Commissioner, "and I refuse to withdraw my charges."

It was clear that the Police Commissioner was acting on principle. Mack was not a prisoner anyone would have kept around for the fun of it. And his disposition did not improve with confinement.

The fact that Frank the Flower did not seem to mind too much being in jail added to Mack's bad humor. Frank was now used to the place, of course, and he received many letters and postcards from his friends among the pushcart peddlers, as well as from the hundreds of Frank-the-Flower fans.

Morris the Florist wrote Frank every day and sent him fresh flowers twice a week. Maxie Hammerman sent him all the latest reports on how the war was going, and General Anna had promised him that he would be made a general, too, as soon as he got out of jail.

None of Frank's friends had told him — they didn't like to worry him — about the Mayor's threat to end the war by revoking the pushcart licenses. So Frank the Flower was under the impression that the pushcarts were still winning the war. Naturally, he did not believe anything Mack told him to the contrary.

Frank the Flower's general cheerfulness and his conviction that the pushcarts were winning were bound to be annoying to Mack. But what drove him wild was Frank the Flower's dart board.

An old lady, whom Frank had never met, but who had read about him in the papers, had crocheted for Frank a large pink and green dart board. Running in circles around the bull's-eye, Frank's friend had crocheted twenty trucks, complete with tires, and she had included with the dart board a generous supply of darts which she had fashioned from darning needles. (She had apologized for the darning needles — "You would probably prefer pea-tacks," she had written Frank, "but, as you know, tacks are very expensive just now." She wrote Frank at the time of the Tacks Tax.)

Frank the Flower had hung the dart board on the side of his cell, and each morning after he had finished reading his mail, he would practice shooting down trucks. Frank's ambition — if he ever got back into action — was to be able to justify his reputation as an ace shot. It embarrassed him that all his fans believed him to be a better shot than he was.

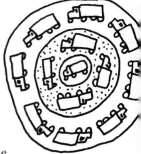

Whenever the prison guards came past Frank's cell, they would call out, "How are you doing, Frank?" And Frank the Flower would report, "Got seventeen out of twenty last time. That's one hundred and sixteen so far today."

Sometimes the guards even came into Frank's cell and had a go at the dart board themselves. Frank the Flower was popular with the guards, who preferred crackpots to criminal types, and they called his cell The Shooting Gallery.

After Mack was arrested, the guards took to calling the truck in the center of the target "The Mighty Mammoth." There was much cheering from Frank's cell every time someone hit The Mighty Mammoth, and medals, in the form of flowers, from Frank's hatband, were given out for every bull's-eye scored. Mack could tell from the number of daisies or bachelor buttons a guard had pinned to his uniform, how many Mighty Mammoths he had hit.

When Mack heard Frank the Flower and the guards laughing and calling out their scores, he would throw his dinner plate into the corridor and demand to be given a quieter cell. At such times, one of the guards would go across the hall and tell Mack to lower his voice as he was disturbing the customers in The Shooting Gallery.

At night when there were no guards around, Mack would call threateningly across the hall to Frank. "You just wait," he'd say. "Just wait. This war is as good as over. And when it *is* — !"

But he did not succeed in worrying Frank the Flower at all. Frank took the very fact of Mack's still being in jail as a sign that things were going very well, indeed, for the pushcarts.

After a week of Frank the Flower's optimism, Mack's own confidence cracked. A guard found him one morning crouched under his bunk, writing a desperate letter to The Three, begging them to surrender.

"An old lady is supplying them with ammunition," Mack wrote, "and thousands of officers are in training, and they will not stop until every Mighty Mammoth is extinct."

The guards confiscated the letter and gave it to the Police Commissioner. The Police Commissioner laughed and said, "Mail it to Moe Mammoth. Special delivery."

CHAPTER XXXIII

The Turning Point: The War of Words

Frank the Flower's faith, unfortunately, could not be shared by any of the pushcart peddlers who knew the facts. Things had never looked worse for the peddlers. From the time the Mayor had threatened to revoke the pushcart licenses, most of them had given up hope. Even Maxie Hammerman, though he was now famous and on a magazine cover as "The Pushcart King of America" and "The Brains Behind the Pushcart Conspiracy," was very glum.

"A great kind of king to be when soon there will be no pushcarts," Maxie said privately to his friends.

"Who is giving up?" said General Anna. "So now we must fight the City Council."

"City Councils you can't fight," Maxie said somberly. "They meet in private. You don't meet them on the streets.

"Until now," Maxie explained, "the pushcarts had a lawful right to be on the streets and we could fight for our rights. But if the City Council makes a law against pushcarts, then we have no rights to fight for. If we fight, we are against the law."

The whole city seemed to accept the fact that the Pushcart War was over. A newspaper ran a story called "The Death of the Pushcarts."

However, there was to be one more battle, and it was to be provoked by a picture, the photograph Marvin Seeley had taken months before, of Mack hitting Morris the Florist the first time. Everyone was curious at this point to know just how the war had begun, and this prompted Emily Wisser to show her husband, Buddy Wisser, Marvin's Honorable Mention picture in her scrapbook.

Buddy, as we know, blew up Marvin's picture to get a clearer view of the situation, and as the facts he discovered by enlarging the picture had human interest, he decided to publish the picture on the front page of his newspaper.

Buddy Wisser was as surprised as anyone else at what happened next. Buddy thought of himself as a hard-working editor putting together a few facts. He had no idea of the chain reaction that would be set off by the Seeley picture.

For Marvin Seeley's photo touched off the most heated, and certainly the oddest, battle of the war. This battle did not take place in the streets. It took place entirely in words, and it was to prove the turning point in the war.

Overnight all the newspapers in the city began to get letters about the pushcarts. The following letters, for instance, all appeared in the June 18th edition of one of the city papers:

Dear Mr. Editor:

If there aren't any pushcarts, where can you get peanuts in the park to feed the squirrels?

Larry Gilbert, Age 8

Dear Editor:

I work in the garment business. I sew the sleeves in coats. I have been sewing in the sleeves for 35 years and I like my job, but I do not make so much money that I can eat my lunch in a restaurant. What I like to do is to buy a hot dog & sauerkraut, or else a hot sweet potato, from the pushcart of Harry the Hot Dog.

Harry comes by my place of business every noon hour. From Harry the Hot Dog, you can buy for twenty cents a good lunch. For twenty-five cents, even a piece of fruit afterward. Several of my friends buy the same.

Bessie Schwartz

Dear Editor:

My husband has a pushcart, and if they make the pushcarts get off the streets, I don't know what I will do because the only peace I get is when he is pushing the cart. I love my husband, but a man should have some work to do.

Mrs. Bertha Beneker

Dear Editor:

Every afternoon when we get out of school, we buy Good Humors from the Good Humor pushcart that stops by our school playground. If we cannot get a Good Humor after a hard day at school, we will be pretty mad.

Sally Beck
Harold Jayne
Keith Amish
Robert Williams
Gene Smith
Mary Wahle
Vivien Vercrouse
George Vogt
Joe Maier
Betty Rosenbauer
Arlene Enderlin
Bernie Schreiber
Ballison Fulton
Warren Heard
Warren Neely
Vera Burkhardt
Eleanor Rojanski
(The Second Grade of P.S. 42)

Dear Editor:

I would be grateful if you would print in your paper that I am 99 years old and cannot walk very far. A pushcart with bananas comes by my door every morning and stops outside my window if I wave my hand. I live almost entirely on bananas, and I do not know what I would do without this pushcart.

Mrs. Clara Washington

Dear Editor:

I am in the plastic objects business, and all the plastic objects I get come packed in big cardboard cartons. After I unpack the merchandise, I have to get rid of the cartons, because I have no room in my shop for such big boxes.

A truck will charge me $10 an hour to take the boxes away, because the truckers cannot be bothered for less. But there is a man with a pushcart who will take away these cartons at no cost to me, because he gets calls from people with merchandise to pack who need the cartons I do not need. If I have to pay a truck $10 an hour, I may as well go out of business.

E. Siegel

Dear Editor:

Last week a truck smashed in the fender of a lovely little car I bought in Paris, France. The driver did it on purpose. I know just how the pushcart men feel, and I think we should do everything we can to help them.

Nancy Raeburn

Dear Editor:

I am in the 2nd-hand and junk line, and I get almost all goods I sell in my shop from the pushcart men who go around the streets picking up things that people have thrown away, but which maybe someone else could use. I would like to ask you how I can stay in business if nobody picks up old toasters and chairs and all kinds of hardware. You'd be surprised what people are throwing out. I got from a pushcart last week an eggbeater practically as good as new. In addition, the pushcarts are cleaning up the streets.

Si Biski

Dear Editor:

I am an artistic person, and I want to say that I think the pushcarts with their striped umbrellas and big old-fashioned wheels are a very pretty sight. I have painted many pictures of pushcarts. All of the trucks are ugly.

R. Solbert

Dear Editor:

Here is a fact I know will be of interest to all animal lovers. My cocker spaniel named Cookie, who has been with me for eleven years, grows very nervous whenever a big truck passes us on the street. But she loves pushcarts and will go right up to one and let the owner pet her. Now that there are so many trucks on the streets, I really dread taking Cookie for a walk.

Arthur Winkle

Dear Editor:

A year ago I retired to the island of Rubanga. There are no trucks on Rubanga. We make our own peanut butter, and I am very happy.

I am sorry to read that you are still having trouble in the city.

Archie Love

Dear Editor:

I have never written a letter to a newspaper before, but the picture of that Mighty Mammoth hitting that pushcart has upset me so much that I cannot sleep at night. The whole thing does not seem right to me.

Jean F. Merrill

Dear Editor:

Is New York being run for trucks or people? Pushcarts are pushed by people who sell goods to other people who buy from the pushcarts out of choice. Who needs 400 cartons of peanut butter?

Committee for the Preservation
of Pushcarts

Dear Editor:

Since crowded streets seem to be our trouble, wouldn't it be more helpful to get rid of 300,000 trucks than 500 pushcarts?

Committee for the Revocation
of Truck Licenses

Dear Editor:

I just hate trucks.

A Loyal Reader

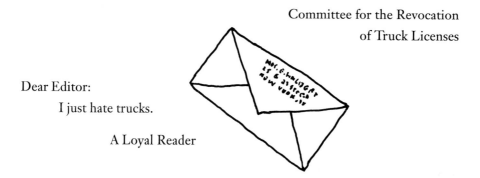

Dear Editor:

I have followed with interest the concern your readers have been expressing over the plight of the pushcart peddlers in your city. It may interest your readers to know that in our city (Harmony, Illinois), we have passed a law which makes the sale, manufacture, or operation of a truck a criminal offense, punishable by a fine of $20,000 or 20 years in jail.

Elmer P. Kusse

Dear Editor:

I have read about Maxie Hammerman, the Pushcart King, in your paper. I am wondering why there isn't any Pushcart Queen. It is my ambition when I grow up to be the Pushcart Queen.

Alice Myles, Age 10

This was only the beginning. Each letter to an editor that was published seemed to inspire a hundred other people to write. Buddy Wisser said that he had never received so much mail in his entire life as an editor as suddenly came to him on the subject of pushcarts. Even though the editors could publish only a very small sampling of the letters they received, about one out of a thousand, the "Letters to the Editor" sections of the newspapers were within a week taking up so much space that several papers had to cut out their sports, news, and comic sections.

The truck drivers did not know what to make of the hundreds of letters in the newspapers. It appeared from the letters that *everyone* who was not a truck driver was on the side of the pushcarts.

Some of the truck drivers tried to laugh off the letters. "What are a few letters to the newspapers?" they asked each other. "Everyone knows only crackpots write to the papers."

Mayor Emmett P. Cudd, however, was not laughing. "Crackpots have a vote like everyone else," he told his wife, Ethel P. Cudd. "And enough crackpots could vote a mayor into office. Or out," he added.

The Three were not laughing either. When Big Moe read Elmer P. Kusse's letter about making the driving of a truck a criminal offense, Big Moe knew it was time to surrender.

It was clear to Big Moe that the people of New York were already on the side of the pushcarts. If the Mayor's threat to revoke the pushcart licenses was carried out, people would be even angrier with the trucks. The possibility of people voting the trucks off the street entirely, as Elmer P. Kusse suggested, was not a risk Big Moe was willing to take.

Louie Livergreen wanted to proceed with the Master Plan. He said that once Operation Krushkar was rolling, people would be afraid to vote against the trucks. However, Big Moe's faith in the Master Plan had not been the same since Maxie Hammerman had captured his bulletproof Italian car. And the word "extinct" in Mack's special delivery letter had sent shivers down his spine.

"How can the Master Plan be carried out," asked Big Moe, "when we are in so much trouble with the pushcarts which you guaranteed would be a push-over?"

The Tiger voted with Big Moe to come to terms with the pushcarts and on July 4th, Big Moe telephoned the Mayor, who was just about to call Big Moe.

Big Moe told the Mayor that he was willing to meet with Maxie Hammerman and work out an agreement that would be acceptable to both sides. This was exactly what the Mayor had been about to suggest and was, of course, exactly what the Peace Army had been fighting for.

"In other words," said Maxie Hammerman, looking more surprised than he had ever looked in his life, "we have won the war."

CHAPTER XXXIV

The Battle of Bleecker Street

If any of the truck drivers thought Big Moe had given in too easily to the letters to the editors, The Battle of Bleecker Street convinced them otherwise. This was a freak battle in that it took place after Big Moe's surrender, but before the Pushcart Peace Conference which spelled out the terms of the surrender.

The day after Big Moe's surrender, all the pushcarts were on the streets again. Wherever they appeared, people cheered wildly, especially down on Bleecker Street.

On Bleecker Street, between Sixth and Seventh Avenues, some dozen pushcarts lined up, end-to-end, along the north curb every day to form a kind of outdoor market. From the pushcarts on Bleecker Street, a housewife could buy anything she needed in the fresh fruit and vegetable line, without ever having to step inside a store.

On the day after Big Moe's surrender, the pushcarts that regularly did business on Bleecker Street were joined by many of their friends. For it seemed likely that the outdoor market would attract many people after all the newspaper stories about the Pushcart War.

There must have been thirty pushcarts in Bleecker Street that morning, and there was still more business than the pushcarts could handle. Women crowded around the carts, exclaiming over the quality of the fruit and comparing bargains.

Papa Peretz, who had come down to join the fun — although fruit and vegetables were not his line — had sold out a cart of pretzels by ten o'clock and was waltzing in the street with one of the customers. At about 10:05, while everyone was cheering the waltzers, half a dozen trucks came down the street.

"Here they come!" shouted an excitable young woman. "Those dirty trucks!" And she picked a ripe cantaloupe out of a sack of cantaloupes she had just purchased and hurled it straight through the open window of one of the trucks.

The driver she hit crashed into the truck ahead of him, and the trucks behind him slammed on their brakes. Then before the pushcart peddlers realized what was happening, their customers were all grabbing cantaloupes and tomatoes and peaches from the crates on the curb where the peddlers threw any spoiled vegetables and fruits they found in unpacking their produce each morning.

"Have a peach," a lady shouted, pitching a mouldy peach at another truck.

"Have a melon," called another.

"A nice soft pear!"

"A rotten apple!"

"A little salad," said someone, tossing out a head of lettuce.

"A nice fresh fish!" The owner of a fish store along the sidewalk could not resist making a contribution and flung a fat flounder into one of the cabs.

"All the tomatoes you want!" said an old lady, generously emptying her whole shopping bag.

The truck drivers leaped from their trucks and tried to run for cover, but they were surrounded. The ladies were pelting them from all sides. A truck driver dodged an overripe mango, only to be conked by a cabbage.

The air was filled with flying fruit and vegetables — peaches, pears, apples, pomegranates, cucumbers, cabbages, and cantaloupes. Mainly cantaloupes, as this fruit had just come into season.

At 10:30, a siren sounded, and a police car screeched around the corner. Two policemen leaped from the car and seized a redheaded woman who was carefully aiming a cantaloupe.

"Hey, lady," said one of the officers, "the war's over. Haven't you heard?"

"Certainly," she said. "We're just celebrating."

"Oh," said the policeman, and looking around, he could see that everyone was laughing and in the best of spirits.

"Well, in that case," the officer said — and he took the cantaloupe from her hand and hurled it with deadly accuracy right into the back of a fleeing truck driver, knocking the fellow headlong into a cart of tomatoes.

"You're wonderful!" shouted the redheaded lady, clapping her hands and kissing the policeman. It was a wild morning.

Fifty police cars had to be dispatched to the scene before any kind of order could be restored. And then it was really only the truck drivers' finally escaping into a subway entrance that brought an end to the fighting.

The police made no arrests. The situation was clearly a case of a city celebrating the end of a long and tiring war.

It was an expensive celebration for the pushcart peddlers. In the excitement, the ladies — when they had used up the spoiled fruit and vegetables — had helped themselves to perfectly good produce from the pushcarts. Most of the ladies offered afterwards to pay the peddlers for what they had used, but many did not know which cart they had taken the fruit from. And the peddlers did not want to take their money anyway.

The pushcart peddlers were grateful for the support of the people of the city. And they told the ladies that a few melons and peaches were the least they could contribute to the celebration.

After the Battle of Bleecker Street, the truck drivers urged Big Moe to press for a peace conference at the earliest date possible. The Mayor was glad to oblige.

It might be mentioned here that one of New York's most colorful holidays, Cantaloupe Day — or The Feast of the Cantaloupes, as it is called in Bleecker Street — is a holiday in celebration of the armistice that marked the end of the Pushcart War.

On this day, July 5th, anyone shopping in Bleecker Street is given a free cantaloupe by the fruit peddlers there. At night the street is lit up and gaily-decorated booths line the street. One can buy Big Moe dolls and paper pushcarts and souvenir maps of the battlegrounds of the Pushcart War (replicas of Maxie Hammerman's famous battle map). There is dancing in the streets and a pea shooter contest for children. The Feast of the Cantaloupes attracts many tourists, and, indeed, no visitor to New York should miss it.

CHAPTER XXXV

The Pushcart Peace Conference & The Formulation of the Flower Formula for Peace

The Pushcart Peace Conference opened on July 13th. After the long summer of bitter fighting, representatives of both sides met in the City Council chambers.

Big Moe and Mack represented the truckers. Maxie Hammerman and General Anna spoke for the pushcart peddlers. Buddy Wisser and Wenda Gambling represented the general public. Mayor Emmett P. Cudd presided over the Conference.

General Anna's terms for peace were simple: "The City Council should revoke all truck licenses."

Big Moe protested. He had come to bargain, he said. "That is not a bargain. That is total surrender."

"Why should we settle for less?" said General Anna.

Maxie Hammerman explained to Big Moe that General Anna had lost two carts in the war and naturally felt a little bitter on that account.

This led to the first two conditions of the peace: the first, that Mammoth Moving must pay for all damages to pushcarts, goods, and peddlers caused by Mack's driving into the Peace Army; second, that Mack was to have his driving license revoked for a period of one year.

The third condition agreed upon had to do with the size of the trucks that should be allowed in the city. There was some difference of opinion as to how big was too big.

The majority of those present at the Peace Conference felt that trucks the size of the Mighty Mammoths (or Leaping Lemas or Ten-Ton Tigers) were "much too big." They also agreed that trucks the size of the Mama Mammoths were "perhaps bigger than they needed to be."

Wenda Gambling insisted to the end that even the Baby Mammoths were too big. Big Moe pleaded that for moving a big item like a power plant, a truck had to be "a little bit big." And it was finally agreed that a few trucks could be as big as the Baby Mammoths, but that *no* truck should be any bigger.

The fourth condition provoked the most argument. This had to do with the number of trucks that should be licensed for use in the city. Even Maxie Hammerman conceded that the city needed a *few* trucks.

"I, myself, will call a truck sometimes," Maxie admitted. "The fact is that if I order a whole truckload of lumber for building pushcarts, I get a better price on the lumber than when I order a few boards at a time."

Big Moe was prepared to agree to a *few* less trucks. General Anna wanted to hold out for a *lot* less. It looked as if the Peace Conference was going to bog down on this point. It might have, if it had not been for Buddy Wisser proposing, after the argument had run on for four days, that the Conference consider a compromise based on the Flower Formula.

The Flower Formula was something Frank the Flower had worked out while shooting darts in jail. He had told Buddy Wisser about it when Buddy went to see him in connection with his study of Marvin Seeley's picture.

The formula was really very simple. So simple, in fact, that many people afterwards said, "*I could have told them that.*" But as no one had, Frank the Flower is given official credit.

Every high school student in New York is now familiar with the Flower Formula. Here is the formula as it appears on page 16 of the new edition of the math book now used in all New York City schools:

$$If: \quad T = trucks$$
$$And: \quad t = time$$
$$Then: \quad 1/2T = 1/2t$$

The example given with the formula on page 16 is the same one that was originally presented to the Pushcart Peace Conference:

If: there are 100,000 trucks (100,000 T) in the city, traffic will be so bad that it will take 10 hours (10t) to deliver a load of potatoes from 1st Street to 100th Street.

But if: there are only 1/2 as many trucks (50,000 T), traffic will only be 1/2 as bad, and it will take only 1/2 as long (5t) to deliver a load of potatoes from 1st Street to 100th Street.

Therefore: one truck can make two trips in one day.

Which means: 50,000 trucks, making two trips a day, can deliver as many potatoes as 100,000 trucks making one trip.

Moreover: if the potato dealer is paying the truckers by the hour, he will be getting two loads delivered for the price of one.

Thus: he can sell the potatoes for less (which his customers will appreciate).

Result: everybody (including pushcart peddlers) will be happier.

Professor Lyman Cumberly has pointed out that the fascinating thing about the Flower Formula is that its principle can be carried even further than was proposed at the Pushcart Peace Conference. For example, says Professor Cumberly:

If: there are only 1/4 as many trucks, traffic will be only 1/4 as bad (that is to say, 4 times faster), and you will get 4 loads of potatoes for the price of one.

Or: if there are only 1/10 as many trucks, traffic will be 10 times as fast, etc.;

Or: if there are only 1/100 as many trucks, traffic will be 100 times as fast, etc.

One could, in fact, Professor Cumberly says jokingly, keep on reducing the number of trucks almost indefinitely without hurting business at all.

It is unlikely, however, that Big Moe would have agreed at the Peace Conference to so drastic a reduction of trucks as Professor Cumberly has visualized. He did agree to the one-half formula, and as Maxie Hammerman pointed out, the fact that the one-half remaining trucks would be approximately one-half as big as most of the trucks had been before the war meant that the pushcarts had won the equivalent of an agreement to four times fewer trucks.

There was an additional condition in the peace treaty. This fifth condition was an amnesty clause; it provided that Frank the Flower, in view of his contribution to the fourth condition of the treaty, should be excused from serving the balance of the sentence he would normally be expected to serve for the willful destruction of 18,991 truck tires.

The final act of the Peace Conference was to draw up the Courtesy Act (which the City Council passed by a unanimous vote the following week). The Courtesy Act made it a criminal offense for a larger vehicle to take advantage of a smaller vehicle in any way.

CHAPTER XXXVI

The Post-War Years: A Few Last Words About Albert P. Mack, Wenda Gambling, Joey Kafflis, General Anna, Harry the Hot Dog, Mayor Emmett P. Cudd, Frank the Flower, Louie Livergreen, and Alice Myles, the Pushcart Queen

In the ten years since the Pushcart War, the Courtesy Act has been strictly observed by most of the truck drivers in New York. There have been exceptions, of course. Albert P. Mack has been arrested nineteen times for violation of the Act and is now serving a life sentence. But, as Professor Cumberly says, that might have been predicted.

What no one would have predicted, however, was that Wenda Gambling would marry a former truck driver. She is now Mrs. Joey Kafflis. A few years ago Joey Kafflis sold his diary to a movie company that was making a movie about the Pushcart War, and by coincidence Wenda Gambling was chosen to play the part of Wenda Gambling, and in this way she met Joey Kafflis.

TITLE: The Pushcart War
STARRING: Wenda Gambling
LOCATION: LOT # 6
PRODUCER: John Wright DATE: 8/6

In the movie version of the Pushcart War, Wenda Gambling *does* fire the opening shot in the historic Pea Shooter Campaign, and she also appears in the front lines of the Peace March, right between General Anna and Morris the Florist. In the Peace March she is shown pushing a cart of secondhand shoes. A few of Wenda's admirers did not recognize her in this scene as she is wearing a shawl over her head.

In the movie it is Wenda Gambling, of course, rather than General Anna, who saves Morris the Florist's life. Although Wenda herself is seriously wounded, she manages to pull Morris to safety.

It is perhaps just as well that General Anna did not live to see the movie version of the Peace March. She died a few years after the Pushcart War at the age of eighty-one, and there is now a statue of her in Tompkins Square Park, the first statue of a pushcart peddler ever to be placed in a city park. The inscription beneath the statue reads simply: "By Hand."

Among the officials who spoke at the dedication of General Anna's statue was the Honorable Harold L. Kugelman, better known to veterans of the Pushcart War as Harry the Hot Dog. At that time, Harry had just been appointed Target Chief for the New York City Moon Exploration Bureau. (This is the department that sent the successful "Pea-Pin" Rocket to the north side of the moon last year.)

Harry was named as Target Chief for the MEB by none other than Mayor Emmett P. Cudd. For Mayor Cudd, despite his questionable role in the Pushcart War, was re-elected after the war for a third term.

In his post-war campaign, Mayor Cudd ran for re-election on a Potato Platform ("Two Potatoes for the Price of One" — a slogan that won him many more votes than his Peanut Butter Platform of the previous election). It was this campaign that earned the Mayor the nickname "Potato Head."

One of the yet unresolved mysteries of the war is the whereabouts of Louie Livergreen. Louie disappeared from his offices on Second Avenue a few days after Big Moe's surrender to the pushcarts.

Louie's secretary told the police that certain documents (among them, the LEMA Master Plan for the Streets of New York) had disappeared from her employer's files at the same time her employer dropped from view. It is widely believed that the AST (Association of Small Truckers) had something to do with Louie's disappearance, but this has never been proved.

There was also a rumor at one point that Louie was alive and hiding out in Dallas, Texas, where he was said to be operating an earth-moving machinery business under another name. New York and Dallas police traced this rumor to the fact that there was a firm in Dallas known as LEMA (Lucky Earth-Moving Associates). However, on investigation, it appeared that the firm was run by a Mr. Jim Lucky, one of the best-liked young businessmen in Dallas. Jim Lucky sued a Houston newspaper for printing the rumor, which he claimed was damaging his business reputation, and since then other papers have been cautious about printing Livergreen stories.

And, finally, we cannot conclude this account of the Pushcart War without mentioning Alice Myles. Alice, who at the age of ten had written to the editor of a newspaper to say that her ambition was to be the Pushcart Queen, is well on her way to getting her wish.

Alice attended a very good vocational school and now has her own pushcart shop. Last year she built almost as many carts as Maxie Hammerman. Maxie says he does not mind the competition. He is about to retire and is glad that Alice will be carrying on the good work.

"That is what we fought the war for," Maxie says, "so that there should always be a few pushcarts in the city of New York."

Responding to *The Pushcart War*

Thinking and Discussing

What features make the novel seem to be the history of an actual event? What clues are given that it is not a true story?

In what ways do Mr. Jerusalem and Old Anna change during the story? What causes these characters to change? How do you think they felt after the Pushcart Peace Conference?

Choosing a Creative Response

Reporting on the War Assemble a newspaper front page containing stories about the Pushcart War. First write one or two short articles about the cause of the war, major battles, key figures, or anything else that might interest readers. Be sure that each lead paragraph tells who, what, when, where, and why about the subject. Then draw pictures to illustrate the stories. Think of catchy headlines for the stories.

Creating Your Own Activity Plan and complete your own activity in response to *The Pushcart War*.

Thinking and Writing

Reread the events surrounding the Daffodil Massacre in Chapter I of *The Pushcart War*, and the Tacks Tax and British Ultimatum in Chapter XIX. Then do some research about the American Revolution.

Write several paragraphs comparing the fictional Pushcart War with the American war for independence. Make the following comparisons: the Daffodil Massacre and the Boston Massacre; the Tacks Tax and the Stamp and Tea acts; the British Ultimatum and Britain's response to rebellion in America.

Thinking About Novels

Satirizing Your Own Experience One way to write a satire is to transform a minor event into something of great importance. In *The Pushcart War*, traffic problems become important enough to cause a war.

Write a story of your own that satirizes a minor incident in your life. Magnify the event's importance by exaggerating the ways it affects your town, or even your country or the world. Give yourself a central role. When you have finished the satire, share it with your classmates.

Comparing Satire with Historical Fiction *The Pushcart War* is based on fictional historical events. How does it compare with novels based on real historical events? Working with a group, complete this chart and use the information to discuss the similarities and differences between *The Pushcart War* and historical fiction. Which novels have realistic settings? Which novels have realistic main characters? Are the plots and outcomes imaginary or real? How does the purpose of satire differ from that of historical fiction?

Satire:	Historical fiction:
The Pushcart War	_____
Time	Time
Place	Place
Main Characters	Main Characters
Plot	Plot
Outcome	Outcome

VANILLA
CHOCOLATE
STRAWBERRY
RASPBERRY
ORANGE
CHOC-CHIP
COCOA CRUNCH
MOCHA
VANILLA/
raisin

COLD
DRINKS

ICE CREAM

About the Author

Jean Merrill

Jean Merrill was born in Rochester, New York, in 1923. She grew up on a farm and spent most of her childhood years, when she was not in school, outdoors. She says, "The only thing that could detain me indoors was a book — though a book could also be carried up into a tree, out to a meadow, down by the lakeside."

After graduating from college, Merrill spent five years working as a writer and editor for Scholastic Magazines, Inc., in New York City. It was during this time that she realized how trucks tyrannized city streets. "My reaction . . . was to take refuge in a fantasy of suitable revenge," says Merrill. "The one that gave me the most satisfaction was imagining myself equipped with an inconspicuous weapon, a kind of miniature blow-gun that propelled a tiny dart sufficiently lethal to penetrate a truck tire. . . . [*The Pushcart War*] is essentially an elaboration of my personal David and Goliath fantasy." In 1965, *The Pushcart War* won the Lewis Carroll Shelf Award and the Boys' Clubs of America Award.

Merrill has written many different types of books for young people. She has published picture books and folktales for early readers, as well as more sophisticated books for older readers, including the fable *The Black Sheep* and the realistic stories *Maria's House* and *The Toothpaste Millionaire*. *The Toothpaste Millionaire* received the Dorothy Canfield Fisher Memorial Children's Book Award and the Sequoyah Award.

Today Merrill lives in Vermont, six months of the year on an old hill farm in Washington, and the rest of the year in the nearby town of Randolph.

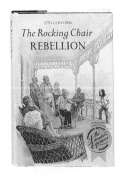

The Rocking Chair Rebellion by Eth Clifford (Houghton, 1978) Opie's parents have firm ideas about what she should be when she grows up, but she takes a course of her own when she starts working at the Maple Ridge Home for the Aged and finds herself in the middle of the Rocking Chair Rebellion.

The Glad Man by Gloria Gonzalez (Knopf, 1975) Mellissa and her little brother, Troy, meet an old man living with his dog in a run-down bus in the city dump. The friendship deepens, but at the same time the old man's life is disrupted. Mellissa and Troy have to find a way to help.

MORE FROM THE

Joan Aiken's Black Hearts in Battersea series begins with **The Wolves of Willoughby Chase** (Doubleday, 1963; Dell, 1987). These nineteenth-century adventures are filled with danger, mystery, and humor. Fifteen-year-old Simon uncovers a wicked plot to overthrow the king of England in **Black Hearts in Battersea** (Doubleday, 1964; Dell, 1981). The series continues with **Nightbirds on Nantucket** (Doubleday, 1966; Dell, 1981), **The Cuckoo Tree** (Doubleday, 1971; Dell, 1988), **The Stolen Lake** (Delacorte, 1981; Dell, 1988), and **Dido & Pa** (Delacorte, 1986; Dell, 1988).

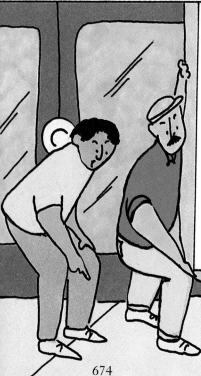

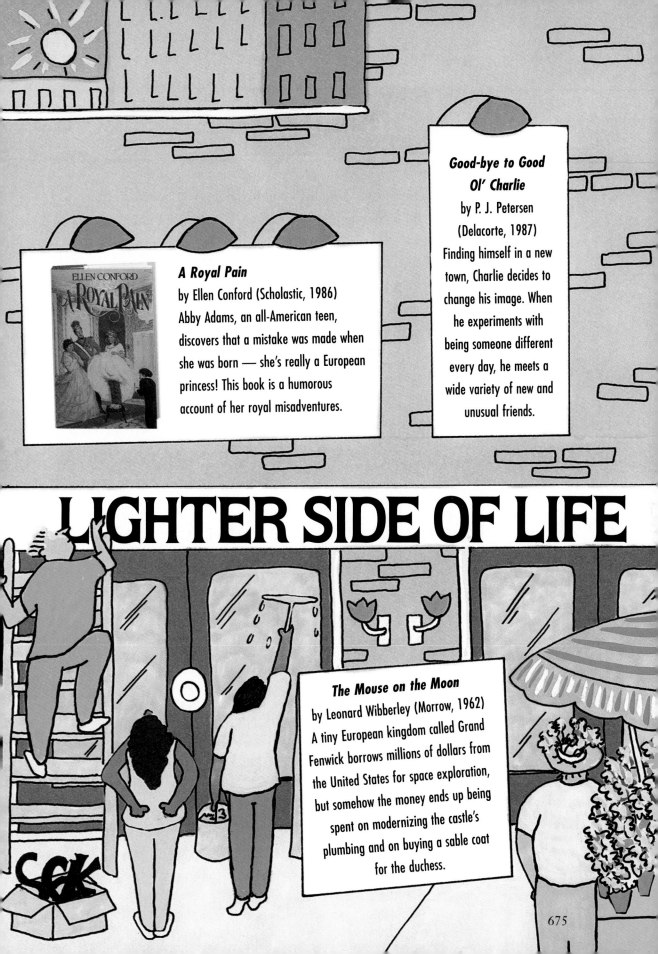

A Royal Pain
by Ellen Conford (Scholastic, 1986)
Abby Adams, an all-American teen, discovers that a mistake was made when she was born — she's really a European princess! This book is a humorous account of her royal misadventures.

Good-bye to Good Ol' Charlie
by P. J. Petersen (Delacorte, 1987)
Finding himself in a new town, Charlie decides to change his image. When he experiments with being someone different every day, he meets a wide variety of new and unusual friends.

LIGHTER SIDE OF LIFE

The Mouse on the Moon
by Leonard Wibberley (Morrow, 1962)
A tiny European kingdom called Grand Fenwick borrows millions of dollars from the United States for space exploration, but somehow the money ends up being spent on modernizing the castle's plumbing and on buying a sable coat for the duchess.

Glossary

Some of the words in this book may have pronunciations or meanings you do not know. This glossary can help you by telling you how to pronounce those words and by telling you the meanings with which those words are used in this book.

You can find out the correct pronunciation of any glossary word by using the special spelling after the word and the pronunciation key that runs across the bottom of the glossary pages.

The full pronunciation key opposite shows how to pronounce each consonant and vowel in a special spelling. The pronunciation key at the bottom of the glossary pages is a shortened form of the full key.

FULL PRONUNCIATION KEY

Consonant Sounds

b	**bib**	k	**c**at, **kick**, pi**que**	th	pa**th**, **thin**
ch	**church**	l	**l**i**d**, need**l**e	*th*	ba**th**e, **th**is
d	**deed**	m	a**m**, **m**an, **mum**	v	ca**v**e, **v**al**v**e,
f	**f**ast, **f**i**f**e, o**ff**,	n	**n**o, sudde**n**		**v**ine
	phase, rou**gh**	ng	thi**ng**	w	**w**ith
g	**g**a**g**	p	**p**o**p**	y	**y**es
h	**h**at	r	**r**oa**r**	z	**r**o**s**e, **s**i**z**e,
hw	**wh**ich	s	mi**ss**, **s**au**c**e, **s**ee		**x**ylophone,
j	**j**u**dg**e	sh	di**sh**, **sh**ip		**z**ebra
		t	**t**igh**t**	zh	gara**g**e,
					plea**s**ure, vi**s**ion

Vowel Sounds

ă	p**a**t	î	d**ea**r, d**ee**r,	ou	c**ow**, **ou**t
ā	**ai**d, th**ey**, p**ay**		f**ie**rce, m**e**re	ŭ	c**u**t, r**ou**gh
â	**air**, c**are**, w**ear**	ŏ	p**o**t, h**o**rrible	û	f**ir**m, h**ear**d,
ä	f**a**ther	ō	g**o**, r**ow**, t**oe**		t**er**m, t**ur**n,
ě	p**e**t, pl**ea**sure	ô	**a**lter, c**au**ght,		w**or**d
ē	b**e**, b**ee**, **ea**sy,		f**or**, p**aw**	yo͞o	ab**u**se, **u**se
	s**ei**ze	oi	b**oy**, n**oi**se, **oi**l	ə	**a**bout, sil**e**nt,
ĭ	p**i**t	o͝o	b**oo**k		penc**i**l, lem**o**n,
ī	b**y**, g**uy**, p**ie**	o͞o	b**oo**t		circ**u**s
				ər	butt**er**

STRESS MARKS

Primary Stress '	*Secondary Stress* '
bi•ol•o•gy [bī **ŏl′**ə jē]	bi•o•log•i•cal [bī′ə **lŏj′**ĭ kəl]

Pronunciation key © 1986 by Houghton Mifflin Company. Adapted and reprinted by permission from *The Houghton Mifflin Student Dictionary*.

A

a·bound·ing (ə **bound**'ĭng) *adj.* Possessing in abundant or plentiful supply: *Because of good weather, the market is **abounding** in fresh vegetables.*

ab·so·lute (ăb'sə lōōt') *adj.* Not limited in any way: *The caged bird longed for **absolute** freedom.*

ab·stract·ly (ăb **străkt**'lē) *adv.* Beyond the concrete or factual: *To understand a theory, one must think **abstractly**.*

a·bun·dance (ə **bŭn**'dəns) *n.* A great amount or quantity; a plentiful supply: *an **abundance** of natural resources.*

a·byss (ə **bĭs**') *n.* A huge emptiness: *From the rim of the canyon, they looked down into the **abyss**.*

ac·com·pa·ni·ment (ə **kŭm**'pə nĭ mənt) *or* (ə **kŭmp**'nĭ-) *n.* Music to be performed along with another presentation, such as a dance: *The loud **accompaniment** overwhelmed the singer's voice.*

ac·count for (ə **kount**' fôr) *v.* **Idiom.** To be responsible for: *Carelessness **accounts for** many accidents.*

a·cous·tic (ə **kōō**'stĭk) *adj.* Of sound or the sense of hearing.

a·cute (ə **kyōōt**') *adj.* Sharp and intense: *an **acute** pain.*

ag·o·ny (**ăg**'ə nē) *n.* Intense and prolonged pain and suffering.

am·bi·dex·trous (ăm'bĭ **dĕk**'strəs) *adj.* Able to use both hands equally well; neither right-handed nor left-handed.

am·ble (**ăm**'bəl) *v.* **am·bled, am·bling.** To walk or move along at a slow, leisurely pace: *My neighbor waved as I went **ambling** by.*

a·mi·a·ble (**ā**'mē ə bəl) *adj.* Friendly; good-natured.

am·nes·ty (**ăm**'nĭ stē) *n.* A governmental pardon, especially for political offenses.

an·tic·i·pate (ăn **tĭs**'ə pāt') *v.* **an·tic·i·pat·ed, an·tic·i·pat·ing.** To foresee, expect, or consider in advance: *We hadn't **anticipated** so many guests.*

Abundance *comes from the Latin word* abundare, *meaning "to overflow." In Latin, the words "abound" and "abundance" have the same origin. In English, both words involve the same concept or idea.*

The Latin for "skillful; on the right side" is dexter. *The Latin prefix* ambi-, *which means "both," was combined with* dexter *to form the word* **ambidextrous,** *meaning "able to use both hands well" or "able to use both hands as well as most people use their right hands."*

ă pat / ā pay / â care / ä father / ĕ pet / ē be / ĭ pit / ī pie / î fierce / ŏ pot / ō go / ô paw, for /

anx•i•e•ty (ăng zī′ĭ tē) *n.* A feeling of uneasiness and distress about something in the future; worry: *He was filled with anxiety about the test.*

ap•palled (ə pôld′) *adj.* Filled with horror and amazement.

ap•pa•ri•tion (ăp′ə rĭsh′ən) *n.* A strange or unusual sight: *The painting of wildflowers captured an apparition of beauty.*

ap•peal (ə pēl′) *n.* The transfer or request for transfer of a case from a lower court to a higher court for a new hearing: *The defendant's lawyer filed an appeal with the Supreme Court.*

ar•chae•o•log•i•cal (är′kē ə lŏj′ĭ kəl) *adj.* Of or concerned with the scientific study of the remains of past human activities, such as burials, buildings, tools, and pottery.

ar•du•ous (är′jōō əs) *adj.* Demanding great effort; difficult.

a•ris•to•crat (ə rĭs′tə krăt′) *or* (ăr′ĭ stə-) *n.* A member of a social class based on inherited wealth, status, and sometimes titles.

ar•mi•stice (är′mĭ stĭs) *n.* A suspension of fighting between two armies by agreement; a truce.

ar•ti•san (är′tĭ zən) *n.* One manually skilled in making a certain product; a craftsman.

as•cent (ə sĕnt′) *n.* The act of climbing up.

as•sert (ə sûrt′) *v.* **as•sert•ed, as•sert•ing.** To state or declare positively; claim: *The witness asserted that his story was true.*

as•trol•o•ger (ə strŏl′ə jər) *n.* One who predicts the course of human events through the study of the positions of the stars and planets, which are believed to have a supernatural influence.

a•vert (ə vûrt′) *v.* **a•vert•ed, a•vert•ing.** To keep from happening; prevent: *A guard was placed at the crossing for the purpose of averting an accident.*

artisan

*An obsolete meaning for **astrologer** was "astronomer" or "one who studies the stars for scientific purposes." Because the English language has changed over many years, "astronomer" now refers to scientific study, and **astrologer** refers to supernatural prediction.*

bar•ren (băr′ən) *adj.* Lacking or unable to produce growing plants or crops.

---

oi **oil** / o͞o **book** / o͞o **boot** / ou **out** / ŭ **cut** / û **fur** / *th* **the** / th **thin** / hw **which** / zh **vision** / ə **ago**, it**e**m, penc**i**l, at**o**m, circ**u**s

679

be•grudge (bǐ grŭj′) *v.* **be•grudged, be•grudg•ing.** To envy (someone) the possession or enjoyment of something: *She **begrudged** him his youth.*

be•rate (bǐ rāt′) *v.* **be•rat•ed, be•rat•ing.** To scold severely.

be•stow (bǐ stō′) *v.* **be•stowed, be•stow•ing.** To give or present, especially as a gift or honor: *The President **bestowed** a medal on the hero.*

be•wil•der•ing (bǐ wǐl′dər ǐng) *adj.* Greatly confusing; puzzling.

bleak (blēk) *adj.* Gloomy; dismal; cheerless: *The dimly lit room was **bleak** and uninviting.*

bril•liant (brǐl′yənt) *adj.* Excellent; wonderful: *She had a **brilliant** plan for the party.*

brine (brīn) *n.* Water that contains a large amount of dissolved salt, especially sodium chloride.

broad•cast (brôd′kăst′) *or* (-käst′) *v.* **broad•cast** *or* **broad•casted, broad•cast•ing.** To make known over a wide area: *He was **broadcasting** the rumor throughout the school.*

bu•reau•crat (byoor′ə krăt′) *n.* An official of a government managed through agencies and departments.

C

cam•paign (kăm pān′) *n.* A series of military operations that achieves a specific purpose in a certain area: *The **campaign** that won the war surprised the enemy.*

cas•u•al•ty (kăzh′oo əl tē) *n., pl.* **cas•u•al•ties.** A person who is killed, wounded, captured, or missing during a military action: *Medics treated the **casualties** after the battle.*

ca•tas•tro•phe (kə tăs′trə fē) *n.* A great and sudden disaster, such as an earthquake or flood.

Bureaucrat *comes from the French word* bureau, *meaning "woolen cover for a writing desk." The definition evolved from "woolen-covered desk" to "government agency where woolen-covered desks are used." From this definition came the word "bureaucracy," meaning "a government made up of agencies." Next came the word* **bureaucrat,** *which means "an official of an agency." In America, the word* **bureaucrat** *is often used in a negative way.*

ă pat / ā pay / â care / ä father / ĕ pet / ē be / ĭ pit / ī pie / î fierce / ŏ pot / ō go / ô paw, for /

cat•e•go•ry (kăt′ə gôr′ē) *or* (-gôr′ē) *n., pl.* **cat•e•go•ries.** A class or division in a system of classification: *The children were divided by age into* **categories** *for the contest.*

char•ac•ter (kăr′ĭk tər) *n.* A symbol, such as a letter or number, used in representing information, as in printing or writing.

cir•cum•spect (sûr′kəm spĕkt′) *adj.* Careful; cautious: *He was* **circumspect** *in shopping for a used car.*

cir•cum•stance (sûr′kəm stăns′) *n.* One of the conditions, facts, or events connected with and usually affecting another event, a person, or a course of action: *Traffic was one of the* **circumstances** *causing him to be late.* —**Idiom. under no circumstances.** In no case; never.

cli•max (klī′măks′) *n.* That point in a series of events marked by greatest intensity or effect, usually occurring at or near the end: *At the* **climax** *of the storm, the wind reached speeds of over fifty miles per hour.*

co•in•ci•dence (kō ĭn′sĭ dəns) *n.* A combination of events that, though accidental, is so unusual it seems to have been planned: *By a strange* **coincidence,** *founding father Thomas Jefferson died on the Fourth of July.*

col•league (kŏl′ēg′) *n.* A fellow member of a profession, staff, or organization; an associate.

com•pa•ra•ble (kŏm′pər ə bəl) *adj.* Capable of being compared; having like traits; similar or equivalent: *The two pumpkins were* **comparable** *in size.*

com•pel (kəm pĕl′) *v.* **com•pelled, com•pel•ling.** To make someone do something, as by force, necessity, or powerful influence: *The sudden storm* **compelled** *us to stay home.*

com•pe•tent (kŏm′pĭ tnt) *adj.* Able to do what is required; capable: *She is a* **competent** *attorney who wins many of her cases.*

com•plex (kəm plĕks′) *or* (kŏm′plĕks′) *adj.* Consisting of many connected parts; organized in a complicated way: *The game is hard to play because of* **complex** *rules.*

Character *comes from the Greek word* kharassein, *which means "to inscribe." The Greek word moved into the Latin language as* character, *meaning "a mark, sign, or distinctive quality."*

Compel *comes from the Latin word* compellere, *meaning "to push or drive together."*

---

oi **oi**l / o͞o b**oo**k / o͞o b**oo**t / ou **ou**t / ŭ c**u**t / û f**u**r / *th* **th**e / th **th**in / hw **wh**ich / zh vi**s**ion / ə **a**go, it**e**m, penc**i**l, at**o**m, circ**u**s

com•plex•i•ty (kəm **plĕk′**sĭ tē) *n., pl.* **com•plex•i•ties.** Something difficult to understand or figure out: *Most people experience* **complexities** *in their lives.*

com•po•sure (kəm **pō′**zhər) *n.* Control over one's emotions; calm: *A hero maintains* **composure** *in the face of danger.*

com•pro•mise (**kŏm′**prə mīz′) *n.* A settlement of differences between opposing sides in which each side gives up some of its claims and agrees to some of the demands of the other.

com•pute (kəm **pyoot′**) *v.* **com•put•ed, com•put•ing.** To work out a solution by mathematics; calculate.

con•clu•sion (kən **kloo′**zhən) *n.* A judgment or decision based on one's experience or one's examination of facts or results: *The jury reached their* **conclusions** *after studying the testimony.*

con•fi•dent (**kŏn′**fĭ dənt) *adj.* Feeling or showing self-assurance; sure of oneself; certain.

con•fine (kən **fīn′**) *v.* **con•fined, con•fin•ing.** To restrict in movement: *The rain* **confined** *the children to the house all day.*

con•fis•cate (**kŏn′**fĭ skāt′) *v.* **con•fis•cat•ed, con•fis•cat•ing.** To seize (private property) from someone in order that it may be withheld, redistributed, or destroyed.

con•flict (**kŏn′**flĭkt′) *n.* A clash of opposing ideas, interests, etc.

con•science (**kŏn′**shəns) *n.* An inner sense in a person that distinguishes right from wrong: *Let your* **conscience** *be your guide.* —*Idiom.* **on (one's) conscience.** Causing one to feel guilty.

con•scious•ness (**kŏn′**shəs nĭs) *n.* The condition of being able to perceive and understand what is happening: *She regained* **consciousness** *after fainting.*

con•so•la•tion (**kŏn′**sə **lā′**shən) *n.* Comfort during a time of disappointment or sorrow: *He turned to his parents for* **consolation**.

Confiscate *comes from the Latin* confiscare, *meaning "to seize for the public treasury." The original form was* com-, *meaning "together" and* fiscus, *meaning "treasury."*

ă pat / ā pay / â care / ä father / ĕ pet / ē be / ĭ pit / ī pie / î fierce / ŏ pot / ō go / ô paw, for /

con·sol·i·date (kən sŏl′ĭ dāt′) *v.* **con·sol·i·dat·ed, con·sol·i·dat·ing.** To make or become secure and strong: *He will* **consolidate** *support for the new school.*

con·spir·a·cy (kən spîr′ə sē) *n., pl.* **con·spir·a·cies.** A secret plan to commit an unlawful act.

con·sul·ta·tion (kŏn′səl tā′shən) *n.* A conference at which advice is given or views are exchanged.

con·tam·i·nate (kən tăm′ə nāt′) *v.* **con·tam·i·nat·ed, con·tam·i·nat·ing.** To make impure, bad, or less good by mixture or contact; pollute; foul.

con·temp·tu·ous·ly (kən tĕmp′chōō əs lē) *adv.* In a way that shows the feeling that someone or something is inferior and undesirable: *The team laughed* **contemptuously** *at their opponents.*

con·test (kən tĕst′) *or* (kŏn′ tĕst′) *v.* **con·test·ed, con·test·ing.** To dispute; challenge: *The heirs bitterly* **contested** *the will.*

con·tra·dict (kŏn′trə dĭkt′) *v.* **con·tra·dict·ed, con·tra·dict·ing.** To assert or express the opposite of (a statement): *The witness seemed to* **contradict** *his previous testimony.*

con·tra·dic·to·ry (kŏn′trə dĭk′tə rē) *adj.* Having elements or parts not in agreement: *The two eyewitness accounts were* **contradictory.**

con·trap·tion (kən trăp′shən) *n. Informal.* A mechanical device; a gadget.

con·tra·ry (kŏn′trĕr′ē) *adj.* Completely different; opposed: *contrary points of view.*

con·trive (kən trīv′) *v.* **con·trived, con·triv·ing.** To bring about through clever scheming: *The contestant* **contrived** *to win by cheating.*

con·tro·ver·sy (kŏn′trə vûr′sē) *n., pl.* **con·tro·ver·sies.** Argument; debate.

con·verse[1] (kən vûrs′) *v.* **con·versed, con·vers·ing.** To talk informally with others: **converse** *about family matters.*

Converse[1] *and* **converse**[2] *are related but separate words.* **Converse**[2] *comes from the Latin* com-, *which means "together or completely," plus* vertere, *"to turn."* **Converse**[1] *is from the Latin* com-, *meaning "together or with," plus* versari, *"to live or move around," which is related to* vertere, *"to turn."*

---

oi **oil** / ŏŏ **book** / ōō **boot** / ou **out** / ŭ **cut** / û **fur** / *th* **the** / th **thin** / hw **which** / zh **vision** / ə **ago, item, pencil, atom, circus**

crochet

con•verse² (kŏn′vûrs′) *n.* The opposite or reverse of something: *Dark is the converse of light.*

con•vey (kən vā′) *v.* **con•veyed, con•vey•ing.** To make known; communicate: *He phoned to convey his love.*

con•vic•tion (kən vĭk′shən) *n.* A strong opinion or belief: *People should act according to their convictions.*

cor•don (kôr′dn) *n.* A line of people, military posts, ships, etc., stationed around an area to protect or enclose it.

coun•ter (koun′tər) *v.* **coun•tered, coun•ter•ing.** To move, act, or speak in opposition to: *They counter the accusation with evidence.*

crav•ing (krā′vĭng) *n.* A very strong desire; yearning.

cre•vasse (krə văs′) *n.* A deep crack, as in a glacier; a narrow gorge.

crev•ice (krĕv′ĭs) *n.* A narrow crack or opening.

cro•chet (krō shā′) *v.* **cro•cheted, cro•chet•ing.** To make a piece of needlework by looping thread or yarn into connected links with a hooked needle.

cross•beam (krôs′bēm′) *or* (krŏs′-) *n.* A horizontal beam or girder.

cudg•el (kŭj′əl) *n.* A short, heavy club.

cul•ti•va•tion (kŭl′tə vā′shən) *n.* The process of tilling or growing: *They plowed the land for the cultivation of corn.*

cum•ber•some (kŭm′bər səm) *adj.* Clumsy and inefficient: *a cumbersome method of rowing.*

cu•ri•os•i•ty (kyo͞or′ē ŏs′ĭ tē) *n., pl.* **cu•ri•os•i•ties.** A desire to know or learn.

cur•ren•cy (kûr′ən sē) *or* (kŭr′-) *n., pl.* **cur•ren•cies.** Any form of money in actual use in a country.

cur•rent (kûr′ənt) *or* (kŭr′-) *n.* A mass of liquid or gas that is in motion: *A current of air leaked through the window.*

ă pat / ā pay / â care / ä father / ĕ pet / ē be / ĭ pit / ī pie / î fierce / ŏ pot / ō go / ô paw, for /

dam·sel (dăm′zəl) *n.* A young girl; maiden.

de·ceit·ful·ness (dĭ sēt′fəl nĕs) *n.* Being given to lying or making a person believe something that is not true: *He was struck by the deceitfulness of the traitors.*

de·cep·tion (dĭ sĕp′shən) *n.* Something that misleads a person, such as a trick or a lie.

de·jec·tion (dĭ jĕk′shən) *n.* Unhappiness; depression: *Her dejection over the loss was obvious.*

dense (dĕns) *adj.* Thick-headed; dull: *I felt dense when talking to the scholar.*

de·pressed (dĭ prĕst′) *adj.* Gloomy; low in spirits: *He feels depressed because his vacation is ending.*

de·scent (dĭ sĕnt′) *n.* The act of moving from a higher to a lower place: *Ice slowed their descent down the mountain.*

de·sir·a·bil·i·ty (dĭ zīr′ə bĭl′ĭ tē) *n.* Being of a pleasing quality; wanted: *The radio sold out quickly because of its desirability.*

des·o·late (dĕs′ə lĭt) *adj.* Having little or no vegetation and few or no inhabitants: *The desert seems a desolate, uninhabitable place.*

de·test (dĭ tĕst′) *v.* **de·test·ed, de·test·ing.** To dislike strongly.

di·ag·no·sis (dī′əg nō′sĭs) *n., pl.* **di·ag·no·ses.** The conclusion reached as a result of an examination to identify the nature of a disease or malfunction.

dif·fuse (dĭ fyoos′) *adj.* Widely spread or scattered: *The topics for the conference are varied and diffuse.*

di·lem·ma (dĭ lĕm′ə) *n.* A situation that requires a person to choose between courses of action that are equally difficult or unpleasant: *He faced the dilemma of giving in or losing his job.*

Desolate *comes from the Latin* de-, *meaning "completely," and* solus, *meaning "alone."*

oi **oil** / o͞o **book** / o͞o **boot** / ou **out** / ŭ **cut** / û **fur** / *th* **the** / th **thin** / hw **which** / zh **vision** / ə **ago, item, pencil, atom, circus**

di·min·ish (dĭ mĭn′ĭsh) *v.* **di·min·ished, di·min·ish·ing.** To make or become smaller or less: *A drought diminished their food supply.*

dis·crim·i·nate (dĭ skrĭm′ə nāt′) *v.* **dis·crim·i·nat·ed, dis·crim·i·nat·ing.** To act on the basis of prejudice; show unfairness: *The employers discriminated against some workers for union activity.*

dis·rupt (dĭs rŭpt′) *v.* **dis·rupt·ed, dis·rupt·ing.** To interrupt or block the progress or functioning of: *Floods disrupted transportation in the town.*

dom·i·nance (dŏm′ə nəns) *n.* Being the most influential or controlling; governing: *The colonists fought to free themselves from foreign dominance.*

doom (do͞om) *n.* A terrible fate, especially death or extinction: *send a person to his doom.*

draw (drô) *v.* **drew, drawn, draw·ing.** To pull or move so as to cover or uncover: *drawing the blankets up to her neck.* —*n.* A ditch or channel in the ground, usually worn by running water after a rain; gully: *The posse rode through the draw after the robbers.*

drone (drōn) *n.* A continuous low humming or buzzing sound: *The fumes from the highway are worse than the drone.*

dude (do͞od) *or* (dyo͞od) *n.* A visitor or newcomer to the American West.

dumb·found (dŭm′found′) *v.* **dumb·found·ed, dumb·found·ing.** Variation of **dumfound.** To make speechless with astonishment; stun: *They were dumbfounded by the surprise.*

dy·nas·ty (dī′nə stē) *n., pl.* **dy·nas·ties.** A succession of rulers from the same family or line: *The Ming dynasty ruled for three hundred years.*

Discriminate has two very different meanings, but neither meaning cancels the other out. One meaning is "to judge sensitively between." From this meaning came another meaning, "to judge unfairly against and act on the basis of prejudice."

Drone means either "a male bee" or "a continuous low humming or buzzing sound." The original meaning was "a male bee." The second meaning came from the sound made by bees.

ă pat / ā pay / â care / ä father / ĕ pet / ē be / ĭ pit / ī pie / î fierce / ŏ pot / ō go / ô paw, for /

e·con·o·my (ĭ kŏn′ə mē) *n.*, *pl.* **e·con·o·mies.** The management of the resources of a country, community, or business: *The American economy was once based on manufacturing.*

ed·i·ble (ĕd′ə bəl) *adj.* Capable of being eaten; fit to eat.

ee·rie (îr′ē) *adj.* Inspiring fear without being openly threatening; strangely unsettling; weird: *Imagining living on the moon was an eerie thought.*

ef·fect (ĭ fĕkt′) *n.* The power or ability to bring about a desired result; influence: *Even studying a little will have an effect.*

ef·fi·cien·cy (ĭ fĭsh′ən sē) *n.*, *pl.* **ef·fi·cien·cies.** The quality of acting or producing effectively with a minimum of waste, expense, or effort: *The antique car is not known for its efficiency.*

ef·fi·cient (ĭ fĭsh′ənt) *adj.* Acting or producing effectively with a minimum of waste, expense, or effort: *an efficient secretary.*

e·lab·o·rate (ĭ lăb′ər ĭt) *adj.* Having rich and complicated detail: *an elaborate map.*

el·lipse (ĭ lĭps′) *n.* A closed plane curve composed of all the points that have the sum of their distances from two fixed points equal to a constant.

e·mo·tion (ĭ mō′shən) *n.* **1.** Any strong excitement or stimulation, such as fright, rage, joy, etc., often involving characteristic chemical and physical changes in the function of the body. **2.** A strong, complicated feeling, such as love, sorrow, hate, etc.

en·a·ble (ĕn ā′bəl) *v.* **en·a·bled, en·a·bling.** To give the means, ability, or opportunity to do something: *Science has enabled us to probe the secrets of the universe.*

en·coun·ter (ĕn koun′tər) *v.* **en·coun·tered, en·coun·ter·ing.** To meet or come upon, especially unexpectedly: *We encountered new words in a book.*

en·deav·or (ĕn dĕv′ər) *n.* A major effort or attempt.

> **Economy** *is from the Greek word* oikonomia, *meaning* "*household management.*"

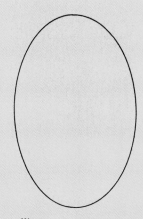

ellipse

oi **oil** / ŏŏ **book** / ōō **boot** / ou **out** / ŭ **cut** / û **fur** / *th* **the** / th **thin** / hw **which** / zh **vision** / ə **ago, item, pencil, atom, circus**

en•mi•ty (ĕn′ mĭ tē) *n.*, *pl.* **en•mi•ties.** Deep hatred or hostility, as between enemies or opponents.

e•ra (îr′ə) *or* **(ĕr′ə)** *n.* A period of time that has a specific point in history as its beginning: *the Revolutionary and Colonial eras in U.S. history.*

err (ûr) *or* **(ĕr)** *v.* **erred, er•ring.** To make a mistake or error; be incorrect: *They err when they say that pollution is not a problem.*

es•ker (ĕs′kər) *n.* A ridge of coarse gravel deposited by a stream flowing in a trough or tunnel in a melting sheet of glacial ice.

eu•pho•ri•a (yoo fôr′ē ə) *or* **(-fōr′-)** *n.* A feeling of happiness and well-being.

ex•ca•va•tion (ĕks′kə vā′shən) *n.* The act or process of uncovering by digging: ***Excavations** in England revealed Roman ruins.*

ex•cel (ĭk sĕl′) *v.* **ex•celled, ex•cel•ling.** To be better than or superior to (others): *The gymnast **excels** on the balance beam.*

ex•tent (ĭk stĕnt′) *n.* The area or distance over which something reaches; size: *Word spread throughout the **extent** of the kingdom.*

fab•ri•cate (făb′rĭ kāt′) *v.* **fab•ri•cat•ed, fab•ri•cat•ing.** To manufacture; fashion or make: *They **fabricated** pins from metal.*

face (fās) *n.* The surface presented to view; the front: *the north **face** of a building.*

fac•tor (făk′tər) *n.* Something that helps bring about a certain result; ingredient: *Many **factors** contributed to his success.*

fan•cy (făn′sē) *n.*, *pl.* **fan•cies.** An impulsive idea or thought; whim: *She had a sudden **fancy** to buy a new hat.*

fer•ment (fər mĕnt′) *v.* **fer•ment•ed, fer•ment•ing.** To undergo or cause to undergo a chemical reaction in which relatively complex organic compounds are broken down into simpler compounds.

Era is from the Latin word aera, *meaning "counters"; because an era is a specific period of history, it is a way of counting time.*

excavation

Fabricate was borrowed into English from the Latin fabricari, *meaning "to construct, to build."* Fabricari *is from* faber, *which means "blacksmith, carpenter, craftsman," and is related to* fabrica, *"blacksmith's workshop," which gave us "forge."*

---

fe•ro•cious (fə rō′shəs) *adj.*
Extreme; intense: *The rocket traveled at a ferocious speed.*

flour•ish (flûr′ĭsh) *or* (flŭr′-)
v. **flour•ished,
flour•ish•ing.** To fare well; succeed; prosper: *The business flourished under new ownership.*

ford (fôrd) *or* (fōrd) *v.*
ford•ed, ford•ing. To cross (a stream or river) by wading, riding, or driving through a shallow place.

fowl•ing piece (foul′ĭng pēs)
n. A gun for shooting birds and other small animals.

frag•ment (frăg′mənt) *n.* A piece or part broken off or detached from a whole: *We heard only a fragment of his speech.*

frol•ic (frŏl′ĭk) *v.* **frol•icked,
frol•ick•ing.** To behave playfully; romp.

G

gaunt (gônt) *adj.* Thin and bony: *He looked gaunt after his illness.*

gen•er•al•i•za•tion
(jĕn′ər ə lĭ zā′shən) *n.* A general statement about a broad subject that is more or less applicable to the whole.

gen•ial•ly (jēn′yə lē) *adv.* In a cheerful and friendly manner.

ges•ture (jĕs′chər) *n.* A motion of the hands, arms, head, or body used while speaking or in place of speech to help express one's meaning: *The librarian silenced the students with a gesture.*

gim•let (gĭm′lĭt) *n.* A small hand tool with a pointed spiral tip, used for boring holes.

glaze (glāz) *n.* A coating applied to pottery before baking or firing in a kiln: *The potter had glazes of every color.*

H

hab•i•tat (hăb′ĭ tăt′) *n.* The area or natural environment in which an animal or plant normally lives or grows: *He will research the animal and its habitat.*

head•way (hĕd′wā′) *n.* Progress toward a goal.

ford

gimlet

Gaunt *came into
Modern English from
Middle English. Its
origin, however,
was probably
Scandinavian. The
word* gand *in a
Norwegian dialect
means "a thin stick."*

---

oi **oil** / o͝o **book** / o͞o **boot** / ou **out** / ŭ **cut** / û **fur** / *th* **the** / th **thin** / hw **which** /
zh **vision** / ə **ago, item, pencil, atom, circus**

her•o•ine (hĕr′ō ĭn) *n.* A woman noted for her courage, special achievements, etc.; the female counterpart of a hero.

hes•i•tate (hĕz′ĭ tāt′) *v.* **hes•i•tat•ed, hes•i•tat•ing.** To be slow to act, speak, or decide; pause in doubt or uncertainty: *He hesitated before giving his reply.*

hi•er•ar•chy (hī′ə rär′kē) *or* (hī′rär′-) *n., pl.* **hi•er•ar•chies.** A body of individuals organized or classified according to rank, capacity, or authority: *Animals that live in groups usually establish a hierarchy with one leader.*

> *The Greek word hierarkhes, meaning "high priest," is the origin of* **hierarchy.** *The Greek word became* hierarkhia, *meaning "the rule of a priest." In English,* **hierarchy** *is often associated with the rank of clergy within a church.*

hov•er (hŭv′ər) *or* (hŏv′-) *v.* **hov•ered, hov•er•ing.** To remain or linger close by: *The mother hovered around her sleeping baby.*

hu•man•i•ty (hyōō măn′ĭ tē) *n., pl.* **hu•man•i•ties.** The quality of being humane; kindness: *We should treat animals with humanity.*

hu•mor (hyōō′mər) *v.* **hu•mored, hu•mor•ing.** To yield to the wishes of (others); pamper: *He isn't feeling well, so please humor him.*

ig•no•rant (ĭg′nər ənt) *adj.* Without education or knowledge: *I love art but am ignorant about music.*

im•mor•tal•i•ty (ĭm′ôr tăl′ĭ tē) *n.* The condition of living forever without having to die.

im•pas•sive (ĭm păs′ĭv) *adj.* Feeling or showing no emotion; calm: *an impassive judge.*

im•per•vi•ous (ĭm pûr′vē əs) *adj.* Not capable of being affected; immune: *Even without a jacket he was impervious to the cold.*

im•pla•ca•ble (ĭm plā′kə bəl) *or* (-plăk′ə-) *adj.* Not to be moved or changed: *The enemy was implacable during the attack.*

im•prob•a•ble (ĭm prŏb′ə bəl) *adj.* Not likely to happen or be true: *It is improbable that he will pass the test without studying.*

ă pat / ā pay / â care / ä father / ĕ pet / ē be / ĭ pit / ī pie / î fierce / ŏ pot / ō go / ô paw, for /

im•pro•vise (ĭm′prə vīz′) *v.*
im•pro•vised,
im•pro•vis•ing. To make,
build, or provide on the spur
of the moment or from materials found nearby: *They*
improvised a plan to save the
crumbling dam.

in•can•des•cent
(ĭn′kən **dĕs**′ənt) *adj.*
Shining brilliantly; very
bright.

in•cite (ĭn sīt′) *v.* **in•cit•ed,**
in•cit•ing. To provoke to action; stir up; urge on: *He*
incited the people to violence.

in•con•gru•ous
(ĭn **kŏng**′grŏŏ əs) *adj.* Not
consistent with what is logical,
customary, or expected: *The*
scream seemed incongruous
in the quiet library.

in•con•spic•u•ous•ly
(ĭn′kən **spĭk**′yŏŏ əs lē) *adv.*
In a manner not readily noticeable or obvious: *The*
stranger slipped
inconspicuously through
the crowd.

in•con•ven•ience
(ĭn′kən **vēn**′yəns) *n.*
Lack of ease or comfort;
trouble; difficulty: *They*
planned ahead to avoid
inconvenience.

in•cor•po•rate (ĭn **kôr**′pə rāt′)
v. **in•cor•po•rat•ed,**
in•cor•po•rat•ing. To
combine or blend into a
unified whole: *The editor*
incorporated the last-
minute changes.

in•cred•u•lous (ĭn **krĕj**′ə ləs)
adj. Disbelieving; doubting.

in•de•ci•sive•ly (ĭn′dĭ **sī**′sĭv lē)
adv. In a manner that shows
inability to make up one's
mind; in a manner that shows
frequent changes of mind:
The hiker paused indecisively
before heading south.

in•dif•fer•ent (ĭn **dĭf**′ər ənt) *or*
(-**dĭf**′rənt) *adj.* Having or
showing no interest; not caring
one way or the other.

in•dig•nant•ly (ĭn **dĭg**′nənt lē)
adv. In a way that expresses
anger aroused by something
unjust, mean, etc.: *She*
slammed the door
indignantly.

in•dis•put•a•ble
(ĭn′dĭ **spyŏŏ**′tə bəl) *adj.* Not
capable of being debated; beyond doubt: *an indisputable*
truth.

in•ev•i•ta•ble (ĭn **ĕv**′ĭ tə bəl)
adj. Not capable of being
avoided or prevented: *an*
inevitable outcome.

Indignantly *comes*
from the Latin
indignari, *meaning*
"to regard as un-
worthy." The definition
in Modern English
might have evolved
from the idea of anger
brought about by the
unworthiness of a
person, idea, or
thing.

---

oi **oil** / ŏŏ **book** / ŏŏ **boot** / ou **out** / ŭ **cut** / û **fur** / *th* **the** / th **thin** / hw **which** /
zh **vision** / ə **ago, item, pencil, atom, circus**

Inferior *comes from the Latin word* inferus, *"below." Also related to this is the Latin* infernus, *"the place below the earth, the lower world, hell." In Italian,* infernus *became* inferno, *"hell," borrowed into English as* "inferno," *meaning "a place suggesting hell, as in being extremely hot."*

in•ex•o•ra•ble (ĭn ĕk′sər ə bəl) *adj.* Not to be altered, avoided, or turned aside: *the inexorable fate of the Titanic.*

in•fe•ri•or (ĭn fîr′ē ər) *adj.* **1.** Low or lower in order, degree, or rank: *an inferior position in the company.* **2.** Low or lower in quality: *inferior merchandise.*

in•hu•mane (ĭn′hyoo mān′) *adj.* Lacking mercy or kindness.

in•quir•y (ĭn kwīr′ē) *or* (ĭn′kwə rē) *n., pl.* **in•quir•ies.** A request for information: *inquiries about the new mail rates.*

in•quis•i•tive (ĭn kwĭz′ĭ tĭv) *adj.* Eager to learn.

in•sig•ni•a (ĭn sĭg′nē ə) *n., pl.* **in•sig•ni•a** *or* **in•sig•ni•as.** A badge of office, rank, nationality, membership, etc.; an emblem.

in•sip•id (ĭn sĭp′ĭd) *adj.* Lacking flavor; bland.

in•sist•ent•ly (ĭn sĭs′tənt lē) *adv.* In a repetitive or continual manner: *"My turn, my turn!" he begged insistently.*

Insignia *is from the Latin* insignia, *a plural noun meaning "marks or badges of office, official decorations." In English,* insignia *was originally used only as a plural noun, but recently it has been used as a singular noun. The new plural "insignias" is felt to be unacceptable.*

in•stinct (ĭn′stĭngkt′) *n.* An inner influence, feeling, or drive that is not learned and that results in complicated animal behavior such as building of nests, incubation of eggs, nursing of young, etc.

in•tent•ly (ĭn tĕnt′lē) *adv.* In a concentrated, deep, or strong manner: *She peered intently through the binoculars.*

in•ter•act (ĭn′tər ăkt′) *v.* **in•ter•act•ed, in•ter•act•ing.** To act on or affect each other: *people who interact peacefully.*

in•ter•cept (ĭn′tər sĕpt′) *v.* **in•ter•cept•ed, in•ter•cept•ing.** To stop or interrupt the course or progress of.

in•ter•pret•er (ĭn tûr′prĭ tər) *n.* A person who orally translates a conversation or speech from one language to another.

in•vol•un•tar•y (ĭn vŏl′ən tĕr′ē) *adj.* Not subject to the control of the will: *Hiccups are involuntary.*

J

ju•bi•lant (joo′bə lənt) *adj.* Full of joy; rejoicing.

ă pat / ā pay / â care / ä father / ĕ pet / ē be / ĭ pit / ī pie / î fierce / ŏ pot / ō go / ô paw, for /

khan (kän) *or* (kăn) *n.* The title of rulers of Mongol, Tatar, or Turkish tribes after the time of Genghis Khan.

lan•guage (lăng′gwĭj) *n.* Any system of signs, symbols, motions, etc., used to communicate: *The deaf use hand signals as language.*

lev•ee (lĕv′ē) *n.* A bank of earth, concrete, or other material raised along a river to keep it from flooding.

li•a•ble (lī′ə bəl) *adj.* Likely: *People in a rush are liable to make mistakes.*

liv•id (lĭv′ĭd) *adj.* Deathly pale or white, as from anger, fear, exhaustion, etc.

man•date (măn′dāt′) *n.* An official command or instruction: *Congress received a mandate to lower taxes.*

man•i•fes•to (măn′ə fĕs′tō) *n., pl.* **man•i•fes•toes** *or* **man•i•fes•tos.** A public declaration of rules and aims, especially those of a political nature: *The President issued a manifesto about the environment.*

mar•gin (mär′jĭn) *n.* An extra amount, as of time, money, area, etc., allowed beyond what is needed: *The cars missed each other by a narrow margin.*

men•ace (mĕn′əs) *n.* Someone or something that threatens harm; a threat: *The jagged rock is a menace to passing ships.* — **men•ac•ing,** *adj.* Being ready to do harm; threatening: *A tornado might drop from the menacing sky.*

mer•i•toc•ra•cy (mĕr′ĭ tŏk′rə sē) *n., pl.* **mer•i•toc•ra•cies.** A system in which workers are promoted or demoted based on ability or achievement.

mim•ic (mĭm′ĭk) *v.* **mim•icked, mim•ick•ing.** To copy or imitate closely, as in speech, expression, or motions: *She can mimic a British accent perfectly.*

Levee was borrowed in eighteenth-century America from Louisiana French levee, *"something raised up, an embankment on the Mississippi," which developed from the French* lever, *"to raise."*

levee

oi **oil** / o͞o **book** / o͞o **boot** / ou **out** / ŭ **cut** / û **fur** / *th* **the** / th **thin** / hw **which** / zh **vision** / ə **ago, item, pencil, atom, circus**

693

mo•men•tum (mō mĕn′təm) *n.*, *pl.* **mo•men•ta** *or* **mo•men•tums.** Speed or force of motion: *The sled gained momentum as it raced downhill.*

mon•ey e•con•o•my (mŭn′ē ĭ kŏn′ə mē) *n.*, *pl.* **mon•ey e•con•o•mies.** A system in which goods and services are purchased with coins and bills rather than in a direct exchange of goods and services: *A money economy exists in the U.S.*

mo•rale (mə răl′) *n.* The state of a person's or group's spirits, as shown in confidence, cheerfulness, and willingness to work toward a goal: *Our team's morale was high as we entered the championship game.*

mu•ci•lage (myoo′sə lĭj) *n.* A glue made from the natural gum of plants.

murk•y (mûr′kē) *adj.* Cloudy and dark with mud: *The divers could not see well in the murky water.*

mute (myoot) *adj.* Silent: *The distress flag was a mute plea for help.*

Murky *developed from the Old English word* mirce, *meaning "dark," and is probably related to* morgen, *meaning "morning, dawn."*

non•de•script (nŏn′dĭ skrĭpt′) *adj.* Lacking distinguishable qualities and thus difficult to describe: *The nondescript rock was one of hundreds.*

nov•el•ty (nŏv′əl tē) *n.*, *pl.* **nov•el•ties.** The quality of being refreshingly new, different, or unusual: *We hopped backward until the novelty wore off.*

ob•li•ga•tion (ŏb′lĭ gā′shən) *n.* A sense of duty as if being held accountable by a promise, contract, or law: *The obligation of friendship carries many responsibilities.*

ob•scure (əb skyoor′) *adj.* Difficult to understand; vague: *The word's meaning is obscure.*

ob•sess (əb sĕs′) *v.* **ob•sessed, ob•sess•ing.** To occupy the mind of; haunt: *The thought of making money obsessed him.*

ă pat / ā pay / â care / ä father / ĕ pet / ē be / ĭ pit / ī pie / î fierce / ŏ pot / ō go / ô paw, for /

oc•cu•pa•tion (ŏk′yə pā′shən) *n.* The conquest and control of a nation or territory by a foreign military force: *The Allies conducted the occupation of Germany after World War II.*

of•fence (ə fĕns′) *or* (ô′fĕns) *or* (ŏf′ĕns′) *n.* Chiefly British form of the word **offense,** meaning a violation of a moral, legal, or social code: *It is an offence to break the speed limit.*

of•fend (ə fĕnd′) *v.* **of•fend•ed, of•fend•ing.** To cause anger, resentment, or annoyance in; insult: *His careless remarks offended her.*

om•i•nous (ŏm′ə nəs) *adj.* Seeming to be a sign of trouble, danger, or disaster; threatening: *Ominous clouds filled the sky.*

op•ti•mism (ŏp′tə mĭz′əm) *n.* A tendency to take a hopeful view of a situation, or to expect the best possible outcome: *We looked forward to the playoffs with optimism.*

or•gan•ism (ôr′gə nĭz′əm) *n.* Any living thing; a plant or animal.

out•crop•ping (out′krŏp′ĭng) *n.* A piece of rock that extends up above the surface of the soil.

out•rage (out′rāj′) *n.* Great anger aroused by an extremely vicious or wicked act: *public outrage over the incident.*

par•a•dox (păr′ə dôks′) *n.* A group of facts, qualities, or circumstances that seem to contradict each other: *Thunder during a snowstorm seems like a paradox.*

par•ka (pär′kə) *n.* A warm fur or cloth jacket with a hood.

pa•tience (pā′shəns) *n.* Calm endurance of a trying, boring, or annoying situation.

pen•du•lum (pĕn′jə ləm) *or* (-dyə-) *n.* A heavy object hanging from a string or rod and swinging back and forth in order to operate a device, such as a clock.

pen•e•trate (pĕn′ĭ trāt′) *v.* **pen•e•trat•ed, pen•e•trat•ing.** To go or enter into or through: *The underbrush was too thick to penetrate.*

For a long time, scientists divided **organisms** into only two kinds, plants and animals. More recently, they have added another group, the protists, many of which are single-celled, such as protozoans and bacteria, and cannot readily be classified as plants or animals.

Patience *developed from the Latin word* pati, *meaning "to endure."*

pendulum

oi **oil** / ͞oo **book** / ͞oo **boot** / ou **out** / ŭ **cut** / û **fur** / *th* **the** / th **thin** / hw **which** / zh **vision** / ə **ago, item, pencil, atom, circus**

695

per•plex•i•ty (pər **plĕk′**sĭ tē) *n., pl.* **per•plex•i•ties.** The condition of being confused or puzzled; bewilderment: *He approached the problem with some **perplexity**.*

pike

phase (fāz) *n.* A distinct stage of development: *the next **phase** of the space program.*

pick•et (**pĭk′**ĭt) *v.* **pick•et•ed, pick•et•ing.** To demonstrate against, as during a strike.

pike (pīk) *n.* A large freshwater fish with a narrow body and a long snout.

plau•si•ble (**plô′**zə bəl) *adj.* Appearing to be true or reasonable: *a **plausible** excuse.*

plead•ing•ly (**plēd′**ĭng lē) *adv.* In a begging manner or tone: *The dog looked at its master **pleadingly**.*

plight (plīt) *n.* A serious condition or a situation of difficulty or danger: *the **plight** of political prisoners.*

Plight *originally meant "a fold, a twist" and later came to mean "situation"; it is from the Old French* pleit *and is related to "pleat."*

pomp (pŏmp) *n.* Showy or stately display: *The crowning of a ruler is an occasion of great **pomp**.*

pon•der (**pŏn′**dər) *v.* **pon•dered, pon•der•ing.** To think or consider carefully and at length: *She **pondered** the meaning of her dream.*

po•ten•tial (pə **tĕn′**shəl) *n.* Capacity for further growth, development, or progress; promise: *He has the **potential** to be a great musician.*

prac•ti•cal (**prăk′**tĭ kəl) *adj.* Serving or capable of serving a useful purpose: *The inventor turned the idea into a **practical** machine.*

prank•ster (**prăngk′**stər) *n.* A person who plays mischievous tricks or jokes.

pre•cise•ly (prĭ **sīs′** lē) *adv.* In a manner allowing very little error or variation: *My shoes must be **precisely** this size.*

pre•dic•a•ment (prĭ **dĭk′**ə mənt) *n.* A difficult or embarrassing situation.

pre•oc•cu•pa•tion (prē ŏk′yə **pā′**shən) *n.* The state of having one's attention deeply or completely held.

prime (prīm) *adj.* First in importance, degree, value, significance, etc.: *his **prime** concern.*

ă pat / ā pay / â care / ä father / ĕ pet / ē be / ĭ pit / ī pie / î fierce / ŏ pot / ō go / ô paw, for /

prin·ci·ple (prĭn′sə pəl) *n.* A rule or standard of behavior: *a woman of dedicated political principles.*

prob·a·bil·i·ty (prŏb′ə bĭl′ĭ tē) *n., pl.* **prob·a·bil·i·ties.** The likelihood that something will be true or will happen: *The probability is that a storm will occur.*

prob·a·ble (prŏb′ə bəl) *adj.* Likely to happen or to be true: *the probable cost of the expedition.*

pro·ces·sion (prə sĕsh′ən) *n.* A group of persons, vehicles, objects, etc., moving along in an orderly line: *a funeral procession.*

pro·claim (prō klām′) *or* (prə-) *v.* **pro·claimed, pro·claim·ing.** To announce officially and publicly; declare: *The governor proclaimed May 15 an official holiday.*

pro·ject (prə jĕkt′) *v.* **pro·ject·ed, pro·ject·ing.** To convey or communicate; transmit: *An actor tries to project emotions that a character feels.*

proph·e·sy (prŏf′ĭ sī′) *v.* **proph·e·sied, proph·e·sy·ing.** To predict (what is to happen) confidently: *Dad prophesied a harsh winter.*

pro·pose (prə pōz′) *v.* **pro·posed, pro·pos·ing.** To put forward for consideration or acceptance; suggest: *Congress proposed a law to increase taxes.*

pros·per·i·ty (prŏ spĕr′ĭ tē) *n.* The condition of being vigorous and healthy; success: *He wishes us good health and prosperity.*

pro·voke (prə vōk′) *v.* **pro·voked, pro·vok·ing.** To bring on; arouse: *His clumsy behavior is always provoking laughter.*

pur·chase (pûr′chĭs) *n.* A secure position, grasp, or hold: *Using the narrow ledge for a purchase, she paused in her climb.*

quad·ran·gle (kwŏd′răng′gəl) *n.* A rectangular area bordered by buildings: *We ate our lunch outside in the library quadrangle.*

The Latin princeps, *"chief, head, leader" (used as a title) became two words: (1) the adjective* principalis, *"leading, first, chief," which is the source of "principal"; and (2) the noun* principium, *"beginning, origin, foundation, basic element"; this became the Old French* principe, *which was borrowed into English as* **principle.**

Proclaim *developed from the Latin words* pro-, *meaning "forward," and* clamare, *meaning "to cry out."*

quadrangle

oi **oil** / o͞o **book** / o͞o **boot** / ou **out** / ŭ **cut** / û **fur** / *th* **the** / th **thin** / hw **which** / zh **vision** / ə **ago, item, pencil, atom, circus**

ran•dom (răn′dəm) *adj.* Having no particular pattern, purpose, organization, or structure.

re•act (rē ăkt′) *v.* **re•act•ed, re•act•ing.** To act in response to a stimulus or prompting: *Firefighters **react** when they hear an alarm.*

rea•son•ing (rē′zə nĭng) *n.* The process of thinking in an orderly way to form conclusions, judgments, etc.: *Sherlock Holmes's powers of **reasoning** helped him solve mysteries.*

re•bel•lious (rĭ bĕl′yəs) *adj.* In open revolt against a government or ruling authority: *The demonstration was considered a **rebellious** act.*

re•cede (rĭ sēd′) *v.* **re•ced•ed, re•ced•ing.** To move back or away from a limit, point, or mark: *We returned home after the flood **receded**.*

rec•og•nize (rĕk′əg nīz′) *v.* **rec•og•nized, rec•og•niz•ing.** To know, understand, or realize: ***recognize** the value of virtue.*

re•con•noi•ter (rē′kə noi′tər) *or* (rĕk′ə-) *v.* **re•con•noi•tered, re•con•noi•ter•ing.** To make an inspection or exploration of an area, especially to gather information about the presence, arrangement, or activity of military forces: *The scout was **reconnoitering** for signs of the enemy.*

re•flect (rĭ flĕkt′) *v.* **re•flect•ed, re•flect•ing.** To reveal as if through a mirror: *Children **reflect** their parents' behavior.*

reg•is•ter (rĕj′ĭ stər) *v.* **reg•is•tered, reg•is•ter•ing.** To create an impression: *It may take a moment before the news **registers**.*

re•lent (rĭ lĕnt′) *v.* **re•lent•ed, re•lent•ing.** To become softer or gentler in attitude, temper, or determination: *Mom **relented** and let us go to the party.*

rel•ic (rĕl′ĭk) *n.* An object or custom surviving from a culture or period that has disappeared: *The pyramids are **relics** of ancient Egypt.*

re•luc•tant (rĭ′lŭk′tənt) *adj.* Unwilling; opposed. —**re•luc•tant•ly,** *adv.* In an unwilling manner.

Relic *is from the Latin* reliquiae, *meaning "remains, relics," which is from* relinquere, *meaning "to leave behind."* Relinquere *also became the Old French* relinquir, *which was borrowed into English as* "relinquish."

ă pat / ā pay / â care / ä father / ĕ pet / ē be / ĭ pit / ī pie / î fierce / ŏ pot / ō go /
ô paw, for /

698

re•mit (rĭ mĭt′) *v.* **re•mit•ted, re•mit•ting.** To cancel (a penalty, etc.): *remitted his fine.*

ren•dez•vous (rän′dā vōō′) *or* (-də-) *v.* **ren•dez•voused, ren•dez•vous•ing.** To meet together or cause to meet together at a certain time and place: *The explorers will rendezvous in the forest.*

re•peal (rĭ pēl′) *v.* **re•pealed, re•peal•ing.** To withdraw or cancel officially: *The legislature repealed the law.*

re•pose (rĭ pōz′) *n.* Rest or relaxation.

re•prieve (rĭ prēv′) *n.* The postponement of a punishment.

re•proach (rĭ prōch′) *v.* **re•proached, re•proach•ing.** To scold severely or sternly; blame.

re•pro•duce (rē′prə dōōs′) *or* (-dyōōs′) *v.* **re•pro•duced, re•pro•duc•ing.** To make an image or copy of: *She reproduced the photograph.*

re•pro•duc•tion (rē′prə dŭk′shən) *n.* A copy: *reproductions of paintings.*

rep•u•ta•tion (rĕp′yə tā′shən) *n.* The general esteem or respect in which a person is held by others or by the general public: *He made his reputation with a great discovery.*

re•sent (rĭ zĕnt′) *v.* **re•sent•ed, re•sent•ing.** To feel angry or bitter about.

re•serve (rĭ zûrv′) *n.* A supply of something available for use when needed.

re•side (rĭ zīd′) *v.* **re•sid•ed, re•sid•ing.** To live or dwell; make one's home: *She resides in Boston.*

re•sist (rĭ zĭst′) *v.* **re•sist•ed, re•sist•ing.** To keep from giving in or yielding to: *resist temptation.*

res•o•lute (rĕz′ə lōōt′) *adj.* Having or showing strong will and determination.

re•sponse (rĭ spŏns′) *n.* A reaction, as that of a living thing or mechanism to a stimulus or action: *Running from danger is a normal response.*

re•trieve (rĭ trēv′) *v.* **re•trieved, re•triev•ing.** To get back; recover: *He retrieved the ball in the end zone.*

Rendezvous *is from the French phrase* rendez vous, *which means "present yourselves." This was originally a command to soldiers, and the English word, which was first borrowed in the sixteenth century, remains in technical military use up to the present day.*

Reputation *developed from the Latin word* reputare, *meaning "to think over."*

---

oi oil / ōō book / ōō boot / ou out / ŭ cut / û fur / *th* the / th thin / hw which / zh vision / ə ago, item, pencil, atom, circus

re•voke (rĭ vōk′) *v.* **re•voked,
re•vok•ing.** To reverse or
withdraw; cancel: *Her driver's license was* **revoked**.

rit•u•al (rĭch′o͞o əl) *n.* Any
procedure faithfully and regularly followed: *Exercise is
part of his daily* **ritual**.

ri•val (rī′vəl) *n.* Someone who
competes with or tries to
outdo another; a competitor.

ru•di•ment (ro͞o′də mənt) *n.*
Usually **rudiments.** The
basic rules or skills of a given
field of learning: *learning the*
rudiments *of grammar.*

rue•ful•ly (ro͞o′fəl lē) *adv.* In a
sorrowful, shameful, or regret-
ful manner: *The boy* **ruefully**
admitted his guilt.

sentry

sage (sāj) *n.* A very wise person, usually old and highly
respected.

sal•vage (săl′vĭj) *v.* **sal•vaged,
sal•vag•ing.** To save or rescue
anything of use or value that
would otherwise be lost,
discarded, damaged, or
destroyed.

scin•til•la•tion (sĭn′tl ā′shən)
n. Spark, flash, or sparkle:
The **scintillation** *of the diamond was almost blinding.*

scoff (skôf) *or* (skŏf) *v.*
scoffed, scoff•ing. To show
scorn or mockery: *They*
scoffed *at his unusual ideas.*

sen•try (sĕn′trē) *n., pl.*
sen•tries. A person, especially a soldier, posted at some
spot to warn of approaching
attackers or to check persons
seeking admittance; a guard.

ser•pent (sûr′pənt) *n.* A
snakelike dragon or monster.

set•back (sĕt′băk′) *n.* An unexpected check or reverse in
progress: *Her* **setback** *meant
a second trip to the hospital.*

share (shâr) *n.* Any of the
equal parts into which the
capital stock of a business is
divided, bought, and sold by
stockholders: *Some people
invest money in* **shares** *of
stock.*

sheer (shîr) *adj.* Extending
straight up or down, or nearly
so; very steep: *They climbed
the* **sheer** *rock cliffs.*

shrewd (shro͞od) *adj.* Clever
and practical: *The* **shrewder**
detective solved the case.

ă pat / ā pay / â care / ä father / ĕ pet / ē be / ĭ pit / ī pie / î fierce / ŏ pot / ō go /
ô paw, for /

si·dle (sīd′l) *v.* **si·dled, si·dling.** To move sideways or edge along, especially in a sneaky way: *The cat sidled up to the bird.*

sig·nif·i·cant (sĭg nĭf′ĭ kənt) *adj.* Important; notable: *July 4, 1776, is a significant date in U.S. history.*

sim·ple·ton (sĭm′pəl tən) *n.* A fool.

singe (sĭnj) *v.* **singed, singe·ing.** To burn off feathers, bristles, or hair by holding to a flame.

skep·ti·cism (skĕp′tĭ sĭz′əm) *n.* A doubting or questioning state of mind: *After hearing their excuse she was filled with skepticism.*

snow·hook (snō′hŏŏk′) *n.* A piece of curved steel attached to a dog sled harness and used to anchor the dogs and sled in place.

so·cial (sō′shəl) *adj.* Of or typical of living together in communities or similar organized groups: *Being polite is acceptable social behavior.*

sol·emn (sŏl′əm) *adj.* Having the force of a religious ceremony; sacred: *a solemn oath.*

sound (sound) *adj.* Sensible and correct: *Her sound idea saved the company from ruin.*

spasm (spăz′əm) *n.* Any sudden burst of energy, activity, etc.

spec·u·late (spĕk′yə lāt′) *v.* **spec·u·lat·ed, spec·u·lat·ing.** To think deeply on a given subject: *The scientist speculates that life might exist in outer space.*

spell·bound (spĕl′bound′) *adj.* Held as if under a spell or charm; fascinated; astonished: *She listened spellbound to the story he told.*

squan·der (skwŏn′dər) *v.* **squan·dered, squan·der·ing.** To use or spend wastefully or extravagantly: *squandered money.*

stag·nant (stăg′nənt) *adj.* Foul or polluted as a result of not moving: *It was hard to breathe the stagnant air.*

stan·dard (stăn′dərd) *n.* A flag or banner used as the emblem of a nation, military unit, corporation, etc.: *The standard flew next to the national flag.*

Sound, *meaning "sensible," is from the Old English* gesund, *or "healthy." The closely related German* gesundheit, *"health," is often said to someone who has sneezed.*

oi **oil** / ŏŏ b**oo**k / ōō b**oo**t / ou **out** / ŭ **cut** / û f**ur** / *th* **the** / th **thin** / hw **which** / zh vi**s**ion / ə **a**go, it**e**m, penc**i**l, at**o**m, circ**u**s

Subjugate *is from the Latin* subjugare, *meaning "to bring under the yoke." An ancient Roman custom called for defeated armies to pass under a symbolic "yoke" formed of spears. The Romans regarded this as a great humiliation.*

Summon *comes from the Latin word* summonere, *which means "to remind privately." It is built from* sub-, *meaning "secretly," and* monere, *meaning "to warn."*

Superior, *meaning "high or higher," is from the Latin word* super, *which means "above." The Latin word that means "highest,"* supremus, *also comes from* super. *It was borrowed into the English language as "supreme."*

sta•tus (stāt′əs) *or* (stăt′əs) *n., pl.* **sta•tus•es.** A relative position in a ranked group or in a social system: *the high **status** of professional people.*

steppe (stĕp) *n.* A vast, somewhat arid plain, covered with grass and having few trees, as found in southeastern Europe and Siberia.

stim•u•lus (stĭm′yə ləs) *n., pl.* **stim•u•li.** Something that results in an action or reaction of an organism, bodily part, etc.: *Pain is sometimes a **stimulus** for tears.*

sub•ject (sŭb′jĭkt) *adj.* Under the power or authority of another: *The defendant is **subject** to the power of the court.*

sub•ju•gate (sŭb′jŏŏ gāt′) *v.* **sub•ju•gat•ed, sub•ju•gat•ing.** To bring under total control; conquer.

sub•or•di•nate (sə bôr′dn ĭt) *adj.* Subject to the authority or control of another.

sub•se•quent (sŭb′sə kwənt) *adj.* Following in time or order; succeeding: *heavy rains and **subsequent** floods.*

sub•stan•tial (səb stăn′shəl) *adj.* Considerable in importance, value, degree, amount, or range: *The patient made **substantial** progress toward recovery.*

suf•fi•cient (sə fĭsh′ənt) *adj.* As much as is needed; enough.

sum•mon (sŭm′ən) *v.* **sum•moned, sum•mon•ing.** To send for; request to appear: *The principal is **summoning** you to her office.*

su•pe•ri•or (sə pîr′ē ər) *or* (sŏŏ-) *adj.* High or higher in order, degree, or rank: *a **superior** officer.*

sur•pass (sər păs′) *or* (-päs′) *v.* **sur•passed, sur•pass•ing.** To be better, greater, or stronger than; exceed: *The cheetah's speed **surpasses** the lion's.*

swamp (swŏmp) *v.* **swamped, swamp•ing.** To burden or flood; overwhelm: *We were **swamped** with homework.*

sym•bol•ic (sĭm bŏl′ĭk) *adj.* Representing something else, as by association, resemblance, custom, etc.: *Applause is a **symbolic** gesture of approval.*

ă pat / ā pay / â care / ä father / ĕ pet / ē be / ĭ pit / ī pie / î fierce / ŏ pot / ō go / ô paw, for /

taut (tôt) *adj.* Pulled or drawn tight: *The sails were* ***taut*** *with the wind.*

tech•nol•o•gy (tĕk nŏl′ə jē) *n., pl.* **tech•nol•o•gies.** The methods and materials used in applying scientific knowledge, especially in industry and commerce: *Laser* ***technology*** *has revolutionized communications.*

ten•sion (tĕn′shən) *n.* A force that tends to stretch or elongate something: *The elastic band snapped when the* ***tension*** *increased.*

ten•ta•tive (tĕn′tə tĭv) *adj.* Not certain or permanent; not definite: *We have* ***tentative*** *plans to travel in July.*

term (tûrm) *n.* A condition or requirement. Usually **terms**: *Both sides agreed on the* ***terms*** *for peace.*

the•o•ry (thē′ə rē) *or* (thîr′ē) *n., pl.* **the•o•ries.** A statement or set of statements designed to explain things observed by the senses, including conclusions drawn from facts and assumptions by mathematical or logical reasoning: *Scientists have proposed* ***theories*** *to account for the Northern Lights.*

thresh•old (thrĕsh′ōld) *or* (-hōld) *n.* The piece of wood or stone placed beneath a door.

thrive (thrīv) *v.* **throve** *or* **thrived, thrived** *or* **thriv•en, thriv•ing.** To be successful; make progress: *The busy community* ***thrived.***

thwart (thwôrt) *v.* **thwart•ed, thwart•ing.** To prevent from taking place; frustrate; block: *Rain* ***thwarted*** *their plans for a picnic.*

tor•rent (tôr′ənt) *or* (tŏr′-) *n.* Any turbulent or overwhelming flow: *A* ***torrent*** *of mail flooded the post office.*

tor•tu•ous (tôr′chōō əs) *adj.* Winding; twisting: *It is frightening to drive along that* ***tortuous*** *road.*

threshold

Thrive, *meaning "to be successful," comes from the Old Norse word* thrifask, *meaning, "to seize." The related Norse word* thrift, *which meant "the condition of thriving," now means in English "wise management of money," a condition that might lead to success.*

oi **oil** / o͞o **book** / o͞o **boot** / ou **out** / ŭ **cut** / û **fur** / *th* **the** / th **thin** / hw **which** / zh **vision** / ə **ago, item, pencil, atom, circus**

703

treadle

tundra

tran•si•tion (trăn zĭsh′ən) *or* (-sĭsh′-) *n.* The process or an example of changing or pass-ing from one form, state, or place to another: *transition from childhood to adulthood.*

trav•erse (trăv′ərs) *or* (trə vûrs′) *v.* **trav•ersed, trav•ers•ing.** To travel across, over, or through: *A caravan can traverse the de-sert safely.*

tread•le (trĕd′l) *n.* A pedal or lever pushed up and down or back and forth with the foot to drive a wheel, as in a sewing machine or a potter's wheel.

trem•or (trĕm′ər) *n.* A shak-ing or vibrating movement: *The earthquake's tremor caused minor damages.*

trib•ute (trĭb′yo͞ot′) n. A sum of money paid by one ruler or nation to another as acknowl-edgment of submission or as the price for protection by that nation.

tun•dra (tŭn′drə) *n.* A cold, treeless area of arctic regions, having only low-growing mosses, lichens, and stunted shrubs as plant life.

ty•rant (tī′rənt) *n.* A ruler who exercises power in a harsh, cruel manner: *The tyrant forbids public gather-ings.*

ul•ti•mate•ly (ŭl′tə mĭt lē) *adv.* Finally; eventually: *We will ultimately have to replace our stove.*

u•nan•i•mous (yo͞o năn′ə məs) *adj.* Based on complete agreement: *Their decision to stay was unanimous.*

un•can•ny (ŭn kăn′ē) *adj.* Arousing wonder and fear; strange: *An uncanny light came from the ruins.*

un•con•scious (ŭn kŏn′shəs) *adj.* Temporarily lacking awareness, as in deep sleep or coma: *The accident knocked him unconscious.*

un•kempt (ŭn kĕmpt′) *adj.* Not neat or tidy; messy.

un•nerve (ŭn nŭrv′) *v.* **un•nerved, un•nerv•ing.** To cause to lose courage, confi-dence, etc.: *The frightening incident unnerved him.*

ă pat / ā pay / â care / ä father / ĕ pet / ē be / ĭ pit / ī pie / î fierce / ŏ pot / ō go / ô paw, for /

un•par•al•leled
(ŭn păr′ə lĕld′) *adj.* Having nothing resembling it; unequaled: *her **unparalleled** beauty.*

urn (ûrn) *n.* A vase, usually with a footed base.

vain (vān) *adj.* Unsuccessful; useless; fruitless. —*Idiom.* **in vain.** To no avail; unsuccessfully.

van•i•ty (văn′ĭ tē) *n., pl.* **van•i•ties.** Excessive pride; conceit.

ve•he•ment•ly (vē′ə mənt lē) *adv.* In a manner marked by forcefulness of expression or intensity of emotion, feelings, etc.: *The employees **vehemently** demanded a raise.*

ve•loc•i•ty (və lŏs′ĭ tē) *n., pl.* **ve•loc•i•ties.** Speed.

ves•sel (vĕs′əl) *n.* A hollow container, as a bowl, pitcher, jar, or tank, especially one for liquids.

vise (vīs) *n.* A device of metal, usually consisting of a pair of jaws that are opened and closed by means of a screw or lever, used in carpentry or metalworking to hold work in position.

vi•tal (vīt′l) *adj.* Having great importance; essential: *Dialogue is a **vital** element in drama.*

vo•li•tion (və lĭsh′ən) *n.* The fact or power of choosing, using one's own will, etc.: *He left the party of his own **volition**.*

vul•ner•a•ble (vŭl′nər ə bəl) *adj.* Open to danger or attack; unprotected.

ward off (wôrd ôf) *v.* To keep from striking; fend off; turn aside: *The boxer managed to **ward off** the blows.*

wave•length (wāv′lĕngkth′) *or* (-lĕngth′) *n.* Understanding of another person's situation, thoughts, or motivations: *Best friends are often on the same **wavelength**.*

wraith (rāth) *n.* An almost invisible mist or gas.

wretch•ed (rĕch′ĭd) *adj.* Full of or attended by misery or woe: *I'm lonely and **wretched**.*

urn

Vital *developed from the Latin word* vita, *meaning "life."*

The prehistoric Germanic word ward- *meant "a guard" or "to guard." It became* weard *in Old English and* **ward** *in Modern English. Separately,* ward- *was borrowed into Old French as* guarder, *or "to guard";* guarder *was borrowed into English as "guard," or "to protect from harm."*

---

oi **oil** / o͞o b**oo**k / o͞o b**oo**t / ou **out** / ŭ c**u**t / û f**u**r / *th* **th**e / th **th**in / hw **wh**ich / zh vi**s**ion / ə **a**go, it**e**m, penc**i**l, at**o**m, circ**u**s

Glossary of Literary Terms

action   The series of events that make up a **plot.**

alliteration   The repetition of a consonant sound, usually the first sound in a group of words, as in "trumpeted two times."

allusion   A brief mention of a person or thing with which the reader is presumed to be familiar.

anecdote   A short account that gives details of an interesting event.

antagonist   The character who opposes the main character, or **protagonist,** in a story, play, or poem.

archaic language   Words and expressions that once were part of the language, but are no longer in use.

author's purpose   What the author means to say or accomplish in his or her work.

autobiography   A person's account of his or her own life.

ballad   A fairly short poem that tells a story. Ballads typically consist of **stanzas** and a **refrain.** They were originally meant to be sung.

biography   The factual account of a person's life, written by someone else.

blank verse   A form of poetry that does not rhyme and has five beats per line.

chapter   One of the main sections of a book, usually labeled with a number or title.

characterization   The process of making a character seem real and lifelike. An author uses description of the character's physical features, personality traits, actions, thoughts, speech, and feelings to achieve characterization.

characters   The people or animals in a story. The main character handles the problem or **conflict** in the story. Minor characters help advance the **plot** and reveal information about the main character's personality.

character traits   Qualities that make one character different from another. Such qualities — bravery, intelligence, stinginess, and so on — are as various in literature as they are in real life.

climax   The point in a play or story where the **conflict** reaches its highest intensity and must be resolved. The climax is the most exciting moment in a story and holds the most interest for the reader. (See also **turning point.**)

comedy Writing that is designed to amuse. Comedy uses such devices as sarcasm, **exaggeration, satire,** and **wit.** Comedies typically have happy endings.

conclusion In dramatic structure, the part of a story or play that gives the final results; the ending.

conflict The problem in a story faced by the main character. The character may face one (or more) of the following four kinds of conflict: a struggle against nature, a struggle against another character, a struggle against society, or a struggle against himself or herself.

connotation The feelings, emotions, and ideas associated with a word, as opposed to its dictionary definition. (See also **denotation.**)

context The words and ideas that surround a particular word. A reader can often figure out the meaning of a new word from its context.

denotation The exact meaning of a word as it might appear in a dictionary. (See also **connotation.**)

description Writing that provides details of time, place, character, and setting. An author uses description to create images of the "world" in which the story takes place.

descriptive language Language that is rich in sensory details. It evokes sights, smells, sounds, and textures.

dialect The way of speaking used by the people of a particular region or group. A writer achieves a dialect by using words that are spelled differently to show local or regional pronunciations, and by using words and sentence structures that are part of local or regional sayings and manners of speaking.

dialogue The words spoken by characters to one another in a story or play.

diction **1.** The choice and arrangement of words in a story or play. **2.** The quality of speech or singing judged by clearness and distinctness of pronunciation.

drama A serious play designed to be acted on a stage.

dramatize **1.** To turn a story into a play or screenplay. **2.** To relate an incident in a very dramatic way.

epic A long poem or literary work, usually written in a formal style, about heroes and their adventures. Ancient epics, such as Homer's *Iliad* and *Odyssey*, are often written versions of the oral legends of a nation or culture.

essay A brief piece of prose writing about a specific topic. An essay usually expresses the opinions of its author.

exaggeration Deliberate overstatement used for emphasis, effect, or **humor.**

expository writing Informational writing that enlightens or explains. Most **nonfiction prose** is expository.

fable A short story, often with animal characters who speak and act like humans, that teaches a lesson about human nature.

falling action In dramatic structure, the part of a story or play that tells what happens after the **climax.**

fantasy Fiction that tells about events that are impossible in the real world because they do not obey known scientific laws. **Science fiction** and fairy tales are types of fantasy writing.

fiction Stories created from the imagination of the author. **Novels, short stories,** and **fables** are all forms of fiction.

fictionalized biography An account of a person's life that is based on facts but includes some imagined elements.

figurative language Writing that uses figures of speech such as metaphors, similes, and personification. (See also **metaphor, simile,** and **personification.**)

figures of speech Various imaginative uses of language that create special effects or meanings. (See also **metaphor, simile,** and **personification.**)

first person The **point of view** from which one of the characters tells the story using the pronoun *I*. This character may experience the events of the story personally or may simply be a witness to them. (See also **narrator** and **third person.**)

flashback A writing technique that interrupts the present action to explain something that happened earlier.

folklore Traditions, beliefs, legends, customs, and stories handed down by a particular people from generation to generation by word of mouth. Folklore includes folk **ballads,** folk **dramas,** folk **heroes,** and **folktales.**

folktale A traditional story of a particular place or people, handed down from generation to generation and eventually written down.

foreshadowing A writing technique involving clues that a writer gives early in a selection to hint at future events.

formal language Careful, precise language, more frequently used in writing than in everyday speech. (See also **informal language.**)

free verse Poetry that does not follow a regular pattern of rhythm or line, and has either irregular rhyme or no rhyme.

genre A category or type of literary work. Works can be grouped into genres by form, technique, or type of subject. Thus, the adventure story, the **folktale,** and the **novel** are all examples of literary genres.

haiku A **lyric** poem of three lines and usually seventeen syllables. Traditionally, a haiku expresses a person's feelings inspired by nature.

hero/heroine 1. The central character in a work of fiction, poetry, or drama. **2.** A strong and courageous man or woman who performs brave deeds or who risks his or her life for a good cause. In mythology, heroes and heroines were descended from gods.

historical fiction A story based partly on historical events and people and partly on the author's imagination.

humor 1. A type of writing intended to make people laugh. **2.** The quality of being funny.

idiom A use of words, such as a **figure of speech** or a common saying, that is unique to one language and cannot be translated literally into another.

image A mental picture of something not present or real.

imagery Word pictures; mental images. In writing or speech, the use of **figurative language,** vivid **description,** or **sensory words** to produce **images.**

informal language Casual language used mainly in conversation. (See also **formal language.**)

interpretation The art of understanding what a work of literature means. Complex works can be interpreted in several different ways.

introduction In dramatic structure, the part of a story or play that creates the mood, presents some of the characters, and supplies background information.

irony The use of words or situations to contrast what is expected with what is actually meant or occurs. In *verbal irony*, the speaker says the opposite of what he or she means. In *dramatic irony*, the audience knows more about events than the characters do, which makes for **suspense** as the characters act out the story.

jargon Special or technical language used by people in a particular job or by people with a particular hobby or interest.

legend An imaginative story that is often connected with a national hero or a historical event and may be based on truth.

literature Imaginative writing that possesses recognized artistic value.

lyric poetry Poetry that expresses personal feelings and thoughts.

memoir A form of **autobiography,** usually written by someone famous or by someone who has witnessed an important event. A memoir focuses on other people and events, rather than on the writer, as in autobiography.

metaphor An implied comparison between very different things, used to add vividness to writing. In a metaphor, the two things compared are said to be the same, as in "Her mind is a computer." (See also **simile**.)

monologue A long speech delivered by one character in a play, story, or poem.

mood The effect of a story, poem, or play on the feelings of a reader or an audience; the emotional **tone** of a piece of writing.

moral A lesson taught by a story or **fable.**

motivation The combination of plot events and personality traits that determines a character's actions.

motive A reason, a need, or an emotion that causes a character to act in a certain way.

mystery novel Fiction that deals with a puzzling event, often a crime. (See also **novel**.)

myth A story handed down from the past that gives an

imaginary explanation of how certain things in nature, such as the moon, the sun, and the stars, came to be.

narration The act or example of narrating, or telling a story.

narrative In an account of an event, the description of characters, scenes, or events that is not dialogue.

narrative poetry A type of poetry, sometimes rather long, that tells a story.

narrator The character who tells the story or, in a play, who explains the events to the audience by addressing them directly. (See also **point of view, first person, third person.**)

nonfiction Writing that is about the real world rather than an imagined one.

novel A long fictional **narrative,** usually showing how a **character** develops as a result of events or actions, and organized around a **plot** or **theme.**

onomatopoeia The use of a word that imitates the sound it describes. *Buzz, splash,* and *honk* are all onomatopoetic words. In poetry, onomatopoeia may be more subtle, as the sound of the verses may help create a particular mood.

oral tradition A tradition in which songs and tales are passed by word of mouth from one generation to another.

outcome The final result; how something ends.

personification A **figure of speech** in which human traits are given to something that is not human.

plot The action or series of events in a story. The plot is traditionally divided into sections. The **introduction** creates the mood, presents some of the characters, and supplies background information. The **rising action** establishes and develops the **conflict.** At the **climax,** or turning point, the conflict is resolved through a key event or through the actions of the main character. In the **falling action,** the reader learns what happens as a result of the climax. The **conclusion** gives the final results.

point of view The position from which a story is told. A story may be told from the point of view of one of its characters, or from the position of an observer who is outside the action. (See also **first person, third person, and narrator.**)

prose Ordinary speech or writing as distinguished from verse or poetry.

protagonist The main character in a story. (See also **antagonist.**)

proverb A sentence or phrase that expresses a truth about life. "The early bird catches the worm" is a proverb.

realism Fiction that tells about true-to-life people, places, or events that could actually exist or happen.

refrain A phrase or verse repeated several times, usually at regular intervals throughout a song or poem.

repetition A writing technique in which a word or phrase is repeated for emphasis.

rhyme The repetition of the same or similar sounds of syllables, often at the ends of lines of verse.

rhyme scheme The pattern in which rhymes occur in a poem.

rhythm In poetry, a regular pattern of accented and unaccented syllables.

rising action In dramatic structure, the part of a story or play that establishes and develops the **conflict.**

romance novels **Novels** about extraordinary events in extraordinary settings. Romance novels are more concerned with action — love, adventure, combat — than with characters.

satire The use of **humor** or **irony** to expose hypocrisy or foolishness.

scene A section of a novel or play that focuses on the actions of one or several characters in one place and time.

science fiction Imaginative writing that has some basis in scientific fact and usually takes place in a time other than the present. Science fiction writing is sometimes used by an author as a vehicle for making a statement about society.

sensory words Words that appeal to one or more of the five senses (hearing, sight, smell, touch, and taste).

setting The time and place in which events in a story or play occur.

short story A brief fictional **narrative** in prose. It has unity in **theme, tone, plot,** and **character.** Often a short story reveals a character's true nature through a series of events.

simile   A comparison of two unlike things, using *like* or *as*. "He was as brave as a lion" is a simile. (See also **metaphor.**)

slang   Words and phrases that occur most often in **informal language.** Slang is often humorous, vivid, and extremely casual. Slang tends to be in a state of constant change, words and phrases experiencing popularity for a time, only to be replaced by new terms.

stage directions   Instructions in the script of a play that tell the characters their movements on the stage. They also describe the use of props and sound effects.

stanza   In poetry, a group of lines united by a pattern of rhyme and rhythm.

subplot   An additional, but secondary **plot,** that makes the action in a work of fiction more complex and more interesting.

suspense   Uncertainty, on the part of the reader or the audience, about what will happen in a story or play. Authors deliberately create suspense to hold the reader's or audience's interest.

symbolism   The use of an object, character, or incident to represent something else.

symbols   Objects, characters, or incidents that represent something else.

synopsis   A summary of a story's events.

theme   The underlying idea or message in a story. The theme may be directly or indirectly stated.

third person   The **point of view** in which the author acts as an unidentified **narrator** to tell the story about the characters. (See also **first person.**)

tone   The attitude toward the subject and the reader in a work of literature. The tone of a work may be formal or informal, for example, or light-hearted or serious. (See also **mood.**)

tragedy   A serious play that ends with a great misfortune that could not have been prevented. In a classic tragedy, the main character, a worthy, noble person, meets his or her fate with courage and dignity.

turning point   An important moment in the **plot,** when events that have led to the moment of greatest intensity in the story come to a peak, and the main conflict must be resolved. (See also **climax.**)

universal themes Themes that occur in the stories of every culture, in every time. The conflict between good and evil is a traditional theme. Universal themes are particularly apparent in traditional tales.

verse **1.** A part of a poem, such as a line or a **stanza.**
2. Rhythmic, and usually rhymed, poetry.

wit The ability to describe events that are amusing or odd, or to point out similarities in things that seem to be very different. Wit is a type of humor that depends mainly on the clever use of words.

Quotations from Authors/Illustrators

Credits

Program Design Carbone Smolan Associates

Cover Design Carbone Smolan Associates

Design 13–107, 483–545 Sheaff Design; 111–189, 191–193, 209–261 Textart, Inc.; 194–208 Ligature, Inc.; 263–295 Martine Bruel; 297–383 Piotr Kaczmarek; 385–481 Liska & Associates, Inc.

Introduction (left to right) 1st row: Piotr Kaczmarek; David Shopper; Ed Parker; 2nd row: David Shopper; Alexander Farquharson; Jim Baldwin; 3rd row: Vince Caputo; Biblioteca Nacional, Madrid; Charlie Hogg; 4th row: Nancy Bernard; Devera Ehrenberg; Theo Rudnak

Table of Contents 4 Michael Melford, The Image Bank; 5 James Grashow; 7 Scala/Art Resource, NY; 8 Piotr Kaczmarek; 9 Theo Rudnak; 10 Robert Roth; 11 Devera Ehrenberg

Illustration 59–67 Bob Brundson; 70–71 Susanah Brown; 72–85 Alexander Farquharson; 111 James Grashow, (calligraphy) Eva Burg; 112–113 Eva Burg; 114–119 James Grashow; 120–125 Ed Parker; 120–121, 125 (woodcuts) James Grashow; 126–127 John Dyess, (borders) Eva Burg; 128–134 Ed Parker; 128, 135–144 (woodcuts) James Grashow; 138–143 Carol Schwartz; 144–153 Ed Parker; 157–159, 163 (woodcuts) James Grashow; 159–162 Carol Schwartz; 164–172 Vince Caputo; 164, 173–187 (woodcuts) James Grashow; 174–179 Vince Caputo; 185 Carol Schwartz; 188–189 Eva Burg; 191–193 Jean and Mou-Sien Tseng; 197 Mapping Specialists; 200–201 Precision Graphics; 218, 232–247, 252, 254, 260–261 Jean and Mou-Sien Tseng; 297 Piotr Kaczmarek; 298–324 Jim Baldwin; 325–327 Piotr Kaczmarek; 328–342 Jim Baldwin; 343 Piotr Kaczmarek; 344–362 Jim Baldwin; 363 Piotr Kaczmarek; 364–376 Jim Baldwin; 377–379, 382–383 Piotr Kaczmarek; 384–387 Theo Rudnak; 388–412 Joan Hall; 414–415 (background) Theo Rudnak; 416–417 Rudi Backart; 418–434 John Hersey; 437 (background) Theo Rudnak; 438–439 (frames) Anne Schedler, (background) Theo Rudnak; 440–455 Maria Stroster; 456–457 Rudi Backart; 458–474 Theo Rudnak; 476–477 Rudi Backart; 478–479 (background) Theo Rudnak; 480–481 Rudi Backart; 484, 488, 495, 509, 510, 528, 532 (display type, technical drawing, and borders), 534–535 (borders), 536–539 (borders and technical drawings) Nancy Bernard; 512–519, 533–535, 537–539 Robert Roth; 520, 524–525 Doug Henry; 527, 529 Mary Ahrndt-Greenhaven Press, Inc.; 547–675 Devera Ehrenberg; 687, 689, 697, 700, 703, 704, 705 George Ulrich

Photography 13 Uli Wiesmeier/Adventure Photo; 16–17 Hans Wendler/ The Image Bank; 20–39 Stock Imagery; 40–41 Michael Melford/The Image Bank; 42–44 Superstock; 45–52 Harald Sund/The Image Bank; 53–55 Steve Pruehl/The Image Bank; 55 (inset) Courtesy of Jacqueline Auriol; 56–57· Courtesy of AKZO/ Transglobe/Zone 5; 58 Courtesy of AKZO/Transglobe/Zone 5; 68 Warren Morgan/West Light; 87 Movie Still Archives; 88–89 Nancy Simmerman/Allstock; 90–91 Jeff Schultz/Leo de Wys; 94–95 Jeff Schultz/Allstock; 102 E. R. Degginger/Bruce Coleman, Inc.; 104– 105 Derek Berwin/The Image Bank; 106 Courtesy of Jacqueline Auriol (top); 106 AP/Wide World Photos (bottom); 107 Bettmann Archive (top); 107 Courtesy of Gary Paulsen (bottom); 186 Courtesy of Little, Brown and Company (top); 186 AP/Wide World (bottom); 187 The Russell Lee Photograph Collection, courtesy of The Barker Texas History Center, The University of Texas at Austin (top); 187 Lionel Cherruault, Camera Press/Globe Photos (bottom); 187 Photo by Charles Adams, courtesy of Margaret K. McElderry Books, imprint of Macmillan Publishing Company (center); 192 Werner Forman Archive, Private Collection; 194-195 ©Wan-go H. C. Weng; 196 Ralph J. Brunke; 199 National Numismatic Society, Smithsonian Institute; 200 National Maritime Museum, Greenwich, London (top); Freer Gallery of Art (bottom); 201 Ontario Science Museum (top); Bibliothèque Nationale, Paris (bottom); 202 © Wan-go H. C. Weng; 203 Biblioteca Nacional, Madrid; 205 Private Collection; 206 Art Resource, NY; 209 (border) Collection, Victoria and Albert Museum, photo ©Michael Holford; 209 National Maritime Mueum, photo ©Michael Holford; 210-211 National Palace Museum, Taipei, Taiwan, Republic of China (border); 212 Xinhua News Service; 212 The University Museum, University of Pennsylvania (border); 213 Xinhua News Service; 214 Courtesy of Cultural Relics Bureau, Beijing, and The Metropolitan Museum of Art, New York City; 214 The University Museum, University of Pennsylvania (border); 215 Courtesy of Cultural Relics Bureau, Beijing, and The Metropolitan